African Societies in Southern Africa

UNIVERSITY OF CONNECTICUT — GROTON, CONN. — SOUTHEASTERN BRANCH LIBRARY —
JUL 10 1970

Historical Studies edited by

LEONARD THOMPSON

African Societies in Southern Africa

Published under the auspices of the African Studies Center University of California, Los Angeles

PRAEGER *PUBLISHERS*

NEW YORK · WASHINGTON

BOOKS THAT MATTER

Published in the United States of America in 1969
by Praeger Publishers, Inc.
111 Fourth Avenue, New York, N.Y. 10003

Library of Congress Catalog Card Number: 72-88353

Printed in Great Britain

Contents

List of Maps vii

Acknowledgements xi

1. The forgotten factor in southern African history 1
LEONARD THOMPSON
Professor of African History, Yale University

2. Early iron-using peoples of southern Africa 24
D. W. PHILLIPSON
Secretary/Inspector, Zambia National Monuments Commission

3. The later Iron Age in South Africa 50
BRIAN FAGAN
Professor of Anthropology, University of California, Santa Barbara

4. Changes in social structure in southern Africa: the relevance of kinship studies to the historian 71
MONICA WILSON
Professor of Social Anthropology, University of Cape Town and Honorary Fellow, Girton College, Cambridge

5. The Sotho-Tswana Peoples before 1800 86
MARTIN LEGASSICK
Assistant Professor of African History, University of California, Santa Barbara

6. The traditions of the Natal 'Nguni': a second look at the work of A. T. Bryant 126
SHULA MARKS
Lecturer in African History, School of Oriental and African Studies, University of London

7. Interaction between Xhosa and Khoi: emphasis on the period 1620–1750 145
GERRIT HARINCK
University of California, Los Angeles

8. The trade of Delagoa Bay as a factor in Nguni politics 1750–1835 171
ALAN SMITH
University of California, Los Angeles

9. The distribution of the Sotho peoples after the Difaqane 190
WILLIAM LYE
Assistant Professor of History, Utah State University

10. Aspects of political change in the nineteenth-century Mfecane 207
JOHN OMER-COOPER
Professor of History, University of Zambia

11. The 'other side' of frontier history: a model of Cape Nguni political progress 230
DAVID HAMMOND-TOOKE
Professor of Social Anthropology, Rhodes University

12. The External relations of the Ndebele kingdom in the prepartition era 259
RICHARD BROWN
Lecturer in African History, University of Sussex

13. The passing of Sotho independence 1865–70 282
ANTHONY ATMORE
Lecturer in African History, School of Oriental and African Studies, University of London

14. Great Britain and the Zulu people 1879–87 302
COLIN WEBB
Senior Lecturer in History and Political Studies, Natal University, Pietermaritzburg

Index 325

Maps

1. *Southern Africa* viii–ix
2. *Sites of the early iron-using peoples* 48
3. *Principal Iron Age sites mentioned in chapter 3* 52
4. *The Sotho-Tswana area before A.D. 1500* 123
5. *Tentative dispersal of chiefdoms in the sixteenth to eighteenth centuries* 124
6. *Sotho-Tswana distribution about 1800* 125
7. *Approximate locations of Khoikhoi and Bantu chiefdoms about 1650–1700* 170
8. *Delagoa Bay* 190
9. *Lesotho 1865–71* 301

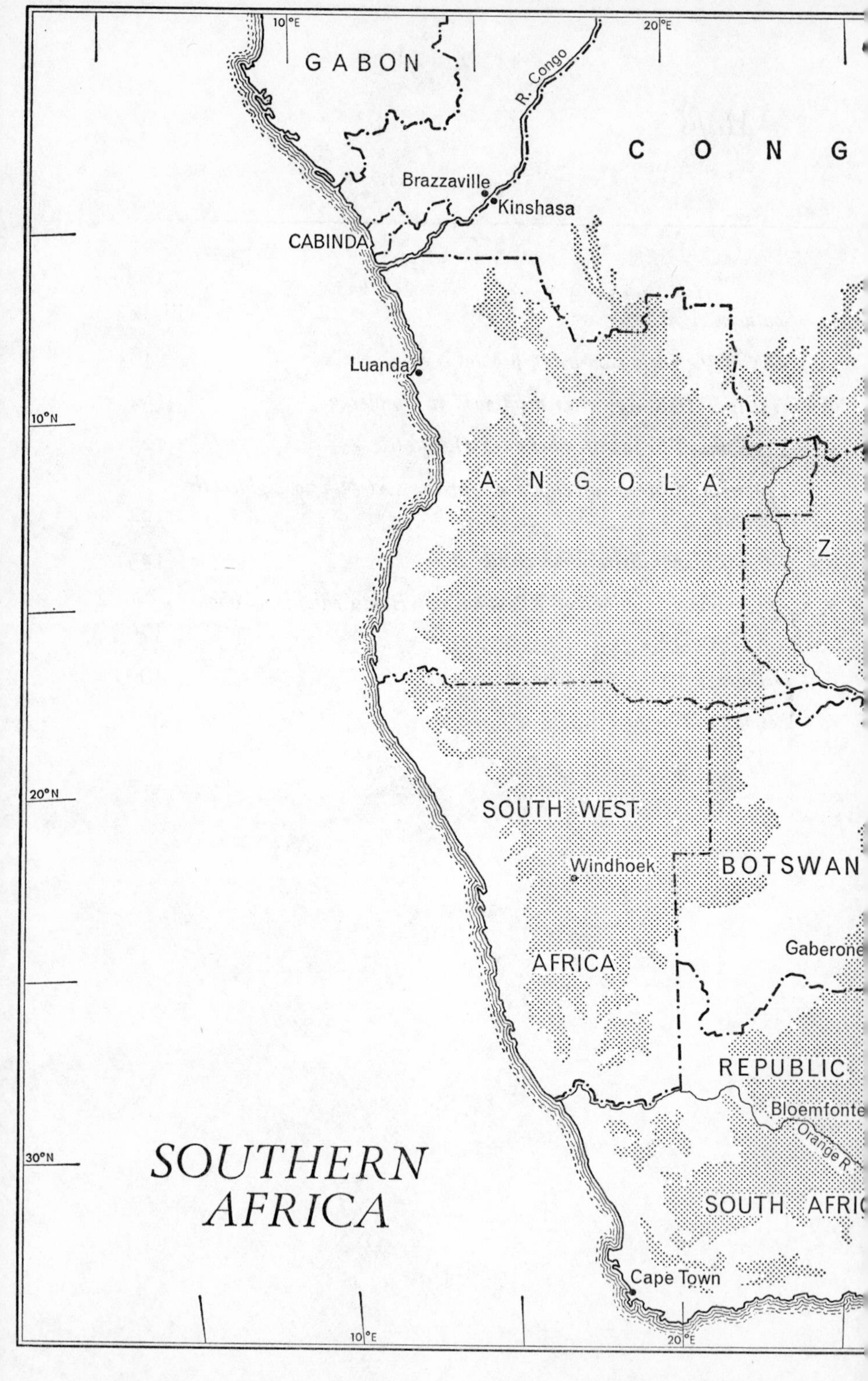

10°E
20°E
GABON
R. Congo
C O N G
Brazzaville
Kinshasa
CABINDA
Luanda
10°N
A N G O L A
Z
20°N
SOUTH WEST
Windhoek
AFRICA
BOTSWAN
Gaberone
REPUBLIC
Bloemfonte
Orange R
30°N
SOUTHERN
AFRICA
SOUTH AFRI
Cape Town
10°E
20°E

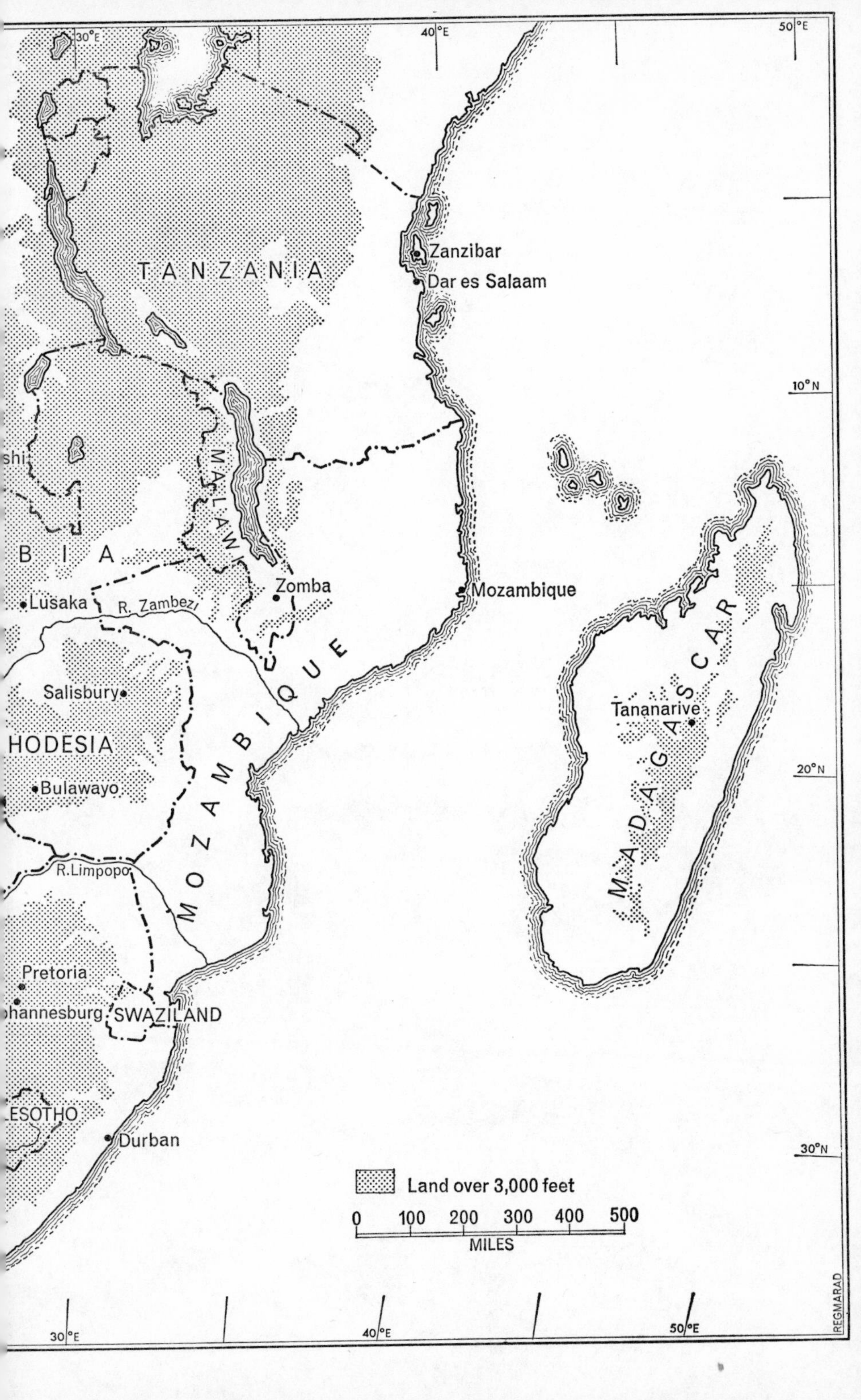

30°E
40°E
50°E
10°N
20°N
30°N
TANZANIA
Zanzibar
Dar es Salaam
MALAWI
shi
B I A
Zomba
Mozambique
Lusaka
R. Zambezi
Salisbury
HODESIA
MOZAMBIQUE
Bulawayo
R.Limpopo
Pretoria
hannesburg
SWAZILAND
LESOTHO
Durban
MADAGASCAR
Tananarive
Land over 3,000 feet
0 100 200 300 400 500
MILES
REGMARAD

Acknowledgements

As is explained more fully in the first chapter, this book is the result of a conference that was held at the University of Zambia, Lusaka in the first week of July 1968.

Cordial acknowledgement is due to Vice-Chancellor Paul Proehl and his fellow-members of the Chancellor's Committee on International and Comparative Studies of the University of California, Los Angeles for providing the funds for the conference. We are also deeply grateful to the University of Zambia for its able and friendly co-operation, and especially to Professor Lalage Bown and Mr Edward Ulzen of the Department of Extra-Mural Studies and Professor John Omer-Cooper of the Department of History, who cheerfully added to their very full programme the responsibility for the local arrangements for the conference. Miss Inez Jarrick of U.C.L.A. was an indefatigable conference secretary; and several other African, British, and American scholars, besides those whose names appear in the contents' sheet, took part in the conference discussions and made contributions that have been taken into account by the authors as they revised their papers for this publication.

All members of the conference would wish me to pay a special tribute to the late Professor A. C. Jordan of the University of Wisconsin—a great-hearted African and a fine scholar—who made his last visit to the continent of his birth to attend the conference. His knowledge, his humour and his courageous bearing were memorable for all of us who were present.

We would also like to thank the U.C.L.A. African Studies Center for its administrative support.

Finally thanks are due to the Royal Commonwealth Society, London for permission to reproduce the photograph on the cover from the print by Samuel Daniell.

Leonard Thompson

Abbreviations

J.A.H. *Journal of African History*
S.A.A.B. *South African Archaeological Bulletin*
P.T.R.S.A. *Proceedings and Transactions of the Rhodesian Scientific Association*
O.P.N.M.S.R. *Occasional Paper of the National Museum of Southern Rhodesia*
S.A.J.S. *South African Journal of Science*
T.R.S.S.A. *Transactions of the Royal Society of South Africa*

1. The forgotten factor in southern African history

LEONARD THOMPSON

The history of southern Africa is now being seen in a new perspective. Until recently, the study and writing of southern African history have reflected the social structure of the area. Historians have been mainly concerned with the activities of the white community, which did not obtain a permanent foothold at the Cape until the second half of the seventeenth century. They have tended to ignore, or to treat very summarily, the history of the African peoples before they were subjected to white over-rule.[1] The pre-conquest African societies are therefore a forgotten factor in southern African history. In so far as they were the subjects of academic enquiry at all, they were left to archaeologists, linguists, ethnologists, and physical and social anthropologists.

It is to social anthropologists that we owe most of our knowledge of African societies before they were subjected to white supremacy;[2] and it is in the departments of social anthropology, rather than the history departments,[3] that a generation of South African students has had the opportunity of studying them. But social anthropologists are not, as such, historians; and most of the works of social anthropologists have been synchronic or comparative

[1] See, for example, C. F. J. Muller, editor *Vyfhonderd Jaar Suid-Afrikaanse Geskiedenis*, Pretoria and Cape Town 1968. This, the most recent Afrikaans history of South Africa, starts with the Portuguese voyages round the Cape of Good Hope and relegates the history of the African peoples to an appendix, pp. 435–55.

[2] See, for example, Max Gluckman 'The Kingdom of the Zulu', in *African Political Systems*, edited by M. Fortes and E. E. Evans-Pritchard London 1940; Hilda Kuper *An African Aristocracy* London 1947; Isaac Schapera *Government and Politics in Tribal Societies* London 1956, *The Ethnic Composition of Tswana Tribes* London 1952 and numerous other works on the Tswana; and, especially, Monica Wilson's four chapters in Monica Wilson and Leonard Thompson, editors *The Oxford History of South Africa* Vol. 1 Oxford 1969.

[3] Hitherto, the Department of History in the University of Rhodesia has given much more attention to the history of the African population than the departments of history in the Republic.

studies, rather than studies of the processes of change in specific societies.[4]

During the last two decades, non-academic writers have also become interested in African societies and have written several books about them—mostly biographies of African rulers.[5] These tend to be somewhat romantic works, mixing fact with fiction and lacking the technical apparatus of scholarly writing. Nevertheless, they are based on solid research. It is regrettable that professional historians in South Africa have been slow to respond to the challenges presented by these non-academic authors as well as by the social anthropologists.

However, as a concomitant of the closure of the colonial era in Africa north of Angola, Rhodesia, and Moçambique, the history of African societies has acquired recognition as a valid and necessary field of study in many history departments outside southern Africa during the last decade. There are now centres of African studies, with history as a major ingredient, not only in tropical African universities such as those in Ibadan and Dar es Salaam, but also in many universities in eastern and western Europe, Asia and America; and it is in those centres, especially, that the history of African peoples, neglected by professional historians during the colonial period, is now being patiently and systematically unravelled. The African historian of today is less influenced than his predecessors by the racial barriers to thought created by the colonial system. He is also transcending the disciplinary barriers that used to deter historians from concerning themselves with the experiences of societies and social groups in the periods before they produced written records.

Culturally, as well as geographically, southern Africa is and always has been part of the continent of Africa. Throughout the ages, ideas, techniques, institutions, goods, and people have crossed the Zambezi and the Limpopo Rivers. Historians of central and eastern Africa disregard southern African history at the peril of leaving gaps in their knowledge of the history of their own

[4] The gap between social anthropologists and historians is no longer as wide as it once was, when anthropologists paid very little attention to discrete historical situations and historians were not much interested in social analysis.

[5] See, for example, P. Becker *Path of Blood: The Rise and Conquests of Mzilikazi, Founder of the Matabele* London 1962 and *Rule of Fear: The life and Times of Dingane, King of the Zulu* London 1964; E. A. Ritter *Shaka Zulu* London 1955; and also the much more scholarly work by Donald R. Morris *The Washing of the Spears: A History of the Zulu Nation under Shaka and its Fall in the Zulu War of 1879* New York 1965.

areas; and historians of southern Africa disregard the history of African peoples, inside and outside the Republic of South Africa and Rhodesia, at the peril of failing to comprehend the majority of the inhabitants of their region. Historical processes in the tropics and sub-tropics have not merely been paralleled, but demonstrably related. This is true of the succession of Stone Age cultures; it is true of the domestication of sheep and cattle, the cultivation of millet, and the mining and smelting of iron, gold and copper; and it is true of the spread of the Negroid peoples and the Bantu languages. It is also true of more recent phenomena. For example, whereas the Fish River area was the ultimate frontier zone produced by the expansion of dark-skinned, Bantu-speaking, herding and cultivating peoples from the north, the Kenya highlands were the ultimate frontier zone produced by the expansion of light-skinned, Afrikaans- and English-speaking peoples from the south, as well as from Europe. Moreover, whereas in the first half of the nineteenth century dark-skinned warrior bands from Natal conquered parts of Rhodesia, Zambia, Tanzania, and Moçambique, in the second half of the twentieth century there was a reverse movement by white people, some of whom retreated from decolonized territories in central and East Africa to the white supremacy bastion in Rhodesia and Africa.

The lacunas in southern African historical knowledge cannot be attributed to a dearth of data. Compared with most parts of sub-Saharan Africa, there is an enormous quantity of relevant source material waiting to be exploited by historians of African societies in southern Africa. Much of this information is available in archives and libraries in Europe and America. It includes books and articles written by white travellers, missionaries, traders, officials, and settlers, who were first-hand observers of African societies, starting with narratives by some of the Portuguese who penetrated the Zambezi valley or were shipwrecked on the south-east African coast in the sixteenth century;[6] a large number of more or less specialized articles in learned journals by archaeologists, ethnologists, anthropologists, and linguists;[7] and several crucial compilations of the oral traditions of African communities, notably those made by the amateur historians A. T. Bryant, D. F.

[6] Some of these are collected and translated into English in G. M. Theal (editor), *Records of South-Eastern Africa* 8 volumes London 1898–1903.

[7] A select bibliography of such articles is soon to be published in Stanford, California, compiled by Leonard Thompson, Richard Elphick and Inez Jarrick.

Ellenberger, J. C. Macgregor, S. M. Molema, J. H. Soga, and G. W. Stow, and the ethnologists P. L. Breutz and N. J. van Warmelo.[8] Moreover, the extensive works of G. M. Theal, notwithstanding his strong bias and (in his *History of South Africa*) his failure to acknowledge his sources, are in one respect much more 'modern' than many more recent writings on South African history: they say a great deal about Africans and much of what they say is based on oral traditions collected in the nineteenth century.[9] There are also rich hoards of unpublished documents: in official archives in London, The Hague, and Lisbon; in missionary archives in Great Britain, France, Italy, Germany, Norway, and the United States; and in other collections scattered through Europe and America, especially in Britain.

Much necessary and significant work can be done on the basis of these materials alone. Nevertheless, many types of problems can only be investigated in depth by research inside southern Africa. There are wide ranges of unique documents in the official archives in Pretoria, Cape Town, Bloemfontein, Pietermaritzburg, and Salisbury; in the South African Public Library, the Parliamentary Library, and the library of the South African Museum in Cape Town; and in the libraries of some of the universities and municipalities (notably the Killie Campbell collection at Natal University and the collections in the Johannesburg Public Library).

In addition, much intensive field-work is still to be done inside southern Africa to uncover various types of latent information. Archaeologists have already made important discoveries in southern African sites that were occupied by man in the more remote millennia and this work must and will continue; but, except in Rhodesia, not nearly so much attention has been given

[8] A. T. Bryant *Olden Times in Zululand and Natal* London 1929, *Bantu Origins* Cape Town 1963 and *History of the Zulu and Neighbouring Tribes* Cape Town 1964; D. F. Ellenberger and J. C. Macgregor *History of the Basuto, Ancient and Modern* London 1912; J. C. Macgregor *Basuto Traditions* Cape Town 1905; S. M. Molema *The Bantu, Past and Present* Edinburgh 1920; J. H. Soga *The South-Eastern Bantu* Johannesburg 1930; G. W. Stow *The Native Races of South Africa* London 1905; P. L. Breutz *The Tribes of the Rustenburg and Pilandsberg Districts* Pretoria 1953 and *The Tribes of the Marico District* Pretoria 1954; N. J. van Warmelo *Contributions towards Venda History, Religion and Tribal Ritual* Pretoria 1932, *History of Matiwane and the Amangwane Tribe, as told by Msebenzi to his kinsman Albert Hlongwane* Pretoria 1938, *The Copper Miners of Musina and the Early History of the Zoutpansberg* Pretoria 1940, and *Transvaal Ndebele Texts* Pretoria 1930.

[9] G. M. Theal *History of South Africa* 11 volumes revised edition London 1919–1926, *Records of the Cape Colony* 36 volumes, London 1897 and 1905, *Basutoland Records* 3 volumes, Cape Town 1883, and *Records of South-Eastern Africa*, op. cit.

to those sites that were occupied in the last millennium or two and that are of major interest to the historian. In this respect South Africa lags far behind Rhodesia, where, thanks no doubt to the conspicuous presence of the Zimbabwe ruins, a great deal of professional work has been done on the archaeological legacy of the ancestors of the Shona peoples. The historian also requires more extensive and systematic comparative studies of the Bantu languages spoken in southern Africa than have so far been made, because historical inferences flow from a clear understanding of the relations between these languages and their differing degrees of incorporation of alien sounds, morphology, and vocabulary.

Historians lack the specialized training of anthropologists, archaeologists, and linguists, but as we define our needs more clearly we shall be able to encourage specialists to do more to satisfy them than they have in the past. Moreover, we historians are ourselves capable of building on the existing body of recorded oral traditions. Most of the major compilations of the traditions of the African peoples of southern Africa were not recorded systematically and have been transmitted to us embedded in the non-scientific assumptions of their compilers.[10] It is therefore necessary to handle these compilations with extreme rigour: to check them for internal consistency, to compare them with other publications, and to search out, record and correlate the traditions that still survive among African communities. Unfortunately, these living traditions are now being distorted and even eliminated at an extremely rapid rate, as a consequence of the drastic changes that the African communities are experiencing. There is, for example, a prodigious feed-back into the living traditions from the published works: the most illiterate informant is liable to cite as tradition facts and interpretations that he has derived at second hand from Bryant, or Soga, or Ellenberger. Nevertheless, rich veins of tradition remain to be tapped and when the work is done by well-informed, skilled and imaginative people the return can be substantial. This has been demonstrated by D. P. Abraham. He has discovered among the Shona peoples of Rhodesia traditions that include valuable information about events in the sixteenth and seventeenth centuries and he has shown that this information dovetails with documentary evidence written in those centuries

[10] This applies to the works of Bryant, Ellenberger, Macgregor, Molema, Soga and Stow listed in footnote 8 on page 4.

by Portuguese who penetrated into Shona country from the East African coast.[11]

As the study of African history has developed in universities in tropical Africa and in Europe and America in recent years, historians have begun to pay attention to the southern as well as the tropical parts of the continent, asking the same sorts of questions and applying the same sorts of techniques that their fellows are using farther north. By 1968 it was evident that the time had come when it would be fruitful for some of these historians, and also some archaeologists and social anthropologists, to meet and pool their ideas and their knowledge. Accordingly, the Chancellor's Committee on International and Comparative Studies of the University of California, Los Angeles, provided funds for a conference which was held in Lusaka with the co-operation of the University of Zambia in July 1968. The other chapters in this book consist of revised versions of thirteen of the papers that were discussed at that conference.

In the rest of this chapter, I indicate the main themes that are dealt with in the succeeding chapters, so that the reader may see the appearance of the wood as a whole before he becomes involved with the individual trees. The chapters fall into four groups. We have two contributions by professional archaeologists. Then there are chapters by a social anthropologist and three historians, dealing with changes in African societies before the nineteenth century. The next three chapters deal with the transformation of African societies related to the career of Shaka. Finally, we have four chapters on aspects of the interactions between African societies and white people during the nineteenth century.

Taking a broad geographical canvas, D. W. Phillipson sums up the archaeological evidence that is now available concerning changes in material culture in southern Africa as a whole during the first millennium A.D. By the beginning of the Christian era, hunting and gathering populations, who used stone tools and were of what is known as bushboskop physical type, were widespread in southern Africa. Then, during the first millennium A.D., a series of crucial changes took place in some areas. Iron, copper and gold were mined and smelted; pottery was made; cattle and sheep were used; and sorghum and other crops were cultivated. Thanks to the radiocarbon dating process, the chronology of the

[11] D. P. Abraham 'Ethno-history of the Empire of Mutapa' in *The Historian in Tropical Africa* edited by J. Vansina, R. Mauny, and L. V. Thomas, London 1964.

beginnings of iron-working and pottery-making at many sites in Zambia and Rhodesia is now approximately established. Well before A.D. 1000, people were working iron at numerous places in Zambia and Rhodesia, and also in the Northern Transvaal. In Swaziland iron was being worked as early as the fifth century. Furthermore, skeletal remains show that these innovations were probably associated with the advent into southern Africa from the north-west of new population elements of Negroid physical type.

In the third chapter, Brian Fagan confines his attention to the area south of the Limpopo and discusses the present state of knowledge concerning developments there after A.D. 1000. At present, this knowledge is depressingly meagre, not because it cannot be found, but because insufficient efforts have been made to find it. However, we do know that in the Limpopo valley and the Soutpansberg there were, in the first half of the second millennium, communities whose material culture was associated with that of the contemporaneous Rhodesian iron-working and food-producing populations, about whom much more is known, at Bambandyanalo in about the eleventh century, at Mapungubwe in about the fifteenth century, and at Palabora from perhaps the ninth century onwards. We also have scattered evidence that at some places in the Transvaal high veld people were smelting iron and making pottery in styles similar to northern Transvaal and Rhodesian pottery from about the eleventh century onwards; and at several sites along the Natal coast there have been considerable finds of pottery, which have not yet been dated and have only been loosely classified.

This archaeological evidence is invaluable; nevertheless, by itself it raises more problems than it solves. If, as seems evident, the San ('Bushmen') are the latter-day heirs of the Stone Age populations, what are the historical antecedents of the Khoikhoi people, whom the whites have called 'Hottentots', who were pastoralists and pottery-makers but not cultivators or iron-workers, who spoke click languages and who were of bushboskop physical type?[12] To what extent was the food-producing and metal-working revolution a product of the immigration of peoples,

[12] Terminology has been a source of great confusion in southern African history. The names 'Bushmen' and 'Hottentots' were coined by white people and have a derogatory connotation; the indigenous names San and Khoikhoi are to be preferred. See the Preface by Monica Wilson and Leonard Thompson (editors) in *The Oxford History of South Africa* Volume 1 Oxford 1969 for a fuller statement on this question.

as distinct from being a local, indigenous development? What sorts of processes lay behind the spread of the Negroid physical type and the Bantu languages in southern Africa? Were immigrations large or small in scale, of short or long duration, from a single source or from more than one? What were the processes of interaction between food-producing and iron-working peoples and the hunting and collecting communities who were previously the sole occupants of the land? What were the processes of change among the food-producing societies once they were established in southern Africa? How, for example, did the Bantu-speaking communities of southern Africa, such as the Shona, the Sotho, and the Nguni, become differentiated from one another? What, furthermore, are the connections between the Iron Age archaeological sites discussed by Phillipson and Fagan and the modern communities of southern Africa?

Both D. W. Phillipson and Brian Fagan speculate about some of these problems. For example, Phillipson suggests that all the crucial ingredients in the Iron Age culture were brought into South and East Africa from the north-west by Negroid peoples in the first millennium A.D. They spread as far as the Transvaal and Natal and a little farther. South and west of that region some of the indigenous peoples took over the stock-raising and the pottery-making innovations, but without the metal-working and the crop-cultivation (the Khoikhoi or 'Hottentots'), while others took over none of the new techniques (the San or 'Bushmen'). However, Phillipson warns us against the concept of a single massive invasion of Negroid peoples. Fagan does not disagree with this. On the other hand, Phillipson and Fagan discern different types of interactions between the food-producing and the hunting and collecting populations at different sites and in different periods. Phillipson finds evidence of culture-contact—for example of symbiotic relations and of miscegenation—but he does not discover signs of acculturation between the two types of communities in the first millennium sites that have been examined. Fagan, on the other hand, suggests that at Bambandyanalo, starting in about the eleventh century, a predominantly bushboskop population may have adopted all the crucial ingredients in the material culture of a relatively small number of iron-working, food-producing, Negroid immigrants.

Our knowledge concerning each of these problems would be vastly increased if there were a great stepping-up of archaeological field-work and laboratory work on the specimens recovered from archaeological sites, especially on the pottery, the iron, the pollens, and the human and animal remains. Nevertheless, archaeologists and related laboratory scientists alone cannot cope with all the issues raised in these questions; and the next four chapters show that we are by no means exclusively dependent on them for our knowledge.

In her chapter, Monica Wilson, writing as a social anthropologist with a deep interest in history, advances four arresting suggestions concerning the problems we have posed. She agrees with D. W. Phillipson that the Khoikhoi are essentially indigenous South Africans, descended from those Stone Age communities who, unlike the San, acquired cattle in South Africa. Secondly, she conceives that there were two distinct streams of immigration to South Africa which jointly were responsible for the food-producing revolution: one stream of iron-working, Negroid peoples from the north-west and another of cattle-keeping people from the north-east. Thirdly, and this constitutes the core of her paper, she shows how comparatively few people, if they were polygynous, patrilineal cattle-keepers with marriage customs involving the transfer of cattle to the bride's kin, might have increased their progeny very rapidly at the expense of other people with whom they were in contact. And finally she suggests why it was that the Nguni and the Sotho became differentiated from one another in their languages, their marriage customs, their settlement patterns, and to some extent in their material cultures: partly because the Sotho were more closely associated with the immigration from the north-west and the Nguni with the immigration from the north-east, and also as a result of different processes of interaction with the indigenous San and Khoikhoi peoples. The last three of these hypotheses are very striking. They are excellent examples of the contributions that social anthropologists are peculiarly well-equipped to make to our understanding of historical processes in societies before they became literate. The reader of Professor Wilson's chapter will observe, in particular, how her speculations, based largely upon cultural comparisons, provide us with different types of insights into the southern African past from those that are derived primarily from a mastery of the archaeological record.

Martin Legassick's chapter is the result of rigorous re-examination of the published oral traditions of the African communities of the Transvaal, the Orange Free State, Lesotho, and Eastern Botswana. He challenges some of the basic assumptions that affected the ways in which the amateur historians, who collected the oral traditions of those communities in the late nineteenth century and the early twentieth century, understood the traditions and synthesized them for publication. In particular, he criticizes the assumption that Sotho society in South Africa was the product of a massive immigration, or a series of waves of massive immigration, of structured groups of people who already had a specific and immutable culture. His own contention is that Sotho society, as it existed in the nineteenth century, was largely the product of local developments inside South Africa. This is, of course, the sort of proposition that makes good sense to the historian. Moreover, one aspect of it is strongly reinforced by Monica Wilson's explanation of the capacity of patrilineal, cattle-keeping lineages to expand at the expense of other communities.

How, then, are we to reconcile the hypotheses of Wilson and Legassick with the archaeological evidence of a series of approximately contemporaneous changes in material culture (the introduction of iron, pottery, sheep and cattle, and crops), in association with the physical anthropologists' evidence of the advent and expansion of the Negroid physical type and the linguists' evidence of the expansion of Bantu languages? The answer seems to be, firstly, that immigration was certainly an important ingredient in these changes in material culture, physical type, and language; but secondly, that the immigrants from the north were not necessarily nearly as numerous as has generally been supposed and that the social and political systems that the Sotho peoples had by the nineteenth century were in large part the product of centuries of interaction and change within South Africa.

Legassick gives substance to his basic contention by attempting to strip the recorded oral traditions of the assumptions in which they have been embedded by their compilers and recognizing them for precisely what they are—the traditions of the ruling lineages of those chiefdoms that were in existence at the time when the traditions were recorded. On this basis, he makes constructive suggestions as to the sorts of research that might still be undertaken to obtain more knowledge of the history of the area before about A.D. 1500; and he gives a highly original reconstruction of the outlines of the subsequent political history of the area. Starting in about 1550, he discerns a complicated process involving the repeated fission of two nuclear ruling lineages—the Kwena and the Kgatla; the continuous expansion of the resulting series of chiefdoms over most of the Transvaal, Orange Free State, eastern Botswana, and northern Lesotho; and the incorporation of most of the previous inhabitants of the area into these chiefdoms in various ways. Finally, he suggests that by the end of the eighteenth century this process of repeated fission and continuous expansion by small Kwena and Kgatla chiefdoms had been slowed up—at least in some parts of the area—as a result of population increase and, perhaps, of the growth of long-distance trade; and that a movement towards political consolidation had begun, notably under the Pedi lineage in the eastern Transvaal.

In the next chapter, Shula Marks does much the same thing for the history of the northern Nguni as Martin Legassick has done for the Sotho peoples. But her problem is more difficult to deal with, because whereas some Sotho traditions have been recorded scientifically (notably those of the western Sotho or Tswana by Isaac Schapera), A. T. Bryant has been the only major compiler of northern Nguni traditions and all his published works are permeated by unscientific assumptions and strong prejudices. Some of Shula Marks's conclusions support those of Legassick. For example, she shows how Bryant (like Stow, Theal, Ellenberger, Macgregor, and Breutz for the Sotho) makes sweeping assertions about migrations into south-eastern Africa, but that his evidence—the traditions he has recorded—says scarcely anything about large-scale or long-distance migrations, and does not extend as far back in time as the period when the material culture of the Iron Age came to south-eastern Africa. The main body of her paper is an ingenious attempt to sift out the wheat from the chaff in Bryant's classification of the Nguni peoples into three main divisions—'Tonga Nguni', 'Mbo', and 'pure Nguni'—each with several sub-divisions. And she, like Legassick, concludes with an exhortation for further archaeological, linguistic, and archival research.

Gerrit Harinck's chapter illuminates one of the most intractable problems in African history—the interactions between communities possessing the material culture of the Iron Age and other communities. The Fish River area, before it became a frontier zone marking the eastern limit of *trekboer* expansion from the Cape, had for many years been a frontier zone marking the southern limit of the Bantu-speaking, Iron Age communities.

Harinck uses linguistic evidence to show that before the seventeenth century the Xhosa chiefdoms, which were subject to fission in much the same way as the Sotho chiefdoms, had pushed Khoi communities out of the country from the Mzimvubu River westwards to the Fish, that their relationships had been intermittently violent but had involved trade, and that some Khoi had been incorporated into the Xhosa chiefdoms. These incorporated Khoi had generally had inferior roles but, as the representatives of the former owners of the soil, they had performed important ritual functions in Xhosa society. Harinck then uses recorded oral traditions to reconstruct some aspects of the interaction in the period between 1620 and 1750, in which he distinguishes two successive phases. In the first phase, a symbiotic relationship was established between a Xhosa chiefdom, newly-created from its parent, and a Khoi chiefdom, each maintaining its autonomy. In the second phase, considerable numbers of Khoi individuals and lineages were incorporated into the newly-created Gqunukwebe chiefdom, which was essentially Xhosa in structure and predominantly Xhosa in culture. Finally, Harinck interprets the evidence in seventeenth- and eighteenth-century documents as showing that when the Dutch founded their settlement at the Cape in 1652, there was a long-distance trade network, extending from the Xhosa chiefdoms westwards, through successive Khoi chiefdoms, to the vicinity of the Cape peninsula, and northwards to the Orange River and thence to the western Sotho or Tswana chiefdoms—a network that was destroyed by white *trekboers* when they occupied the Khoi territories in the eighteenth century.

This chapter is an interesting example of what can be done to reconstruct the pre-colonial history of an area where virtually no evidence has so far been supplied by archaeology. However, two statements of caution are necessary concerning the implications of the case that Harinck has studied. The two successive phases that Harinck distinguishes as marking the relations between contiguous Xhosa and Khoi chiefdoms in the seventeenth and eighteenth centuries should not be regarded as constituting a complete succession of those relationships, because contact between the Xhosa and the Khoi had begun several centuries earlier. Secondly, we have no reason to assume that this case illustrates the process of interaction between hunting and collecting societies and societies with the Iron Age material culture, since the Khoi possessed sheep and cattle and had social and political institutions with some resemblances to those of the Xhosa. Indeed, Harinck considers that the relationships between the Khoi and the Xhosa were largely determined by the what he calls the 'cultural compatibility' of the two societies, a compatibility that could not be said to have existed between the Xhosa and the San. There is a great deal of evidence in oral traditions and documents concerning interaction between Nguni and Sotho chiefdoms and the hunting and collecting peoples in South Africa. It is to be hoped that some scholar will soon bring this evidence together into a comprehensive study of the process.

Nobody would claim that Chapters 4 to 7 have provided definitive solutions to all the problems that were posed on pages 7–8. But these chapters hack away a great deal of the nonsense that has previously been handed down as historical knowledge; they bring out much relevant information in a scientific perspective; and they show several ways in which imaginative and rigorous research may lead to fresh contributions in the future, building progressively towards a clearer and fuller understanding of the key processes in the history of African societies in southern Africa before the age of Shaka.

In *The Zulu Aftermath*, John Omer-Cooper has recently summarized and integrated what is known of the rise of the Zulu Kingdom and its drastic effects upon African peoples living as far north as the Equator.[13] Nevertheless, many aspects of those remarkable events remain obscure. We are still groping towards a satisfactory explanation for the collapse of the apparently long-lived Nguni system of small, autonomous, fissiparous chiefdoms. We are still short of evidence concerning the beginnings of the process of amalgamation under the ruling lineages of the Ndwandwe, Mthethwa, and Ngwane chiefdoms, that preceded the emergence of Shaka's Kingdom.[14] We still need precise and full information about the effects of the Mfecane (Difaqane in the Sotho dialects) upon the Nguni and Sotho communities that were not incorporated by Shaka, and about the processes of incorporation of

[13] J. D. Omer-Cooper *The Zulu Aftermath: a Nineteenth-century Revolution in Bantu Africa* London 1966.

[14] I use the word 'chiefdom' for the *comparatively* small, homogeneous, and simple political communities that existed in south-eastern Africa before the time of Dingiswayo and Shaka; and the word 'kingdom' for the *comparatively* large, heterogeneous, and complex political communities that were then created by men such as Shaka, Mzilikazi, Soshangane, Zwangendaba, Moshweshwe, Sobhuza, and Sekwati. By any definition, there are of course borderline cases.

conquered peoples in the Zulu Kingdom and the Kingdoms of the Swazi, the Gaza, the Kololo, the Ndebele, and the Nguni group of Kingdoms. The chapters by Alan Smith, William Lye, and John Omer-Cooper illuminate these problems.

As a result of work on the published sources of European commercial activity in Delagoa Bay during the period when northern Nguni society was being transformed, Alan Smith explores 'the Northern Factor in Nguni history'. He demonstrates that during this period from 1750 to 1835 there was a considerable seaborne trade in and out of Delagoa Bay; that the principal export was ivory; that an appreciable quantity of this ivory came from the south, that is to say, from the Nguni area; and that the Nguni received beads and brass in return. He is able to show that the Ngwane of Sobhuza, the Ndwandwe, and the Mthethwa, and later the Zulu of Shaka and Dingane, were all involved in this trade; and he deduces that commercial competition by rulers exercising monopolies within their areas was a major factor in the process of political consolidation. He also indicates that Shaka and Dingane played off British traders operating from Port Natal against the Portuguese trade system from Delagoa Bay, channelling their trade in accordance with their satisfaction with the goods received in return for their ivory—and especially, latterly, with the traders' willingness and ability to supply firearms and ammunition. This chapter at last gives us some firm evidence of the economic factor in state-making among the northern Nguni, evidence which, from the analogies of state-making in some other parts of Africa, had been expected but had not previously been accumulated and presented.

As with all new research, Alan Smith's chapter still leaves a series of unsolved questions. The Ndwandwe and Mthethwa states were short-lived; if ever they were visited by literate observers, none of their accounts have been discovered; and, after they were destroyed by Shaka, the institutions which would have been the instruments for the preservation and transmission of their traditions were eliminated. We can only conjecture about the extent to which commerce was a motive for political action with the Ndwandwe and Mthethwa chiefs and councillors, and about their techniques for regulating trade—for example, for distributing the imported goods among their subjects; and our knowledge of these things within the Zulu Kingdom is only comparatively strong. Alan Smith also stimulates us to examine the extent to which the Nguni chiefdoms south of Natal were involved in the trade system emanating from Delagoa Bay, and to ask why it was that the southern Nguni chiefs did not establish internal monopolies over ivory, and what was the relationship between this fact and the absence of an amalgamative process among the southern Nguni chiefdoms. One also wonders whether, as Smith's researches proceed in the Portuguese documents, he will be able to enlarge upon the suggestion made by Martin Legassick that during the second half of the eighteenth century a similar amalgamative process was taking place among some of the Sotho chiefdoms, and that it, too, was related to trade with the east coast.

William Lye's study of the distribution of the Sotho peoples after the Difaqane is a corrective to the view that is endemic in much of the white South African literature, that the period from 1822 to 1836 was exclusively a time of social destruction for the majority of the inhabitants of the high veld. He doubts whether many Sotho chiefdoms were wholly destroyed and, by implication, whether the loss of life was really as prodigious as has been represented. He focuses attention on the ways in which the Difaqane triggered off or, as Legassick would say, 'accentuated', a process of political amalgamation on the high veld. This was marked not only by the rise of the Ndebele state in the central Transvaal, but also of the Sotho states of Sekonyela, Moroka, and Moorosi, as well as Moshweshwe, in the Caledon valley, the expansion of some of the Tswana chiefdoms in the western Transvaal and Botswana, and the recovery of the Pedi chiefdom in the eastern Transvaal. All of them were distinguished from their predecessors by their comparative largeness and by the fact that they incorporated individuals, families, and lineages of diverse antecedents. He concludes that during the Difaqane Sotho society was not so much destroyed as it was re-deployed—individuals, families, and lineages being territorially displaced in many cases, but integrated into larger political units comprising more varied groups than previously.

We must, of course, avoid the trap of overcompensation. The evidence of heavy loss of life is copious in the writings of literate observers of the high veld during and immediately after the Difaqane period. Nor should we underestimate the extent to which the Sotho chiefdoms were composed of groups of diverse origins before the time of Shaka. In the Caledon valley area, at any rate, each little chiefdom already comprised peoples of the most diverse origins, including San and Nguni as well as Sotho. Nor should we ignore Legassick's suggestion that the process of political amalgamation had begun on the high veld in the eighteenth century. Nevertheless, Lye is making an important point when he stresses the integrative, state-building process that was part of the high veld experience during the Difaqane.

John Omer-Cooper's chapter is an essay in comparative politics. He seeks to identify, compare, and show the historical relationships between the essential features of the political system of the northern Nguni before the time of Dingiswayo, the Zulu Kingdom of Shaka, and the kingdoms of the Ndebele and the Swazi and the Ngoni group of Kingdoms. In Shaka's Zulu Kingdom, he discerns only two real innovations—the institution of a standing army and the invention of the short stabbing spear. For the rest, he considers that the Zulu Kingdom developed out of institutions, practices, and techniques that had previously existed among the Nguni and their Sotho neighbours, though with a different balance between them. He finds that the structures of the offshoot kingdoms contained some elements from the Nguni past and some from the Zulu Kingdom, plus diverse adaptations to the exigencies of their different local situations—and especially to their need to absorb and control relatively large numbers of subject peoples whose culture and language were not Nguni. Finally, he contends that over the years the Ndebele and Ngoni kingdoms regressed, in different ways, towards the decentralized norms of the traditional Nguni political system—a tendency that was carried to the extreme of repeated fission among the Ngoni.

Perhaps the evidence for some of the steps in Omer-Cooper's bold analysis is rather sparse. For example, it remains to be demonstrated that the military system in the small pre-Difaqane Sotho chiefdoms was as closely geared to the age grades produced by the educational system as he supposes; and that Dingiswayo or Shaka consciously borrowed this ingredient in Sotho institutions when they created their armies with regiments based upon age grades. But the historian performs a valuable service in essaying an over-view with the data available to him, even if, in some particulars, the connections are not proven and later research may necessitate modifications. In constructing a framework, he helps us to see the relations between events and institutions, and inspires further research.

One aspect of all these Nguni kingdoms that requires very close examination is the ways in which they incorporated subject peoples. The parameters of the problem differed from case to case: the conquerors and their subjects were present in different proportions, and there were different cultural distances between them. We need to know much more about what happened in each particular case. For example, Omer-Cooper reminds us that the Ndebele took over aspects of the religion of their Shona subjects, ust as Harinck has told us that the Xhosa took over aspects of Khoi religion. What, more precisely, was involved in this process? How did Shaka adapt the traditional Nguni religious beliefs, rituals, and institutions to the needs of his situation as amalgamator, conqueror, and despot? And what sorts of accommodations did the Ngoni leaders make with the religions of the diverse peoples they conquered? We also want critical assessments of the roles of the key individuals in these new kingdoms, based upon personality studies of men like Shaka and Sobhuza, Mzilikazi and Zwangendaba. The bold over-view that Omer-Cooper has provided constitutes a necessary starting-point for such studies.

The last group of chapters deals with the process that culminated in the incorporation of the African peoples of southern Africa into white-controlled polities. This process had two aspects. One aspect was white expansion. As Professor Sir Keith Hancock has shown,[15] white expansion in southern Africa was extremely complicated because its different agents—hunters, traders, missionaries, farmers, soldiers, speculators, and administrators—had different interests and methods and, often, different objectives. Moreover, these occupational differences were compounded by differences of national affiliation and loyalty: to Britain, to a British Colony, to an Afrikaner Republic or even, in some cases, to Germany. The process of white expansion was therefore marked by continuous competition and even occasional bloodshed among the expansionists. Nevertheless, cultural pride and racial consciousness were sufficiently prevalent among all categories of white expansionists to set limits to these rivalries. Even when the Republics and Great Britain fought a devastating two-and-a-half years' war, neither side exploited the vast potential of its African subjects as fighting men. A great deal of work is still to be done to increase our knowledge of this aspect of the process. To

[15] W. K. Hancock *Survey of British Commonwealth Affairs* 2 volumes in 3, London 1937–42.

take but one example: the role of the missionary in white expansion in southern Africa has not been systematically examined so far.[16] We need thorough studies of the relationships between missionaries, Africans, and the white men who made the political decisions for expansion.

However, the main gap in present knowledge concerns the inner workings of African polities during the period of interaction culminating in their political subordination to white authorities.[17] However sophisticated their handling of the white elements, the existing accounts are more or less deficient in dealing with the structure of African society and its tensions and conflicts. We need to understand the internal politics of the African chiefdoms and kingdoms; and this involves investigating such phenomena as the modes of recruitment to political offices, the powers of chiefs and councillors, the methods of decision-making, the relationships between ruling and commoner lineages, the roles of age grades versus those of kin groups, the customs concerning the incorporation of aliens and the secession of subjects, and the value system and its associated rituals. We also need to understand the external politics of the chiefdoms and kingdoms: the relationships between chiefdoms of the same cluster (like the Xhosa), between chiefdoms of different clusters (like the Xhosa and the Thembu), and between chiefdoms of different languages and cultures (like the Nguni and the Sotho). The more we can discover about these phenomena, the better we shall be able to understand the process of interaction between white people and Africans.

The African response was just as complex as the white expansion. Traditional tendencies to the fission of chiefdoms and traditional rivalries among chiefdoms, accentuated in many cases by the Mfecane and Difaqane wars, impeded concerted resistance. Whites were able to form alliances with disaffected segments of chiefdoms, with chiefdoms that sought assistance against their African enemies, and with communities which, like the Mfengu, had been disrupted by Shaka and wanted protection. In almost every case of physical conflict, whites were able to recruit Africans as allies against their African enemies.

We can distinguish two phases in the process of interaction. In

[16] There is, however, a polemical work, N. Majeke *The Role of the Missionaries in Conquest* Johannesburg 1952.

[17] Nevertheless, Isaac Schapera *Government and Politics in Tribal Societies* London 1956 which is based on southern African data, is an excellent introduction to the subject.

the first phase, the agents of white expansion were comparatively small numbers of hunters, traders, prospectors, and missionaries, operating at a distance from their bases. African governments did not at first regard such people as constituting a threat to their survival and they sought to accommodate their presence by admitting, controlling, and assimilating them, as they were accustomed to do with aliens. But in no case did this attempt at accommodation produce stability. Scarcely any white people became assimilated. Moreover, traders, by selling guns and liquor, disturbed the power relationships within and among the chiefdoms, and affected African morale; and missionaries created new African communities in the heart of the chiefdoms, with new values and divided loyalties. Thus, during the first phase of interaction fundamental changes were initiated in African society.

The beginning of the second phase was usually marked by the arrival of white farmers, who proceeded to occupy land and to employ Africans as labourers. African governments, realizing that their control over their land and their subjects was threatened, then sought African allies and tried to play off missionary versus farmer, and Briton versus Boer. Sooner or later, many kingdoms and chiefdoms resorted to force to try to preserve their land and their autonomy. The Xhosa chiefdoms fought intermittently for a hundred years; the Zulu kingdom engaged in sharp wars against both the Voortrekkers (1838) and the British (1879); the southern Sotho defied the Orange Free State, successfully in 1858 and unsuccessfully in the 1860s; the Pedi and the Venda resisted the South African Republic for many years; and the Ndebele and the Shona challenged the British South Africa Company regime when it was still in its infancy in the 1890s. Other African governments, like those of the Mpondo, the Swazi, and some of the Tswana chiefdoms, succumbed without a fight. By the end of the nineteenth century, all the kingdoms and chiefdoms in southern Africa had submitted to white over-rule. They had been subjected, not only because of the ultimate solidarity and the vast technological superiority of the whites, but also because of the persistence of the old divisive forces in African society and the creation and exploitation of new cleavages by the agents of white expansion.

David Hammond-Tooke's chapter is a significant contribution to our knowledge of that part of the process of interaction which is at present most obscure. Drawing upon his own field research as well as documents written at the time by white missionaries, he reconstructs the political system of the Mpondomisi chiefdoms during the decade or so immediately preceding their annexation to the Cape Colony in 1875. He emphasizes the autonomy of each Nguni chiefdom *vis-à-vis* chiefdoms of the same as well as other clusters, and thus lays bare the foolishness of British and colonial officials who repeatedly tried to control an entire cluster of Nguni chiefdoms by subjecting the genealogically superior chief and imposing upon him the duties of a non-existent paramountcy. He then analyses the internal structure of an Mpondomisi chiefdom, showing how power was divided regionally between the chief, the sub-chiefs in charge of districts, and the heads of wards or sub-divisions of districts, and institutionally between the chief, his councillors, and the adult men of the entire chiefdom. Finally, he explores the decision-making process, showing that, though political decisions were proclaimed by the chief, it was the accepted theory, and to a great but variable extent the actual practice, that a decision was the formal expression of a consensus derived from a series of consultations and discussions with councillors and also, if the subject was important, with the men of the entire chiefdom assembled in a mass meeting. In this respect, too, white people repeatedly erred, by assuming that a chief was an autocrat, able to bind his subjects to accept conditions that had been imposed upon him from without.

For the Mpondomisi, this chapter answers most of the questions we have posed about African political systems, and has probably answered them in more substantial detail than has previously been provided for any of the pre-colonial chiefdoms of southern Africa. Moreover, although his data relate specifically to the Mpondomisi and to the period 1865–75, Professor Hammond-Tooke suggests firstly, that the principles of the system he has described had long been present among the Mpondomisi, and secondly, that they were to be found among the other Nguni chiefdoms, including those in Natal before the time of Dingiswayo and Shaka. This seems to be a reasonable extension. Moreover, the basic principles in the political systems of the Sotho, the Shona, and the other Bantu-speaking peoples of southern Africa before the Mfecane and the Difaqane wars were probably very similar.

While the main thrust of David Hammond-Tooke's chapter concerns the internal political system of an Nguni chiefdom, Richard Brown focuses on the external relations of the Ndebele

Kingdom, from its origins in secession from Shaka in 1822 to about 1880.[18] He emphasizes the great range of the diplomatic contacts and involvements of the Ndebele state. He also demonstrates the intricate connections between the internal tensions of the kingdom and its foreign policy. In particular—and this was typical of African states—the disputed succession after the death of Mzilikazi in 1868 resulted in internal cleavages which were exploited by others, both black and white. Brown also shows how the attempt of Mzilikazi and Lobengula to apply to white intruders the traditional African methods of admitting, controlling, and assimilating aliens was doomed to failure, because the white traders and missionaries declined to be assimilated and remained loyal to alien governments, institutions and ideologies.

Two important aspects of the foreign relations of African states are only dealt with by inference in this chapter. One is the conduct of diplomacy. White observers often referred to the presence of 'messengers' at African capitals. In fact, the term 'ambassadors' would be more appropriate. These were men of high status and they possessed exceptional skills—the physical capacity to travel long distances very rapidly and the intellectual capacity to remember very precisely extremely detailed instructions. In nineteenth-century southern Africa ambassadors were constantly on the move from state to state, and a ruler like Mzilikazi or Moshweshwe received and dispatched many ambassadors each year.[19] The second aspect is a consequence of the first. As a result of the extensive diplomatic network, an African king or chief and his councillors were always very much better informed about the situation in southern Africa as a whole than the mass of their subjects. This meant that they had a clearer grasp of the formidable military resources which were ultimately associated with the comparatively small number of white people who were actually present in their state. It was partly for that reason that African rulers and their councillors were generally more cautious in their dealings with white people than their subjects, especially their young warriors.

Anthony Atmore's chapter is a case study in the interaction of white expansionists and an African kingdom during the transition

[18] The final defeat and subjection of the Ndebele and the Shona has recently been described in T. O. Ranger *Revolt in Southern Rhodesia 1896–7* London 1967.

[19] My data come from research in the history of Lesotho, where Moshweshwe had diplomatic contacts extending from the Ndebele in the north to the Xhosa in the south.

from autonomy to white over-rule. It is an excellent subject for such a study, because many different interests, both white and African, were involved. Among the whites, there were rival groups of French Protestant and French Catholic missionaries, each hoping to reap a spiritual harvest in Lesotho. The Orange Free State under President J. H. Brand was anxious to consummate its military victories by driving the southern Sotho off the land it claimed to have conquered. The British Cabinet was willing to allow British influence to be used to protect the southern Sotho from virtual annihilation by the Boers, provided that could be done without cost to the British taxpayer. The Colony of Natal, dominated by its Secretary of Native Affairs, Theophilus Shepstone, wanted to get control of Lesotho for itself. Finally, Sir Philip Wodehouse, Governor of the Cape Colony and British High Commissioner in South Africa, thought it was desirable to protect the southern Sotho, and saw through the expansionist schemes of Natal. The southern Sotho were at a very low ebb. Their country had been devastated, their cattle decimated. Moshweshwe, their founder-king, was dying. Each of his sons of the first house—Letsie, Molapo, and Masopha—had distinct interests, including a territorial base and a following. Some of his junior sons, especially those like Sekhonyana and Tsekelo who had had a good Western education, were acting independently. His allies, such as Moletsane and Moorosi, had never been integrally incorporated in his kingdom. The nation was also ridden with religious conflicts between traditionalists, Protestants, and Catholics. Out of these varied elements arose a series of tentative and often short-lived alliances between white and Sotho interests. Two men emerged triumphant from the prolonged crisis. One was Wodehouse, who incorporated Lesotho in the British Empire without incurring physical resistance, even though his military resources were minute and he was in one way or another defying not only the Orange Free State, but also the British Government, the Natal Government, and those Sotho who had committed themselves to Natal. The other was Letsie, who succeeded his father peacefully and, under British over-rule, proceeded to become the effective paramount chief over most of his father's followers and allies.

Finally, Colin Webb presents a case study of the events preceding the annexation of another African kingdom. The contrasts between the situations explored by Atmore and Webb illustrate the vital significance of the unique, specific context of each relationship. In the one case, British authority, as exercised by Wodehouse, preserved the southern Sotho from complete disruption by the victorious Orange Free State Republic. In the other case, it was British forces that conquered the Zulu Kingdom, a British official who imposed an utterly disruptive settlement upon the Zulu people, and British Cabinets, of both parties, who then compounded the work of destruction by declining for eight long years to assume the responsibility for making that settlement work. Colin Webb's chapter is also a demonstration of the value of the contributions that can still be made to our understanding of *African* history by historians who continue to place the spotlight on imperial policy, provided that, as Webb has done, they relate policy-making in the metropolis to the facts of life in the societies to which the policy was applied. This is what imperial historians have not often achieved.

This volume, together with the *Oxford History of South Africa*,[20] constitutes an interim report on the state of historical knowledge flowing from the new approach to the history of southern Africa. The chapters that follow show that many of the assumptions and assertions that have previously been disseminated must be discarded or radically modified. They also illustrate the sorts of questions that are now being asked by historians; they indicate why it is that at this stage the responses to some of these questions can only be in the form of tentative hypotheses; and they suggest types of investigations that should be conducted in the future if we are to attain greater precision and greater certainty. It is hoped that the book will stimulate scholars resident in southern Africa to exploit their incomparably rich storehouse of information about the African past and to persuade their universities, their foundations, and their government agencies to provide increased support for Iron Age archaeology and for the recording of the oral traditions that still exist among the African communities, but are so rapidly being distorted and eliminated. It is hoped, too, that it may help scholars, students, and others who are interested in Africa, wherever they may live, to appreciate the broader dimensions of the complex history of the southern part of the continent.

[20] Volume II will be published in 1970.

2. *Early iron-using peoples fo southern Africa*

D. W. PHILLIPSON

INTRODUCTION

Two thousand years ago central and southern Africa was occupied by a stone-using hunter-gatherer population lacking any knowledge of metallurgy and probably practising no, or only very rudimentary, techniques of food production. The next five hundred years saw the establishment of immigrant communities with a markedly contrasting way of life. Remains of the villages occupied by these settlers have been found widely distributed in Rhodesia and Zambia and in parts of Malawi, Botswana and the Transvaal. They are marked by a common ceramic tradition and appear to be both contemporary with, and successive to, sites of the aceramic stone-using communities. Metallurgy first appears in association with this widespread type of pottery, iron being found in all areas while the distribution of copper and gold follows that of the mineral deposits. At many Early Iron Age sites domestic animal bones and indications of plant cultivation give evidence of food production. Neither of these traits is represented in the Late Stone Age.

The great economic contrast between the Early Iron Age people and those of the Late Stone Age marks a cultural development which has been of paramount importance in determining the later history of the subcontinent, and archaeological discoveries relating to this period have considerable significance for other fields of study. Southern African archaeology has often been studied in three watertight compartments: Stone Age, Iron Age and rock paintings. All these have bearings on the present topic. As much of the work on Early Iron Age sites has been published only recently, and as the reports are widely scattered, I feel that a provisional synthesis is now desirable. What follows is, therefore, a general review of the available archaeological evidence for the inception and initial development of the Early Iron Age societies.

This will be followed by a consideration of this evidence in the light of that obtained by parallel disciplines, and a discussion of the relationships between these societies and their geographical and chronological neighbours. No apology is offered for spreading this discussion over a wider area of Africa than is covered by the general theme of this volume. Early Iron Age communities almost certainly had their origins far outside southern Africa and they cannot profitably be considered as *dei ex machinis* stepping over an arbitrarily chosen line of latitude or equally arbitrary modern political boundary.

THE ARCHAEOLOGICAL EVIDENCE

Zambia and northern parts of Rhodesia

A summary of Early Iron Age sites in Zambia has recently been published, so only an outline need be given here.[1] Over seventy sites are now known. Although the pottery assemblages from these sites have many features in common, they are divisible into at least five geographical and typological groups, all of which appear to be contemporaneous. These are the Kalambo group of north-eastern Zambia; the Chondwe group (Copperbelt); the Kapwirimbwe group (Lusaka region); the Kalundu group (Southern Province plateau) and the Dambwa group (Zambezi valley). The possibility should be borne in mind that, when further discoveries are made, these groups may prove to be less clearly defined than they now appear. Other groups will doubtless be discovered in areas at present unexplored.

The Kalambo group is heterogeneous and future work may demonstrate the need for further subdivision. It is represented by eleven sites in the area lying north and east of the Congo pedicle and west of the Luangwa River. With one exception these sites have yielded only small assemblages of artefacts, but the pottery appears to belong to a single group, characterized by shallow undecorated bowls and by necked vessels decorated with broad grooves and false-relief chevron stamping and often bearing decoration on the bevel of the rim. Seven radiocarbon dates from the extensive Kalambo Falls site range from the fourth to the fourteenth or sixteenth centuries A.D. (GrN-4646, GrN-4647,

[1] D. W. Phillipson 'The Early Iron Age in Zambia: Regional Variants and some Tentative Conclusions' *J.A.H.* IX (1968), pp. 191–211.

L–395c, L–395b, L–395a, GrN–3580, GrN–3189).[2] Iron working was practised throughout the occupation but copper and other trade goods were absent. Although bones were rarely preserved the remains of cattle and dogs are reported while rubbing stones suggest the grinding of grain.[3]

Most of the other sites in the Kalambo group are caves and rockshelters where pottery of Early Iron Age type occurs in association with Late Stone Age artefacts. This association has been dated at Nakapapula rockshelter, Serenje, where the Late Stone Age occupation probably began in about the fourth millennium B.C.[4] At a time represented by the deposition of the level six to nine inches below the present surface, Early Iron Age pottery was first introduced into the shelter. A charcoal sample from this level gives a date in the seventh to ninth centuries A.D. (GX–535); and it can be demonstrated that the schematic paintings at the site were not executed before that date. The three to six inch level, which is dated to the tenth to twelfth centuries A.D. (GX–767), contained a reduced amount of pottery. The stone industry continues unchanged through both these levels and evidently survived well into the present millennium.

During the first millennium A.D. the iron-using population of this northern region appears to have been sparse and impermanent. Much of the area is thickly wooded and less fertile than the more densely settled areas farther south and it is therefore less suitable for the prolonged occupation of single village sites.

In the Copperbelt area fourteen Early Iron Age sites are known from the fringes of the Kafue headwater *dambos* and have been designated the Chondwe group. In contrast to the northern area, all but one of these are open village sites. Chondwe pottery lacks undecorated bowls and decorated rim-bevels. Comb stamping is very much more common than it is on Kalambo pottery and is frequently used to fill the spaces between broad grooves arranged in horizontal bands with pendant loops. False-relief chevron

[2] Radiocarbon age determinations are referred to in the text by their laboratory reference numbers only. The actual dates are listed in an appendix to this paper (pp. 46–47) in alphabetical order of laboratories and numerical order of analyses.

[3] J. D. Clark 'The Kalambo Falls Prehistoric Site: an Interim Report' *Actes IV Congrès Panafr. de Préhistoire* Tervuren 1962 pp. 195–202; F. van Noten 'Archeologische Opgravingen in Rhodesië, 1963' *Africa-Tervuren* X (1964) pp. 1–7; B. M. Fagan 'The Iron Age Peoples of Zambia and Malawi' *Background to Evolution in Africa*, ed. W. Bishop and J. D. Clark, Chicago 1967 pp. 659–86.

[4] D. W. Phillipson 'The Prehistoric Sequence at Nakapapula Rockshelter, Zambia' *in press*.

stamping is also frequent. Copper is associated with Early Iron Age pottery at the eighth to tenth century Chondwe site (GX–1009, GX–1010), and it is likely that the first exploitation of the Zambian copper deposits dates from this period.[5] Pottery from other sites in the area, such as Kangonga and Roan Antelope, is thought on typological grounds to be earlier and Kangonga has been dated to the eighth to ninth centuries (GX–1327)[6]. The Early Iron Age occupation at Chondwe had come to an end by the eleventh to twelfth centuries (GX–1330, GX–1331).

Two excavated sites provide substantial information about the Early Iron Age of the Lusaka area. Excavations at Kapwirimbwe, eight miles east of the city, have revealed a substantial village whose apparently brief occupation occurred around the fifth century A.D. (GX–1012, GX–1013a, GX–1013b). A number of post-holes had been dug into the natural subsoil but ant and root disturbance prevented the recovery of a meaningful architectural plan. There were extensive traces of collapsed *daga* structures, most of which were probably iron-smelting furnaces. Enormous quantities of iron slag and bloom confirmed that extensive iron working had been conducted very close to the site. Iron tools, including a spear-point, a ring, a razor and probable thumb-piano keys were much more common than is usual on Zambian Iron Age sites. Copper, on the other hand, was not found. Bone was rare, but poorly preserved fragments from a sealed refuse pit indicate the presence of domestic cattle. The Kapwirimbwe pottery is distinctive, comprising mainly necked vessels and hemispherical bowls with internally thickened rims. Decoration consists of horizontal bands of grooved or incised hatching and false-relief chevron stamping is common.[7] Similar but more elaborately decorated pottery from a site in Twickenham Road, Lusaka, is clearly a later development of the Kapwirimbwe tradition. It is associated with dates of the ninth to twelfth centuries A.D. (GX–662, GX–1329).

The only Early Iron Age site so far discovered in the Eastern

[5] Copper artefacts are recorded from many Early Iron Age sites in Zambia but no finds of this period have yet been made at any mining site. See D. W. Phillipson 'Prehistory of the Copper Mining Industry in Zambia' *South African Mining Journal* (1968) pp. 1332–1339.

[6] A further date from Kangonga, GX–1328, gave a reading in the third-fifth centuries A.D. This is considered less reliable than GX–1327 because of the sample size available.

[7] D. W. Phillipson 'Kapwirimbwe' *Inventaria Archaeologica Africana* series Z5 Tervuren 1968; D. W. Phillipson 'The Early Iron Age Site at Kapwirimbwe, Lusaka' *Azania* III (1968) pp. 87–105.

Province of Zambia is the Makwe rockshelter on the Moçambique border. Here Early Iron Age pottery occurs in the upper levels of a so far undated Late Stone Age deposit. The pottery shows more affinities both with East African material and with the Ziwa ware of Rhodesia than it does with contemporary Zambian pottery. Its possible connection with Malawi finds cannot yet be ascertained and details of Robinson's recent discoveries in the latter country are awaited with interest.

In the more fertile country of Zambia's Southern Province large, permanent or semi-permanent Early Iron Age villages were well established by the middle of the first millennium A.D. They seem to have brought about a rapid displacement of the previous stone-using inhabitants whose counterparts farther north survived the arrival of agriculture and metallurgy for another thousand years. In this southern area more research has been conducted than in other areas of Zambia and evidence is beginning to appear of a gradually merging cultural continuum during the Early Iron Age, displaying clear links with the contemporary inhabitants both of the Rhodesian plateau and of the areas to the north.

On the Zambian Batoka Plateau Inskeep and Fagan have demonstrated the presence of Early Iron Age deposits underlying those of the 'Kalomo Culture' at such sites as Gundu and Kalundu.[8] The material culture of these sites shares some features with those of the Kapwirimbwe group, but the pottery is distinguished by the rarity of false-relief chevron stamping and of bowls with internally thickened rims. Cowrie shells indicate contacts with the coastal trade but glass beads are absent. The lowest levels of Kalundu yielded abundant animal bones of which less than 40 per cent are of domestic cattle and small stock. Hunting evidently played an important part in the economy. Iron was used for the manufacture of such objects as razors, arrowheads, rings and probable thumb-piano keys. Copper fragments were also present. These sites were evidently occupied between the third and sixth centuries A.D. (GX–1114 and GX–1115 at Gundu; SR–65 and SR–123 at Kalundu). The small Situmpa assemblage is best regarded as allied, and possibly ancestral, to these pre-Kalomo culture Early Iron Age groups.[9]

[8] R. R. Inskeep 'Some Iron Age Sites in Northern Rhodesia' *S.A.A.B.* XVII (1962) pp. 136–80; B. M. Fagan *Iron Age Cultures in Zambia—I* London 1967.

[9] J. D. Clark and B. M. Fagan 'Charcoals, Sands and Channel-Decorated Pottery from Northern Rhodesia' *American Anthropologist,* LXVII (1965) pp. 354–71.

A large number of sites in the Zambezi valley share features both with the Kalundu group and with the Gokomere sites in Rhodesia. The most intensively investigated sites in this group are Dambwa and Kumadzulo near Livingstone.[10] Both are securely dated: Dambwa to the seventh to eighth centuries A.D. (SR–106, SR–62, SR–110, SR–97, SR–98, SR–96) and Kumadzulo to the fifth to seventh centuries (N–409, N–411, N–410, N–412, N–413, N–414). Iron and copper were found at both sites and there were substantial remains of pole and *daga* huts at Kumadzulo. The pottery assemblages at both sites are dominated by necked pots with an externally thickened rim decorated with diagonal comb stamping.

Three sites in the north-western area of Rhodesia appear to be closely related to the Dambwa Early Iron Age group whose Zambian distribution extends along the Zambezi valley from Mambova to Chirundu. An open village site in Kapula Vlei, Wankie Game Reserve, has yielded a single radiocarbon date (SR–73) of the eighth to ninth centuries A.D. which is in close agreement with the Dambwa dates.[11] More problematical is the 100 B.C. to A.D. 100 date (UCLA–929) from Calder's Cave near Gokwe.[12] The date comes from a level containing Late Stone Age artefacts associated with sherds of a single Early Iron Age vessel of a common Dambwa type. Since this is an isolated find rather than a well-defined horizon it is inadvisable at present to attach great significance to the associated radiocarbon date. The third site is a surface scatter some miles to the south of Calder's Cave.

Since Inskeep first published the material from the mound sites around Kalomo in Zambia the area of the distribution of the Kalomo culture has been stated to extend south of the Zambezi into Rhodesia.[13] More recent work has suggested that, if the Kalomo Culture is to be a meaningful entity, it should be re-defined to the exclusion of the pottery from the lowest levels of the Kalundu site, which is now recognized as being of Early Iron

[10] S. G. H. Daniels and D. W. Phillipson 'The Early Iron Age Site at Dambwa near Livingstone' in B. M. Fagan, D. W. Phillipson and S. G. H. Daniels *Iron Age Cultures in Zambia—II* London, 1969. J. O. Vogel, *personal communication.*

[11] K. R. Robinson 'The Iron Age Site in the Kapula Vlei near the Masuma Dam, Wankie Game Reserve, Rhodesia' *Arnoldia* (*Rhod.*) II (1966) No. 39.

[12] C. K. Cooke 'The Archaeology of the Mafungabusi Area, Gokwe, Rhodesia' *P.T.R.S.A.* LI (1966) pp. 51–78.

[13] R. R. Inskeep 'Some Iron Age Sites in Northern Rhodesia' *S.A.A.B.* XVII (1962) pp. 136–80.

Age type quite distinct from the fine wares found at Isamu Pati and in the upper levels at Kalundu.[14]

As far as I am aware the affinities of all the Rhodesian sites which have been attributed to the Kalomo culture are with the basal Kalundu material or with related Early Iron Age groups. The Calder's Cave find, described as 'Kalomo' by Summers[15] has already been discussed. The finds from Lukuzulu and Siachelaba's kraal exhibit grooving and false-relief chevron stamping.[16] They appear to be of Early Iron Age type comparable to finds from sites of the Kalundu and Dambwa groups and quite distinct from the Kalomo pottery as here defined. In the present state of our knowledge, therefore, the Kalomo culture has no place in the Iron Age sequence of Rhodesia.

Several widely differing views have been published on the affinities of the finds from Sinoia Cave sixty-five miles north-west of Salisbury.[17] Recent work on the site by Robinson has demonstrated the Early Iron Age character of much of the pottery and its association with copper smelting.[18] Ancient copper workings are reported from the area of the nearby Alaska Mine. The Sinoia pottery shares many features with that from Ziwa and there are also many sherds which recall those from Early Iron Age sites in the Lusaka area, especially Twickenham Road. This Early Iron Age attribution has been strengthened by a recently-announced radiocarbon date of the sixth to eighth centuries A.D. (SR–118).[19]

Rhodesia

Over most of the central and southern parts of Rhodesia the Early Iron Age cultures show considerable basic similarity. Wide general acceptance has been given to a tripartite division of the pottery with Ziwa ware in the eastern areas around Inyanga, Leopard's Kopje I (Zhiso) in the south-west centred on Bulawayo,

[14] B. M. Fagan *Iron Age Cultures in Zambia—I* London 1967.

[15] R. Summers 'Iron Age Industries in Southern Africa, with Notes on their Chronology, Terminology and Economic Status' in *Background to Evolution in Africa*, ed. W. Bishop and J. D. Clark Chicago 1967 pp. 687–700.

[16] See note 13.

[17] R. R. Inskeep 'Some Iron Age Sites in Northern Rhodesia' *S.A.A.B.* XVII (1962) pp. 136–80; J. F. Schofield *Primitive Pottery* Cape Town 1948; R. Summers, K. R. Robinson and A. Whitty 'Zimbabwe Excavations, 1958' *O.P.N.M.S.R.* III (1961) No. 23a.

[18] K. R. Robinson 'The Sinoia Caves, Lomagundi District, Rhodesia' *P.T.R.S.A.* LI (1966) pp. 131–55.

[19] K. R. Robinson, *personal communication*. I am grateful to Mr T. N. Huffman for his comments on this and other Rhodesian topics discussed in this paper.

and Gokomere ware widely distributed in the south-central area. The typology shows that the three groups are closely related: in an early classification they were grouped together, with some later derivatives, under the heading 'stamped ware'. In many cases there is considerable typological overlap between groups. The Early Iron Age in Rhodesia is thus probably best regarded as a gradually changing continuum within which clustering is readily apparent but less easily defined.

There is, however, one group of finds which does not fit easily into the general picture but which has been claimed to represent the earliest Iron Age occupation of Rhodesia. Bambata ware is the name which has been given to a loose grouping of pottery finds characterized by thin-walled vessels bearing areal decoration, often of massed stamp-impressions, which frequently extends over the rim.[20] No sealed horizon containing Bambata ware has yet been located, and nowhere is it demonstrably associated with iron. All the finds except one are from caves or rockshelters where it is usually associated with Late Stone Age material and sometimes also with pottery which clearly belongs with Gokomere and related Early Iron Age wares. Robinson has argued that at Dombozanga rockshelter near Beit Bridge[21] Bambata ware may postdate Early Iron Age sherds of the late first millennium A.D. Malapati type (see below, p. 34). A single pot of Bambata type from Inyanga comes from the same site as a third to fourth century date (SR–17).[22] At no other site in Rhodesia is there evidence for the age of Bambata ware other than its association with Late Stone Age material.

In view of the total absence of comparable pottery from Zambia, suggestions that Bambata ware is intrusive into Rhodesia from the north must be treated with reserve.[23] Bambata ware's affinities, like its date and cultural associations, must remain problematical pending further discoveries.

[20] J. F. Schofield 'Report on the Pottery from Bambata Cave' *S.A.J.S.* XXXVII (1940) pp. 361–72; K. R. Robinson 'Bambata Ware: its Position in the Rhodesian Iron Age in the Light of Recent Evidence' *S.A.A.B.* XXI (1966) pp. 81–85.

[21] K. R. Robinson 'Dombozanga Rockshelter, Mtetengwe River, Beit Bridge, Southern Rhodesia: Excavation Results' *Arnoldia* (*Rhod.*), I (1964) No. 7.

[22] F. O. Bernhard 'A Bambata-type Pot from Inyanga' *S.A.A.B.* XVIII (1963) p. 72.

[23] R. Summers 'Iron Age Industries of Southern Africa, with Notes on their Chronology, Terminology and Economic Status' in *Background to Evolution in Africa*, ed. W. Bishop and J. D. Clark Chicago 1967 pp. 687–700; K. R. Robinson A Preliminary Report on the Recent Archaeology of Ngonde, Northern Malawi' *J.A.H.* VII (1966) pp. 169–88.

Much firmer evidence is available for other Early Iron Age settlements in Rhodesia, as illustrated by Robinson's excavations at Mabveni in the Chibi district.[24] Remains of three pole and *daga* structures were located; one of these is interpreted as a storage bin which was originally raised above the ground on stones. A small enclosure of dry-stone field walling and a forty-five feet length of similar wall, crossing a watercourse at right angles as if to dam it, could not be linked unequivocally with the Early Iron Age occupation but are of a type distinct from structures of known late date. A shallow midden deposit yielded a substantial quantity of pottery, figurines of sheep and humans, and iron objects including a ring and eight iron beads. Beads were also made of copper, ostrich egg and snail shell. Trade with the coast is demonstrated by pierced marine shells and three imported glass beads. Sheep was the only domestic animal represented in the small faunal collection, but wildebeest, buffalo, impala and zebra were hunted. The two radiocarbon dates for Mabveni (SR–43: first to third centuries A.D., and SR–79: fifth to seventh centuries) are not in close agreement but a date somewhere in the first two-thirds of the first millennium is indicated.

Parallel evidence for much of that from Mabveni is provided by Robinson's re-examination of the Tunnel site at Gokomere.[25] Overlying a Stone Age horizon and sealed by a deposit containing fairly recent Karanga material were three feet of apparently redeposited midden containing Early Iron Age pottery, copper and iron fragments and glass beads of types paralleled in the earliest series from the Acropolis at Zimbabwe. Trade with the east coast is attested by, in addition to the glass beads, a complete conus shell, most probably *Conus ebraeus*, a species which does not occur in the Atlantic. The base of the Gokomere Early Iron Age midden yielded a date in the fifth to seventh centuries A.D. (SR–26). The end of the comparable earliest occupation of Zimbabwe is dated to the third to fifth centuries (M–913).[26]

The characteristic Early Iron Age pottery of the north-eastern

[24] K. R. Robinson 'An Early Iron Age Site from the Chibi District, Southern Rhodesia' *S.A.A.B.* XVI (1961) pp. 75–102.

[25] T. Gardner, L. H. Wells and J. F. Schofield 'The Recent Archaeology of Gokomere, Southern Rhodesia' *T.R.S.S.A.* XVIII (1940) pp. 219–53; K. R. Robinson 'Further Excavations in the Iron Age Deposits at the Tunnel Site, Gokomere Hill, Southern Rhodesia' *S.A.A.B.* XVI (1961) pp. 75–102.

[26] R. Summers, K. R. Robinson and A. Whitty 'Zimbabwe Excavations, 1958' *O.P.N.M.S.R.* III (1961) No. 23a.

parts of Rhodesia has been termed Ziwa ware.[27] It shows many points in common with Gokomere ware and Summers's work at the 'Place of Offerings' has provided valuable information about its associations.

The 'Place of Offerings' is a large open site where sherds and associated finds mainly occurred in shallow pits. The pottery recovered was of the more elaborately decorated type of Ziwa ware which has been named Ziwa 1. Associated finds include shell beads and part of an imported cowrie shell. There were probable fragments of an iron hoe and an iron clamp, while MacIver recovered a thumb-piano key from the same site.[28] Copper wire was not rare and a fragment of a copper ingot came from one pit. Millet and pumpkin seeds and bones of buffalo and various antelope were recovered.

No glass beads have been found associated with Ziwa 1 pottery but rare examples do occur with the closely related, perhaps slightly later, pottery which Summers has named Ziwa 2. Crude terrace walling is associated with Ziwa 2 pottery.

The absolute dates for these Ziwa 1 and 2 sites are not easy to establish with precision. No radiocarbon dates are available for the sites investigated by Summers, but Bernhard has obtained four dates for closely related sites in the same area. A date of the third to fourth century A.D. (SR–17) and one of two late first millennium dates (SR–32, SR–38) are associated with human burials which are described as showing Negroid physical features.[29] A final date, of the tenth to eleventh centuries A.D. (B–233), from the lowest levels of the stone enclosure at Nyahokwe, dates a final phase, Ziwa 3.[30]

Centred on Bulawayo, the early phase of the Leopard's Kopje culture has much in common with the Early Iron Age cultures further east.[31] Like Gokomere and Ziwa sites, those of Leopard's Kopje 1 are associated with simple low stone walling. Sherds of this type have been found in gold and copper workings as, farther east, have Ziwa 2 sherds. A single date (TX–228) in the ninth to

[27] R. Summers *Inyanga* Cambridge 1958.
[28] R. MacIver *Mediaeval Rhodesia* London 1906.
[29] F. O. Bernhard 'Notes on the pre-Ruin Ziwa Culture of Inyanga' *Rhodesiana* XII (1964).
[30] F. O. Bernhard 'The Ziwa Ware of Inyanga' *Native Affairs Department Annual* (Southern Rhodesia) XXXVIII (1961) 84–92.
[31] K. R. Robinson 'The Leopard's Kopje Culture, its Position in the Iron Age in Southern Rhodesia' *S.A.A.B.* XXI (1966) pp. 5–51.

twelfth centuries A.D. from Zhiso Hill in the Matopos is the only date so far reported for a site attributed to Leopard's Kopje 1. Leopard's Kopje 2, which was formerly regarded as a development from 1, but whose pottery seems far removed from the Early Iron Age tradition and whose distribution is restricted to south-western Matabeleland, has been dated to the seventh to eighth centuries A.D. (SR–55) at the type site near Khami and slightly later (SR–68) at Taba Zikamambo. These dates suggest that the hypothesis of a Leopard's Kopje 1–Leopard's Kopje 2 succession may be an oversimplification and that the 'Leopard's Kopje Culture' of the literature may not represent a single cultural entity.

The earliest Iron Age occupation of south-western Rhodesia is probably represented in the archaeological record by sites such as Mandau[32] and Madiliyangwa[33] where the pottery has close parallels both in early Gokomere wares and in the so-called channel-decorated pottery which may antedate the Dambwa settlements of southern Zambia. These Matabeleland sites may prove to be ancestral to Leopard's Kopje 1 which should then be regarded as a localized development from the general Early Iron Age continuum. The apparent scarcity of very early sites in this area may be fortuitous or it may indicate that the population, prior to the development of Leopard's Kopje 1, was comparatively sparse. The later phases of the Leopard's Kopje culture are outside the scope of this paper.

At Malapati on the Nuanetsi River in the extreme south-east of Rhodesia a village site investigated by Robinson has yielded a date in the last quarter of the first millennium A.D. (SR–33).[34] The pottery shows affinities with both Gokomere and Leopard's Kopje 1 wares, while Robinson also suggests that it has links with material described by Schofield from Maokagani Hill in Botswana.[35] Little archaeological work has so far been done in the Rhodesian Lowveld or in the Limpopo valley but Malapati and Dombozanga show that the area was inhabited by Early Iron Age peoples before the first settlement of Bambandyanalo.

[32] K. R. Robinson 'Bambata Ware: its Position in the Rhodesian Iron Age in the Light of Recent Evidence' *S.A.A.B.* XXI (1966) pp. 81–85.

[33] N. Jones 'Excavations at Nswatugi and Madiliyangwa' *O.P.N.M.S.R.* I (1933) No. 2 pp. 1–44.

[34] K. R. Robinson 'Further Excavations in the Iron Age Deposits at the Tunnel Site, Gokomere Hill, Southern Rhodesia' *S.A.A.B.* XVIII (1963) pp. 155–71.

[35] J. F. Schofield *Primitive Pottery* Cape Town 1948.

During the first millennium A.D. virtually every area of Rhodesia which has been archaeologically investigated appears to have supported an Early Iron Age population of remarkably similar type. However, no other country south of the Zambezi can match the degree to which the Iron Age archaeology of Rhodesia has been investigated. An almost complete lack of evidence confronts us when we seek to discover the extent to which Early Iron Age settlement extended beyond the southern borders of the present Rhodesia.

Botswana and South West Africa

As Summers has pointed out, much of southern Africa, particularly in the western regions, is climatically unsuited to farming settlement. Recent economic patterns tend to support this view and it is likely that climatic change during the last two thousand years has not been on a sufficient scale radically to change this picture. The available evidence suggests that most of Botswana was occupied largely, if not exclusively, by hunting-gathering people of Late Stone Age stock until very recent times. From the eastern strip of Botswana, adjacent to the Rhodesian border, finds of pottery of Leopard's Kopje and Malapati type suggest that this area may be regarded as part of the Rhodesian culture zone.

A recent survey of the pre-European pottery of South West Africa has failed to locate any material for which there is any reason to suggest an antiquity greater than a very few centuries.[36] The affinities of this pottery appear to be with Khoikhoi wares rather than with any Early Iron Age tradition. The presence of copper beads in a Late Stone Age site dated to the beginning of the second millennium A.D. (SR–46) which was investigated by MacCalman in the Brandberg north-west of Windhoek, perhaps indicates the presence of metallurgists in the area at this early date, but the beads could have been traded for a very considerable distance.[37]

South Africa

For the Transvaal and Swaziland we have a little more to go on,

[36] W. Sydow 'The pre-European Pottery of South West Africa' *Cimbebasia memoir I* Windhoek 1967.

[37] H. R. MacCalman 'Carbon–14 Dates for South West Africa' *S.A.A.B.* XX (1965) p. 215.

but here too the picture is very incomplete. Pottery similar to that from Malapati has been discovered by de Vaal on the farm Happy Rest in the Soutpansberg of the Northern Transvaal.[38] The site is undated but presumably precedes the occupation of Bambandyanalo. This and the similarity with the dated Malapati site make a date in the second half of the first millennium appear likely. Farther south in the Transvaal, Iron Age occupation distinct from the Early Iron Age tradition appears to have been established on the Witwatersrand by the beginning of the second millennium.[39] That this was not the first Iron Age settlement so far south is demonstrated by two recent investigations, on neither of which are full data yet available. At Castle Peak in western Swaziland Beaumont has obtained a single date of the fourth to fifth century A.D. (Y–1712) from charcoal associated with sherds of vessels 'typified by a carinated profile and single or multiple channelled lines lying parallel to and immediately below the rim. Various types of stone mining tools, ground stone fragments, rare iron tools and Late Stone Age artefacts came from the same levels.'[40] Although no further details of the Castle Peak finds are yet available, the description of the pottery suggests that it is markedly dissimilar to that of the Uitkomst or Buispoort sites and other more recent wares. It could well prove to be a representative of the Early Iron Age lying several hundred miles to the south of the previously known distribution. Whatever the cultural affinities of the pottery, the Castle Peak finds do seem to indicate the presence in Swaziland, around the middle of the first millennium A.D., of iron-using, pot-making people in contact with Late Stone Age folk. No other site south of the Limpopo has produced evidence for the presence of such people at such an early date.

In keeping with the Castle Peak evidence is a series of dates obtained by van der Merwe from iron and copper working sites at Palabora in the eastern Transvaal.[41] Mine workings at Loolekop reach depths of seventy feet and have given dates in the seventh to eleventh centuries A.D. (Y–1635, Y–1636). Two successive occupations of clay huts at Kgopolwe have been dated: the lower floor to the ninth to eleventh centuries (Y–1637,

[38] J. B. de Vaal ' 'n Soutpansbergse Zimbabwe' *S.A.J.S.* XL (1943) pp. 303–18.
[39] R. J. Mason *Prehistory of the Transvaal* Johannesburg 1962.
[40] Quoted in B. M. Fagan 'Radiocarbon Dates for sub-Saharan Africa-V' *J.A.H.* VIII (1967) p. 525.
[41] M. Stuiver and N. J. van der Merwe 'Radiocarbon Chronology of the Iron Age in sub-Saharan Africa' *Current Anthropology* IX (1968) pp. 54–8.

Y–1638), and the upper floor to the tenth to twelfth centuries (Y–1639, Y–1662). No details of the pottery and associated finds are yet available. The presence, through much of the Transvaal, of Iron Age communities well before the end of the first millennium A.D. seems amply demonstrated by the available evidence. That these peoples were related to the Early Iron Age folk from north of the Limpopo seems likely but cannot yet be demonstrated.

COMPARISON WITH OTHER AREAS

Any discussion of the affinities of the Early Iron Age communities just described is hampered by the fact that many vast areas remain archaeologically unexplored. The Zambian and Rhodesian evidence is sparse and incomplete but the situation elsewhere is generally worse. This should be remedied in the near future as a great deal of valuable work is now under way in Malawi and East Africa.

Studies of the later prehistory of Moçambique are almost completely lacking. The few finds of Iron Age pottery which have been described do not appear to resemble known Early Iron Age types from elsewhere.[42] On the other hand, dos Santos has drawn attention to the distribution in Moçambique north of the Zambezi of schematic rock paintings.[43] These closely parallel Zambian paintings which appear to be of Iron Age date but to predate the arrival of most of the present Iron Age communities.[44] Of the Iron Age archaeology of the coastal plain of Moçambique and of the lower Zambezi valley virtually nothing is known which predates Portuguese settlement. In view of suggested Indonesian influences reaching the African mainland via the Comoros and/or Madagascar during the first millennium A.D.[45], the lack of knowledge about the Moçambique coast is particularly lamentable.

In Angola the situation is little better, despite the great strides that Stone Age studies have taken. A few radiocarbon dates are available but hardly any details of the associated pottery have

[42] L. H. Wells 'Relatorio sobre objectos encontrados em restos de cozinha perto da foz do Limpopo' *Moçambique documentario trimestral* 1943 pp. 13–23.
[43] J. R. dos Santos Junior 'Les Peintures Rupestres de Moçambique' in *Actes du II Congrès Panafricain de Préhistoire* Paris 1955 pp. 747–58.
[44] D. W. Phillipson 'The Rock Paintings of Zambia: their Age and Cultural Associations', paper presented to *Sixth Panafrican Congress on Prehistory* Dakar Senegal 1967.
[45] M. Posnansky 'The Iron Age in East Africa' in *Background to Evolution in Africa* ed. W. Bishop and J. D. Clark Chicago 1967 pp. 629–49.

been published. We can be reasonably sure that Iron Age communities inhabited much of Angola during the first millennium A.D., but of the affinities of these communities we can say nothing. Only 200 miles north of the Kunene the radiocarbon dates from Feti la Choya (Y–587, Y–588) show that a very substantial Iron Age settlement was established at least as early as the seventh to eighth centuries A.D. Beyond the fact that iron was present, no details of the associated finds are available.[46]

In northern Angola there is a single date which suggests very early Iron Age activity. A stream gravel at Furi Mine contained a Late Stone Age industry together with potsherds and charcoals which have been dated (UCLA–170) to the first to third centuries A.D. Two other sites in the same area, a buried land surface in Kalahari sand at Dundo Airfield (UCLA–716) and a rockshelter at Ricocco (UCLA–717), yielded late first millennium dates for similar pottery.[47]

This thin scatter of incompletely published sites extends northwards into the Congo. In Kinshasa Province there are two tantalizing associations of undescribed pottery with radiocarbon dates in the fourth to second century B.C. (LV–167) and the fourth to fifth century A.D. (LV–168).[48] Published Congolese Iron Age sites are mainly from the eastern part of the country. In Rwanda and Burundi the earliest known pottery bears many typological resemblances to the 'dimple-based ware' of south-western Kenya. At several sites this pottery has been found associated with Late Stone Age industries or with iron-smelting debris.[49] It presumably pre-dates the highly developed culture revealed by Nenquin's excavations at Sanga.[50] Although similarities with the local Congolese Early Iron Age are slight, the

[46] J. Vansina *Kingdoms of the Savanna* Madison 1966; B. M. Fagan 'Radiocarbon Dates for sub-Saharan Africa—III' *J.A.H.* VI (1965) pp. 107–16.

[47] C. J. Ferguson and W. F. Libby 'UCLA Radiocarbon Dates—II' *Radiocarbon* V (1963) p. 17; R. Berger, C. J. Ferguson and W. F. Libby 'UCLA Radiocarbon Dates—IV' *Radiocarbon* VII (1965) pp. 358–9.

[48] B. M. Fagan 'Radiocarbon Dates for sub-Saharan Africa—IV' *J.A.H.* VII (1966) pp. 495–506.

[49] J. Hiernaux and E. Maquet 'Cultures Préhistoriques de l'Age des Métaux au Ruanda–Urundi et au Kivu, Congo Belge: Première Partie' *Bull. des Séances Acad. Roy. des Sci. Coloniales* Bruxelles 1957 pp. 1126–49; J. Hiernaux and E. Maquet 'Cultures Préhistoriques de l'Age des Métaux au Ruanda–Urundi et au Kivu, Congo Belge: Deuxième Partie' *Mém. Acad. Roy. des Sci. d'Outre-Mer* X Bruxelles 1960; J. Nenquin *Contributions to the Study of the Prehistoric Cultures of Rwanda and Burundi* Tervuren 1967.

[50] J. Nenquin *Excavations at Sanga, 1957* Tervuren 1963.

late first millennium (B–263, B–264) Sanga pottery shares many features with the Zambian Kalambo material and it should probably be regarded as a specialized development of the general Early Iron Age tradition. Pottery finds of this same general tradition extend far to the west through the Congo basin, as finds at Tshikapa in Kasai[51] and near Thysville in Bas-Congo indicate.[52] Until more extensive Iron Age research is conducted in the central and western Congo, little more than this bare catalogue of pottery finds will be possible.

The close connections between the Rwanda-Burundi Early Iron Age pottery and that from East Africa has long been recognized. Soper recognizes three basic subdivisions of the latter material.[53] That from Kwale, inland from Mombasa, is dated to around the third century A.D. (N–291, N–292).[54] Kwale pottery appears closely related to that from Sandaweland[55] which is at present undated, although Sutton[56] has recently obtained dates in the fourth to eighth centuries A.D. (N–463, N–465) for very similar wares at Uvinza in western Tanzania. Recently obtained radiocarbon dates[57] show that the 'dimple-based ware' from Kavirondo in Kenya[58] is contemporary with Kwale. Unfortunately hardly any associated finds are recorded from these East African Early Iron Age pottery sites. Iron is reported only from Kwale and faunal remains are so far completely absent.

This bare summary of finds is sufficient to show that the Zambian and Rhodesian Early Iron Age is no isolated phenomenon. Traces of related cultures are known from almost all the adjacent areas where any Iron Age research has been done. The available dating evidence shows that the East African Early Iron Age settlements are approximately contemporary with those in Zambia and Rhodesia. Over this huge area, most of Africa south of the Equator, a remarkably consistent picture is beginning to

[51] J. Nenquin 'Dimple-Based Pots from Kasai, Belgian Congo', *Man,* LIX 1959, article 242.

[52] G. Mortelmans 'Archéologie des Grottes Dimba et Ngovo' in *Actes du IV Congrès Panafricain de Préhistoire,* Tervuren 1962 pp. 405–26.

[53] R. C. Soper 'Early Iron Age Pottery Types from East Africa: Comparative Analysis' paper presented to *Sixth Panafrican Congress on Prehistory* Dakar Senegal 1967.

[54] R. C. Soper 'Kwale, an Early Iron Age Site in South-Eastern Kenya' *Azania* II (1967) pp. 1–17.

[55] G. Smolla 'Prahistorische Keramic aus Ostafrika' *Tribus,* VI (1956) pp. 35–64.

[56] J. E. G. Sutton, 'Report on excavations at Uvinza' *Azania* III (1968) pp. 45–86.

[57] R. C. Soper *personal communication.*

[58] M. D. Leakey, W. E. Owen and L. S. B. Leakey 'Dimple-Based Pottery from Central Kavirondo, Kenya' *Coryndon Museum Occasional Paper No. 2* Nairobi 1948.

emerge of the appearance of iron-using, pot-making, food-producing communities whose way of life contrasted markedly with that of the Late Stone Age hunters. The scale and completeness of this contrast leave little doubt that we are dealing with the arrival of a new population element, which probably began to spread through the area early in the first millennium A.D. and by the middle of that millennium had established itself, often in not inconsiderable numbers, over much of the area north of the Vaal.

INTERACTION WITH LATE STONE AGE PEOPLES

From very early times the Iron Age cultures appear to have been practised by a considerable number of people. Occupation by the early farmers was particularly dense in reasonably fertile areas such as southern Zambia. Here Early Iron Age finds come from substantial village sites where there is no residual trace of Late Stone Age technology. It seems likely that in these areas the Late Stone Age population was largely displaced by the second half of the first millennium A.D. No doubt a certain amount of the Late Stone Age population was absorbed into the society of the new arrivals but their cultural contribution appears to have been minimal. Elsewhere in Zambia the Early Iron Age population was probably sparse and in many areas Late Stone Age people survived in their traditional way of life well into the present millennium. The evidence from Nakapapula[59] again provides little indication of acculturation between the two groups, yet the frequency with which potsherds identical to those which occur in Early Iron Age sites which lack any sign of Late Stone Age technology are found in Late Stone Age deposits suggests that some contact may have taken place.

In many areas of Rhodesia, particularly the Matopo Hills, the chronological break between the Late Stone Age and Early Iron Age can be shown to be no more distinct than it is north of the Zambezi. The presence of Early Iron Age sherds in association with Late Stone Age artefacts is common in caves and rock-shelters: Amadzimba[60], Dombozanga, Bambata[61], Madiliyangwa[62]

[59] D. W. Phillipson 'The Prehistoric Sequence at Nakapapula Rockshelter, Zambia' *in press*.

[60] C. K. Cooke and K. R. Robinson 'Excavations at Amadzimba Cave, Matopo Hills' *O.P.N.M.S.R.* II No. 19 (1948) pp. 699–728.

[61] J. F. Schofield 'Report on the Pottery from Bambata Cave' *S.A.J.S.* XXXVII (1940) pp. 361–72.

[62] N. Jones 'Excavations at Nswatugi and Madiliyangwa' *O.P.N.M.S.R.* I No. 2 (1933) pp. 1–44.

and Tshangula[63] may be quoted as examples. The late first millennium A.D. radiocarbon dates from Dombozanga (SR–15) and Tshangula (SR–69) are further evidence for the late continuation of the Late Stone Age industries.

The rock art provides further evidence for the late survival of Late Stone Age peoples into the period of Early Iron Age settlement. Cooke has argued convincingly for a late date for the majority of the surviving paintings in Matabeleland and there is no reason to doubt a similar date for the art in other parts of the country.[64] There is general acceptance that the great bulk of the naturalistic art in both Zambia and Rhodesia was executed by people at a Late Stone Age stage of development. In Rhodesia much of the subject matter of the naturalistic paintings indicates that the artists had contact with Iron Age people who practised an economy different from their own. Partly contemporary but generally later than the naturalistic art in Zambia is a large series of schematic paintings which appear to be the work of Iron Age peoples.[65] Such paintings, although present in Rhodesia, are less common there and have received comparatively scant attention.

Precisely what were the relationships between the two groups in the area, where they remained in contact is not easy to determine. Physical anthropology suggests that miscegenation was not particularly common after the early centuries of the Iron Age. Archaeology does not provide evidence for significant acculturation in either direction.

Recent relationships between Negroid farmers and residual hunting-gathering groups have been studied among both the Bushmen[66] and pygmies.[67] In both these cases a client relationship has been shown to exist in which the hunters, while clients of the farmers, are drawn into the farming economy but often do not themselves adopt such an economy. Objects from the material culture of the farmers will come into the possession of their clients

[63] C. K. Cooke 'Report on Excavations at Pomongwe and Tshangula Caves, Matopo Hills, Southern Rhodesia' *S.A.A.B.* XVIII (1963) pp. 73–150.

[64] C. K. Cooke 'The Rock Paintings of Matabeleland' in *Prehistoric Rock Art of the Federation of Rhodesia and Nyasaland*, ed. R. Summers London 1959 pp. 112–62; C. K. Cooke 'Iron Age Influence in the Rock Art of Southern Africa' *Arnoldia* (*Rhod.*) II (1964) No. 12.

[65] D. W. Phillipson 'The Rock Paintings of Zambia: their Age and Cultural Associations' paper presented to *Sixth Panafrican Congress on Prehistory* Dakar Senegal 1967.

[66] G. Silberbauer *Bushman Survey: Report to the Bechuanaland Government* Gaberones 1965.

[67] C. Turnbull 'The Lesson of the Pygmies' *Scientific American* CCVIII (1963) No. 1.

but the appropriate technology will often remain the prerogative of the former group.[68] The evidence is slender, but it may be that such a situation was prevalent in Central Africa during the first millennium A.D. On the margins of the Negroid distribution it has continued to the present day.[69]

In the extreme south of the continent there is evidence for the spread of pottery and animal domestication beyond the distribution of the Iron Age cultures. The only dates available for early pottery on the coast of the Cape Province are those from Scott's Cave in the Gamtoos valley[70]. The start of the occupation is dated to the seventh to ninth centuries A.D. (SR–82) and the terminal stage to the sixteenth to seventeenth centuries (Y–1425). These suggest an age which is not so early as to rule out the probability that the impetus for the development of this pottery was acquired by contact with Iron Age groups. No domestic animal bones were recovered from Scott's Cave, but Seddon and Vinnicombe have recently published references which show that cattle, sheep and goats had reached the Cape of Good Hope by 1505–8.[71] Both pottery and domestic animals were, of course, important aspects of the material culture of the Khoikhoi who were recorded by early European visitors as occupying much of the area lying to the south of the country of the Iron Age peoples.

ORIGIN AND SPREAD

Although the Early Iron Age groups are obviously closely related, considerable regional variation is apparent from the earliest time. This is clear in Zambia and Rhodesia where the coverage of research is less incomplete. The contrast between the Early Iron Age pottery from northern Zambia and that from East African sites is also marked. The distribution of the regional variants has led the writer to postulate a general north-western origin for the Early Iron Age in Zambia and Rhodesia.[72] Posnansky, concentrating his study on the East African material, has reached a

[68] J. D. Clark 'Bushman Hunters of the Barotse Forests' *Northern Rhodesia Journal* I No. 3 (1951) pp. 56–65.

[69] See note 66.

[70] H. J. and J. Deacon 'Scott's Cave: a Late Stone Age Site in the Gamtoos Valley' *Ann. Cape Prov. Mus.* III (1963) pp. 96–121; H. J. Deacon 'Two Radiocarbon Dates from Scott's Cave, Gamtoos Valley' *S.A.A.B.* XXII (1967) pp. 51–52.

[71] J. D. Seddon and P. Vinnicombe 'Domestic Animals, Rock Art and Dating' *S.A.A.B.* XXII (1967) pp. 112–13.

[72] D. W. Phillipson 'The Early Iron Age in Zambia: Regional Variants and some Tentative Conclusions' *J.A.H.* IX (1968) pp. 191–211.

similar conclusion.[73] This hypothesis does not, of course, preclude the possibility that some of the cultural traits of the Early Iron Age may have various, widely scattered, origins. African population movements within the recent past appear exceedingly complicated and are difficult to unravel. Not only are very many groups mobile, but the composition of the groups is in a continuous state of flux. A comparable situation probably prevailed among Early Iron Age communities.

The archaeological evidence therefore points to the conclusion that Iron Age culture was brought into eastern and southern Africa by a largely immigrant population around the beginning of the first millennium A.D. The available physical anthropological data are in keeping with this hypothesis. Skeletons found associated with Late Stone Age industries pre-dating the introduction of the Early Iron Age are almost invariably of Bush type[74], although it may be that some of the Late Stone Age folk of northern Zambia and Malawi showed some physical similarity to modern pygmy groups.[75] Negroid features are, however, apparent in skeletons recovered from Iron Age sites, although most are claimed to show varying degrees of Bush mixture, as at Inyanga[76] and Dambwa.[77] Tobias's suggestion that 'metal culture diffused down the east coast of Africa mainly before the "negrotization" of the population' does not seem to be in accord with the more recent discoveries.[78] There is not sufficient evidence to prove that Negroid peoples definitely were those responsible for the introduction of Iron Age culture, but it seems probable that they were. Certainly the arrival of the Negroids was chronologically close to that of the Iron Age.

The correlation between the spread of the central and southern African Early Iron Age and that of the Bantu languages is frequently postulated. We have argued above that the arrival in

[73] M. Posnansky 'Bantu Genesis—Archaeological Reflexions' *J.A.H.* IX (1968) pp. 1–11.

[74] C. Gabel 'Further Human Remains from the Central African Late Stone Age' *Man* LXIII (1963) article 44.

[75] L. H. Wells 'Late Stone Age Human Types in Central Africa' *Proceedings of the Third Panafrican Congress on Prehistory* London 1957 pp. 183–5.

[76] F. O. Bernhard 'Notes on the Pre-Ruin Ziwa Culture of Inyanga' *Rhodesiana* XII (1964).

[77] S. G. H. Daniels and D. W. Phillipson 'The Early Iron Age Site at Dambwa near Livingstone' in B. M. Fagan, D. W. Phillipson and S. G. H. Daniels *Iron Age Cultures in Zambia—II* London 1969.

[78] P. V. Tobias 'Skeletal Remains from Inyanga' in R. Summers, *Inyanga* Cambridge 1958 pp. 159–72.

central and southern Africa of such cultural traits as pottery, metallurgy and food production was approximately synchronous and that it was due to the arrival of a new population element. Whether or not the spread of the Bantu languages can also be linked to the same movement there is not sufficient evidence to say, but the directions of spread of the Iron Age cultures and of the Bantu languages do appear to be remarkably similar. Purely archaeological evidence is, of course, incapable of determining the language spoken by a preliterate community and the problem of language is one with which the archaeologist does not normally concern himself. However, linguists have been able to postulate historical reconstructions and this both provides a means for attempting a correlation between linguistic and archaeological evidence and, if such a correlation can be accomplished, opens up valuable possibilities for future research.

Ehret has argued that the spread of cattle in our area preceded the spread of the Bantu languages.[79] He argues 'that the three Bantu forms of the *(k)umbi* root for cattle cannot be explained on the basis of Bantu sound-changes. It follows from this that the root was borrowed into Bantu languages independently in at least three original forms in different locations; that is that cattle were known by these names in these locations when Bantu-speakers arrived in them'.[80] Before Ehret's conclusions can be accepted unreservedly we should perhaps inquire whether or not this borrowing of the root into Bantu languages must necessarily have taken place in the area of the present distribution of the respective roots within the Bantu language structure. If it is agreed that the Bantu languages spread into central and southern Africa from elsewhere, might not the *(k)umbi* words have spread with them, having been borrowed from non-Bantu languages within, or immediately peripherally to, a primary or secondary centre of dispersal? It seems to the present writer that very little is yet known concerning the dynamics of linguistic spread in Africa. Argument from the present distribution of languages[81] presupposes that many traditionally recorded population movements have not greatly affected the linguistic pattern. Examples can be cited both to support and to refute this assumption.

[79] C. Ehret 'Cattle Keeping and Milking in Eastern and Southern African History: the linguistic Evidence' *J.A.H.* VIII (1967) pp. 1–17.

[80] Op. cit. p. 6.

[81] e.g. R. O. Oliver 'The Problem of the Bantu Expansion' *J.A.H.* VII (1966) pp. 361–76.

Ignorance of the dynamics of cultural spread is, of course, not limited to the linguistic field. Archaeology can provide us with information concerning the distribution of traits of material culture and it is all too easy, and too frequent, for the archaeologist to interpret the apparent spread of cultural traits in terms of a physical population movement, whereas there is often no theoretical reason to prefer such an interpretation to the concept of cultural diffusion through a static population or by means of a very small group of migrant individuals. Even in the field of traditional history there is, as Vansina[82] has demonstrated, considerable doubt about the amount of population movement involved in the migration of political entities. Our sources of evidence thus deal with technological, linguistic and political units, all of which are apparently fluid and none of which need be conterminous with a physical population unit. Historians and archaeologists should beware of conceptualizing prehistoric data into tidy culture areas and stratigraphic units. Insufficient evidence can too easily lead to false assumptions based on the apparent concurrence of what may in fact be unrelated traits.

It was once popular to visualize the spread of the African Iron Age in terms of a massive, swift invasion in which the technical superiority of iron weapons gave an immediate advantage to their owners. Advantageous as iron tools and weapons may have been, they were almost certainly very scarce and the wide but sparse distribution of the Early Iron Age makes an invasion hypothesis unlikely. The diversity within the common pottery tradition suggests that we are dealing with a substantial number of independent but related groups whose arrival took place gradually over a period of several centuries. The detailed definition and dating of these groups over an area of more than two million square miles is an enormous task but one which must be accomplished, at any rate in outline, to provide a foundation for our knowledge of the subsequent history of African societies in central and southern Africa.

[82] J. Vansina *Kingdoms of the Savanna* Madison 1966.

Appendix

RADIOCARBON DATES

B–233	Nyahokwe	A.D. 1010±110
B–263	Sanga	A.D. 710±120
B–264	Sanga	A.D. 880±200
GrN–3189	Kalambo Falls	A.D. 1350/1580±50
GrN–3580	Kalambo Falls	A.D. 1020±40
GrN–4646	Kalambo Falls	A.D. 345±40
GrN–4647	Kalambo Falls	A.D. 430±40
GX–535	Nakapapula	A.D. 770±100
GX–662	Twickenham Road, Lusaka	A.D. 1055±110
GX–767	Nakapapula	A.D. 1040±85
GX–1009	Chondwe	A.D. 815±130
GX–1010	Chondwe	A.D. 890±95
GX–1012	Kapwirimbwe	A.D. 505±95
GX–1013a	Kapwirimbwe	A.D. 425±110
GX–1013b	Kapwirimbwe	A.D. 410±85
GX–1114	Gundu	A.D. 440±85
GX–1115	Gundu	A.D. 540±85
GX–1327	Kangonga	A.D. 765±85
GX–1328	Kangonga	A.D. 340±115
GX–1329	Twickenham Road, Lusaka	A.D. 940±110
GX–1330	Chondwe (post-E.I.A.)	A.D. 1155±85
GX–1331	Chondwe (post-E.I.A.)	A.D. 1110±85
L–395a	Kalambo Falls	A.D. 980±150
L–395b	Kalambo Falls	A.D. 870±180
L–395c	Kalambo Falls	A.D. 550±150
LV–167	Funa	270 B.C.±90
LV–168	Ile des Mimosas	A.D. 410±100
M–913	Zimbabwe	A.D. 330±150
N–291	Kwale	A.D. 270±110
N–292	Kwale	A.D. 260±110
N–409	Kumadzulo	A.D. 430±110
N–410	Kumadzulo	A.D. 560±110
N–411	Kumadzulo	A.D. 550±110
N–412	Kumadzulo	A.D. 620±110
N–413	Kumadzulo	A.D. 630±110
N–414	Kumadzulo	A.D. 690±105
N–463	Pwaga, Uvinza	A.D. 420±160
N–465	Nyamsunga, Uvinza	A.D. 590±200

SR-15	Dombozanga	A.D. 750±100
SR-17	Ziwa Farm, Inyanga	A.D. 300±100
SR-26	Gokomere	A.D. 530±120
SR-32	Ziwa Farm, Inyanga	A.D. 850±100
SR-33	Malapati	A.D. 850±100
SR-38	Ziwa Farm, Inyanga	A.D. 900±100
SR-43	Mabveni	A.D. 180±120
SR-46	Numas Entrance Shelter	A.D. 1080±100
SR-55	Leopard's Kopje	A.D. 700±110
SR-62	Dambwa	A.D. 620±110
SR-65	Kalundu	A.D. 300±90
SR-68	Taba Zikamambo	A.D. 870±100
SR-69	Tshangula	A.D. 830±90
SR-73	Kapula Vlei	A.D. 810±90
SR-79	Mabveni	A.D. 570±110
SR-82	Scott's Cave	A.D. 760±100
SR-96	Dambwa	A.D. 860±95
SR-97	Dambwa	A.D. 750±95
SR-98	Dambwa	A.D. 780±90
SR-106	Dambwa	A.D. 600±100
SR-110	Dambwa	A.D. 660±120
SR-118	Sinoia Cave	A.D. 650±95
SR-123	Kalundu	A.D. 455±95
TX-228	Zhiso Hill	A.D. 1040±130
UCLA-170	Furi Mine	A.D. 150±80
UCLA-716	Dundo Airfield	A.D. 760±80
UCLA-717	Ricocco II	A.D. 940±80
UCLA-929	Calder's Cave	20 B.C. ±80
Y-587	Feti la Choya	A.D. 710±100
Y-588	Feti la Choya	A.D. 1250±65
Y-1425	Scott's Cave	A.D. 1590±80
Y-1635	Loolekop	A.D. 1000±60
Y-1636	Loolekop	A.D. 770±80
Y-1637	Kgopolwe	A.D. 1040±60
Y-1638	Kgopolwe	A.D. 960±80
Y-1639	Kgopolwe	A.D. 1100±60
Y-1662	Kgopolwe	A.D. 1130±80
Y-1712	Castle Peak	A.D. 410±60

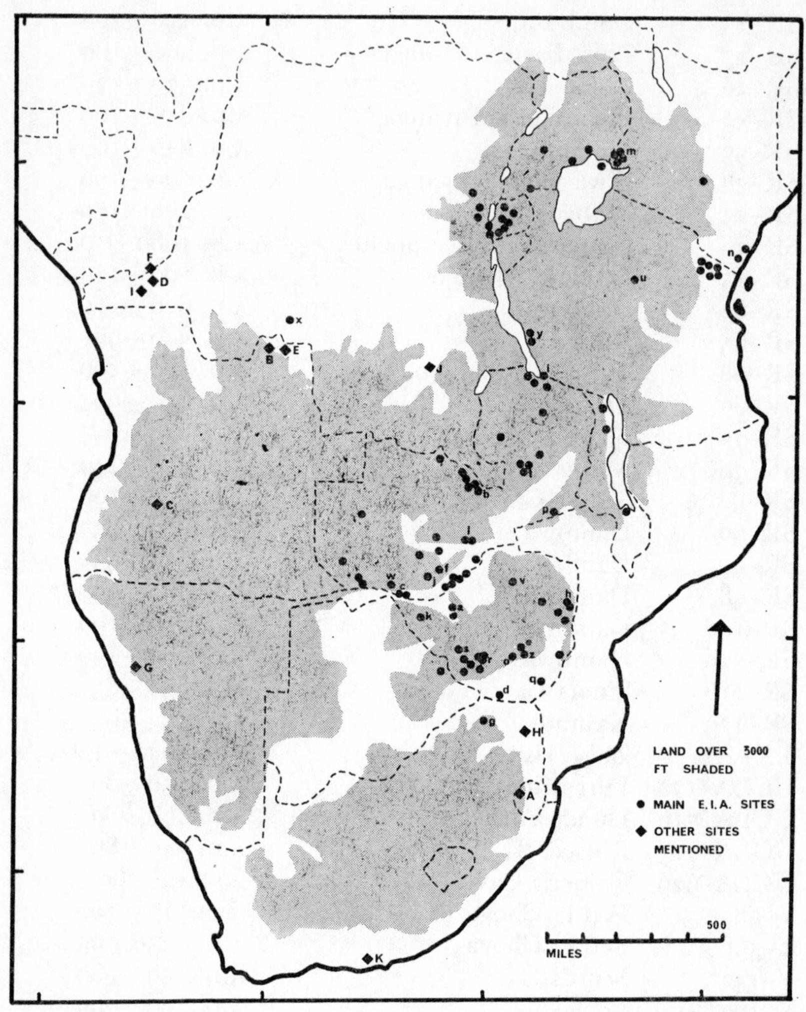

2. *Sites of the early iron-using peoples*

EARLY IRON AGE SITES:

a—Calder's Cave
b—Chondwe and Kangonga
c—Dambwa and Kumadzulo
d—Dombozanga
e—Gokomere
f—Gundu
g—Happy Rest
h—Inyanga, Nyahokwe and 'Place of Offerings'
i—Kalambo Falls
j—Kalundu
k—Kapula Vlei
l—Kapwirimbwe and Twickenham Road
m—Kavirondo sites
n—Kwale
o—Mabveni
p—Makwe
q—Malapati
r—Matopo Hills (Amadzimba, Bambata, Madiliyangwa, Tshangula and Zhiso)
s—Mandau
t—Nakapapula
u—Sandaweland
v—Sinoia Cave
w—Situmpa
x—Tshikapa
y—Uvinza
z—Zimbabwe

OTHER SITES, *including possible but not proven Early Iron Age occurrences*:

A—Castle Peak
B—Dundo Airfield
C—Feti la Choya
D—Funa
E—Furi Mine
F—Ile des Mimosas
G—Numas Entrance Shelter
H—Palabora
I—Thysville
J—Sanga
K—Scott's Cave

3. *The later Iron Age in South Africa*

BRIAN FAGAN

The study of Iron Age culture south of the Limpopo has always been overshadowed by the richness of the Stone Age archaeological record in South Africa. Descriptions of stone implements and rock paintings fill the pages of scientific journals, but the literature on the closing centuries of South African prehistory is sporadic, speculative, and frequently of dubious quality. Although early travellers such as Moffat[1] and Campbell[2] described the 'stone towns' of Iron Age, Bantu-speaking peoples in the Transvaal and Orange Free State in the nineteenth century, and stone implements were collected as early as 1858,[3] the first systematic attempts to study Iron Age sites in South Africa were not made until the 1920s and 1930s when a number of investigators published superficial accounts of stone-built cattle kraals in the treeless areas of the Highveld. Despite some dissenting views,[4] van Riet Lowe and others ascribed them to early Bantu-speaking peoples. At the same time Laidler[5] and Schofield began their studies of South African ceramics, which led to the latter's monograph on the subject in 1948.[6] This study is still the basis for the classification of Iron Age wares over much of southern Africa, although the conclusions reached by its author are based on highly inadequate evidence.

World attention was focused on the South African Iron Age with the discovery of the Mapungubwe site in 1933.[7] The long campaigns of excavations in the Limpopo valley were completed

[1] R. Moffat *Missionary Labours and Scenes in South Africa* London 1842.

[2] J. Campbell *Travels in South Africa* London 1822.

[3] J. Desmond Clark *The Prehistory of Southern Africa* London 1958 p. 24.

[4] Summarized in P. L. Breutz 'Stone Kraal Settlements in South Africa' *African Studies* (1956) 15 4 pp. 157–75.

[5] P. W. Laidler, various references, mostly in select bibliography, but especially 'South African native ceramics: their characteristics and classification' *T.R.S.S.A.* (1938) XXVI pp. 93–172.

[6] J. F. Schofield *Primitive Pottery* Cape Town 1948.

[7] L. Fouché *Mapungubwe* Cambridge 1937.

immediately before the war, but only finally published in 1963.[8] Schofield and others were quick to recognize that the northernmost parts of the Transvaal had close cultural connections with the north, but many details of the Limpopo sequence remain unstudied.

For many years it was assumed by the ignorant that the first Bantu-speaking peoples crossed the Limpopo at approximately the same time as Van Riebeeck landed at the Cape.[9] This view, sometimes still glimpsed in obscure or nationalistic literature has been completely disproved by the researches of Revil Mason, Monica Wilson, and others. Mason has investigated a number of Iron Age sites in the Transvaal, making extensive use of air photographs to locate stone structures and obtaining an important series of radiocarbon dates for various settlements.[10] His excavations on the Witwatersrand showed that Iron Age peoples have been living in the Transvaal for over a thousand years, while Monica Wilson's masterly analysis of the early history of the Transkei and Ciskei demonstrated the antiquity of Bantu settlement in the south-eastern parts of the country.[11]

This paper is an attempt to summarize the later Iron Age archaeology of South Africa. The unsatisfactory archaeological evidence means that our conclusions are speculative and liable to extensive modifications. In the interests of clarity, I consider the data area by area.

THE LIMPOPO AND NORTHERN TRANSVAAL

The dry and *mopane*-covered country between the Limpopo and the Soutspansberg mountains formed an important cultural province during the Iron Age. Copper and iron outcrops were abundant and much exploited,[12] salt pans were found in the mountains, while other commodities such as tin for alloying could be readily traded from south of the Berg.

The sites which have been extensively examined come from the farm Greefswald, fifty-five miles west of Messina near the Limpopo.

[8] G. A. Gardner *Mapungubwe* Vol. II Pretoria 1963.

[9] The literature is diverse. A recent manifestation is: R. Gayre of Gayre 'The Bantu homelands of the Northern Transvaal' *Mankind Quarterly* 1962 pp. 98–112.

[10] R. J. Mason 'The origin of South African Society' *S.A.J.S.* 1965 61 pp. 255–67.

[11] Monica Wilson 'Early history of the Transkei and Ciskei' *African Studies* (1959) 18 4 pp. 167–79.

[12] N. J. van Warmelo 'The copper miners of Musina and the early history of the Zoutpansberg' *Ethnol. Publ.* Government Printer Pretoria (1940) p. 8.

The cultural sequence from Mapungubwe Hill, and the nearby Bambandyanalo site, were fully described in the two monographs on the area, but the interpretation of these important localities by Gardner, who was responsible for the second volume, was controversial. Elsewhere I have attempted a reassessment of the sites.[13]

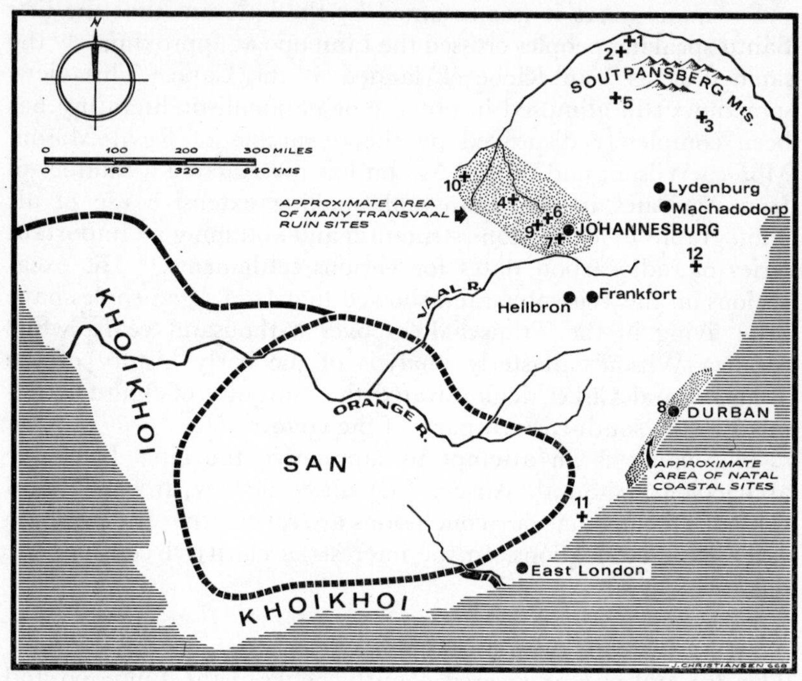

3. *Principal Iron Age sites mentioned in Chapter 3*

1. Mapungubwe; 2. Bambandyanalo; 3. Palabora; 4. Chwenyane; 5. Happy Rest; 6. Uitkomst; 7. Melville Koppies; 8. Karridene; 9. Aasvogelskop; 10. Buisport; 11. Umgazana; 12. Zeerust.

Bambandyanalo is the earlier of the two settlements, a circular mound of occupation debris some 200 yards in diameter and twenty feet deep at its highest point. Stratigraphical profiles have shown that the centre of the village was used for cattle enclosures while huts were built around the edge. The mound was accumulated as a result of successive occupation of the village site, and there is a radiocarbon date of A.D. 1050±65 (Y–135. 17) from Beast Burial Number 6. The material culture is simple, and metal

[13] B. M. Fagan 'The Greefswald sequence: Bambandyanalo and Mapungubwe *J.A.H.* (1964) V 3 pp. 337–62.

tools are rare or non-existent. Seventy-four human skeletons were found, most of them buried in a flexed position surrounded by pots. The human remains were studied by Alexander Galloway who declared them to be non-Negro.[14]

Gardner ascribed Bambandyanalo and its remains to a Khoikhoi population. In so doing he was strongly influenced by the findings of the physical anthropologists, arguing that the site was occupied in its closing stages by Nguni peoples, who introduced hoe-agriculture and hut building, as well as the use of iron. At the time when Gardner studied the Bambandyanalo material little was known of the contemporary cultures north of the Limpopo. He was led to draw parallels between the badly documented economy of the inhabitants of Bambandyanalo and that of the Khoikhoi. In fact the economic evidence from Bambandyanalo appears very similar to that from Rhodesian and Zambian Iron Age sites, where agriculture is inconspicuous in the archaeological record, although thought to be a vital part of the economy. The settlement at Bambandyanalo is much larger than any known Khoikhoi village, while the bone arrowheads and link-shafts from the deposit can be paralleled in Rhodesian Iron Age horizons. The Bambandyanalo pottery, classified as M2 by Schofield[15] has connections with Leopard's Kopje II wares from southern Matabeleland,[16] and is unlike the Khoikhoi pottery to which Gardner compares it.[17] Thus Bambandyanalo belongs within a group of Iron Age industries which are widespread in Rhodesia, Botswana, and to which the Uitkomst pottery of the Central Transvaal is stated to have some parallels.[18]

There remains the question of the human skeletons which were thought, admittedly many years ago, to be of non-Negro type. Under Brothwell's classification they would be labelled as large Khoisan,[19] part of the indigenous physical type, whereas their material culture and economy belong to the Iron Age. This is not

[14] A. Galloway *The skeletal remains of Bambandyanalo* Johannesburg 1959.

[15] J. F. Schofield 'The work done in 1934: pottery' in L. Fouché op. cit. 1937 pp. 32–102.

[16] K. R. Robinson 'Further excavations in the Iron Age deposits at the Tunnel site, Gokomere Hill, Southern Rhodesia' *S.A.A.B.* (1963) 18 (72) pp. 155–71.

[17] G. A. Gardner op. cit. (1963) p. 60.

[18] Roger Summers 'Iron Age industries of Southern Africa, with notes on their chronology, terminology, and economic status' in W. W. Bishop and J. Desmond Clark *Background to African Evolution* Chicago 1967 pp. 687–700.

[19] D. R. Brothwell 'Evidence of Early Population Change in Central and Southern Africa' *Man* (1963) 63 art. 132.

as unexpected as has been made out, for Tobias's studies[20] on Rhodesian crania have indicated that hybridization between large Khoisan and Negro took place during the Iron Age, and there is evidence of this in the Mapungubwe population. Thus it is not inconceivable that the large Khoisan indigenous population adopted the material culture and perhaps the language of the early Negro groups who brought Iron Age economy and culture with them, the newcomers rapidly becoming assimilated into the indigenous population.

There was extensive mining and smelting of both copper and iron at Palabora in the north-eastern Transvaal by the end of the first millennium. Schwellnus's[21] descriptions of Palabora furnaces have been followed by Mason and van der Merwe's investigations from which have come a series of radiocarbon dates for Iron Age metallurgy in this region. They range from A.D. 770±80 (Y–1636) and A.D. 1000±60 (Y–1635) from charcoal in a mine shaft at Loolekop to a date of A.D. 1890±120 from a furnace standing on the surface. An occupation level at the Kgopolwe III site reads A.D. 960±80 (Y–1638) and A.D. 1040±60 (Y–1637).[22] Unfortunately, almost no details of the sites have been published, although the excavator stresses the continuity in pottery tradition between the older sites and modern wares.[23] The final report on this material should throw considerable light on one of the central problems of South African history, the date at which the first Sotho peoples crossed the Limpopo.

Everyone who has worked at Mapungubwe agrees that it was occupied later than Bambandyanalo, and on the radiocarbon dating it is clearly later than the earlier settlements at Palabora. Mapungubwe consists of two entities, the hill itself, the summit of which has been extensively excavated, and the terrace, which is largely unstudied, although it might be expected to yield stratigraphical evidence of the greatest importance. According to Gardner the first occupants of the hill were those who lived at Bambandyanalo in its final stages. Their occupation was sealed from the later hill levels by a layer of black ash, above which

[20] P. V. Tobias 'Skeletal remains from Inyanga' in R. Summers *Inyanga* Cambridge 1958 pp. 159–72.

[21] C. M. Schwellnus 'Short notes on the Palabora smelting ovens' *S.A.J.S.* (1937) 33 pp. 904–12.

[22] M. Stuiver and N. J. van der Merwe 'Radiocarbon chronology of the Iron Age in Sub-Saharan Africa' *Current Anthropology* (1968) IX 1 pp. 54–58.

[23] Personal communication.

occur spindle whorls, abundant iron tools, and traces of more elaborate occupation. Gold and copper ornaments are associated with burials and a distinctive type of pottery named M1 by Schofield.[24] In fact both M1 pottery and M2 (Bambandyanalo-type) ware are found on the hill, the latter being more common at the base of the deposits, while M1 ware is also found in the uppermost levels of Bambandyanalo. There is no indication from Schofield's pottery sequence that there was a major break in culture during the occupation of the hill, but merely a gradual enrichment of the Mapungubwe material culture and economy in the later stages of occupation.

Schofield's M1 pottery, dominant in the upper levels of the hill, has strong Shona influences and can be connected with Leopard's Kopje III pottery. Trading activity is well attested in the hill deposits. Copper and ivory are abundant in the Limpopo valley, gold is readily obtainable; glass beads, sea shells, cloth and other imported objects are common. Two radiocarbon dates from the three- and five-foot levels, of A.D. 1420±60 and A.D. 1380±60 (Y–135, 9, 14)[25] respectively, place the sacred hill contemporary with Period III at Zimbabwe, when much stone construction was in progress and the site was at the zenith of its prosperity. Zimbabwe was an important centre of the *Mwari* cult; Mapungubwe with its prominent hill was perhaps a similar religious headquarters.

The pottery typology and trade goods from the hill show the close connections between the Limpopo valley and the Shona kingdom to the north of the river. Unfortunately, the stratigraphical evidence from the hill is still inadequately recorded, but there is mingling of several distinct pottery traditions, including that of Bambandyanalo and M1 ware.[26] This may reflect a gradual change in the nature of the population, with immigrants living amicably alongside an indigenous population. John Schofield has compared Bambandyanalo pottery with that from Transvaal stone enclosures and also to Sotho vessels. He even makes a parallel between M2 ware and Ngwato pottery.[27] Schofield himself admits that the connections between Sotho wares and M2 pottery are based on inadequate evidence, but the Bambandyanalo finds *might* be grounds for postulating a

[24] J. F. Schofield op. cit. (1937) pp. 32–102.
[25] A. Galloway op. cit. (1959) p. ix.
[26] J. F. Schofield op. cit. (1948) p. 107.
[27] J. F. Schofield op. cit. (1937) pp. 32–102.

Sotho settlement of the Limpopo valley by the eleventh century, if Schofield's conclusions were confirmed by future investigations.

M2 ware may be a uniform pottery tradition.[28] It has connections both to the north and to the south of the Soutspansberg mountains, and, in the case of the latter area, with industrial activities which can almost certainly be attributed to Sotho peoples. The later peoples who exploited the riches of the Limpopo in the fourteenth and fifteenth centuries are superimposed on an indigenous population which had connections to the south, was apparently mining, and had a general level of culture somewhat similar to that of their southern neighbours. Presumably they traded with them, for mineral outcrops are abundant at Rooiberg and other localities, while salt was exploited in recent times.[29] There is no archaeological evidence at present available to document this statement, and the Shona do not appear to have dominated their southern neighbours.

THE HIGHVELD

South of the Soutspansberg the nature of the archaeological record changes, with building in stone a conspicuous feature. The high altitude Bushveld and Highveld country has less arduous topography and a temperate climate. At the present time there are fewer trees on the Highveld, with parkland vegetation occurring north of the latitude of Pretoria. Game abounded in prehistoric times, but the scarcity of trees in many areas today has led to a shortage of firewood and building materials. But as Acocks[30] has pointed out, studies of modern vegetational patterns indicate major changes within the last 500 years, simply as a result of processes of change still in progress. The Bushveld had a far wider distribution about A.D. 1400, and the condition of bareness found over much of South Africa today is the result of human activity, and possibly some changes in surface water supplies. Acocks goes so far as to suggest that most of South Africa was originally covered with either forest or closed scrub forest. Thus it is very difficult to argue from the modern vegetation patterns as to the significance of one of the most striking features

[28] J. F. Schofield op. cit. (1937) pp. 32–102.

[29] G. W. Bates 'A preliminary report on archaeological sites on the Groot Letaba river, North-Eastern Transvaal' *S.A.J.S.* (1947) 43 pp. 365–75.

[30] J. P. H. Acocks 'Veld Types of South Africa' *Botanical Survey of South Africa Memoir No. 28* (1953) pp. 10–13 and Maps 1 and 2.

of the Iron Age archaeology of this region, the prevalence of building in stone.

The Iron Age sequence for this enormous area is inadequately known, and consists of scattered finds of pottery associated with rockshelters and caves, traces of ironworking, mining activities, and numerous stone structures. Stratigraphy and radiocarbon dates are rare, while no large-scale excavations have been made.

Mr Phillipson has mentioned the Early Iron Age site at Happy Rest, which, on the basis of pottery typology alone antedates the main Iron Age sequence south of the Soutspansberg. The closest affinities of the potsherds are said to be with the Gokomere-type pottery from Malapati in Rhodesia which dates to the ninth century.[31] Unfortunately, this important collection has not been analysed in detail, although de Vaal drew attention to the resemblances between the Happy Rest material and Gokomere ware many years ago.[32]

The earliest dated site from this area is at Melville Koppies on the Witwatersrand where Mason found two Iron Age levels overlying a Middle Stone Age floor.[33] The lower of the two, at a depth of twelve inches, contained an iron smelting furnace, charcoal from which was dated to A.D. 1060±50 (Y–1338). Potsherds and other occupation debris associated with the furnace have been assigned by the excavator to the so-called Uitkomst culture, best known from the cave of that name near Hekpoort, some twenty-five miles north-west of Melville Koppies. At Uitkomst two iron-smelting furnaces overlay a Later Stone Age occupation level, the upper of the two being dated by radiocarbon to A.D. 1650±300 (Y–1323B). The furnaces were associated with the type series of Uitkomst pottery, which has now been found over a wide area of the central and southern Transvaal. Uitkomst sites extend as far north as Warmbaths, but the main focus of the culture lies between the Magaliesberg and the Witwatersrand.

Deep bowls and shouldered pots are characteristic of Uitkomst ware, with simple rims and a certain amount of burnishing on the

[31] B. M. Fagan 'Radiocarbon dates for sub-Saharan Africa, 4–III' *J.A.H.* (1965) VI 1 p. 108.

[32] J. B. de Vaal ''n Soutspansbergse Zimbabwe' *S.A.J.S.* (1943) 40 pp. 303–22.

[33] R. J. Mason and N. J. van der Merwe 'Radiocarbon dating of Iron Age sites in the Southern Transvaal: Melville Koppies and Uitkomst cave' *S.A.J.S.* (1960) 60 p. 142.

surface of vessels. Stamped and incised decorations are predominant, with parallel incised or stamped lines or variants on these motifs being especially frequent. Unfortunately, no one has yet published a full description of Uitkomst ware, although a number of authors consider that it has connections with the Leopard's Kopje wares of Rhodesia and the Limpopo.[34]

Uitkomst potsherds are found with a stone-walled structure on the lower slopes of the Melville Koppies hill as well as with the dated furnace. Thus, the tradition of stone building, so strongly established over a large area of South Africa during later centuries, may have already been practised at the end of the first millennium.

Schofield[35] describes two pottery types from the many stone structures found between the Magaliesberg and Winburg, labelled ST 1 and ST 2. ST 1 wares are imperfectly known, most of the potsherds coming from unstratified contexts at Chwenyane and Aasvogelskop. Spherical and necked pots are common, with chevron and triangle decoration frequent. Colouring was used to delineate the decoration. Oblique impressions and comb stamped bands are common. Schofield compares ST 1 to his BP 3 wares from Botswana, both being characterized above all by the use of colour contrasts. The Transvaal sites from which these wares come are undated, although the Chwenyane structures are said to have been destroyed in the Difaqane in about 1823. Although detailed studies using modern analytical methods remain to be completed, ST 1 probably belongs in the Uitkomst tradition; many sites representing late expressions of the culture, which, if the accounts of nineteenth-century travellers are to be relied on, were abandoned during the wars of the early nineteenth century.[36]

ST 2 pottery also comes from stone-walled settlements, which are very similar to those associated with Uitkomst pottery. The sites are to the west of the Uitkomst settlements, and the pottery is of the same general type as Uitkomst ware, but the decoration is simpler and confined to short vertical strokes or gashes on the rims of vessels. The type site is Buispoort, where the ware is heavy, with wide-mouthed bowls and deep pots with vertical or flared sides dominant. Some ST 1 sherds are also found. Pipes, spoons,

[34] For example: Roger Summers op. cit. (1967) and R. J. Mason, *The Pre-history of the Transvaal* Johannesburg 1962. Uitkomst sites, see Mason (1962, 1965).

[35] J. F. Schofield op. cit. (1948) pp. 142–9.

[36] J. F. Schofield op. cit. (1948) pp. 144–5.

and some figurines, as well as a limited range of iron tools have been found in these sites.

Some settlements in the northern Orange Free State resemble the southern Transvaal villages. The region is now largely treeless, and corbelled roofs were sometimes constructed instead of thatched ones. Evidence for iron working is rarely found, perhaps owing to the treeless environment, while the pottery is coarser than in the Transvaal. Maggs has recently investigated a large number of settlements in the province using air photographs, combined with ground survey and limited excavations. Unfortunately, his findings are not yet ready for publication, but radiocarbon dates of A.D. 1445±95 (GX–1014) and A.D. 1495±110 (GX–1015) have been obtained from two stone structures in the Vrede district.[37] He has also distinguished several architectural styles.

Uitkomst and Buispoort wares are probably later than the earliest Iron Age occupation of South Africa,[38] and the pottery types found with the stone structures everywhere have no connections with Khoikhoi wares. The dated finds of Uitkomst pottery from the Witwatersrand and the type site are for pottery types which also occur in the middens associated with the Transvaal ruins.[39] The typological links between this ware and the Buispoort pottery forms are established by both Mason and Schofield.[40] Such pottery, including moulded forms, is said to be found in the corbelled structures of the Orange Free State, but Maggs's recent findings should provide more information. Uitkomst occupation levels are associated in at least one case with stone walling, but we lack the accurate dating evidence and stratigraphy to trace the later development of this ware, and indeed, of stone walling in South Africa.

Both Uitkomst and Buispoort wares are of Iron Age association, even if traces of metallurgy are rare. Early travellers' records carry mixed accounts as to the association of the stone structures with any particular people. Many structures throughout the highveld area were abandoned during the Difaqane and the wars of Mzilikazi in the 1820s.[41] A substantial proportion of the more

[37] Personal communication, also: T. Maggs in B. M. Fagan, 'Radiocarbon dates for sub-Saharan Africa–VI' *J.A.H.* (1968) IX p. 4. *In the press.*

[38] B. M. Fagan *Southern Africa* London and New York 1965 p. 153.

[39] R. J. Mason op. cit. (1962).

[40] For example: J. F. Schofield op. cit. (1948) pp. 142–9.

[41] J. Campbell op. cit. (1822) describes the results of Nguni raids.

recent stone ruins are to be associated with Sotho peoples. The stone-walled settlements in the Zeerust area have been shown by Van Hoepen to be the work of Hurutshe,[42] while those of the area to the north of Machadodorp[43] in the Lydenburg District are thought to be of Pedi workmanship. Schofield, who studied most of the pottery from the Transvaal sites, ascribes Aasvogelskop to the same chiefdom, and alleges that the Magaliesburg site was the work of a nearly related group.

The stone-hut settlements are harder to assign to a particular chiefdom. Van Riet Lowe and Walton ascribe many of them to the Ghoya,[44] the grounds for the latter's conclusion being similarities in architecture between recent and more ancient huts. Laidler on more tenuous evidence ascribed some of them to the Taung,[45] a related people.

The criteria for connecting a particular people with archaeological sites have not been at all strictly applied to South African Iron Age sites. Schofield's views, based on a so far unrivalled knowledge of modern South African pottery, must command respect pending the completion of more detailed studies of modern ceramics in relation to ancient wares from a large number of well-dated sites. Oral traditions have not been collected at all systematically; their relevance to the archaeological record is obvious, while the criteria for the differentiation of, for example, modern Fokeng and Hurutshe pottery, have not been established.

Any statements relating to the relationship between stone structures and individual chiefdoms must be provisional and extremely cautious. We can state that the stone structures are not of Nguni workmanship, for they are not found east of the Drakensberg mountains.[46] That they are in general terms associated with Sotho peoples seems unquestionable, especially in view of the many travellers' accounts which demonstrate such a linkage. The ultimate origins of the stone structures lie in the earlier Iron Age, and *may* be associated with early Sotho chiefdoms. Mason's

[42] E. C. N. van Hoepen and A. C. Hoffman 'Die Oorblysfsels van Buispoort en Braklaagte Noordwes van Zeerust' *Argeol. Navorsing van die Nasionale Museum, Bloemfontein* (1935) II pp. 1–25.

[43] J. F. Schofield op. cit. (1948) p. 148.

[44] C. van Riet Lowe 'A preliminary report on the stone huts of Vechtkop' *Journ. Roy. Anthrop. Inst.* (1927) 57 pp. 217–33. Also: James Walton 'Early Ghoya settlement in the Orange Free State' *Res. Nat. Mus. Bloemfontein* (1965) p. 2.

[45] P. W. Laidler 'The archaeology of Certain Prehistoric settlements in the Heilbron Area' *T.R.S.S.A.* (1935) 23 pp. 23–70.

[46] J. F. Schofield op. cit, (1948) p. 155.

association of Uitkomst wares and later occupation in the Central Transvaal is an argument for indicating that the Sotho have been living in that area since the eleventh century, if not earlier. The Iron Age peoples of the Transvaal lacked the elaborate iron tools and ceremonial regalia of the Shona, even if they were engaged in mining activities at Rooiberg and elsewhere.[47] Stone was abundantly available, and used for the construction of cattle enclosures and huts, which give their sites some superficial resemblances to the stone buildings of Rhodesia. Some have even suggested that stone building was introduced to the area by the migration of peoples with a tradition for this type of construction.[48] Archaeological evidence for this is lacking, but surely a more logical explanation lies in the necessity of protecting stock and settlements in areas where the most convenient building material is the stone boulder, the architectural styles of the walls being evolved from practical experience. Walton's studies[49] of Sotho stonework tend to confirm this supposition. Sotho stone construction is characterized by the use of the 'pilled-pen' double wall combined with orthostats, by round wall terminations, the two ends of the wall being built in two sections at the same time, the builders working towards each other. Although differences in style are evident, the fundamental building techniques are the same in most stone structures in South Africa. A circular cattle enclosure wall often forms the focus of the settlement; alternatively smaller enclosures are linked by common walls. The huts of the village may be grouped around the kraal in a circle, or a number of small enclosures may be associated with the huts and grouped round a central open space. Such types of settlement are found in Lesotho and the Orange Free State. In the Transvaal, wattle and mud huts were built in a circle, each hut being within a semi-circular alcove of the outer wall, with a number of large, circular stone-walled cattle enclosures in the central open space. Irregular enclosure walls were sometimes linked together. Burials were often deposited near the entrances of cattle enclosures. Stonework was also used among some southern Sotho groups, as well as by the Pedi and others for defensive purposes, and for fortifying hills.

The Venda also make use of stone construction, and were still

[47] R. J. Mason op. cit. (1962).
[48] P. L. Breutz op. cit. (1956).
[49] James Walton 'Sotho cattle kraals' *S.A.A.B.* (1958) 13 52 pp. 133–43.

building in this material in recent times.[50] They are probably culturally related to the Shona, but may have been using stone as a convenient building material, as did the Sotho, rather than reflecting the southward extension of the architectural styles of the Rhodesian plateau.

The importance of the stone structures of the Bushveld and Highveld has perhaps been exaggerated in the literature. The primary problem is that of population movements rather than architectural practices. The archaeological evidence from the Natal Coast has more relevance in this connection.

THE NATAL COAST

The coast of Natal is bordered by lines of sand dunes, covered for the most part with dense bush, which gives way to open grassy tracts or areas of wind-blown, drifting sand. These less well-covered areas yield abundant traces of human occupation, especially where the sea borders rocky beaches rich in small shellfish. Shell middens are to be found wherever partly submerged rocks are rich in oysters, mussels and limpets, of which the accumulations are almost wholly composed. Similar middens extend northwards into the Lourenço Marques area and all the way down the south-east African coast to the Cape although the archaeological associations of the shell accumulations vary considerably.

We owe to John Schofield a considerable body of information on the Iron Age pottery found on Natal middens in 'promiscuous profusion'.[51] He studied small, mainly surface, collections of potsherds from a considerable number of localities, most of them over a distance of more than sixty miles between Karridene and Tinley Manor on the Natal and Zululand coasts. His classification of Iron Age pottery in this region is still in use, for little new research has been carried out since the late 1940s.

Farther to the south, Stone Age middens are more common, including strandlooper settlements. Laidler was able to work out a long sequence of shell collecting activity in the East London area, extending back into the Middle Stone Age. Late Stone Age middens were stated to be stratigraphically earlier than Khoikhoi

[50] P. R. Kirby 'The building in stone of a new kraal for the paramount chief of the Venda' *S.A.J.S.* (1956) 52 7 p. 167.

[51] J. F. Schofield 'Natal Coastal Pottery from the Durban District, Parts I and II *S.A.J.S.* (1935) 32 pp. 508–27 and (1936) 33 pp. 993–1009.

occupations with pottery, which in their turn are overlain by midden levels containing what he calls 'Bantu' pottery at Buffalo and Bland River.[52]

At Umgazana Cave on the Pondoland coast, fishing communities occupied the site intermittently for a considerable period of time.[53] The upper layers of the cave yield pottery, whereas the lower horizons contain only stone and bone tools. While there is no apparent stratigraphical break between the two occupations, and the arrival of pottery in the site is undated, Schofield was able to classify the potsherds at Umgazana within his NC 2 group from the Natal shell middens. Other excavations in similar caves combined with the systematic collection of radiocarbon samples should enable the dating of the interface with a considerable degree of accuracy in the future.

Schofield's analysis of the coastal Iron Age pottery was based both on the internal typology of the various collections and on direct comparison between modern wares from a wide area of the Republic. He distinguished four different classes of Natal Coastal pottery, designated NC 1–4.[54] I have ignored his minor subdivisions of these classes for the purposes of this paper.

NC 1 ware is very uncommon, consisting for the most part of isolated potsherds from the Umhloti Road midden. The pottery is rough, the most meaningful fragment being a pierced lug from Umhloti Dune which may be of Khoikhoi type. Schofield regards NC 1 as 'pre-Bantu', but the quantity of material is in fact far too small for such a conclusion.

NC 2 pottery came from many localities. It is usually made from a grey or blackish clay, with both plain and decorated vessels. Rough incisions and bands of comb-stamped triangles are common, while notched rims are found. Moulded decoration also occurs. Many of the Natal Coast middens are associated with NC 2 potsherds, important sites including the University site in Durban, all the sites at Umhloti, and Tinley Manor.

Schofield[55] and Walton[56] are of the opinion that NC 2 wares

[52] P. W. Laidler 'Shell Mound Cultures' *S.A.J.S.* (1935) XXXII pp. 560–71.

[53] J. F. Schofield 'A description of the pottery from Umgazana and Zig Zag caves on the Pondoland Coast' *T.R.S.S.A.* (1937–38) 25 pp. 327–32.

[54] For a detailed analysis of his classifications see op. cit. (1935, 1936) and also 'Pottery from Natal, Zululand, Bechuanaland, and South West Africa' *S.A.J.S.* (1958) 35 pp. 382–95.

[55] J. F. Schofield op. cit. (1948) p. 156.

[56] James Walton 'Early Bafokeng settlement in South Africa' *African Studies* (1956) XV pp. 37–43.

can be assigned to the Fokeng of Ntsuanatsasti, while other Mbo groups such as the Mphetla, Mpolane, and Mphunthi may have played their part in the development of this pottery. The former compares NC 2 to some rim shapes from Cala, East London, and to modern Mpondo pottery. Comb-stamped decoration is common on Sotho ware, as well as on NC 2. Some of his resemblances are based on comparisons between isolated vessels from sites many miles apart. Such criteria are not regarded as acceptable today. His most important comparison is, however, between NC 2 and the pottery from Uitkomst and Buispoort sites in the far interior.[57] Schofield does not give a detailed analysis of his reasons for such a conclusion, but the literature implies that it was based on a comparison of vessel forms, the presence of notched rims in both pottery types, and also on some similarities in incised and stamped motifs. He goes so far as to say that 'all the types of NC 2 pottery were found in conditions which make it impossible to attribute it to any other people than the Bahurutsi'.[58] The Transvaal pottery is known to extend back as early as the eleventh century, but unfortunately no NC 2 sites have yet been radiocarbon dated.

Schofield's statement that the makers of NC 2 were iron-users rather than iron-workers is based on observations at a large number of sites where iron tools were apparently very rare in contrast to later settlements.[59] Without large-scale excavations, this statement cannot be taken as entirely valid. Certainly iron weapons were in use by 1593 when Lavanha of the *San Alberto* recorded that the people of Natal valued iron and copper for which they bartered cattle.[60] A date of 1550–1650 for the floruit of NC 2 ware was reached by using this reference and Perestrello's observation that Bantu peoples near Port St John were still using wood assegais in 1554. In truth, however, both NC 2 ware and its successors are undated.

NC 3 pottery is found on some sites with NC 2, as well as over a wide area of the Natal north coast. The pots tend to be coarse, with globular pots and bowls being common. Hatched triangles and herringbone incisions are frequent with elaborate motifs in use. Iron smelting was commonly practised, with iron workings

[57] J. F. Schofield op. cit. (1948) p. 155.
[58] J. F. Schofield op. cit. (1935–36).
[59] J. F. Schofield 'Pottery from Natal, Zululand, Bechuanaland, and South West Africa' *S.A.J.S.* (1958) 35 pp. 382–95.
[60] Monica Wilson 'Early history of the Transkei and Ciskei' *African Studies* (1959) 18 4 pp. 167–79.

in the Tugela valley yielding plentiful NC 3 sherds. This pottery is very different from that of the Nguni peoples who live in Natal today. Schofield assigns NC 3 to the Lala on the basis of Soga's statement that they came from Karanga stock, and makes some tenuous connections between NC 3 and Inyanga wares.[61] If Bryant's definition is accepted,[62] the Lala are a Tonga-Nguni amalgam, with connections to the north.[63]

The Karridene site has yielded NC 4 potsherds somewhat similar to modern vessels. Schofield regards the ware as Hlubi, making a far-reaching comparison with Ndebele pottery from the Potgietersrus area of the Transvaal.

The Natal sequence is based on the most tenuous of archaeological evidence. The pottery is undated and found in small, often unstratified collections. Information on the economy and settlement pattern of the Natal Coastal peoples is almost totally lacking except for statements that they lived near the shell midden heaps, kept domestic stock, and probably cultivated crops. Two skeletons from NC 3 levels at the Tinley Manor Dune site are stated to be a Bush/Negro mixture,[64] and include an adult with an iron ring on his left ankle.

Stratigraphical proof of a Late Stone Age–Khoikhoi Iron Age succession on the south-east African coast was possibly established by Laidler, while Khoikhoi pottery is extremely rare in Natal. The earliest Iron Age pottery type identified by Schofield is assigned on flimsy grounds by two investigators to Fokeng,[65] some of whom later settled in the eastern Cape among the Mpondo. These iron-using Sotho were followed by NC 3 and NC 4 pottery-makers whose tribal identity may be Mbo, and later by pure Nguni. There is no trace of Early Iron Age occupation in the Rhodesian sense within the Natal or eastern Cape areas.

Thus, archaeology cannot as yet contribute much depth to the exciting historical data now emerging from Natal and the eastern Cape.[66] Monica Wilson has pointed out that from 1554 there were people 'very black in colour' south of the Mthatha River, while the survivors of the wreck of the *San Alberto* recorded Nguni

[61] J. F. Schofield op. cit. (1948) p. 161.
[62] A. T. Bryant *Olden Times in Zululand and Natal* London 1929.
[63] Shula Marks 'The Nguni, the Natalians, and their History' *J.A.H.* (1967) VIII 3 pp. 529–95.
[64] J. F. Schofield op. cit. (1958) pp. 382–95.
[65] For example, James Walton, op. cit. (1956) pp. 37–43.
[66] Monica Wilson op. cit. (1959) pp. 167–79.

speech in the same area in 1593. None of the recorded traditions indicate any substantial movement of Nguni peoples southwards into the south-eastern Cape since 1300. Archaeological excavation and reconnaissance for Iron Age sites has hardly begun. The critical problem for the archaeologist remains the date for the introduction of iron-using and smelting. The coastal regions from which most of the archaeological data has come are not the best of grazing grounds for large herds. Future research is best concentrated inland, where the pastures are sweeter, and the population was denser in the sixteenth century, a pattern that is still true today, and presumably was in earlier times. Midden sites, cattle kraals, and chiefs' burial places probably await discovery in this archaeologically unexplored region.

DISCUSSION

Although the details of the South African Iron Age are almost completely unknown, the very general nature of this vital and formative period of South African history can be seen. Early Iron Age settlement appears to be connected with that of Rhodesia, for there are typological links between the pottery from Happy Rest and that from Gokomere-type sites north of the Limpopo. The earliest radiocarbon dates for metallurgy south of the Limpopo come from unpublished sites in Swaziland and assign metallurgy to as early as the fifth century A.D.[67] Iron was certainly being smelted by the Palabora miners by the eighth century, although their cultural associations are still unpublished.

The main part of the South African Iron Age sequence appears to belong to different cultural traditions. North of the Soutpansberg, Iron Age peoples of Leopard's Kopje associations were living at Bambandyanalo by the eleventh century; their pottery differs significantly from that of the earliest Iron Age inhabitants of Rhodesia. The pottery of the Limpopo site has some, albeit completely unstudied, connections with Uitkomst wares from the central Transvaal, which may either be the result of trade or of migration.

Revil Mason has produced evidence for linking Uitkomst and the related Buispoort wares to the Sotho occupation of South Africa. If this connection is justified then the Sotho have been settled in the Transvaal for at least nine centuries. Much of the

[67] B. M. Fagan 'Radiocarbon dates for sub-Saharan Africa–V' *J.A.H.* (1967) VIII 3 p. 525. This site is described by D. W. Phillipson in Chapter 2.

mining and trading activity of that Province can be attributed to the Sotho occupants before the time of the Difaqane, but the stratigraphy and chronology of the late first and early second millennia are almost totally unknown.

Much of the Buispoort and Uitkomst pottery comes from stone structures, many of which are associated with different Sotho chiefdoms, speculations ranging from Ghoya to Fokeng through the Hurutshe. The stone structures are particularly common in the areas to the south of the Vaal River. Schofield has drawn attention to the apparent resemblances between his NC 2 ware from the Natal coast and Buispoort wares. These resemblances are deduced from quite inadequate potsherd samples and cannot be taken as a definite indication that the Sotho preceded Nguni-speakers in this area of South Africa.

Archaeological evidence for Nguni-speakers in Natal and elsewhere in South Africa consists of Gardner's dubious conclusions on the Greefswald sites, already discussed elsewhere and of Schofield's NC 3 wares, which are in all probability of Lala associations.

The basis of any archaeological inquiry is stratigraphy and chronology at the regional level. Future studies of the South African Iron Age are certain to be based on such research, hopefully carried out over increasingly wide areas of the country. On the overall view, however, a number of major and urgent problems relating to South African history are awaiting intensive research.

A first millennium date for the introduction of the Iron Age in South Africa is now generally accepted, but exact chronological information is still lacking. Of primary importance are the exact datings of the introduction of metallurgy and agriculture. Systematic small-scale excavations and reconnaissance combined with radiocarbon dating should reveal the extent of Gokomere-type sites south of the Limpopo, for the pottery is characteristic and there is no reason why it should not have had a much wider distribution than appears on the present evidence.

The early history of the Sotho and Nguni people appears to extend back further than the frontiers of oral tradition or even the largest genealogies; archaeology must be a primary source of information on the critical problems of early origins and precedence in migration. Present archaeological information, beyond

Schofield's inadequate evidence from the Natal Coast, is totally non-committal, although there are no signs of Nguni-type wares in the Limpopo, and the Sotho have probably been established in the Central Transvaal for most of the second millennium.

John Schofield's classic but somewhat superficial study of South African Bantu and Khoikhoi pottery was based on a vast and intuitive knowledge of vessels from many different areas of South Africa. He assigned prehistoric pottery industries to Sotho, Nguni, Venda, and indeed to individual chiefdoms with considerable confidence. While some of his correlations were obviously based on quite inadequate criteria, his intuitive judgement, based on very long experience, must command a degree of respect. Schofield distinguishes between Pedi and Hurutshe, Fokeng and Ghoya on the basis of the general features of their pottery.

Even with the rapid change in, and disappearance of, a pottery industry in South Africa, by utilizing existing museum collections and records as well as field methods it should be possible to amass a far greater body of information regarding the potting habits of both modern and ancient Sotho and Nguni peoples. Without this data the Iron Age archaeologist can never hope to produce any detailed analyses of the early history of the two principal Bantu peoples of South Africa. This must be regarded as an urgent research project for the future.

Questions of trade and contact are susceptible to solution by archaeological methods. Although there may conceivably have been a pre-Portuguese trading chiefdom near Port St Johns,[68] most of the major East Coast trading activity took place north of Delagoa Bay. Imports of any kind are comparatively rare to the south of the Limpopo valley, although scattered caches of beads are sometimes found.

But extensive prehistoric trade in copper and iron, as well as in salt and tin, flourished in the Transvaal, based on such localities as Klein Letaba and Rooiberg where initial investigations have revealed evidence of intensive salt and metallurgical activity. Wagner[69] mapped areas of iron and copper working, while Trevor[70] has estimated that a major area of metallurgical activity extended from the Limpopo to the Highveld at the

[68] Shula Marks op. cit. (1967) p. 531.

[69] Wagner's map was published posthumously in L. Fouché op. cit. (1937).

[70] T. G. Trevor 'Some observations on the relics of Pre-European culture in Rhodesia and South Africa' *Journ. Roy. Anthrop. Inst.* (1930) 60 pp. 389–99.

latitude of Pretoria. While some of the output of these mines was perhaps exported, much of it was probably used for local trade and consumption, for imports are rare or almost non-existent in Sotho sites in the Transvaal while spindle whorls do not occur south of the Limpopo valley. In the areas south of the Vaal, iron tools were apparently rarer, perhaps as a result of a scarcity of firewood in an area with fewer trees. The Iron Age communities living in this region depended on trade for their iron implements, as well as a range of other raw materials. Iron Age settlement in the Highveld must have depended to a considerable degree on a comparatively efficient and well-established system of barter and trading contact for essential raw materials, as indeed must have settlement on the Natal and Cape coasts. Schofield's attribution of iron-using to his NC 2 (Sotho) people is based on quite inadequate data by modern archaeological standards, although it has been quoted in recent literature. At the present time we have no means of telling when Iron Age peoples first settled in the treeless or less iron-rich areas of Bantu-speaking South Africa, although the date is probably earlier than A.D. 1400. By the eleventh century iron-smelting was well established in the central Transvaal. Without a strongly based iron-working industry in surrounding areas the Iron Age settlement of more southerly and easterly areas might never have taken place. The archaeologist's task is to study the centres of the iron and copper trade and to trace distributions of artifacts and occurrences of raw material relative to their date and ultimate place or origin.

The fourth major archaeological problem is the critical one of contact between different racial groups. Both Sotho- and Nguni-speakers have a long history of contact with Khoisan peoples. Such contacts are reflected in their physical types, language, and in the archaeological record, where traces of mixed material culture are sometimes found. Contact can arise from direct confrontation, competition, sporadic or regular trading, or by long-term mutual tolerance in the same base area. The historical record is rich in accounts of trading contact between San and Sotho over long periods of time, with resulting intermarriage and cultural change.

Such processes have been in progress for a long time, and may be studied by careful selection of prehistoric sites which might be expected to yield evidence of contact between farmer and hunter, and agriculturalist and pastoralist. From such studies one would learn much of the processes of diffusion of Iron Age culture, obtain evidence for the length of Bush-Bantu contact, a problem of crucial importance to students of Khoikhoi history, as well as valuable data on individual chiefdoms, and on the extent of penetration of Iron Age culture into the heartlands of South Africa. On the south-east coast, one might expect to find sites where both early foreign imports and Early Iron Age materials occur, as well as, in later centuries, evidence for Portuguese contact with the Natal coast.

Lastly, a great deal of valuable information of critical use to the archaeologist can be gleaned from historical records. The story of the South African Iron Age is one of continuous trade and contact between different peoples. The archaeologist must correlate his data with the existing documentary sources such as early travellers' accounts, and Portuguese records. He should make use of the oral tradition collected by such authorities as Ellenberger and Bryant, as well as more recent workers. Some of the historical problems posed by oral and written records can only be solved by application of archaeological methods in conjunction with those of other disciplines.

All these points are generalities, for the basic task of the archaeologist remains at the regional level, with the erection of Iron Age sequences in the major regions of South Africa. The research that has been conducted to date has hardly scratched the surface. But it serves to show the richness of the Iron Age archaeological record in South Africa, a country that should become the methodological laboratory of the sub-continent, so varied and fascinating are the archaeological problems within its borders. Let us hope that one day it will.

4. *Changes in social structure in southern Africa: the relevance of kinship studies to the historian*

MONICA WILSON

Here I write as myself, an anthropologist, seeking to communicate with historians. I am not pretending to be a well-brought-up historian who holds fast to chronology and frowns on comparisons which stray out of time. Anthropologists are all concerned with what is and why it is, and some of us with *how it becomes*—that is with an analysis of *process*. If a similar process occurs in different places at different times we think comparison is illuminating. But we gain greatly from the insistence of historians that we should think in terms of the chronicle of events and take due account of their sequence.

Studies of certain changes in economy and social structure which anthropologists have made in Africa are relevant to the historian. I think particularly of the shift from hunting and collecting to cultivation or herding, and the kind of society that emerges as the hunters are partially absorbed by the community with a more secure food supply. What has repeatedly emerged is a society with patrons and clients. The process in the Ituri forest has been brilliantly documented by Colin Turnbull.[1] We have eye-witness evidence on it also for Botswana[2] and the Western Cape,[3] and there are oral traditions of it happening over a very wide area among people like the Nyakyusa, Lobedu, Tsonga and others.

This century there has been a further shift from a subsistence economy to large-scale production for markets. Some of us have watched it happening and tried to record the changes in social structure that accompany it. It has also tended to a stratified society with a period of increasing difference in consumption.

[1] C. M. Turnbull *The Forest People* New York and London 1961 and *Wayward Servants* New York and London 1965.

[2] London Missionary Society *The Masarwa* Lovedale 1935; G. B. Silberbauer and A. J. Kuper 'Kgalagari Masters and Bushmen Serfs' *African Studies* 25 4 (1966) pp. 171–9.

[3] D. Moodie *The Record* Cape Town 1960 I pp. 402, 403; H. J. Wikar *The Journal of Hendrik Jacob Wikar* (1779) V.R.S. Cape Town 1935.

In the political field we have an eye-witness account of the establishment of the institution of chieftainship where none previously existed,[4] and again many traditions of how chiefs first arrived in this area or that, and gradually established themselves. They are commonly depicted as having brought such benefits as fire, new crops, cattle, iron, the power to make rain, a power of creating fertility, and the rule of law, and in at least some areas they were welcomed for their gifts. There is little doubt that incoming groups in fact brought new crops, and cattle, and iron, though the knowledge of fire and fertility are to be interpreted symbolically rather than materially. The technical changes were probably a condition of a denser population and political development.[5]

For thirty years anthropologists have been analysing the growth of kingdoms when one chief or priest-chief became pre-eminent and established a hegemony over what were independent political units. A study of the Ngonde kingdom which was centred in Malawi but stretched into Zambia and Tanzania was published in Zambia in 1939 by Godfrey Wilson,[6] and Max Gluckman first published on the Zulu kingdom in 1940.[7] This theme, the growth of kingdoms, has been fruitfully elaborated by historians[8] who can handle the wider relations—the coastal end of the ivory trade, the effect of changes in the British Government on frontier policies, and so forth—of which the anthropologist is ignorant.

What anthropologists concerned with process particularly want to know is why kingdoms developed among some people and not among others. Why did a kingdom not develop among the Nyakyusa, just north of the Songwe, who shared a common

[4] A. W. Southall *Alur Society* Cambridge 1953 pp. 189–228, esp. p. 185.

[5] E. E. Evans-Pritchard 'A Contribution to the Study of Zande Culture' *Africa* XXX 4 (1960) p. 322; Monica Wilson *Peoples of the Nyasa–Tanganyika Corridor* Cape Town 1958 and *Communal Rituals of the Nyakyusa* London 1959; E. J. and J. D. Krige *The Realm of the Rain Queen* London 1943; and J. D. Krige 'Traditional Origins & Tribal Relationships of the Sotho of the Northern Transvaal' *Bantu Studies* XI (1937) pp. 321–56.

[6] Godfrey Wilson *The Constitution of Ngonde* Livingstone 1939.

[7] Max Gluckman 'The Kingdom of the Zulu' *African Political Systems* ed. M. Fortes and E. E. Evans-Pritchard London 1940.

[8] Roland Oliver 'The Traditional Histories of Buganda, Bunyoro, and Nkole' *J.R.A.I.* 85 (1955) pp. 111–17; J. Vansina *Kingdoms of the Savannah* Madison 1966; J. D. Omer-Cooper *Zulu Aftermath* London 1966; and Leonard Thompson 'Co-operation and Conflict: the Zulu Kingdom and Natal' and 'Co-operation and Conflict: The High Veld' *The Oxford History of South Africa* edited Monica Wilson and Leonard Thompson I Oxford 1969.

language and common customs with the people of Ngonde, and whose chiefs came from the same stock as the Kyungu, the divine king of Ngonde? Why did a kingdom not develop among Xhosa who spoke another dialect of Nguni and sprang from the same stock as the Zulu? It has been shown that in Ngonde the growth of centralized authority was linked with the development of external trade controlled by one chief.[9] I believe that the monopoly of trade is one clue to centralization. I have tried to show that it existed in Zululand but not among the Xhosa.[10] (See Chapter 8 where this view is endorsed.)

Recent archaeological work by Desmond Clark and K. R. Robinson gives a date of 1410±80 for pottery on Mbande hill indicating the arrival of the first Kyungu in Ngonde in the fifteenth century,[11] at least a hundred years earlier than I had supposed, calculating from genealogies.[12] If the theory of trade monopoly supporting a kingdom is correct we must suppose that it continued in Ngonde for four hundred years. Oral traditions assert this and I believe that the monopoly was why the kingdom lasted so long.

On these three processes: the shift from hunting to herding or cultivation; the establishment of chieftainship; and the growth of kingdoms—anthropologists can provide comparative evidence which illuminates oral tradition and historical documents for other areas. For example I had heard the Nyakyusa traditions of the establishment of chieftainship repeated again and again, and was familiar with the ritual re-enactment, but I understood the tradition much better after reading Southall's accounts by eye-witnesses of the establishment of chiefs in Alur.

I now want to explore another field: that of kinship. I suggest that it also is relevant to the historian, for the forms of marriage and kinship directly affect the power of certain lineages, the growth of kingdoms and the spread of languages. The topic of *change* in kinship systems is not a respectable one among anthropologists: we were put off by the speculations of an earlier

[9] Godfrey Wilson *passim*.

[10] Monica Wilson *The Oxford History of South Africa* I, pp. 250–1.

[11] K. R. Robinson 'A Preliminary Report on the Recent Archaeology of Ngonde, Northern Malawi' *J.A.H.* VII 2 (1966) pp. 169–88, and personal communication.

[12] Monica Wilson *Communal Rituals* p. 2 and genealogies facing pp. 3, 27. The genealogies are not of the Kyungus whose reigns were often short, but of the royal line in fifty-four Nyakyusa chiefdoms among whom transfer of power occurred once in a generation. The Kyungus came from the same royal line as the Nyakyusa chiefs.

generation—speculations divorced from observation and dogmatically asserted as fact. The speculations told one more about the speculators than about kinship systems—the armchair men were preoccupied with what they called 'primitive promiscuity', the 'precedence of mother right', 'marriage by capture' and so forth. But change in kinship systems is something we can watch happening, and the range of possible change in kinship is one of the pressing questions of African history, particularly in the south.

As you will know there are two major groups in Africa south of the Limpopo: the Nguni and the Sotho, using Sotho in the wide sense to include the Tswana. Nguni and Sotho differ in language; they differ in the form of local grouping, the Sotho ancestors having lived concentrated in large settlements and the Nguni in scattered homesteads; and they differ in their kinship systems. Nguni have exogamous clans and among most of them there is a rigid taboo on marriage into a mother's clan as well as into the father's, and sometimes a taboo on marriage into a grandmother's clan. Among the Sotho there is preferred cousin marriage, both parallel and cross-cousin marriage being permitted amongst most Sotho speakers. The Nguni and Sotho are contiguous and each has absorbed groups of refugees from the other over many centuries. Those so absorbed tend to take over the kinship usages along with the language of their hosts. There has also been mingling and mutual influence along common boundaries, but Nguni and Sotho remain distinct.

The question we keep asking ourselves in the south is this: have the Nguni and Sotho a common origin with the last thousand years or have they a diverse origin? The archaeologists discuss this in terms of pottery, the linguists discuss it in terms of morphology and syntax. I have been thinking about it in terms of economy and local grouping, and finally in terms of kinship.

Could a system with preferred cousin marriage, and a rigid system of exogamous clans be derived one from the other, or from a common source? I cannot pretend to answer that yet but I pushed the question further and asked myself: what do we know about the dynamics of kinship systems? What evidence have we about change in kinship systems in Africa? There is a wealth of comparative material on kinship systems in Africa and some on developmental cycles—the fruit of forty years field-work by anthropologists—but studies of the dynamics of kinship systems are meagre.

The best evidence is from areas where two types of marriage exist, and one is becoming more common at the expense of the other. For example, the Amba who live in the Ituri forest west of the Ruwenzori practise sister exchange, A marrying B's sister and B marrying A's. But the Amba have come into close relations with the Toro who marry with stock and a man finds he has more choice, and it is altogether more convenient if he receives stock (goats) for his sister and in turn gives goats for his bride, instead of exchanging sisters with one brother-in-law. Moreover, marriage on the Toro pattern carries prestige. So marriage with stock is increasing, sister exchange diminishing.[13]

Again, among a number of peoples of central and east Africa, notably the Shona,[14] Nyakyusa, Safwa,[15] Nyamwezi[16] Tumbuka, Ndamba,[17] and Kikuyu,[18] there are or have been, two forms of marriage[19]: marriage by service with matrilineal descent, and marriage with stock, preferably cattle, and patrilineal descent. The second type was more honourable. The first was referred to derogatively by my Nyakyusa friends as 'cock marriage' because, they said, 'chickens are the hen's, the cock goes about alone'. As opportunity for acquiring cattle increased 'cock marriage' disappeared among the Nyakyusa and diminished among the Safwa. Whether it has wholly disappeared among Shona and Kikuyu I do not know. Both types still existed among the Nyamwezi in 1965.

Among the Bemba a rather different change occurred. Twenty years ago, as men began to work for long periods on the Copperbelt and failed to perform the traditional period of service for a bride, marriage payments increased. Inheritance and descent remained matrilineal but marriage was virilocal at a much earlier

[13] E. H. Winter *Bwamba* Cambridge n.d. pp. 21–46.

[14] H. Kuper 'The Shona' in H. Kuper, A. J. B. Hughes and J. van Velsen *The Shona and Ndebele of Southern Africa* London 1955.

[15] Monica Wilson 'Nyakyusa Kinship' *African Systems of Kinship and Marriage* ed. A. R. Radcliffe Brown and D. Forde London 1950 p. 121. Information on the Safwa was given by Nyakyusa informants.

[16] R. G. Abrahams *The Peoples of the Greater Nyamwezi, Tanzania* London 1967 pp. 44–45.

[17] Monica Wilson *Peoples of the Corridor* p. 60.

[18] Information on the Kikuyu from Dr L. S. B. Leakey, personal communication.

[19] Patrilineal Gogo share clan names with matrilineal Kaguru indicating a shift either to patrilineal descent or to matrilineal. Peter Rigby 'Time and Social Structure in Gogo Kinship' *Cahiers d'Etudes Africaines* VII 28 (1967) p. 640.

stage. The bride went to live with her husband instead of his coming to her home.[20] Since family relationships are modified by where a young couple settles, this was an important change. A young man became far more independent of his wife's family than he had been traditionally, but a shift to patrilineal descent and inheritance had not occurred up to 1941.

Marriage with stock does not invariably drive out marriage by service when the two forms exist side by side. The Ceŵa who were matrilineal lived mingled with Ngoni who were patrilineal, but in 1946–9, and perhaps still, Ceŵa fathers might refuse cattle for their daughters even when offered, because they preferred to keep control of their grandchildren. They refused because a man's status depended upon his following and the approved way of building up a following was to establish a village with daughters and granddaughters whose husbands attached themselves but could not take the women away.[21] This was particularly interesting because the Ngoni generally had a high status, and it might have been expected that following their marriage customs would carry prestige. Similarly, the Ambo in South West Africa have long owned cattle, but they are still matrilineal, though neighbours of the patrilineal Herero. Economy alone does not determine kinship.

A shift from patrilineal to matrilineal descent and inheritance can and does occur. It was observed to happen among the Ngindo of Tanzania by Robin Cross Upcott where Ngindo, of the Ndonde sub-group, who were patrilineal settled near Makonde who were matrilineal.[22] G. P. Murdock admitted that change from patrilineal to bilateral could occur but he denied any 'direct transition to a matrilineal form of organization'.[23] In this I think he was mistaken.

There are other situations where a shift to matrilineal descent and inheritance is visible. Among the strongly patrilineal Xhosa in South Africa the illegitimacy rate is now 30 to 60 per cent in towns and 25 per cent in some country districts. Girls who were themselves illegitimate tend to have illegitimate children, and mother-centred families, often comprising three generations, are

[20] A. I. Richards *Bemba Marriage and Present Economic Conditions* Livingstone 1940.
[21] M. G. Marwick *Sorcery in its Social Setting* Manchester 1965 pp. 169–70, 178–9; J. A. Barnes *Marriage in a Changing Society* Cape Town 1951 pp. 18, 35–37 *et passim*.
[22] A. R. W. Cross Upcott *The Social Structure of the KiNgindo-speaking Peoples* University of Cape Town, unpublished Ph.D. thesis 1955 pp. 144 ff., 169 ff., 500–62.
[23] G. P. Murdock *Social Structure* New York 1949 p. 218.

common. The ideal is still strongly patrilineal; the practice is towards an increasing proportion of matrilineal families. The causes of this change include the disruption created by migrant labour, and the decline in polygyny. Polygyny has diminished with the spread of Christian teaching, but it also diminishes as shortage of land increases, and as a man's wealth and power cease to depend upon the number of his children. Other facts also contribute to the decline but there is a clear connection between the availability of land and the polygyny rate. Men still marry older than women, so apart from any difference in the expectation of life between men and women, and there almost certainly is a difference among the Xhosa, marriageable women outnumber men. The anthropologists will remember that seven years difference in the marriage age allows 20 per cent of the married men to have more than one wife.[24]

Not only has illegitimacy greatly increased among Sotho and Nguni, but there is greater freedom of choice in marriage. Among the Sotho the obligation to marry a cousin is questioned and in town preferred marriages have virtually disappeared.[25] The levirate, which was once obligatory among Mfengu and Mpondo has ceased to be accepted custom, and Nguni girls have a freer choice in first marriage. The old limitations on choice are eroding before what a Nguni informant giving evidence in 1882 referred to as 'a thing called love'.[26] Even the taboo on marriage within the same clan or the mother's clan is questioned by some young Xhosa people in Cape Town.[27]

Lineages and clans diminish in importance where they cease to control heritable property, such as breeding stock or land, that is essential to the founding of a family,[28] and the decline in their importance is reflected in kinship usages. For example in Langa, a suburb of Cape Town the Xhosa terms for parents and siblings

[24] H. Sonnabend 'Demographic Samples in the Study of Backward and Primitive Populations' *South African Journal of Economics* 2 (1934) pp. 319–21.

[25] Personal communication from Sotho students; J. F. Eloff 'n *Volkekundige Studie van Aanpassing en Ontwikkeling in die Gesinslewe van die Naturelle van Atteridgeville.*' Unpublished M.A. thesis University of Pretoria 1952.

[26] *Cape of Good Hope Report on Native Laws and Customs* 1883 (G.4–'83) I 304.

[27] M. Wilson and A. Mafeje *Langa* Cape Town 1963 p. 77.

[28] M. Fortes 'The Structure of Unilineal Descent Groups' *American Anthropologist* 55 (1953) pp. 17–41; M. E. Elton Mills and Monica Wilson *Land Tenure* Pietermaritzburg 1952 pp. 133–4; Monica Wilson *Peoples of the Corridor* p. 60. Rigby p. 68, argues that the correlation is with economic conditions which allow a 'certain degree of stability and density of population'.

are being used in a much more restricted sense than they were in Pondoland or the Ciskei in 1931.[29]

Another change occurs when it becomes possible for a man to earn property by his own exertions. Inheritance by a son replaces inheritance by a brother. I saw this happening in BuNyakyusa in 1935. Wealthy Nyakyusa refused to inherit from an elder brother because they did not wish their own accumulated cattle to be confused with lineage stock. They wanted their own sons to inherit what they themselves had earned. A similar process is reported from Ashanti.[30]

All the discussion of patrilineal and matrilineal, polygyny and monogamy, lineages and forms of inheritance may seem remote from the field of most historians. I am happy to note that there are now historians such as Peter Laslett in Cambridge, and Pierre Gaubert and Louis Henry in France, who find changes in family structure a fit subject for study,[31] for kinship structures profoundly affect other social relationships. I want particularly to draw your attention to the connection between changing kinship and political structures in Africa.

Marriage with stock and polygyny allows a wealthy lineage to increase much faster than poorer lineages. John Dunn, the Scottish trader who became a sub-chief in Zululand under Cetshwayo and married forty-eight Zulu wives, had over a hundred children.[32] He could marry many wives because he commanded wealth in cattle. This is how certain lineages expanded very fast in Africa. I think of the lineage of Nyakyusa and Ngonde chiefs which spread through the hills and on the plain to the north of Lake Malawi,[33] or of the Dlamini in Swaziland,[34] or the Avongara who spread through Zande country,[35] and of the Alur who spread through one north-west corner of Uganda.[36] The Dlamini went so far as to claim that the king differed from ordinary men in that he might legally take women as wives without giving *lobola*, and kinsmen of the king sometimes claimed the same right,[37] so the Dlamini increased even faster than their wealth in cattle permitted.

[29] Wilson and Mafeje pp. 87–88.

[30] Personal communication from Professor Meyer Fortes.

[31] P. Laslett *The World We have Lost* London 1965 *passim*.

[32] University of Natal Research Team *The Dunn Reserve* Pietermaritzburg 1953 p. 3.

[33] Monica Wilson *Communal Rituals* pp. 1–21, 40–48 and *Peoples of the Corridor* pp. 1–2.

[34] H. Kuper *An African Aristocracy* London 1947 pp. 11–18.

[35] Evans-Pritchard p. 309.

[36] Southall pp. 5–7.

[37] I am indebted to Professor Hilda Kuper for this point.

It is no accident that the royal lineage is sometimes patrilineal where commoners are matrilineal for the increase in a matrilineage is limited by the number of daughters; it cannot recruit child-bearers from a poorer lineage. Hence, I suggest, we find that when the Lunda were expanding one of the royal lines became patrilineal.[38] Even if a society is patrilineal and polygynous the number of a man's wives is limited if marriage is by sister exchange.[39] Only the combination of patrilineal descent, polygyny, and marriage with stock allows wealthy lineages to increase fast at the expense of the poor.

The Arab historian, Atiya, suggested in 1955 that polygyny tended to fission in a society, for Arab history was full of tales of conflict between half-brothers and their descendants. He interpreted differences in development between Europe and the Arab world partly in terms of monogamy and polygyny.[40] I think he overstated the argument: potential conflict between full brothers is doubtless less than between half-brothers who may mobilize their mothers' lineages to support them, but the conflict may emerge as a territorial, or class, or religious one. Nevertheless, Atiya's argument must be met.

Among both Nguni and Sotho oral tradition tells of incoming groups which spread through the country, and had a superior status. I suggest that these were lineages which increased faster than the previous occupants because they commanded wealth, could marry many wives, and traced descent in the patrilineal line. It is in this fashion that a small group of cattle-owners establishing themselves among hunters or cultivators could increase fast. They married women of the group among whom they settled, and their offspring became part of the dominant group.

Polygyny does not affect the reproduction rate, except in so far as it may reduce the marriage age of women and ensure that all women marry; it only means that wealthy men have more descendants than poor men. But increase in population may well have occurred as Bantu-speakers moved southward out of the zone in which malaria and trypan somiasis (sleeping sickness) were endemic,[41] that is from the central Transvaal southward on

[38] V. Turner 'A Lunda Love Story and its Consequences' *Rhodes Livingstone Journal* XIX (1955) p. 26.

[39] Winter p. 25.

[40] E. Atiya *The Arabs* Harmondsworth 1955 p. 47.

[41] F. L. Lambrecht 'Notions Concerning the Evolution of Communicable Diseases in Man' *S.A.J.S.* 64 2 (1968) pp. 64–71.

the Highveld, and St Lucia Bay on the Natal coast. A marked increase in population probably occurred also after groups acquired stock and learnt to drink milk. Remains of sheep are reported from Mabveni, 140 miles north of the Limpopo in A.D. 180±120 and cattle from 'an unknown date between A.D. 300 and 1085'.[42] If the acquisition of stock and milk-drinking coincide we may postulate a population rise north of the Limpopo somewhere between the fourth and eleventh centuries, and I suggest that the increase would be faster once the stock owners were as far south as the Mohalesberg (Magaliesberg), in the Transvaal, the area to which Sotho traditions of origin point.

Cattle-owners who spread fast and established themselves as rulers were not necessarily as skilled craftsmen as the people they dominated. In three areas on which we have evidence: Rwanda, Namaqualand, and BuNyakyusa, the potters and/or iron-workers were not of the dominant lineages but subordinate or absorbed groups. In Rwanda both potters and iron-workers were Twa (pygmy) hunters.[43] In Namaqualand the iron-workers were Negro Dama, not the cattle-owning Nama,[44] and in BuNyakyusa the potters were Penja[45] who were absorbed by the incoming cattle-owning Kukwe who established chieftainship. Thus the anthropological evidence is compatible with the hypothesis that iron-working spread with Bantu-speakers from the southern savannah, and cattle came with other lineages who established themselves as rulers, from East Africa.

There is some evidence to suggest that when two groups speaking different languages mingle the form of marriage determines which language will become dominant. Commonly, children learn their mother-tongue but when the mothers are slaves, or serfs, or prisoners taken in war, and have the status of concubines rather than of wives then, it seems, children learn the fathers' language. Some Nguni groups who moved into the Transvaal kept their own language, others learnt Sotho and lost their Nguni tongue. It is suggested that those groups which kept their language were those which did not marry Sotho women with cattle, but only took captives as concubines. Where a Sotho woman was a

[42] R. R. Inskeep 'The Archaeological Background' *The Oxford History of South Africa* Vol. I pp. 30–31.

[43] J. J. Maquet *The Premise of Inequality in Rwanda* London 1961 p. 10.

[44] Monica Wilson 'Hunters and Herders' *The Oxford History of South Africa* Vol. I.

[45] Monica Wilson *Good Company* pp. 2, 61. The Penja were associated by some Nyakyusa informants with the earlier pygmy population of the Rungwe forests.

wife, and her children visited her family, then the child learnt Sotho rather than Nguni. It is noticeable also that the people of mixed descent at the Cape learnt Dutch in the form of Afrikaans and not a Khoikhoi language: the 'Basters', as they were called, were characterized by their use of Dutch from the eighteenth century.

We need a great deal more evidence on change in language, and the various Nguni offshoots which moved north offer an excellent field for study. For example, at what date and why did mission schools in north Nyasa stop using Zulu school books? Donald Fraser noted that Ngoni was already disappearing in 1919, though fifteen to twenty years earlier it had been widely spoken.[46] For how long did the various Ngoni groups continue speaking a form of Zulu? Some old Ngoni women from Songea were still speaking Zulu in BuNyakyusa in 1938, but the children knew none. What is the extent of Sotho influence on Lozi? What proportion of Lozi people speak a form of Sotho intelligible to Sotho-speakers? Members of Chief Lewanika's family of my generation who went to school at Lovedale had no difficulty in talking with Sotho-speakers there.[47] When and why did Bisa moving eastward across the Luangwa valley begin to speak Tumbuka?[48] I believe study of language change of this sort would throw much light on African history.

We know from both oral tradition and eye-witness evidence that Nguni and Sotho cattle-owners spread among and absorbed hunters who spoke click languages. The hunters' languages had most influence on Nguni, rather less on Southern Sotho, and still less on Northern Sotho and Tswana. The Sotho, particularly the Tswana, were more stratified than the Nguni. Marriage of Tswana with Sarwa women was prohibited and it is likely that children of mixed descent learnt Tswana not Sarwa. The influence of Sarwa on Tswana remained minimal. But some southern Sotho and some Nguni did marry click-speaking hunters, and the influence of click languages, particularly on Nguni, is conspicuous. We know that Xhosa fused with Khoikhoi, the wives of eighteenth-century Xhosa chiefs often being Khoikhoi. The Khoikhoi were herders not hunters, but their language is similar to the language of various

[46] Donald Fraser *Winning a Primitive People* London 1914 p. 86.
[47] Personal communication from the late Dr Gladstone Letele (linguist) of his experience at school in Lovedale. His home language was Sotho.
[48] Fraser p. 86.

hunting groups. We know that the Sotho-speaking Tlhaping also married Khoikhoi women in the eighteenth century, but it seems that this had not continued over a long period as it had with Xhosa and Khoikhoi.

Pushing the argument a stage further you may ask why the Sotho generally, and especially the Tswana, were more stratified than the Nguni. I relate their stratification to trade. The Sotho were miners with an ancient tradition of metal work, and export of metal and of furs. The chiefs claimed a monopoly of the trade. The wealth of the chief attracted followers, both hunting people who attached themselves as clients, and Sotho commoners who concentrated round the chief because he had milk, cattle, and later trade goods to distribute.

Eugène Casalis wrote in 1835: 'Cattle is the foundation of power with the Kaffir and Bechuana chiefs. As the people live almost exclusively on the milk of their chief's cows, the population of the towns increases at the same rate as the number of cattle which the chief has at his disposal.'[49] In this passage Casalis does not distinguish between Sotho and Nguni; by 'Kaffir' he probably meant Xhosa or Thembu, but the people he really knew were the Sotho. I suggest that among the Sotho a chief controlled relatively more of the stock than among the Nguni where ownership was more widely distributed. He achieved this through a trade monopoly and it was the most important factor influencing both the form of local grouping, and stratification.[50]

There may be other factors which contributed to stratification among the Tswana. Perhaps they encountered a relatively greater number of hunters than the Nguni did and a more numerous people are more difficult to absorb, but on this we can only speculate.

In terms of Malcolm Guthrie's hypothesis on the spread of Bantu languages from the southern savannah (North Zambia and Katanga), Nguni (i.e. Zulu and Xhosa) and Sotho spread southward at more or less the same time. Both groups must have had

[49] E. Casalis, Morija, May 1835, quoted R. C. Germond *Chronicles of Basutoland* Morija 1967 p. 437.

[50] Monica Wilson 'The Sotho, Venda, and Tsonga' *The Oxford History of South Africa* I. The Songhe lived in large settlements in the nineteenth century (Vansina p. 29). Was this a fruit of the enormous metal trade of Katanga? Ntusi in south Uganda is thought to have been occupied by 'a population of several thousands' (Oliver p. 18). Linyati on the Chobe had between six and seven thousand inhabitants in 1853 and Lunda, Kazembe's capital, was 'two miles across' in 1831.

contacts with cattle-owners after separating from the Bantu nuclear area because the cattle words in Nguni and Sotho are not the roots most common in Bantu languages. They are roots which appear only in the south. Furthermore, they appear also in Khoikhoi, therefore Nguni, Sotho, and Khoikhoi acquired cattle from the same source or from each other. This has been demonstrated by my colleague, Ernst Westphal.[51] Christopher Ehret argues that the Nguni and Sotho did not borrow their term for cattle from 'Hottentot' (Khoikhoi).[52]

The Sotho were markedly less dependent upon cattle than the Nguni. This is reflected both in their form of marriage and in ritual. Sotho marriage resembles marriage by service with an uxorilocal stage rather than the typical marriage with cattle. Sotho ritual is less tied to cattle sacrifice than Nguni ritual, and the symbols for most Sotho descent groups were *wild* animals important to a hunting people. The Sotho economy seems to have been dominated by hunting, cultivation, and mining, with cattle-keeping added whereas the Nguni, or most of the Nguni, were cattle-owners first and foremost. The Khoikhoi show very close cultural, including linguistic, connections with various hunting people and it seems likely that they are the descendants of southern hunters who obtained breeding stock—sheep and cattle. I suggest that culturally the Nguni are closest to the people who brought stock from East Africa. On the basis of law and custom I look for connections between Nguni and the pastoralists of the Kenya, Uganda, and Sudan borderlands. Matrilineal cultivators were dispersed in a broad belt across Central Africa from the Congo to the Tanzania coast much in the form reflected in Guthrie's map of language spread. The most likely hypothesis on our present evidence is that pastoralists from East Africa fused with Bantu-speaking cultivators spreading out from the southern savannah. One of the factors affecting the fusion and spread was the form of kinship.

Kinship studies suggest an ancient differentiation between Nguni and Sotho, but there is one fact which indicates a common experience. The Nguni and most of the Sotho share a characteristic which differentiates them on the one hand from the yellow-skinned hunting people and the Khoikhoi who, I believe, are

[51] E. O. J. Westphal 'The Linguistic Prehistory of South Africa' *Africa* 33 iii (1963) pp. 253–6.

[52] C. Ehret 'Cattle Keeping in Eastern and Southern Africa' *J.A.H.* 81 (1967) p. 7.

hunters who acquired cattle,[53] and on the other from the Bantu-speakers of Moçambique and most of Zambia. They rigidly avoid eating fish.

Now food taboos have commonly been an expression of differentiation between groups. Non-pork-eaters distinguished themselves from pork-eaters; non-beef-eaters from those who ate cows; non-horse-flesh-eaters from those who feasted on horses. I suggest that those who avoided fish lived in contact with, but distinguished themselves from, the hunters who ate fish whenever it was available, and from the Bantu-speakers who spread from the southern savannah, and who perhaps first spread along rivers.[54] Bantu-speakers of the Congo and the Zambezi basins prized fish as a food and used fish symbols in their art. I first saw the gulf in symbolism between fishermen and cattle-men ten years ago when visiting an exhibition of African art in Lubumbashi, then Elizabethville. I suggest that cattle-owners coming into the southern grasslands distinguished themselves as non-fish-eaters in the same way as the Hima have distinguished themselves from Hutu in Rwanda until the last decades,[55] and as Christians distinguished themselves from horse-eating pagans in Hungary, or Jews from Gentiles in Palestine many centuries ago.[56]

According to this argument both Sotho and Nguni are heirs of incoming cattlemen, but one section of the Sotho, the Tlhaping, rejected the taboo during a famine and assert that fact in their name. They call themselves 'the fish-eaters'. Other small groups in Lesotho who mingled with hunters also began eating fish. But there is a song in the Sotho initiation ritual rejecting fish as a food,[57] and Livingstone tells of Tswana starving at Kolobeng in 1842 rather than eat fish from the drying river.[58] The Shona are said also to avoid fish, but confirmation is needed of practice of the various Shona-speaking sub-groups.

The fish-taboo is not a general mark of Bantu-speakers, and it is not observed by all cattle-owners. Khoikhoi prized fish and so

[53] Hunters and Khoikhoi were distinguished from Bantu-speakers by many characteristics, among them a radical difference in kinship structure. The hunters and Khoikhoi practised brother-sister avoidance, something known in other parts of the world, but peculiar to them in central and southern Africa, whereas the Bantu-speakers all expect and allow a close familiarity between brother and sister.

[54] M. Posnansky 'Bantu Genesis' *J.A.H.* IX (1968) p. 3.

[55] M. Maquet *Le Système des relations sociales dans le Rwanda ancien* Tervuren 1954 p. 27.

[56] F. J. Simons *Eat Not this Flesh* Madison 1961 p. 113.

[57] Monica Wilson 'The Sotho, Venda and Tsonga' *The Oxford History of South Africa*, I.

[58] D. Livingstone *Missionary Travels* London 1857 pp. 20–21.

did many Bantu-speakers who owned cattle north of the Zambezi, but the presumption that it was a mark of incoming cattle-owners in the south is strong. It is strong enough for me to press the archaeologists to look closely for the remains of fish when they excavate a site. This my colleagues from Cape Town are already doing.

Studies of food taboos do not therefore fit exactly with studies of Nguni and Sotho kinship. The conclusion is familiar: classifications using different criteria—whether economy, language, political structure, kinship structure, forbidden foods, or symbolic associations—do not coincide precisely, but there are links between them, and the history of Africa can only be understood by a patient disentangling of these links.

5. *The Sotho–Tswana Peoples before 1800*

MARTIN LEGASSICK

Sotho, or Sotho–Tswana, is a linguistic sub-division of the Southern Bantu languages. The Sotho–Tswana peoples who speak the language are also commonly regarded as a distinct cultural group characterized by 'totemism, the possession of cattle, with a cattle complex and extensive cattle terminology, a type of round hut with conical roof, and the pre-emptive right of men to marry their maternal cousins. Besides these there are many smaller, but no less significant features, for instance in material culture (as dress, pottery, weapons and so forth) which are equally characteristic'.[1] However, the Sotho–Tswana peoples share clear physical, linguistic and cultural affinities with other Bantu-speaking peoples, and more particularly with the southern Bantu-speakers, who may broadly be classified as those lying south of the 'matrilineal belt' and through the Kalahari desert.[2] On Guthrie's classification, for example, Sotho, Venda and Nguni are presumed to derive from Zezuru, a Shona language.[3] A recent study of the skull bones of Sotho, Nguni, and Shangana–Thonga peoples, attested as sound by other physical anthropologists, reaches the significant conclusions that variation in skull-type among these peoples is negligibly related to tribal grouping, and that the most distinctive variation from other Negroid populations consists in the incidence of Khoisanoid characteristics.[4]

[1] N. J. Van Warmelo *A Preliminary Survey of the Native Tribes of South Africa* Pretoria: Native Affairs Department Ethnological Publications No. 5 1935 p. 96. This series of publications, produced since 1959 by the Department of Bantu Administration and Development, will be cited as NAD/BAD with the volume number.

[2] For the cultural similarities and differences among the Southern Bantu see, for example, G. P. Murdock *Africa: Its Peoples and their Culture History* New York: McGraw-Hill 1959 pp. 364–91. See also the less general and earlier collection edited by I. Schapera *The Bantu-speaking Tribes of South Africa* Routledge and Kegan Paul 1937.

[3] See, for example, M. Guthrie 'Some developments in the pre-history of the Bantu languages' *J.A.H.* III (1962) 2 pp. 273–82.

[4] H. de Villiers *The Skull of the South African Negro: A Biometrical and Morphological Study* Witwatersrand University Press 1968. The physiological aspect of this work, which forms the bulk of it, is based on measurement of the different bones within the

It is the task of the historian to examine the processes which led to the emergence of the Sotho–Tswana as a distinctive linguistic and cultural group, as well as the processes of structural and cultural change which the Sotho–Tswana have undergone subsequently; to examine, in other words, the movement of peoples, the diffusion and evolution of cultural ideas, techniques, and institutions, and processes of intercultural adaptation and interaction. Ideally, such an examination should encompass the whole history of the Iron Age in the area over which Sotho–Tswana peoples are now settled: a history which can now be regarded, from the recent excavations in Swaziland, as beginning in the fifth to sixth centuries A.D.[5] For though it is not necessary, and perhaps even unlikely, that the first South African iron-workers were Bantu-speaking, there do not appear to be any abrupt cultural discontinuities from that time through to the development of Bantu-speaking iron-working societies. Such a study, however, would have to incorporate evidence derived for the most part from archaeology, linguistics, comparative ethnography and other disciplines appropriate to a time-depth of some 1,300 to 1,400 years. The present essay will be confined largely to an examination of existing accounts of pre-1800 Sotho–Tswana history and the oral traditions on which they are largely based, and will attempt to lay down a preliminary framework within which the accumulation and analysis of evidence from other disciplines can be integrated. Specifically, it will be argued that almost all existing theories, based as they are on a deficient methodology, are unfruitful as well as unreliable and further, that evidence from most types of oral tradition alone is unlikely to be of value, with certain exceptions, for the period prior to A.D. 1600 to 1700.

THE SOURCES OF PRE-1800 SOTHO–TSWANA HISTORY

The earliest syntheses of Sotho–Tswana history prior to 1800 were published at the start of the present century by George Stow, a settler who arrived in 1843, and George McCall Theal, widely

[5] D. W. Phillipson 'Early Iron-Using Peoples of Southern Africa' *supra* p. 36.

skull. The linguistic and historical data are outdated but are not central to the work. See also studies which have shown no significant intertribal variation of gene frequencies among South African Bantu-speakers, namely M. Shapiro 'The ABO, MN, P and Rh blood group systems in the South African Bantu' *South African Medical Journal* XXV (1951) pp. 165–70; 'Further evidence of the homogeneity of blood group distribution in the South African Bantu' ibid XXV (1951) pp. 406–11.

regarded as the pioneer of scientific South African history. *The Beginning of South African History* (1902) by Theal does little more than to mention the 'Batlapin, the Batlaro, the Barolong, the Bahurutsi, the Bangwaketsi, the Bakwena, the Bamangwato, all the sections of the Makalanga, and the whole of the Basuto, north and south' as the 'interior tribes', separate from the coastal and the western tribes.[6] But three years later Theal edited and published, without footnotes, large sections of *The Native Races of South Africa*, which had been completed by Stow in about 1880,[7] and after that time Theal's continuing revisions of his *History of South Africa* contain far greater detail on the Sotho–Tswana which, if not derived directly from Stow, show a dependence on very similar sources.[8]

In 1905 there also appeared two compilations, derived mainly from oral traditions, which attempt to provide for the Southern Sotho of Lesotho and the Sotho of the Transvaal a history similar to Stow's, whose published sections focus largely but not entirely on the Sotho–Tswana of Botswana: these were the *Short History of the Native Tribes of the Transvaal*,[9] and *Basuto Traditions*.[10] Seven years later the material of *Basuto Traditions*, written by J. C. MacGregor an official of the British Administration of Basutoland, was for the most part incorporated within *A History of the Basuto, Ancient and Modern*, written by D. Frederick Ellenberger, a missionary with long experience among the Southern Sotho and substantial familiarity with their traditions; it was MacGregor

[6] *The Beginning of South African History* T. Fisher Unwin 1902 pp. 31–32. This is the revision of an 1896 version, on the basis of Theal's researches in European archives.
[7] George W. Stow *The Native Races of South Africa: A History of the Intrusion of the Hottentots and Bantu into the Hunting Grounds of the Bushmen, the Aborigines of the Country* Chs. XXI–XXVI London Swan Sonnenschein, New York Macmillan 1905 reprinted Cape Town Struik *Africana Collecteana* Vol. VII 1963. Certain sections of the manuscript omitted by Theal are housed in two bound volumes in the South African Public Library. These are relevant mainly for the Southern Sotho and the Nguni peoples. The section on the Ghoya may be found in James Walton *Early Ghoya Settlement in the Orange Free State* Bloemfontein National Museum, Memoir 2 1965 pp. 19–36.
[8] See, for example, G. M. Theal *The Yellow and Dark-Skinned People of Africa South of the Zambezi; History and Ethnography of South Africa before 1795*, III, ch. LIX; *Ethnography and Conditions of South Africa Before 1505* esp ch. IX George Allen and Unwin 1910. William Lye claims to have found further information on the Sotho–Tswana in early, pre-Stow, editions of Theal's writings. I have not discovered them.
[9] Transvaal Native Affairs Department *Short History of the Native Tribes of the Transvaal* Pretoria Government Printing Office 1905; F. H. W. Jensen 'A Note on the Bahurutshe' *African Studies* VII (1947) p. 4, is a revised version of Chapter 2 of this work. It was summarized, and fresh ethnographical and conquest-period history added, in R. H Massie, *The Native Tribes of the Transvaal* London General Staff of the War Office 1905.
[10] J. C. MacGregor *Basuto Traditions* Cape Town 1905.

who translated this work into English.[11] These works were followed by several more in the same amateur tradition by A. J. Wookey *Dico tsa Secwana*, 1919, S. M. Molema *The Bantu: Past and Present* 1920, and J. T. Brown *Among the Bantu Nomads* 1926. The historical contributions of these works are of variable standard, but from this time concern with Bantu-speaking peoples was to pass largely from historians, professional or amateur, to anthropologists of the functional school. Significantly, Brown's book has an introduction by A. R. Radcliffe-Brown, then Professor of Anthropology at Cape Town University.[12]

The writing of this period, which has provided the base on which more detailed subsequent studies have been built, suffers from at least three methodological deficiencies:

1 *The Differential quality and quantity of knowledge of Sotho–Tswana groups*

The amount and quality of relevant information gathered during the nineteenth century, on which the syntheses were based, was historically determined by the accessibility of different Sotho–Tswana communities to those in a position to record their history, who were, for the majority of the century, missionaries. The famous and valuable works by, among others, John Campbell, Robert Moffat, Thomas Arbousset, Eugéne Casalis, and David Livingstone were based on their experiences among the southern Tswana and the communities of the 'missionary road' to the north, or among the southern Sotho. These were either, as in the case of the Tlhaping and Rolong, 'atypical' societies, or, as with the Southern Sotho, the Kwena, the Ngwato and the Ngwaketse, recently consolidated in a new form.[13] Although from about 1830

[11] D. F. Ellenberger *A History of the Basuto: Ancient and Modern* Caxton 1912. Subsequent volumes of this work, which would have continued the history after about 1830, were not published.

[12] S. M. Molema *The Bantu Past and Present: an Ethnographical and Historical Study of the Native Races of South Africa* Green 1920, reprinted Cape Town Struik *Africana Collecteana* Vol. V 1963; J. T. Brown *Among the Bantu Nomads* London Seeley and Service 1926; A. J. Wookey *Dinwao leha e le dipolelo kaga dice tsa Secwana* Tigerkloof second edition 1921. Brown and Wookey were missionaries among the Tswana while Molema was a Christianized Morolong.

[13] John Campbell *Travels in South Africa* London 1813, Andover Flagg and Gould 1813; J. Campbell *Travels in South Africa . . . being a narrative of a second journey* London Westley 1822 2 vols.; Robert Moffat *Missionary Labours and Scenes in Southern Africa* London Snow 1842; T. Arbousset *Narrative of an Exploratory Tour* Cape Town 1846, reprinted Cape Town Struik *Africana Collecteana* Vol. XXVII 1968; E. Casalis *The Basuto* first edition Paris 1859, London Nisbet 1861; reprinted Struik *Africana Collecteana*

one finds fragmentary information on the Sotho–Tswana peoples within the present Transvaal, a combination of historical factors led to smaller interest in the histories of these communities, and less ready accessibility to available information in Dutch or German. Nor was this deficiency repaired by the other sources of evidence available. The important oral testimony given by Sotho–Tswana and others to the series of commissions and courts which met to settle boundary disputes from the 1840s to the turn of the century was equally weighted towards the Southern Sotho and the westernmost Sotho–Tswana communities, as was the fresh oral testimony on which the synthesizers drew.

The value of this nineteenth-century evidence is well recognized, as is apparent from the increasing number of reprints of relevant works, as well as the publication of the letters and journals of missionaries, officials and others who were in the Sotho–Tswana area in the period.[14] Much more along these lines remains to be done, however, and it is clear that future publications of this type should be judged by the amount of new light which they shed on the history of the societies in the area rather than the fame of the author. The archives of German missionary societies—the Hermannsborg, Hanover, and Berlin missions—remain, for example, almost completely unexplored. And the wealth of material on African peoples scattered through the published government documents and the official South African archival collections will remain hard for any one person to utilize over a manageable time period unless they are gathered together into carefully chosen document collections.

2 *Parallel chains of transmission of historical testimony*

From the early part of the nineteenth century there have existed written accounts of Sotho–Tswana oral traditions drawn from a differentially accessible cross-section of groups. Each successive

[14] Amongst the most valuable of these should be mentioned the *Family Letters*, *Missionary Correspondence* and *Private Journals* of David Livingstone, and Moffat's *Apprenticeship at Kuruman*, all superbly edited in the 1950s by Isaac Schapera. Also the less well-edited *Diary of Andrew Smith* Van Riebeeck Society Vols. 20–21 1939–40 ed. P. Kirby, and ed. J. P. R. Wallis *Matabele Journals of Robert Moffat* Chatto and Windus 1945 2 vols.

Vol. XVI 1965; David Livingstone *Missionary Travels and Researches in South Africa* first edition London 1856, New York Harper 1858. These are only the most well-known and widely used of a whole collection of similar nineteenth-century works.

writer has drawn on these already published traditions in addition to gathering fresh oral tradition in the field. For the most part, moreover, there is no citation of sources to enable the critic to separate what was freshly gathered by the author from what was not, what was reconfirmed from what was surmised, what was reliably obtained from what was not. Such dissection of the syntheses can only be achieved from a detailed knowledge of all the nineteenth-century material. In Stow's work, for example, long extracts from Campbell, Moffat and Arbousset and others can be found, which are sometimes, due, perhaps, to Theal's editing, taken past the relevant passage to entirely extraneous material which could only be confusing to the unknown reader. Elsewhere two passages from different books, referring to different communities with a similar name, are telescoped together to give a coherent but entirely erroneous narrative.[15]

This period over which oral traditions have been recorded, longer than for most parts of Africa, has resulted in the emergence of a chain of transmission of traditions from one written account to the next parallel to the normal oral chain of transmission. The written chain, furthermore, because of the inadequate methodology and techniques of citation, is almost impossible to validate by the usual correlation with social structure along the lines developed by African historiography. Further, there has been an interpenetration between the two chains of transmission to the extent that literate Sotho–Tswana have read written versions of their own history and transmitted this version to non-literate persons: 'many of them [the Tlhaping] are not on top of [historical] affairs any more, and the evidence of those that can read agrees overwhelmingly with the account by Wookey', writes a recent historian of the Tlhaping.[16]

The extent to which the existence of the parallel chain and its interpenetration with the oral chain has prevented and will prevent further collection of traditions will vary according to the degree of literacy of the group concerned, as well as the rapidity with which traditional structures are changing. In South Africa a further distortion has been induced by the artificial

[15] See, for example Stow, *Native Races* pp. 501–3, in comparison with M. Legassick 'Mokalaka, Regent of the Rolong boo Ratlou boo Mariba: A synthesis of oral and written sources'. Unpublished paper of School of Oriental and African Studies London 1967.

[16] F. J. Language 'Herkoms en Geskiedenis van die Tlhaping' *African Studies* I (1942) 117.

'retribalization' which has been proceeding over the last twenty years, which appears to have created autonomous communities which did not exist before and induced them to produce traditions to support their new status. Yet the work of persons in the field even within the last decade, notably, for the Sotho–Tswana, P.-L. Breutz and N. J. van Warmelo, suggest that at least for the eighteenth century onwards it is still possible to gather fresh information, and to validate such traditions as have already been recorded. Nevertheless there is no doubt that the systematic collation and analysis of the voluminous body of traditions that now exist is a task at least as important as the gathering of fresh material.

3 *A Priori assumptions in Sotho–Tswana historiography*

The damaging but powerful assumptions of late nineteenth-century social philosophy, and particularly those of the German and Austrian Kulturhistorische Schule, predominant in the colonial era of African historiography, were and remain prevalent in historical accounts of the African peoples of South Africa. Thus it has generally been assumed that peoples sharing a common culture and language must have moved to South Africa in a single wave of migration, conquering or exterminating those with whom they came in contact, and preserving their identity intact and static over time through some mysterious genetic process. Or, if it appears evident that the migration was not some single movement, then it consisted in successive waves of a group that had been a unit at some other place and earlier time. 'The pioneers appear to have been comparatively insignificant tribes,' writes Stow, 'the advanced guard of the still greater body which was following, and which, when it overtook them, swept over them, and reduced the greater portion of the fugitives to a state of vassalage.'[17] 'It was during the sojourn in Rhodesia,' we are told by Ellenberger, 'that [the Fokeng and the Rolong] threw off all the numerous offshots which in course of time came to occupy the whole of South Africa.'[18]

Such assumptions have recently been subjected to detailed and rigorous examination and criticism by African historians.[19]

[17] Stow *Native Races*, p. 420. Also *ibid*, pp. 405–7, 433–4.

[18] Ellenberger, *Basuto*, xviii–xx.

[19] For recent examples, see A. Southall 'The Peopling of Africa: the Linguistic and Sociological Evidence' in M. Posnansky (ed.) *Prelude to East African History* London Oxford University Press 1966; Jan Vansina *Kingdoms of the Savanna* University of

Their persistence in South Africa can be accounted for only by the relative isolation of its academic community from trends in African history, and by the necessity of such assumptions to underpin not only the philosophy of apartheid, but the mythical version of the emergence of the Afrikaner community. It is now well recognized that not only do changes in culture, language, physical type, and economy occur independently of one another, but that the change of each is a complex problem requiring sophisticated analysis. 'Migrations', defined as a large body of people moving a considerable distance over a short period of time, are a relatively rare phenomenon, and cannot be used to explain each change of culture or structure. All cultures and populations are mixed, absorbing new elements and evolving *in situ*. Such a perspective alters considerably the questions which it seems relevant to ask about Sotho–Tswana history. In particular it should direct attention away from the 'quest for origins' towards a study of the cultural and structural changes undergone by the Sotho–Tswana peoples during their occupation of South Africa between the Limpopo and the Orange, and the causes of such changes.

From about the late 1920s the nature of inquiry about Bantu-speaking peoples in South Africa underwent a transition from a concern for exotic customs and a semi-speculative history based on such *a priori* diffusionist or evolutionist conceptions, towards a study of the institutions of the societies concerned and their functional relationship. The writings of missionaries and officials began to give place to those of trained anthropologists, whose work over the succeeding decades has provided us with a solid understanding of Sotho–Tswana social institutions which is indispensable for further evaluation of oral traditions, as well as giving a base-line against which to reconstruct institutional development. Such work has been focused predominantly around the anthropology departments of a limited number of South African universities and the journal *African Studies* from 1942 (*Bantu Studies* 1921–41) on the one hand, and on the other the Ethnological Section of the Native Affairs Department (Bantu Administration and Development since 1959), whose series of

Wisconsin Press 1966. 'Some basic concepts' pp. 14–18; H. Lewis 'Ethnology and African Culture History' in C. Gabel and N. R. Bennett (eds.) *Reconstructing African Culture History* Boston University Press 1967 pp. 25–44.

publications commences in 1930. Outstanding among the ethnographic analyses is the work of Isaac Schapera, though since his field-work has been entirely among the peoples of the present-day Botswana it cannot be generalized in space or time without due caution. The ethnography of the Southern Sotho and, especially, the Sotho of the Transvaal is less extensive and less penetrating. Furthermore these anthropologists, unlike many of their contemporaries elsewhere in Africa, paid some attention to the histories of the particular communities with which they were concerned, modifying or amplifying on a detailed level the earlier historical accounts. In 1940 Schapera edited a volume of histories of the Tswana in the vernacular[20] which were mostly republished in English elsewhere, and from 1944 onwards N. J. Van Warmelo and P.-L. Breutz in particular, supplemented by others, have published similar histories of Sotho–Tswana communities in the northern Cape and Transvaal. Though uneven in value according to how far the conventional historical apparatus of critical appraisal and citation of sources, written and oral, has been adopted, these have added a new wealth of detail to our knowledge of the Sotho–Tswana past. The need for new synthesis is made apparent, however, by the continued reliance in historical accounts on compilations of the existing state of knowledge in the 1930s made by N. J. Van Warmelo (*A Preliminary Survey of the Native Tribes of South Africa* 1935) and I. Schapera (*The Bantu-Speaking Tribes of South Africa* 1937) if not on Theal and Stow themselves.[21]

THE TERMS 'SOTHO' AND 'TSWANA' AND THEIR RECOGNIZED CULTURAL SUB-DIVISIONS

Were it not for the Platonic 'ideal-type' attitude which persists among writers on the Sotho–Tswana, it would not be necessary to examine the history of denominative terms such as 'Sotho' or 'Tswana'. The absence of a common self-designated name is a necessary, but not a sufficient, condition for the absence of a common culture. But the fact that the 'Sotho' and the 'Tswana'

[20] I. Schapera (ed.) *Ditirafalo tsa Merafe ya BaTswana* Lovedale 1940. The English translations of these accounts, and other more recent historical writings, will be cited as relevant.

[21] Thus the main citations in I. Schapera's account of the Sotho–Tswana in E. A. Walker (ed.) *Cambridge History of South Africa* Vol. VIII Cambridge second edition 1963, and J. D. Omer-Cooper *The Zulu Aftermath* Longmans 1966 are to Van Warmelo's 'Grouping and Ethnic History' in Schapera *Bantu-Speaking Tribes* pp. 58–63.

have only comparatively recently, and with rather variable applicability, designated themselves as such, does at least throw open the question as to what collective entities the 'Sotho–Tswana' peoples saw themselves as belonging prior to the nineteenth century. Indeed might not comparative ethnography, studied in conjunction with the known history of these peoples, throw light on significant clusterings of deviant culture-traits which might give leads to the formative processes which resulted in existing Sotho–Tswana culture?

It is not intended here to provide a complete historiographical account of the meaning or use of 'Sotho' or 'Tswana'. It has been suggested that the term 'Sotho' was first applied by Mbo Nguni to chiefdoms living on the Usutu River in Swaziland, though it is unclear whether the term, meaning brownish-black, light-black, dark-brown, was applied first to the river, the people or their clothing.[22] From here it may have spread west and south to the communities who would later be amalgamated by Moshweshwe. The first recorded use of it, to my knowledge, is in an 1824 letter by John Melvill at Griquatown.[23] There is no comparably satisfactory account of the meaning or origin of the word 'Tswana' or 'Bechuana'. Indeed the most convincing criticism of the usual explanations can only suggest that, since the Xhosa called the interior Bantu-speakers 'Abetswana'.

It seems possible that someone who knew Sixosa, but very little Secwana might have used the word first. The Becwana are expert corrupters of words whose significance they do not fully understand, or such as they have reason to believe are ridiculous, questionable, doubtful or foreign; and so it would follow that once they heard a Moruti or traveller say 'Becwana' it would be a joke (and jokes speedily become fashions of the day . . .) and they would indulge in a sportive or wanton use of it.[24]

[22] Evidence of E. Jacottet in A. T. Bryant *Olden Times in Zululand and Natal* Longmans Green 1929, reprinted Cape Town Struik *Africana Collecteana* Vol. XIII 1965 pp. 308–10; Ellenberger *Basuto* p. 34. See also N. J. Van Warmelo in A. C. Myburgh *The Tribes of Barberton District* (NAD/BAD, No. 25, 1949) p. 10 and Smith *Diary* II p. 278. Ellenberger and Bryant give different dates to this event, but neither considers the possibility of a lengthy 'Sotho' occupation of the Usutu River.

[23] John Melvill 17 December 1824 in British Parliamentary Papers [50 of 1835, 216–17].

[24] D. M. Ramoshana 'The Origin of Secwana' *Bantu Studies* III (1927–9) pp. 197–8. See also Arbousset *Narrative* p. 271; E. Solomon *Two Lectures on the Native Tribes of the Interior delivered before the Mechanics Institute Cape Town* Saul Solomon 1855 pp. 40–41; Stow *Native Races* p. 407; Brown *Bantu Nomads* p. 25–26.

The earliest recorded use of the name is in 1779, when the traveller Gordon inscribed 'Moetjooaanas' on a map; prior to this the Sotho–Tswana had been known to whites by Khoi-derived names such as 'Briqua'.[25] Early whites among the present-day southern Tswana record very variable usages of the name, and indeed the tendency seems to have been to describe more distant Sotho-Tswana groups generally as 'Bakuen', which may refer to the communities whose *siboko* (totem) was *kwena* (the crocodile), but is also used by Robert Moffat interchangeably with 'Bakone', a term cognate to 'Nguni' but also apparently applied by the southern Tswana to the communities north and east of the Marico River.[26]

As whites, particularly missionaries, began to spread from the southern Tswana farther to the east and north after 1830, the term 'Bechuana' came to be generally applied to all the Bantu-speaking peoples of the South African interior, sometimes, indeed, too extensively. 'The Bechuana,' wrote the missionary Archbell, 'are known to commence in the east about Delagoa Bay and to extend southward and westward to the colony of the Cape ... They incline to the north and are found on the western shores about the 23° of southern Latt, under the denomination of Damaras ... If there are many dialects of Bechuana, the differences are very small.'[27] And the 'Sotho' were regarded as 'one of the most considerable sub-divisions of this [the Bechuana] family'.[28] It was only as a wedge was driven by white settlement between the communities neighbouring the Kalahari desert and those of the Caledon valley and foothills, with the intermediate communities largely subjected, that 'Bechuana' came to be used more narrowly for the communities of present-day Botswana and the northern Cape. 'These people,' wrote Mackenzie of the 'Bechuana', 'do not use this word of themselves, or of one another; nevertheless they accept of it as the white man's name for them, and now begin to use

[25] See C. Saunders 'Early Knowledge of the Sotho: Seventeenth and Eighteenth Century Accounts of the Tswana' *Quarterly Bulletin of the South African Library* (1966) p. 293. But see also J. Edwards 22 July 1802 [LMS 2/2/A] who, among the Tlhaping, wrote of the surrounding peoples 'the whole Nation they called in general Cabitikwa ... there are 22 capital places'.

[26] See R. Moffat *Apprenticeship at Kuruman* ed. I. Schapera Chatto and Windus 1951 p. 282; R. Moffat 30 January 1827 [LMS 11/1/A]; R. Moffat *Missionary Labours* ch. XXIV. For other uses of the term Bakoni see Arbousset *Narrative* p. 271; Bryant *Olden Times* pp. 6, 14, 308–9.

[27] J. Archbell 6 September 1830 [MMS: Box V–Unnumbered].

[28] Casalis *Basuto* xviii. Also Stow *Native Races* p. 519.

it of themselves.'[29] Meanwhile the term 'Sotho' has, in the twentieth century, been extended to include all 'Sotho–Tswana' peoples, with 'Bechuana' or 'Tswana' now representing a sub-division.[30]

The question of current terminology leads on to the cultural and linguistic sub-divisions commonly recognized among the Sotho–Tswana. These, when closely examined, can be seen to derive in large part from forces which have moulded the historical experience of the Sotho–Tswana peoples in relatively recent times. The 'Southern Sotho', for example, owe their cultural and linguistic homogeneity largely to the post-Difaqane state-building by Moshweshwe and his successors. The rather lesser homogeneity of the 'Central Sotho' of the eastern Transvaal can be explained by the era of Pedi hegemony, at its height in the eighteenth century. The 'Northern Tswana', 'Southern Tswana' and 'Eastern Tswana' underwent different historical experiences in the nineteenth century also, and it is recognized that these groupings, and even more the 'Northern Sotho' grouping, are culturally and linguistically unsatisfactory.[31] 'There is no dialect which describes itself as Tswana and the grouping of the Western dialects as Tswana is not acceptable to the author. There is similarly no valid Northern or Pedi group,' wrote a linguist recently.[32]

That cultural divisions which appear to stem from so recent a historical experience have been found to be unsatisfactory is encouraging. For it suggests that, if the right questions are posed, a systematic study of dialect differences among the Sotho-Tswana, and of clusters of culture-traits, could still unearth evidence relevant to an earlier historical experience. It is in an attempt to guide such investigations, which can be conducted both in the field and by more systematic investigation of the existing documents, published and unpublished, that the remainder of this essay is formulated.

[29] J. Mackenzie *Austral Africa* Sampson Low 1887 I p. 22. For the restricted use of Bechuana see also, for example, John Brown 'The Bechuana Tribes' *Cape Monthly Magazine* New Series XI (July 1875) pp. 61, 1–5.

[30] See, for example, Van Warmelo *Preliminary Survey* p. 96; I. Schapera *The Tswana* Ethnographic Survey of Africa, Southern Africa, Part III, London: IAA, 1953; V. G. J. Sheddick, *The Southern Sotho* Ethnographic Survey of Africa, Southern Africa, Part II, London: IAA, 1953. E. H. Ashton, *The Basuto* London O.U.P. 1952.

[31] For the subdivisions see Van Warmelo *Preliminary Survey* pp. 96–116 and, in slightly different form, Van Warmelo 'Grouping and Ethnic History' in Schapera *Bantu-Speaking Tribes* pp. 57–63. Van Warmelo is at great pains to point out the artificial nature of the divisions, with the exception of the Southern Sotho.

[32] E. Westphal 'The linguistic pre-history of Southern Africa' *Africa* XXXIII July 1963.

THE SOTHO–TSWANA PEOPLES FROM ABOUT 1500 TO 1800

The recorded oral traditions of Sotho-Tswana communities are almost entirely those associated with the ruling lineages of the chiefdoms which form the Sotho–Tswana political community. The lineages in which the office of chieftainship was vested, by means of succession rules which it is not necessary to discuss here,[33] were the skeleton of the political community for as far back as we can determine. The office of chief was the ritual, judicial, administrative, economic and political focus of the community, and membership of a chiefdom involved first and foremost allegiance to the office of the chieftainship. These communities were subject to periodic fission by which sometimes perhaps a number of sons, but more usually a single son or brother of the ruler would, in a succession dispute, or even during a ruler's lifetime, leave the community with his followers and establish himself in autonomy. The process which produced a cluster of chiefdoms, which will be termed a lineage-cluster, is, as Omer-Cooper has pointed out, appropriate to a situation in which relatively uninhabited territory was being colonized by an expanding population.[34] It appears that, as among the Cape Nguni, the senior chief in the cluster of chiefdoms would retain some social and ritual authority, though it is difficult to determine at this stage the nature of this or the extent to which geographical distance and the rise or fall of political power led to decay in this regard.[35] Certainly with regard to judicial affairs, and command of the allegiance of his subjects, each chief enjoyed autonomy and equality of status. But though one can find indications of ritual respect paid to the senior chief, there are also cases in which such ritual respect was paid to the powerful chief of a sub-cluster.[36] On the other hand, of course,

[33] Though in theory these identified a single legitimate heir, they were in practice fluid enough to give ample scope for dispute and fission. This was in particular because there could be doubt as to who was the 'chief' wife, because of the practice of the levirate and the existence of regencies, and because, in certain areas, there could be female rulers. The use of the term 'lineage' to describe this structure is controversial (Adam Kuper, personal communication).

[34] Omer-Cooper *Zulu Aftermath* p. 23.

[35] W. D. Hammond-Tooke 'Segmentation and Fission in Cape Nguni Political Units' *Africa* April 1965 pp. 143–67, discusses the lineage-cluster (which he calls the 'Tribal cluster') among the Cape Nguni.

[36] A clear example of this is the 'tribute' apparently paid by Sekgoma of the Ngwato to Sechele of the Kwena, see Livingstone *Missionary Travels* p. 51. Another case apparently revolves around the ritual seniority of the Hurutshe in first-fruits ceremonies, though they seem in fact to have been junior to the Kwena–Magopa, and possibly

obligations of a political kind could become transformed in historical memory into those due to lineage-cluster membership.[37] It is primarily the distortion of lineage-cluster relationships by factors of territorial association and relative political power, which have become amplified by inadequate understanding of political structure in the written chain of transmission, which complicates the reconstruction of lineage-clusters.

Around the skeleton of the ruling lineage are grouped today, in every Sotho-Tswana community, sub-units whose nuances are many, but whose basic feature is a reproduction of the chiefdom on a smaller scale. The crucial units are the *kgoro*, *kgotla*, *moze* or *motse* and so on, the ward or hamlet, governed by a hereditary headman, and enjoying a substantial separate corporate life.[38] In some cases these were grouped within a single settlement, and in others scattered over the countryside. The 'hamlet' would be likely to contain people who were not members of it, whether or not the headman was a member of the chief lineage. In certain cases, as for the chiefdoms of present-day Botswana, we have considerable knowledge of the history of the peoples of these wards.[39] In other cases we have at least an enumeration of them, with some details which can provide clues to the ancestry of their populations. Sometimes, too, it is evident that a presently existing autonomous chiefdom was at one time in the recent past contained as a ward, or series of wards, in another, and that the 'fission' has come in the

[37] This was certainly the case with the Fokeng ba Thekwane who became politically subject to the Hurutshe at Kaditshwene, which led Ellenberger, the TNAD *Short History* and others to assume a genealogical relationship. It is also likely to be true of the supposed relationship between the Kgatla and the Hurutshe, for some at least of the Kgatla were in the eighteenth century subordinate to the Hurutshe. See Breutz *The Tribes of Rustenburg and Pilansberg District* (NAD/BAD, 28, 1953) p. 61; Ellenberger *Basuto* pp. 15–16; H. Methuen *Life in the Wilderness* London 1846 p. 254; evidence of Gasietsewe in *Bloemhof Bluebook* p. 190. Ellenberger, *Basuto*, pp. 15–16.

[38] Burchell *Travels* II pp. 347, 491–2, 513, was the first, when among the Tlhaping, to distinguish the 'ward'. See also, for example, Casalis *Basuto* chs. IX, XII; I. Schapera 'The social structure of the Tswana ward' *Bantu Studies* IX (1935) pp. 203–24; E. H. Ashton 'The Social Structure of the Southern Sotho Ward' *Communications of the School of African Studies* UCT n.s., 15 (1946); E. J. Krige 'The Place of the North-Eastern Transvaal Sotho in the South Bantu Complex' *Africa* XI (July 1938) 3 pp. 265–93.

[39] See, in particular, I. Schapera *The Ethnic Composition of the Tswana Tribes* London School of Economics, Monograph in Social Anthropology 11 1952.

junior to other Kwena groups. See ibid p. 51; Smith *Diary* II pp. 221–2; Stow *Native Races* pp. 520–1, which appears to misinterpret Livingstone; TNAD *Short History* pp. 11–13; Brown *Bantu Nomads* pp. 260–2; P.-L. Breutz *Die Stamme van die Distrik Ventersdorp* (NAD/BAD, 31, 1954–5) pp. 76, 113–19; *The Tribes of Marico District* (NAD/BAD, 30, 1953–4) pp. 25–27.

disruption of the nineteenth or twentieth centuries and not earlier. But for the most part the histories of non-lineage groups are not available, particularly in the case of the important communities in the eastern part of the Sotho-Tswana area.[40]

In about 1500 two such chiefdoms began to divide into clusters which, taken together, form the dominant communities over most of the Sotho–Tswana area at the present time. One of these lineage-clusters consists of those communities who trace their descent from an apical ancestor Malope and his father Masilo who, according to the traditions, appear to have 'lived' about twelve generations before 1800, or about 1440 to 1560.[41] Though it is often difficult to determine whether the traditions present a true genealogy, or simply a ruler-list, the internal consistency in this case suggests that the generation-depth is reliable. At some time around 1500 the original chiefdom of this cluster began to undergo fission, so that within three hundred years its members were spread from the centre of the Highveld near Brits to the borders of the Kalahari, and as far south as the upper Caledon River.

A precise chronology of the dispersal is not possible at this stage, because questions of precedence in the cluster naturally affect the genealogies. But the most plausible reconstruction would suggest that dispersion commenced from Rathateng, a site near the junction of the Marico and Crocodile Rivers whose precise location is unknown.[42] From here it would appear that the Hurutshe moved up towards the headwaters of the Marico, while another group moved up the Crocodile River to Mabjaba-Matswane, now Zwartkoppies, in the Brits district. At the same time a third group moved farther south, across the Vaal to Ntsanatsatsi, which is variously located at Stoffberg, or between Frankfort and Vrede in the Orange Free State.[43] During the

[40] J. D. Krige 'Traditional Origins and Tribal Relationships of the Sotho of the Northern Transvaal' *Bantu Studies* XI (1937) p. 327.

[41] The genealogies used, estimating twenty to thirty years to a generation until a more exact figure can be given, are those of the Hurutshe, the Kwena–Magopa, and the Kwena of Sechele: these are not inconsistent either with those in Ellenberger. See Breutz *Rustenburg* pp. 82–83; *Marico* pp. 92–93; Ellenberger *Basuto* pp. 334–7, 374–88; I. Schapera *A Handbook of Tswana Law and Custom* Oxford University Press revised edition 1955 p. 302.

[42] See Breutz *Rustenburg* pp. 20–21, 80–81, 83–84, 107–8, 125, 144, 425; *Marico* pp. 17–18; *Ventersdorp* pp. 92–94; *Mafeking* pp. 23–24; Schapera *Ditirafalo* 33. A variant version has Mabjaba–Matswana as the earliest site, from which dispersion took place in a westerly direction: this is less satisfactory.

[43] See Arbousset *Narrative* 131; Ellenberger *Basuto* pp. 17–20, 68; Breutz *Ventersdorp* p. 119.

seventeenth and eighteenth centuries each of these chiefdoms was to divide further, and indeed there are communities in the north-west Transvaal and Botswana, notably the Khurutshe and Gananwa, whose relationship to this lineage-cluster appears clear though the chronology is not, and who may have been other pre-seventeenth century offshoots.[44]

By the end of the eighteenth century, the chiefdoms of this lineage-cluster were spread over the western part of the Transvaal Highveld, from near the present Brits in the east to Kanye, on the borders of the Kalahari, in the east.[45] In many of the traditions there is little mention of the existence of other non-related communities until the eighteenth century, which may be accounted for by elision or by the relative sparseness of previous habitation of the area concerned. Such non-related communities do, however, exist today. Some of them are the so-called 'Transvaal Ndebele', and other communities whom we must presume to have been earlier inhabitants of the area. The nature of the Sotho–Tswana political structure and traditions is such that it is almost impossible to tell whether a now independent community was once subject to another or not, since a hamlet headman fulfills the same structural function in miniature to the chief, and hence can reproduce a similar tradition.[46] It seems likely, however, as will be discussed later, that existing inhabitants were in some cases absorbed into the dominant communities ruled by members of the lineage-cluster, and in other cases, as groups or families, were in some form of subject relationship to these communities or their members.

In one area, at least, we have evidence of the existence of earlier inhabitants. The Kwena chiefdoms who are now dominant among the Southern Sotho have a tradition of crossing the Vaal to the south in about 1550–1650 and legitimizing their occupation

[44] See Breutz *Marico* pp. 19–21; F. Jensen 'Note on the Baharutse'; Schapera *Ethnic Composition* pp. 354–5; TNAD *Short History* p. 37; J. D. Krige 'Traditional Origins' pp. 354–5.

[45] See Ellenberger *Basuto* pp. 17–20, 70–85, 374–88; Breutz *Marico* pp. 18–22, 54–88 236–9; *Rustenburg* pp. 78–105, 106–58, 321–53, 424–37; *Ventersdorp* pp. 91–99, 101–7 For lineage-cluster members in Botswana see I. Schapera 'A short history of the Bangwaketse' *African Studies* I (1942) pp. 1–26; Schapera *Ditirafalo* and others. Lineage-cluster members whose traditions do not appear to have been published include post-Difaqane Kwena–Magopa offshoots in the Brits and Pretoria districts, and several groups, such as the Kwena ba Moletse, Tlhaloga, Kopa, and Kwena ba Mongatane, in the Pietersburg and Middleburg districts whose membership of the lineage-cluster is debatable.

[46] For discussion of this point, see M. Legassick 'Mokalaka'.

of the territory south of the river by intermarriage with the Fokeng inhabitants at Ntsuanatsatsi.[47] According to Ellenberger, in about 1600–80 the now mixed Kwena and Fokeng recrossed the Vaal to the north and settled in the present Heidelberg district, from where after a short time there was a secondary dispersal southward.[48] Ellenberger's evidence is complemented by more recent traditions gathered by Breutz from members of the Fokeng ba ga Motlatla and Kwena Mare-a-Phogole, groups which were destroyed as communities at the time of the Difaqane.[49] From the two sets of traditions together it is evident that, over a wide area of the southern Transvaal and northern Orange Free State, in precisely that region which is characterized by Walton as the home of 'early Ghoya culture' there was, from the sixteenth to the eighteenth centuries, a process of intermingling and presumably acculturation between the members of the newly-arrived lineage-cluster and the earlier inhabitants, with the Fokeng continuing to command respect but not enjoying power.[50] A few of the resultant communities continued to call themselves Fokeng, but apart from the Fokeng ba Thekwane in the Rustenburg district in the extreme north of the area concerned, they would all appear to have been thoroughly intermingled.

The other lineage-cluster which began to proliferate over approximately the same period as that of the Kwena was the

[47] Ellenberger *Basuto* pp. 17–20, 68. The tradition relates the southward migration of Napo, son of Mochuli of the Kwena lineage, and his marriage with the daughter of a Fokeng chief. 'Napo' is, however, a name associated with the early Fokeng rather than the Kwena lineage-cluster. The Kwena–Fokeng alliance dissolved when a later Fokeng chief took a San wife.

[48] Ibid pp. 17–20, 70–85. Ellenberger claims the cause of the dispersal was the arrival in the area of a separatist Hurutshe group under Motebeyane. However, it is evident from Hurutshe traditions that they were not as far east as this at any time, and while Ellenberger thinks that Tsuenyane, which was indeed founded by Motebeyane, was the present Heidelberg, it was in fact a settlement in the Zeerust area.

[49] Breutz *Ventersdorp* pp. 75–121; *Marico* pp. 25–27. The traditions were obtained from a relative of the last, pre-Difaqane, chief of the Kwena by Mare-a-Phogole, who appear indeed to have been the most senior of all the Kwena chiefdoms. The traditions, related when the community no longer exists as such, lack structural controls. When these traditions are compared with Ellenberger's, it is impossible to accept Breutz's theory that these are either simply another part of the Kwena lineage-cluster or another Kwena lineage-cluster. They are a clear example of Kwena–Fokeng intermingling. Another part of this community were the Khudu, also dispersed at the start of the nineteenth century, but who are reported to have included the Kwena ba Mongatane in Middleburg district and some Fokeng groups now termed Southern Sotho. For these see also TNAD *Short History* p. 42.

[50] Ellenberger *Basuto* pp. 17, 25–26, 60; Walton *Early Ghoya Settlement* especially map 3.

Kgatla. A number of sources have suggested that the Kgatla communities are a part of the Kwena lineage-cluster, but it seems likely that this is a reflection of later political and territorial association between certain Kgatla and Kwena groups. Thus the TNAD *Short History*, the earliest systematic account I have been able to trace, gives as evidence of such connection the fact that the Kgatla look on the Hurutshe as Bakgatla-Ba-Bagolo ('High Bakgatla') and that the Kgatla were formerly called Ba-Kgabo-Ea-Melle ('the people of the fire flames') by which name the Kwena-Magopa were also known.[51] Attempts to find a genealogical connection between the Kwena lines and the early Kgatla chiefs have not been noticeably successful.[52] Furthermore, there are certain cultural differences between the Kgatla chiefdoms and the Kwena communities in the Western Transvaal, such as the manner of building huts, which suggest a possible difference of origin.[53]

The traditions of Kgatla dispersal are even less studied than those of the Kwena lineage-cluster. Early settlement sites mentioned include Schilpadfontein (Pretoria District) and Dirolong (Rustenburg District), though there are deviant traditions suggesting a movement to this area from the Vaal sources, which is more likely to refer to a subsequent area of Kgatla settlement. Kgatla dispersal during the sixteenth and seventeenth centuries occurred predominantly over the area north of the Vaal and eastward of the Kwena-lineage cluster, with the Phuthing and the Kholokoe, later to join the Southern Sotho, the southernmost of the chiefdoms.[54] One Kgatla chiefdom at least, the Kgatla-Kgafela, moved into the Pilansberg district during the eighteenth century, where it appears that at first they paid tribute to the Tlhako, a 'Transvaal Ndebele' group, but later asserted their independence.[55] The most successful part of this lineage-cluster was, however, the Pedi chiefdom which, moving eastward from the present Pretoria district to the Lulu mountains in about

[51] TNAD *Short History* p. 27.

[52] Ibid p. 30; Ellenberger *Basuto* pp. 20, 31 ff., 347–55 (who derives his data from TNAD and elaborates it); Schapera *Handbook* p. 306; Van Warmelo (NAD/BAD, 17, 1944) pp. 4–5.

[53] Van Warmelo *Preliminary Survey* p. 106; 'Grouping . . .' pp. 60–61.

[54] TNAD *Short History* pp. 27–30; Ellenberger *Basuto* pp. 31–32, 34–38; Van Warmelo *Preliminary Survey* pp. 107–8, 45, 49–50, 53; Van Warmelo (NAD/BAD, 17, 1944).

[55] I. Schapera 'A short history of the Bakgatla ba ga Kgafela of Bechuanaland Protectorate' *Communications of the School of African Studies* UCT, n.s., 3, 1942; Breutz *Rustenburg* pp. 244–85.

the mid-seventeenth century, was able to incorporate a large population spread over a considerable area into a state during the eighteenth century. The Pedi state, indeed, is one which demands considerably more attention, particularly as its development appears at least contemporary with, and possibly earlier than, the state-building process among the Northern Nguni.[56]

The dispersal of the Tlokwa chiefdoms, who are commonly regarded as a sub-cluster of the Kgatla, is rather anomalous. They are to be found today among the Southern Sotho, in the Rustenburg and Pilansberg districts, and in the northern Transvaal Highveld and northern Botswana, and their traditions claim that this degree of geographical spread dates from at least the early part of the eighteenth century.[57] It may be significant that the Tlokwa, as well as other groups associated with the Kgatla whose genealogical connections are uncertain, were important iron-working groups: the Mmanaana-Kgatla in the Marico district, for example, and the people of the Tswapong hills in northern Botswana who for the most part call themselves 'Pedi'.[58]

THE 'TRANSVAAL NDEBELE': MOVEMENT INTO THE SOTHO–TSWANA AREA FROM THE SOUTH-EAST

Spread widely through the Sotho–Tswana area are a set of chiefdoms whose ultimate origins almost certainly lie over the Drakensberg to the south-east in the coastal area inhabited by the Nguni. The most well-known of these groups are the Manala and Ndzundza chiefdoms of the central Transvaal, who have

[56] The earliest account of the Pedi appears to be in Arbousset *Narrative* pp. 169–84. See also TNAD *Short History* pp. 31–35; D. R. Hunt 'An account of the Bapedi' *Bantu Studies* IV (1931) pp. 275–326; Van Warmelo *Preliminary Survey* pp. 108–10; J. R. Brown 'Foreign Relations of the Pedi Chiefs Sekwati and Sekhukhuni'. Unpublished seminar paper, UCLA 1965. For an example of the means by which the Pedi gained hegemony over other communities, see H. O. Monnig 'The Baroka ba Nkwana' *African Studies* XXII (1963) pp. 172–3.

[57] For Tlokwa histories see Ellenberger *Basuto* pp. 38–51; Breutz *Rustenburg* pp. 196–213, 354–388; J. D. Krige 'Traditional Origins . . .' pp. 350–2; Van Warmelo (NAD/BAD, 29, 1953) pp. 3–22; V. Ellenberger 'History of the Batlokwa of Gaberones' *Bantu Studies* XIII (1939) p. 3; TNAD *Short History* pp. 39–40.

[58] For the Tswapong Hills people see J. Mackenzie *Ten Years North of the Orange River* Edmonston and Douglas 1871 p. 266; Schapera *Ethnic Composition* pp. 65–84. For the Mmanaana–Kgatla see, for example, Schapera 'Bangwaketse'; Breutz *Marico* pp. 23, 95; there are also references to them in the published correspondence of David Livingstone and the letters of Roger Edwards, for it was among this people that the two men established the LMS mission station of Mabotsa in 1843.

'clung to Ndebele [i.e. Nguni] custom and language with extraordinary tenacity', though they have adopted from the Sotho–Tswana the custom of taboos against a given animal.[59] They may be found, however, as far north as Pietersburg and Potgietersrus, and stretching into the western Transvaal from where, in the nineteenth century, one chiefdom moved into the present Botswana. They include the Moletlane, Laka, Sebetiele and Seleka, the Tlhako, the Po and the Lete.[60]

Neither the precise relationships of these communities to particular elements in the present Nguni area, nor the chronology or manner of their dispersal is known at present. They have been associated with the Hlubi, a Mbo-Nguni group, and indeed the 'Po' are simply the Sotho cognate of Mbo. From such traditions as are available, however, it is clear that their general line of movement has been from south-east to north-west. All the chiefdoms of the western Transvaal, for example, can trace their movements back to Pretoria, from where the Tlhako and Lete had moved to the Magaliesberg area by the mid-seventeenth century, and the Po shortly afterwards. This would suggest that a movement from the Nguni area across the Drakensberg, and subsequent dispersal north and west across the Highveld must have occurred at roughly the same time, or perhaps even earlier, than the dispersal of the Kwena and Kgatla lineage-clusters.

Had such a dispersal taken place one would expect to find similar chiefdoms scattered south and east from the central Transvaal towards the Natal border. Over the last two hundred and fifty years, however, this part of the Sotho–Tswana area has been subject to considerable disruption: the state-building of the Pedi and the Swazi, the passage of Mzilikazi, the settlement of whites who in many cases in this part dispersed communities as labour on white farms. In the 1905 surveys of Transvaal tribes, however, there is mention of 'Zulu' in the districts of Wakkerstroom, Ermelo and Standerton which, in the context, appear to

[59] See Van Warmelo 'Grouping . . .' pp. 53–54, 86. See also TNAD *Short History* pp. 53–56; Massie *History* pp. 33–35; (both of whom assume that they are nineteenth century arrivals); N. J. Van Warmelo *Transvaal Ndebele Texts* (NAD/BAD, 1, 1930). One of the Ndzundza chiefdoms, near Roos Senekal in the Middelburg district, was that of 'Mapoch', which waged fierce resistance against the white Transvalers and was broken up in 1882–3.

[60] See Van Warmelo *Preliminary Survey* pp. 45, 48, 49–50, 52–53, 55, 57; Breutz *Rustenburg* pp. 175–95, 286–320, 389–97; *Marico* pp. 208–22; V. Ellenberger 'Di Robaroba Matlhakola-tsa ga Masodi-a-Mphelo' *T.R.S.S.A.* XXV (1937) pp. 1–72.

be similar Nguni-related migrants.[61] And the Lete, for example, trace their origins to the Volksrust district.

Furthermore, in the eastern and north-eastern Transvaal there are to be found a number of groups called 'Koni', the Sotho cognate of Nguni whose origin 'is everywhere regarded to be in the east or south-east' of where they are settled.[62] It must be presumed that these, and other communities in the same area with different names but who may be associated with them, were part of the same north-eastern movement from the Nguni area, or possibly a movement at a different time. Again, it is fairly clear that this movement was at latest contemporary with the Kwena and Kgatla dispersals. When the Pedi arrived in the Lydenburg district they found Koni in the south of the area, though these were not the dominant community of the region.[63]

THE EIGHTEENTH CENTURY

The period between about 1500 and the early eighteenth century is characterized in the Sotho–Tswana area, as we have seen, by the fragmentation of a number of chiefdoms into lineage-clusters which dispersed themselves widely over the present Transvaal and northern Orange Free State. It is evident that such a process implies an expanding population, though it is not necessary to assume that the rate of population increase accelerated at the time the dispersion began. The possible causes of this dispersal, and the fact that the new communities appear often to have exerted a dominance over such groups as were already in the areas occupied, will be considered below. By the eighteenth century, however, it would appear that the increase of population was sufficient, when taken together with other factors, to accelerate processes of a different kind in the Sotho–Tswana area.

Stated briefly, it would appear that in the eighteenth and early

[61] TNAD *Short History* pp. 59–61; Massie *History* pp. 85–86, 91 f. See also Van Warmelo *Preliminary Survey* pp. 44–45, 49–50, 58; A. C. Myburgh *Die Stamme van die Distrik Carolina* (NAD/BAD, 34, 1956) pp. 281–3.

[62] See J. D. Krige 'Traditional origins' pp. 346–50. Also, for the 'Koni', see Van Warmelo (NAD/BAD, 12, 15, 1944); (NAD/BAD, 29, 1953) pp. 15–82; Van Warmelo *Preliminary Survey* pp. 45, 50, 52, 54–55; TNAD *Short History* p. 48.

[63] Hunt 'Pedi . . .' pp. 275–7. The dominant community, to whom the Pedi intially paid tribute, were called Mongatane. See also Monnig 'Baroka ba Nkwana' p. 171. The Mongatane have been variously described as 'Roka' and 'Kwena' (see also footnotes on pages 101–102). Monnig's suggestion, on the basis of traditions collected among them, is that they were Roka who adopted the crocodile (*kwena*) as 'totem' at the Olifant's river.

nineteenth century in much of the Sotho–Tswana area, the division of chiefdoms into separate and autonomous units had begun to give place, as a dominant process, to amalgamation of separate communities into larger 'confederations'. It is not necessary to assume that such a process began in the eighteenth century, or that fission ceased; it is more a question of the degree to which each process was dominant. The trend towards amalgamation was fostered for two reasons. In the first place, if a chief could secure a monopoly on the trade, especially the trade in ivory, which was by that time an important item of the Sotho–Tswana economy, he would attract followers to him. Secondly, except south of the Vaal, where there still appears to have been territory occupied only by San, the degree to which population had increased made it easier for a dissident group leaving one chiefdom to join another rather than establishing themselves autonomously.

To give a clear picture of the manner and the extent to which amalgamation was occurring would require more extended treatment than is possible here. It has already been pointed out that the nature of Sotho–Tswana traditions makes it easy for a community that has somehow managed to regain its autonomy to *elide* an earlier period of incorporation in a larger unit. However, the very ward or hamlet structure, which permits such a manipulation of tradition, also facilitates amalgamation. It is easy for a ward, a group of wards, or a sub-division of a ward, to add or subtract itself from the chiefdom without disturbing the overall structure. This is true even in the case of a chiefdom situated at a single settlement, and even more so where the chiefdom is geographically dispersed with its limits defined by the ritual and political obligations of headmen and members of hamlets to the chief. It is very likely that such a political structure emerged much earlier than the eighteenth century, and that it was perhaps designed to facilitate the incorporation of peoples occupying the territory over which the dispersal of about 1500 to 1750 took place.

There is, certainly, some correlation of the amalgamative processes of the eighteenth century with the lines along which long-distance trade appears to have been carried. Though I hope at some later stage to draw together the evidence on Sotho–Tswana trade, a little of the evidence may be mentioned here. It would appear that at least one, and maybe more routes, passed inland eastwards and slightly north from Delagoa Bay to the Pedi. Indeed the assumption that the Pedi were able to secure a monopoly over this trade would go a long way towards explaining their rise to hegemony in the present Eastern Transvaal.[64] 'Their ornaments,' wrote Arbousset of some Pedi visitors to the Southern Sotho in 1837, 'consist of . . . collars and bracelets of blue, red, and yellow beads of Portuguese manufacture, proving that they have communication with the traders at Delagoa; but this only by means of natives belonging to other tribes, as they have assured us . . . the Matlekas [to the east of Pedi country] procure copper, beads, and stuffs at Laurent Marques and go to exchange these for ivory, horns, cattle, and furs in the interior. It is from them, for example, that Sekuate has purchased the red scarf, with which he is said to deck himself on fête days.'[65]

West of the Pedi, stretching across the Highveld as far as the Kalahari, were a series of 'Transvaal Ndebele', Kgatla, and Kwena chiefdoms who appear to have been linked also to the Delagoa Bay trade routes. Though one finds many mentions of such trade in the early travellers, the first person to provide a circumstantial base was Joseph Arend, an escaped slave, who in about 1818 travelled through the Transvaal to a Kwena-Modimosana chiefdom, from whom he had been told he could buy linen. 'On reaching that nation, Aaron could not obtain what he wanted, wherefore he continued his journey to the eastward. In two days he came to the Maquaina nation; but they were in a state of warfare with the nation beyond, and would not permit him to proceed forward . . . [they] told him there were Macuas (or white people) residing beyond them, who sold guns, powder, horses, waggons, clothes, pots, etc., but that cattle in that country were scarce . . . the town stands on the opposite side of a wide water, which they cross on rafts . . . on the near side of the water there was a nation with long hair and brown complexion, among whom a white woman lives, who receives goods from a town on the opposite side of the water, and sells them to the natives.'[66]

[64] For mention of such trade routes see Van Warmelo (NAD/BAD, 15, 1944) p. 48 which mentions a 'Portuguese' person living in the Lebombo mountains in the eighteenth century, apparently along a trade route used by the Koni.

[65] Arbousset *Narrative* pp. 170, 180. See also Casalis *Basuto* p. 213; J. Backhouse *A Narrative of a Visit to the Mauritius and South Africa* Hamilton Adams 1844 p. 398.

[66] Campbell *Second Journey* II pp. 356–9. See also R. Hamilton 19 April 1819 [LMS Journals 3/68]; Thompson *Travels* pp. 117–9; Smith *Diary* I 356.

The Kwena-Modimosana were one, or more probably two, chiefdoms in the area of the Magaliesberg and Pilansberg which contained, by the eighteenth century, a considerable population.[67] Indeed it is only in this century that one finds the first mention of any extent of inter-chiefdom warfare, which may reflect simply elision, or increased population density, or an attempt to win control of the trade routes. Certainly, however, by the start of the nineteenth century it would appear that Pedi raiding parties were fighting in this area, which may well indicate an attempt by the Pedi to win control over the hinterland on which their trade was based.[68] West of the Pilansberg, around the headwaters of the Marico, were the Hurutshe, a community of whom a detailed history is urgently needed. At least as early as the eighteenth century, under their ruler Thekiso, they appear to have been amalgamating a number of lesser communities, including those who mined and worked the abundant iron of the region and, as is apparent from Campbell's account of them in 1820, they were heavily engaged in the exchange of beads for ivory, with the ruler exerting a rigid control over such trade.[69]

Still farther to the west were a section of the Kwena-Magopa whose settlement of the territory west of the Notwani River is dated in the seventeenth or early eighteenth century. During the eighteenth century this chiefdom spawned two offshoots, the Ngwaketse and the Ngwato, whose traditions of origin pose a curious anomaly. It is usually maintained in the traditions that Ngwaketse and Ngwato were two sons of Kwena, a chief who immediately followed Masilo and Malope.[70] Were this true, it

[67] Breutz describes four Kwena–Modimosana chiefdoms and dates their separation in the first part of the eighteenth century. It would appear, though, that until the Difaqane there were only two Kwena–Modimosana settlements, at Molokwane and Boitsemagano, sufficiently close to one another to suggest they were not completely autonomous, and possibly grouping under them other communities. See Breutz *Rustenburg passim*.

[68] See ibid. pp. 63–64, 87–88, 181, 328.

[69] See Breutz *Marico* pp. 94–95; Campbell *Second Journey* I pp. 220–77 *passim*; S. Kay *Travels and Researches in Caffraria* Mason 1833 pp. 225–34.

[70] The earliest account I have found which elevates these communities to this position is in Stow *Native Races* p. 518, who says 'the Bahurutsi branch is called Bahurutsi a Malope, the Bamangwato, Bamangwato a Malope, and the Bangwaketse, Bangwaketse a Malope, the people or men of a son of Malope, while the Bakuena are called Bakuena a Masilo'. It is evident that this could be a misinterpretation of kinship terminology, though the terminology clearly permits such misinterpretations. It would be interesting to find earlier such references. Those I have encountered simply discuss Kwena–Ngwato–Ngwaketse relations. See, for example, Smith *Diary* I pp. 349, 406, II, 170, 180, 196, 202; Livingstone *Missionary Travels* p. 51.

would mean that the members of what by the eighteenth century would have been a very junior section of the royal lineage were able to become autonomous. Such an event would be very unusual, and indeed the elevation of Ngwato and Ngwaketse to this position may simply reflect the nineteenth-century importance of these communities. Even so, the fission and rapid growth of the Ngwaketse and Ngwato to importance in the eighteenth century is itself unusual. It may be assumed that the necessities of trade encouraged the subjugation of the Kgalagadi peoples who appear to have been the occupants of the area prior to the Kwena-Magopa, and that sufficient of them became incorporated in some way into the community, as clients and client communities rather than members, for the most part, to enable the chiefdom to split in three without noticeable effects on its prosperity. While the Ngwaketse moved southward towards the Molopo, where they encountered further Kgalagadi communities, the Ngwato moved to the north. In the late eighteenth and early nineteenth centuries the Ngwato not only underwent further fission to produce the Tawana, who moved to Lake Ngami, but began, under the chief Kgari, to incorporate into their community the 'Kalaka' peoples of the present south-west Rhodesia.[71] Indeed it must remain an open question at this time whether in fact these communities bordering the Kalahari had not opened an independent trade route through the Rozwi area with the Portuguese, perhaps at Inhambane.[72]

These were only some of the processes at work in the eighteenth and early nineteenth centuries. It appears also to have been during this period that the Lobedu arrived from the north and began to establish their ritual and social, if not political, domination over the area of the Transvaal Lowveld around Leydsdorp, whose inhabitants now share what has been described as

[71] See I. Schapera 'Bangwaketse'; M. Legassick 'The Ngwato under Sekgoma' Unpublished seminar paper UCLA 1965; A Sillery *The Bechuanaland Protectorate* Oxford University Press 1952 contains sections on these communities which rely in part on unpublished material.

[72] The most striking early evidence for this is that the travellers Cowan and Donovan, going northwards from the Cape in 1808 with the intention of reaching the Portuguese settlements, did not turn eastward across the Highveld, but proceeded via the Ngwaketse, Kwena, and Ngwato, north of which community they died, probably of fever. Having gone this far north, it is unlikely that they would have returned south-eastward to Delagoa Bay: possibly they were heading for Inhambane. See, for example, Moffat *Missionary Labours* ch. XIV.

the 'Lobedu culture complex'.[73] In this area, as well as farther north-west in the northern Transvaal, there was a rather complex local movement of peoples, which appears to have had a general direction from east to west.[74] Though the significance of this movement cannot be assessed, and indeed the traditions have not yet been sufficiently studied to examine how far they relate to the arrival on the Highveld of Mzilikazi and other events of the Difaqane, it seems likely that they are associated with groups fleeing, perhaps, the expanding Pedi state or the Lobedu culture complex. And south of the Vaal it is necessary to reassess the significance of Mohlomi as an 'enlarger of political scale', as well as the hints in Ellenberger that other persons, such as Moletsane of the Taung, were also engaged in the preliminaries of state-formation prior to the Difaqane.[75]

PEOPLES OF THE SOTHO–TSWANA AREA PRIOR TO ABOUT A.D. 1500

The question of the habitation of the Sotho–Tswana area prior to the dispersal of the Kwena and Kgatla lineage-clusters and the 'Transvaal Ndebele' has been left until last because, with certain exceptions, the oral traditions we are analysing cannot give much help in this regard. Indeed the problem is rather one of questioning the assumptions of almost every one of the syntheses of Sotho–Tswana history, and thus reopening the question of the Early Iron Age peopling of South Africa to research by archaeologists, linguists, physical anthropologists, and comparative culture historians untrammelled by unfounded historical statements.

The general assumption of historians from Stow and Theal to Breutz, derived mainly from evidence among the westernmost Sotho–Tswana groups, has been that the Sotho–Tswana area was populated by a series of rather distinct migrations. The last of these was represented by the Kwena lineage-cluster, who were preceded by a series of others, usually including the Kgalagadi,

[73] See J. D. Krige 'Traditional origins . . .' pp. 329–35; E. J. Krige 'The Place of the North-Eastern Transvaal Sotho . . .'; E. J. and J. D. Krige *The realm of a Rain Queen; a study of the pattern of Lobedu society* London 1943.
[74] See J. D. Krige 'Traditional origins . . .'; Van Warmelo *Preliminary Survey*; TNAD *Short History*; Massie *History*; Van Warmelo (NAD, pp. 10–11, 13, 15, 1944); (NAD/BAD, p. 29, 1953, pp. 50–54); and others.
[75] Ellenberger *Basuto* pp. 23–115 *passim*. See also Arbousset *Narrative* pp. 272–85.

the Dighoya, the Rolong and the Fokeng.[76] Only in certain specific cases does this evidence rest on a lengthy genealogy, all of whose names are presumed to have lived within the Sotho–Tswana area. Apart from some linguistic analysis, the evidence is usually no more specific than the presumed degree of admixture with Khoisan peoples, or the subordination of the 'earlier arrivals' to the Kwena-cluster chiefdoms by the time that written records became available. Such evidence, by itself, is by no means satisfactory.

It would seem preferable, in fact, to pose the questions which these hypotheses attempt to answer in a different way. It has already been suggested that it is the clustering of significant culture traits, and differences of dialect which, in conjunction with the historical traditions, are likely to provide the best clues outside archaeology to the process of cultural formation of the Sotho–Tswana. It is the introduction and diffusion of these features over parts of the Sotho–Tswana area, rather than population movements themselves, which need to be considered. It might emerge, indeed, that the more important developments have occurred *in situ*, stimulated perhaps from outside, rather than as the result of 'migrations'. Furthermore, such a method would discuss the emergence of the Sotho–Tswana culture in the context of the cultures of the surrounding southern Bantu-speakers and the indigenous Khoisan-speakers. These cannot fail to have been the major influences on the Sotho–Tswana, as well as the major cultures from which the Sotho–Tswana distinguished themselves.

Thus it seems likely that the nuclear Kwena and Kgatla communities, whatever the causes of their dispersal and subordination of other groups, were simply two among a number of contemporary groups of similar culture. The strongest evidence for this is perhaps the 'totem', an emblem which is usually but not always an animal, which is widely dispersed among Sotho–Tswana groups. The Kwena and Kgatla lineage-clusters have such emblems, and where segmenting chiefdoms have altered the eponymous emblem (*kwena* means crocodile, and *kgatla* is a type of monkey), there are usually traditions explaining this fact. Communities unrelated to these lineage-clusters also have such emblems, though each is widely dispersed through different

[76] See, for example, Stow *Native Races* pp. 420–1, 432–4, 518–9, 544–6; Theal *Ethnography and Condition* pp. 181–6; Ellenberger *Basuto* xviii–xx p. 15; TNAD *Short History* pp. 8, 16–17; Breutz *Marico* p. 25; *Rustenburg* p. 57; *The Tribes of Mafeking District* (NAD/BAD, 32, 1955–6) pp. 23–24; *The Tribes of Vryburg District* (NAD/BAD, 4 (1959) p. 16.

chiefdoms, and in all cases a chiefdom, or even a sub-division of it, may contain persons of many different 'totemic' allegiances. It is unlikely that their diffusion is a consequence of Kwena and Kgatla dispersal, simply because, although taboos are in some cases attached to the emblem, it has for the most part lost the ritual, and possibly once more extensive significance, which it once must have had. Indeed, though it could be argued that the number of possible emblems is sufficiently limited to allow coincidental duplication, it is possible that the emblems relate to an earlier, clan-based, social organization which has been overshadowed by structural change. Whether this is so or not, the wideness of their spread and their common lack of significance mark the emblems as an early common cultural feature.

Can any present communities other than the nuclear Kwena and Kgatla chiefdoms be clearly identified with this common culture of about 1500? The question is not easy to answer, for the groups whose histories can be traced and who are unrelated to the Kwena and Kgatla groups have undergone historical experiences influenced by the post 1500 dispersal. Broadly speaking, the autonomous or subordinate communities who have some continuity from that time were either subordinated to the Kwena or Kgatla or living in close association with them, in which case cultural features could have been diffused to them. Or else they were pushed outwards from the centres of dispersal, usually coming in presumed contact with other cultures which have interacted with them. It is the traditions of these communities which will now be examined.

It has already emerged that at the time of the Kwena dispersal, Fokeng groups were living north and south of the Vaal. Not only is their habitation of this area affirmed by the 'legitimization' of Kwena political power through the accordance of respect to, and intermarriage with, Fokeng in this area. The legend of the marsh of Ntsuanatsatsi, from which mankind is supposed to have emerged, also suggests a story explaining why the Kwena found the area occupied.[77] Furthermore there is, in the Rustenburg district, at least one Fokeng chiefdom, the ba Thekwane, who appear to have maintained continuity from those times, despite the Kwena-Fokeng penetration and the disruption which the Difaqane and subsequent white settlement exerted over this area. Although for a period tributary to the Hurutshe, their ruler-list

[77] See Arbousset *Narrative* pp. 131–2 and *supra* p. 100.

extends for some twenty-eight names prior to 1800 which, even if this does not represent generations, suggests considerable age for the community in its present form.[78]

The Fokeng, then, represent a community contemporaneous with the early Kwena and Kgatla, though how closely related in culture it is impossible to tell. At the same time we can trace a wide area over which 'Fokeng' culture was spread. It is the region which traditions indicate was occupied by the Fokeng which, as has been mentioned, includes many of the stone-hut settlements classified by Walton as 'early Ghoya'. The latter name is anachronistic and if a classificatory name held by a present-day group is required, 'Fokeng' would be more appropriate. There seems to be evidence of similar settlements, though also undated, as far east as the Ermelo and Carolina districts of the Transvaal.[79] It would be interesting to know how closely associated the pottery across this area is, bearing in mind that it would be likely to be classified by Walton as 'Ghoya', since the pottery he regards as 'Fokeng' is probably derived from the areas where Fokeng and Kwena have been living in close acculturative association. It might then be possible to trace the relationship of Fokeng to Kwena and Kgatla pottery.

A part of the Fokeng culture area was inhabited by those Walton calls 'Ghoya'. In 1839, however, James Backhouse wrote of the 'Batauw, or Bataung . . . also sometimes called Ligoya, from a Chief, whose power is now broken, and who, with the remnant of his people had taken up his residence in this part of the country . . . Makwana [is] the principal Chief of the Batauw',[80] which seems to imply that Ligoya was still alive or but recently

[78] See TNAD *Short History* pp. 16–17; Massie *History* pp. 20–21; Breutz *Rustenburg* pp. 53–77. Breutz writes 'the present chief was told by his father that all these names do not represent the real line of his ancestors, but that they were the names of chiefs of other branches and brothers of chiefs . . . I found several old men who knew the abovementioned traditions . . . One sub-chief knew about the ancient chief mentioned in old praise-songs. An unpublished manuscript by a MoFokeng in the NAD/BAD files relates that the first chief, Nape, settled east of the Marico river 'and to the east of Nape mountain'. West of them there lived Rolong and San.

[79] See Myburgh *Barberton* pp. 11–13; *Carolina* pp. 22–45.

[80] Backhouse *Narrative* p. 390. See also Ellenberger *Basuto* pp. 52–54; Campbell *Second Journey* II pp. 350–1; S. Kay 20 June 1821 [MMS Box 2–1821/21]; S. Broadbent 8 June 1823 [MMS Box 2–1823/5]. The Ghoya–Fokeng confusion is indicated by the doubt over the 'ethnicity' of the community at Kurutlele attacked by the Tlokwa at the start of the Difaqane; they appear to have lived in precisely the area described by Campbell as Ghoya, but are often called Fokeng, indeed the Fokeng from whom Sebetwane came. The error on the dating of the chief Lighoya appears to derive from Stow (as quoted in Walton *Ghoya settlement* p. 19 f.).

dead. Hence, when taken with other contemporary evidence on the Dighoya or Taung, the implication is that these people were simply one of a number of 'Fokeng culture' chiefdoms south of the Vaal, who had not been subject to interpenetration by Kwena groups, and our only knowledge of whom dates from a time after they had been dislocated by the Difaqane and subsequently regrouped. It seems, therefore, that the term 'Dighoya' should not be used prior to the late eighteenth century. This calls for the reassessment of the linking of the Dighoya, by various writers and in various traditions, with a series of other communities around the western and southern peripheries of the Kwena dispersal area: the Phiring, the Kubung, the Kolobe, the Thamaga, the Tlhaping, the Nogeng, the Tlhaloga and so on. Where the traditions of these groups have been studied, they do not go back much further than the eighteenth century, and their names appear to be of comparably recent origin.[81] The relevant question is whether they, or parts of them, formed a part of the Fokeng culture. In some cases, such as the Thamaga and possibly the Tlhaping, these appear to have been communities who had been subjected, and managed to reconstitute themselves as autonomous entities in the eighteenth century.

In other cases we have rather more evidence of interaction between Kwena chiefdoms and non-related communities. The ruler list of the Rolong goes back fourteen generations before their famous chief Tau (*c.* 1700–1760) to the two mythical ancestors Morolong and Noto, who might therefore have lived about 1300 to 1400.[82] It would seem that the Rolong were forced south-westward from the Mosega area across the Molopo by the Hurutshe in about 1500 to 1600. From this time until the time of Tau their traditions relate almost nothing more than the names of rulers, indicating probably a lengthy period of isolation both from events north and east of the Molopo, and even across the Vaal to the east.[83] The curious fact about the Rolong is their 'totems' which, in addition to *tholo* (the kudu), from which the

[81] See, for example, Breutz *Rustenburg* pp. 214–28, 448–56; *Marico* pp. 233–5; *Dis Stamme van die Distrik Ventersdorp* (NAD/BAD, 31, 1954–5) pp. 45–73; *Die Stamme van die Distrikte Lichtenburg en Delareyville* (NAD/BAD, 37, 1957); *The Tribes of the Districts Kuruman and Postmasberg* (NAD/BAD, 49, 1963) pp. 188–94, 215–24. See also Ellenberger *Basuto* pp. 113–15 and Schapera *Ethnic Composition passim.*

[82] See Breutz *Mafeking* pp. 26–27 for analysis of several traditions. My dating is later than his by about a hundred years.

[83] Breutz *Marico* pp. 23–24; *Mafeking* pp. 24–28; *Vryburg* p. 20. There are also Hurutshe traditions of a residence at Taungs about this time.

name Morolong derives, are *tsepe* (iron) and *noto* (hammer). It was at one time assumed that the early Rolong were therefore celebrated iron-workers. More recently it has been suggested that there was in fact a taboo on iron-working, with the smiths having different totems. But totems are not necessarily taboo, so the question remains open. Perhaps, however, the totems relate to the time when the Rolong were displaced from the iron supply around Mosega by the Hurutshe who were to establish a great reputation as workers and traders in metal.[84]

A similar series of events occurred rather later when in the early eighteenth century the Kwena-Magopa entered the present Botswana. Though the traditions of their descendants, who have become generically known as Kgalagadi, are confused, it would seem that the Kwena-Magopa and their offshoots forced to the west a series of chiefdoms situated along the borders of the Kalahari. These communities, unable to sustain their independence in the arid desert, fragmented and, together with groups presumed to be offshoots from the Rolong, all became subject as clients to the Kwena, Ngwato and Ngwaketse. However, the chiefdoms from which they came appear to have been similar in structure and culture to the Kwena chiefdoms.[85] They had a ward structure. They had, and continued to have, clients of their own called 'Lala' (serfs), and many of them, like almost all the communities of the Kwena cluster and others besides, had tales of origin centring around a hole at Lowe near the present Mochudi.[86]

Cumulatively this evidence, sketchy though it is, is not inconsistent with the picture of a number of separated communities prior to 1500, possibly sharing a largely common culture, and each, no doubt, interacting with the indigenous Khoisan inhabitants. As the Kwena dispersal began over this western part of the Sotho–Tswana area some of these communities became incorpor-

[84] See Breutz *Mafeking* p. 25; Brown *Bantu Nomads* p. 216; Ellenberger *Basuto* xviii–xix, quoting the *Journal des Missions*.

[85] See I. Schapera and F. van der Merwe *Notes on the Tribal Groupings, History, and Customs of the Bakgalagadi*. Communications of the School of African Studies UCT n.s. No. 13 1945. Also Schapera 'Notes on the History of the Kaa' *African Studies* IV (1945) pp. 109–21 and Adam Kuper, personal communication. Adam Kuper has made helpful comments on this chapter.

[86] For origin stories relating to Lowe see Campbell *Travels* p. 181; *Second Journey* I pp. 303, 306–7; Smith *Diary* I p. 409; II pp. 221–2; Livingstone *Missionary Correspondence* p. 63; Brown *Bantu Nomads* pp. 260–1; Breutz *Mafeking* pp. 76–77; *Rustenburg* pp. 83, 426–7.

ated in various different ways. Others were pushed outwards, chiefly west and south, where they would have encountered further communities of Khoisan peoples. Sekalagadi is now distinguished as a dialect of Sotho–Tswana separate from 'Tswana' (which is, more accurately, the language of the Kwena lineage-cluster), and is most closely related to Tlhaping/Rolong. But it is possible to conceive of this differentiation as occurring from prior to the Kwena dispersal, if it is assumed that population at that time was sparse and widely dispersed. Similarly 'Southern Sotho', which is in fact the dialect of the Kwena-Fokeng interaction, could derive some of its differentiation from the pre-dispersal differences between Fokeng and 'Kwena' (i.e. Tswana).

The Kgalagadi, as also the Rolong and possibly other communities on the periphery who were linked with the long-distance trade routes, had clients of their own. In some cases it may be assumed that these were the 'fringe groups' of the period before the Kwena–Kgatla dispersal: that is, those who through slow expansion of population had been pushed ahead and forced into contact with Khoi. However, when such a time-depth is being considered, it may be necessary to consider the effects on the western part of the Sotho–Tswana area of a possibly less infertile Kalahari, and the evidence of peoples now or recently spread around the desert, such as the Kattea and Bergdama, who may be related and who appear to differ in language, culture and physical type from both Khoisan peoples and the 'Bantu' populations.[87] Finally, in this early period especially, though also later, it would seem that the Middle Zambezi Bantu-speakers could have been an important influence on Sotho–Tswana cultural development in the west.

The picture in the eastern part of the Sotho–Tswana area prior to the dispersal of the Kgatla, particularly the Pedi, and the 'Transvaal Ndebele', is even less clear than in the west. The impact of these two dispersals, together with the later advent of the Swazi, the Lobedu, and the Ndebele, has almost completely overlaid any traces of earlier occupation. From the traditions of arrival of the Pedi and others, however, it is clear that such earlier occupation did exist.[88] It has been suggested, moreover,

[87] For the Kattea and their possible relationship with the Bergdama, see Breutz, *Vryburg* pp. 15, 18–19; *Kuruman* pp. 24–30; 'Ancient People of the Kalahari' *Afrika und Ubersee* XLII (1959) pp. 51–54. See also M. Wilson, in *The Oxford History of South Africa* I p. 133.

[88] See Hunt 'Pedi...' pp. 275–7; J. D. Krige 'Traditional origins...' pp. 322, 330, 336.

that certain characteristic features of the 'Lobedu culture complex' derive from earlier 'Sotho' inhabitants, particularly the cult of the sacred drums associated with the *komana* ceremonies, and the particular form of the initiation ceremonies.[89] Such evidence must be analysed in conjunction with the archaeological record, which seems to indicate at Palabora a possible cultural continuity extending for more than a thousand years, which cannot be attributed to the recently migrant Palabora ruling group.[90] Again, to the south of the Lobedu and Palabora area, in northern Swaziland, Early Iron Age sites have recently been dated.[91] Evidence of the cultural associations of these sites should be sought among the pre-Swazi populations in this region, whom recent research has identified not only as incorporated into the Swazi, but also to be found today in the Pietersburg district. The Pai, Kutswe and Pulana, together with other 'Swazified Sotho', were clearly the occupants of pre-1800 northern Swaziland, the Barberton Nelspruit and possibly Carolina districts, and extended into Moçambique not far from Delagoa Bay.[92]

Clearly the cultural history of this complex eastern Sotho–Tswana region needs further investigation before any conclusions can be drawn. But on the one hand there is a need to trace the relationship between these 'early Sotho' peoples and the 'Fokeng' culture farther to the west. The Pulana-Kutswe and Pai dialects, for example, a distinct sub-group of Sotho–Tswana, bear certain resemblances to 'Western Sotho' and the Kutswe have vague traditions of coming from the west. On the other hand, it would seem that agriculture plays a much larger part in the lives of these eastern Sotho, with cattle sometimes absent altogether until recently, than is the case with the western Sotho. Furthermore, there are certain elements in the preferred marriage patterns and lineage relationships which suggest a distinctively different

[89] E. J. Krige 'The Place of the North-Eastern Transvaal Sotho . . .' especially pp. 286–7.

[90] See D. W. Phillipson 'Early Iron-Using Peoples . . .' *supra* pp. 36–37; Krige 'Traditional origins . . .' pp. 335–9; E. J. Krige 'Notes on the Phalaborwa and their Morula Complex' *Bantu Studies* XI (1937) pp. 357–67.

[91] D. W. Phillipson 'Early Iron-Using Peoples . . .' *supra* p. 36.

[92] See Van Warmelo *Preliminary Survey* pp. 51, 98, 111–13; D. Ziervogel *The Eastern Sotho: A Tribal, Historical and Linguistic Survey (with Ethnographic Notes) of the Pai, Kutswe, and Pulana Bantu Tribes* Van Schaik 1954; Myburgh *Carolina* pp. 45–46, 146 f., 183 f.. 222 f, 256 f.; *Barberton* pp. 10–11, 107 f., 118 f,, 126 f. Van Warmelo also includes the Phetla, Polane and Phuthi, the first Bantu-speakers to reach the present Lesotho, with these 'early Sotho', though Ellenberger *Basuto* pp. 21–29, classified them as Zizi Nguni.

development of social structure.[93] It is perhaps not implausible to suppose that the eastern Sotho area has been influenced, via the lowlands of Moçambique, by the Central Bantu-speaking peoples. Whether or not population elements might have passed down early in the history of the Bantu dispersal to interact in the eastern Sotho area with populations from the Highveld can be determined only by further research among peoples such as the Thonga, the Ndau, and the Ronga (a name cognate to the Sotho-speaking Roka).

CONCLUSIONS

To digest the immense volume of existing literature on the culture and history of the Sotho–Tswana into any clear conclusions on historical process is at this stage an impossible task. The answers to many significant questions are either diffused through the literature and need to be gathered together or, in many cases, require renewed research. Furthermore, as other chapters in this volume indicate, the archaeology of the South African Iron Age is not as yet on a firm basis. Nevertheless, if only as a stimulus to future hypothesis, some tentative suggestions may be made.

For the period prior to about 1500 there exists very little evidence from oral traditions, and that which has been deduced from traditions is entirely speculative and usually untenable. The scanty evidence from cultural reconstruction and archaeology suggests that it was in about the mid-first millennium that the first iron-using and iron-working cultures began to replace Stone Age cultures south of the Limpopo. It might not be erroneous to assume that it was also at this period that agriculture began to supplement hunting and gathering. Such new techniques were probably diffused from other similar cultures south of the Zambezi. The diffusion may have passed to Khoisan groups without population movement, but it is more likely that there were small movements of population, who may have been related to the ancestors of the Ila-Tonga peoples, the Shona peoples, or the Thonga peoples. Such movements could have occurred from the middle Zambezi south into the Kalahari (assuming it was more fertile at that time), from the present Rhodesia southward across the Limpopo, or closer to the east coast along the lowlands.

[93] See Ziervogel *Eastern Sotho* p. 5; Krige 'Place of North-eastern Transvaal Sotho . . .' pp. 287–8.

At this period there was, almost certainly, considerable interaction with Khoisan peoples and subsequent acculturation.

Over the following centuries it is possible to detect the emergence of a broad sub-stratum of cultural similarities, despite continued differences among regions of the Sotho–Tswana area. Of particular importance in this regard are 'totemism' and distinctive forms of preferential cousin marriage. This suggests that, despite the vast area over which what must have been a relatively sparse population was spread, there was considerable interchange or else a rise to cultural hegemony of one of the groups.

In about 1500, as has been outlined, two chiefdoms which were probably a part of this common cultural grouping (though most authorities to date have regarded them as a migrant grouping, possibly from Rhodesia),[94] began to segment, disperse, and attain a dominance over the surrounding populations. The most likely explanation for this dispersal is the process described by Monica Wilson in Chapter 4, namely the expansion of patrilineal and polygynous lineages with cattle at the expense of those without stock.[95] However, there are certain chronological difficulties since it would seem that, were such a process connected with the introduction of stock and milking, it probably began earlier than 1500.

In the Sotho–Tswana area this process of expansion of wealthy lineages may be related to two other phenomena. On the one hand, the increasing desiccation of the Kalahari may have reduced some groups settled in it from agriculturalists or stock-owners to hunter-gatherers. In the second place the 'ward' or hamlet structure, prevalent over the whole Sotho–Tswana area except the most eastern part, may have grown at this time out of a clan-system as wealthy lineages recruited poorer peoples to herd their stock, or to hunt for them. Certainly the Kwena and Kgatla dispersal period, and possibly the times prior to this, are to be associated in the Sotho–Tswana case with the stratification of communities as well as the increase of two lineage-clusters at the expense of other lineages.[96]

[94] See, for example, Theal *Ethnography and Condition* p. 186; Breutz *Vryburg* p. 121. For a Shona tradition implying some connection with the Hurutshe see F. P. [osselt?] 'The Barozwi' *NADA* 1924 pp. 88–91.

[95] See Monica Wilson 'Changes in Social Structure in Southern Africa' *supra* pp. 71–85.

[96] Murdock, for example, describes the Sotho–Tswana structure as 'a decadent system of agamous patrisibs'. Murdock *Africa* pp. 368, 388. A similar postulate is made for the Cape Nguni in Hammond-Tooke 'Segmentation and fission . . .'. Such a structural

The Kwena lineage-cluster, as has been mentioned, traces its settlement to Rathateng, and claims its 'origins' in the cave of Lowe in present Botswana. The Kgatla lineage-cluster appears to have its origins in the central Highveld. This may imply, as Monica Wilson suggests, that such expansion of population by wealthy lineages was feasible only as cattle percolated as far south as this latitude. For the Kgatla, however, another possibility that should be considered is access to iron. The Melville Koppies iron-smelting site, dated in the eleventh century, is not far from their presumed place of origin.[97] Access to iron resources, and iron-working knowledge, would allow a lineage to recruit clients, giving the clients iron weapons if they faithfully handed over the skins of animals.

Confirmation or rejection of these tentative suggestions on the pre-1600 history of the Sotho–Tswana area awaits evidence from other disciplines. Such further evidence is urgently needed, for it was this early period which saw the introduction of agriculture, of iron-working, and of cattle to the area. It was almost certainly during this pre-1500 period too that the Sotho–Tswana peoples acquired many of their distinctive cultural and structural characteristics. As yet we do not know to what extent these can be traced to indigenous peoples such as the Khoisan, or to movements of population or cultural stimuli from surrounding Bantu-speaking peoples or from such mysterious groups as the Bergdama and Kattea. In contrast the history of the seventeenth and eighteenth centuries is clearer.

The seventeenth and eighteenth centuries were characterized by a wide dispersal of chiefdoms from the Kwena and Kgatla lineage-cluster, which over much of the western and central Transvaal Highveld appear to have absorbed most traces of previous inhabitants within themselves, though through this area they lived alongside chiefdoms of the 'Transvaal Ndebele' dispersion from the south-east. In the south, along the Vaal valley,

[97] See Brian Fagan 'The Later Iron Age in South Africa' *supra* p. 57. It would also be interesting to determine whether it is possible to relate the 'Uitkomst' culture to the Kgatla dispersal and the 'Buispoort' culture to the Kwena dispersal.

---

change implies the existence of persons and families poor enough, and with their political structure sufficiently disintegrated, to become incorporated into 'wards'. This structural change also needs to be considered in the context of the functional reasons for forms of preferential cousin marriage, and other distinctive Sotho–Tswana institutions. For some comparative examples see Murdock ibid pp. 84–85, 287–9, 298, 301, 358, 362–3, 376–9.

the Kwena (and perhaps the Kgatla) chiefdoms intermingled with the previous Fokeng inhabitants who may not have differed significantly in culture. In the west the Kwena forced the Rolong farther south, and later forced the 'Kgalagadi' chiefdoms into the desert where they fragmented and became subordinated. Towards the close of this period the dispersal began to give way to amalgamation, based partly on an increased population density in certain areas, but also on the development of long-distance trade routes with the Portuguese settlements. Though it is impossible to say at this stage when the exchange of beads for ivory began to spread across the Highveld, the control of this by chiefs of the Kwena and Kgatla clusters encouraged the growth of their communities and the association to them in some form of previously autonomous groupings. The major example of this was the Pedi, though others exhibited it on a lesser scale.

It is this latter period on which the immediate attentions of the historian of pre-1800 Southern Africa should be focused. On the basis of the material that already exists, and despite the deficiencies in it which have been outlined, it should now be possible to write a more systematic political and economic history of the Sotho–Tswana in the two centuries preceding the Difaqane. Not only might this shed more light on the cataclysmic events which were to occur over the whole of South Africa in the time of Shaka, but such history of the seventeenth and eighteenth centuries would provide a base line on which to reconstruct, with the aid of other disciplines, the remoter Sotho–Tswana past.

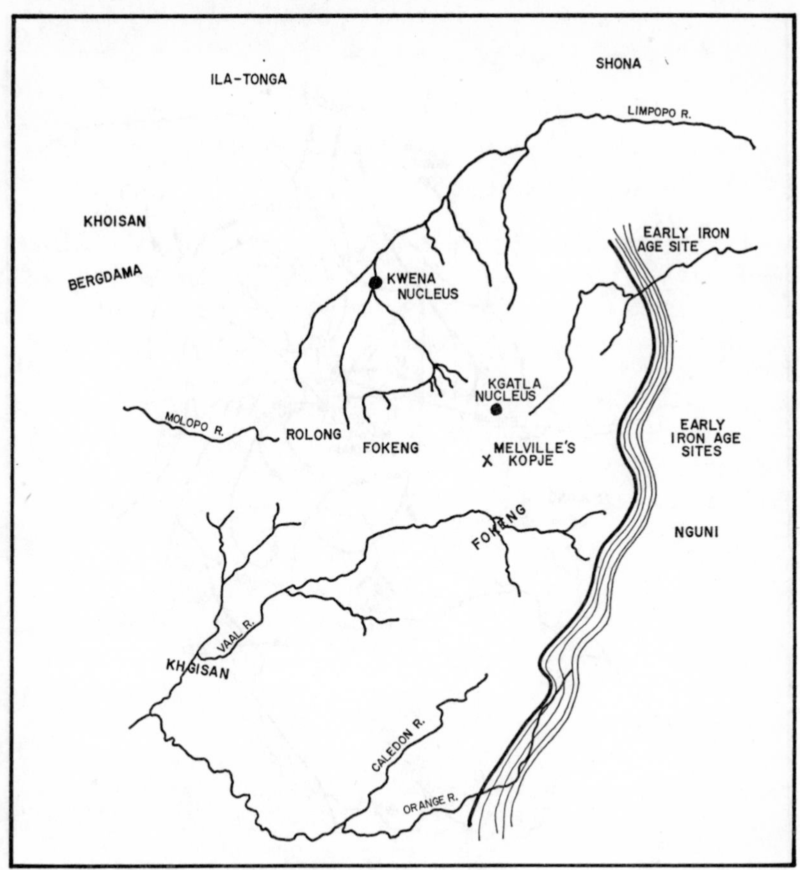

4. *The Sotho–Tswana area before A.D. 1500*

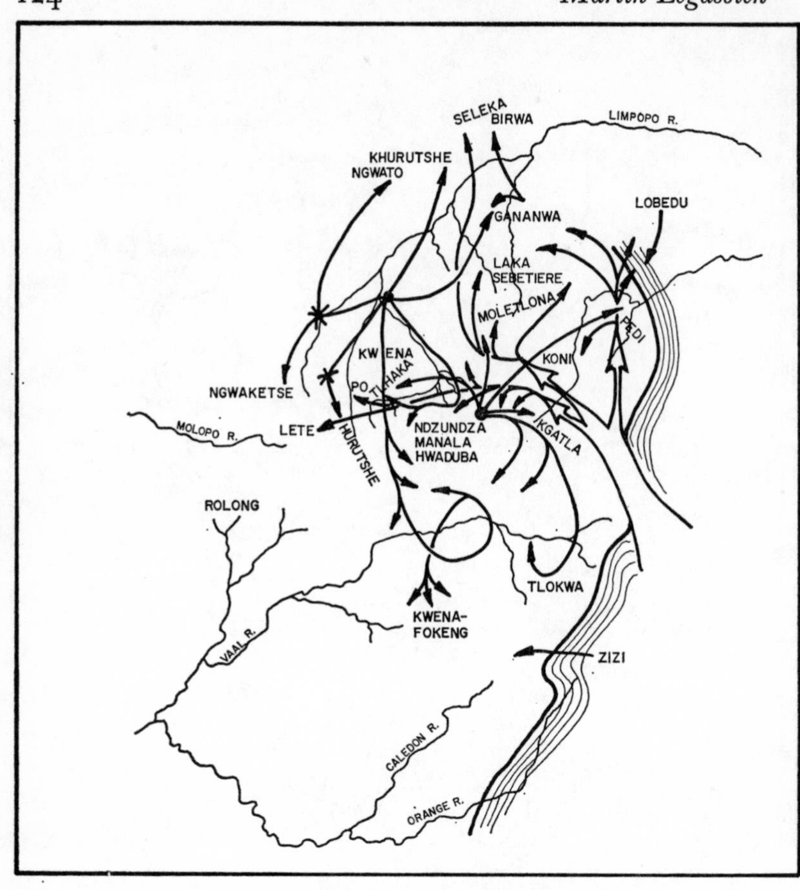

5. *Tentative dispersal of chiefdoms in the sixteenth to eighteenth centuries*

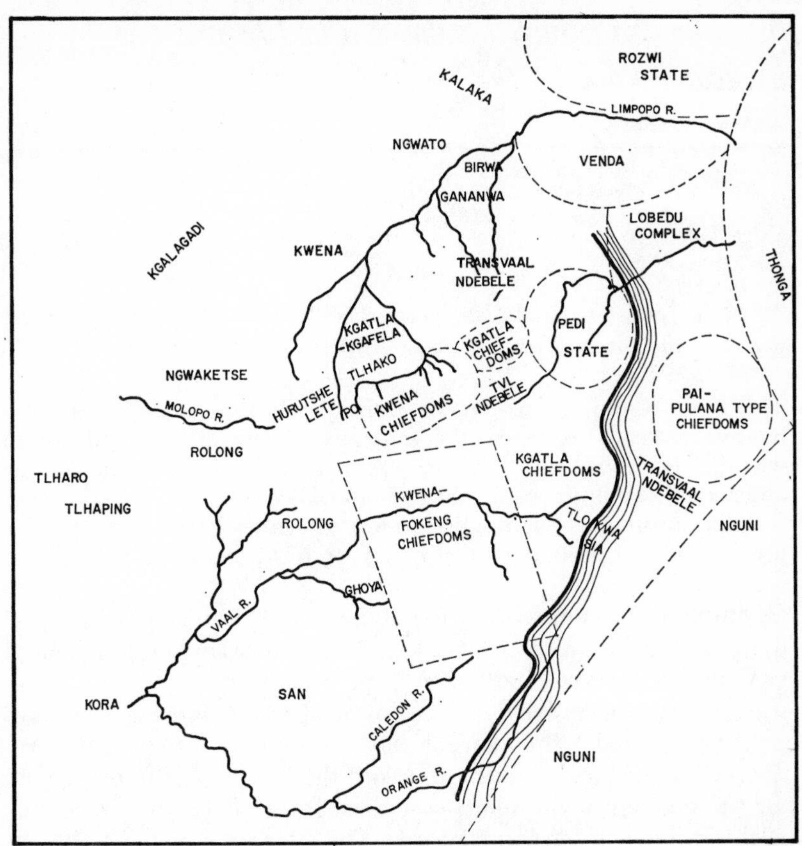

6. *Sotho–Tswana distribution about 1800*

6. *The traditions of the Natal 'Nguni': a second look at the work of A. T. Bryant*

SHULA MARKS

As N. J. Van Warmelo has remarked in his valuable *Preliminary Survey of the Bantu Tribes of South Africa*:

> The term Nguni is used in an entirely arbitrary sense, which has however already received the sanction of several years' usage in scientific literature. . . . The main reason for its adoption lies in the absence of any other name that would be equally suitable. However valid the arguments that might be adduced against its use as a collective term, these will probably have to yield to this necessity.[1]

Certainly the contemporary use of the term to describe the peoples living along the south-east coast of Africa, speaking closely related variants of the same language, and practising the same culture seems inescapable. Nevertheless, as Anthony Atmore and I have recently argued,[2] the present day widespread use of the term 'Nguni' by historians trying to avoid the anachronistic term Zulu for the peoples of the south-east coast in pre-Mfecane times may itself do much to distort the past. This all-inclusive term with its connotation of timeless homogeneity may well be the first obstacle in the way of our understanding the origins of the layers of people that make up the present day Nguni.

As we have suggested, the wide-ranging use of the term is probably 'due to white intervention and invention, not least on the part of [A. T.] Bryant'. Insofar as the term was used by Africans in the nineteenth century, it appears to have either had a very general or a very specific connotation: according to Arbousset, the Tswana generally called the Zulu 'Bakoni', the Sotho equivalent for the term Nguni, and the same term Bakoni appears to have

[1] Department of Native Affairs Ethnological Publications Vol. V Pretoria 1935 Part 3 p. 59.

[2] S. Marks and A. E. Atmore 'The Problem of the Nguni: An Examination of the Ethnic and Linguistic Situation in South Africa before the Mfecane' to be published in D. Dalby (ed.) *Collected Papers of the London Seminar on Language and History in Africa.*

been applied also to those small groups of non-Sotho in the Transvaal who trace their origin to the south-east.[3] Moreover, in the same way as the Sotho call their neighbours Bakoni, the Thonga peoples of Delagoa Bay transform the term into VaNgoni,[4] a term which has received complete recognition for those break-away groups who made their way northward and eastward during the Mfecane.

This, however, may not be the result of the Thonga usage; it could have more specific origins. Both Zwangendaba and the Msane leader, Nxaba, were accompanied on their journeys northward by members of the associated Nzimela clan, who had the address name or *thakazelo* 'Mnguni'.[5] This same address name is found amongst the Qwabe and Cunu of Natal, and amongst the Xhosa, where according to some authorities Mnguni is the quasimythical founder figure at the head of a very long and respectable genealogy. J. H. Soga argues from this that the term Nguni should apply only to the Xhosa and their off-shoots, amongst whom he includes the Nzimela clan;[6] on the other hand, however, according to Bryant the Nzimela are an offshoot of the Ncwangeni, who in turn broke away from the Ndwandwe people. These latter are classified by Bryant in the later versions of his work as part of the Mbo grouping of the Nguni.[7]

If Bryant was the man responsible for 'inventing' the term 'Nguni', no man could have had greater claim to doing so. For any reconstructions of the Nguni past his two major works on tradition, *Olden Times in Zululand and Natal* and *A History of the Zulu*, form the essential starting-point. They represent almost fifty years of work gathering the oral traditions throughout the length and breadth of Natal from old and knowledgeable African informants who no longer exist. His work is, and must remain, the most important single source of Nguni history before and

[3] T. Arbousset *Relation d'un Voyage d'Exploration* Paris 1842 p. 269; N. J. Van Warmelo *Bakoni ba Maake* and *Bakoni ba Mametsa* Native Affairs Ethnological Publications 12 and 15 Pretoria 1944.

[4] A. T. Bryant *Zulu–English Dictionary* Natal 1905.

[5] A. T. Bryant *Olden Times in Zululand and Natal* London 1929 Struik 1965 pp. 276–81. Henceforth *Olden Times*.

[6] J. H. Soga *The South-Eastern Bantu* Johannesburg 1930 pp. 81–83.

[7] See A. T. Bryant *Olden Times* p. 161. In *A History of the Zulu and Neighbouring Tribes* Bryant gives a different version of Ndwandwe history. See below p. 141. *A History of the Zulu*, published by C. Struik in 1964, first appeared as a series of articles in the Mariannhill periodical *Izindaba Zabata* in 1911 and 1913.

during the Mfecane, and is of very considerable importance to anyone trying to understand the structure of the Zulu state throughout the nineteenth century. This, despite the fact that, as a research student has recently put it:

> The nature of Bryant's published work has probably been a barrier to a general understanding of Zulu history. He adopted, in the hope that his books would be financially successful, 'a light and colloquial style . . .' which is at its best quaintly eccentric, but more often leads to ambiguities and confusion. To this must be added the complex nature of the subject, the intricacies of interdependent clan histories, the formidable mass of detail, the unsystematic method of presentation and the annoying value judgements of a social evolutionist.[8]

Clearly Bryant's work is sorely in need of rewriting and reclassification. His cumbersome style and flights of fantasy interpose themselves constantly between the reader and his subject matter. Nevertheless, when one examines the actual traditions which Bryant has recorded amongst the chiefdoms of Natal and Zululand, which he calls tribes and clans, one cannot but be impressed by his scrupulous care. In addition to having gathered every scrap of tradition, he also combed the secondary literature on his subject in a manner that can only occasionally be faulted. Where more than one variant of a tradition existed, they were usually all transcribed. In handling genealogies over seven generations in depth he constantly advises his reader to be on his guard, and on the whole he is probably over-cautious rather than under-cautious in his handling of traditional material. Thus in allowing only eighteen years to an average generation he appears to be out of tune with most other scholars in south-east Africa, who feel that twenty-five to thirty years is probably a fairer average in view of the nature of succession amongst Nguni chiefs. In this case Bryant appears to be arguing from the somewhat false analogy of the nineteenth century, where rules of succession were honoured in the breach rather than the observance.

If this paper does no more than serve as a guide-line to others daunted by the sheer bulk and intricacy as well as by the formid-

[8] J. J. Guy 'An approach to a Study of the Civil War in Zululand during the 1880s'. Unpublished paper presented to the African History seminar on 22 May 1968 Institute of Commonwealth Studies.

able style of A. T. Bryant, it will have served its purpose. It claims to be no more than a preliminary attempt to make sense of *Olden Times in Zululand and Natal* and *A History of the Zulu*,[9] to sort out Bryant's theories from the traditions he records, and to assess the validity of both.

Before taking a closer look at the traditions of the individual chiefdoms, it is necessary to outline Bryant's general theory of the peopling of south-east Africa, for it is here that fact and fantasy are most closely intermingled. It is not necessary to follow Bryant's Nguni farther afield than the headwaters of the Limpopo, through their meanderings along the Zambezi and from the Great Lakes of East Africa: this aspect of his work is so obviously the result of building on straws (or, as the case may be yams),[10] that it is best ignored for the moment. On the other hand, his views on population movements south of the Limpopo have a certain plausibility which have led to their being widely accepted, even although they do not always tally strictly with, or are not essential to, an interpretation of the local traditions he has recorded.

Like Soga, Bryant sees the migration of peoples into south-eastern Africa in three streams, all of which he regards as Nguni, although with different admixtures of alien blood and culture and speaking different variants of the same language. Bryant's 'wandering Nguni' arrive in the Transvaal via the headwaters of the Limpopo. Here one group remained to give rise to the local *Bakoni*, amongst whom he would include the various Tswana offshoots of the Hurutshe–Kwena chiefdoms. (He cites the somewhat dubious identification of *Bakoni* and *Bakwena* made by Stow and Moffat.[11]) In the north-western Transvaal he believes these

[9] I simplified the operation by tracing all sub-groups back to their parent people where this was known. This eliminated the vast majority of people listed at the back of *Olden Times* and left a residuum of the older groups, likely to have been of importance in the early days of 'Nguni' settlement. Underlining the chiefdoms of different groupings in different colours on Bryant's map of the Nguni before the Mfecane also proved an interesting exercise.

[10] See for example 'Part Seven: The Great Nguni Trek,' in *A History of the Zulu* pp. 113–24.

[11] According to Stow, Moffat called the tributary streams of the Upper Limpopo, stretching from the northern flanks of the Magaliesberg to the streams forming the main sources of the Oliphants River, Bakone country. G. W. Stow *The Intrusion of the Stronger Bantu Races* Unpubl. MSS (South African Library), n.d. The same identification of Kwena and Koni is made by the Rev. E. Solomon *Two Lectures on the Native Tribes of the Interior* Cape Town 1855 II p. 53. He may also have been using Moffat as his source however.

Nguni mixed with Venda–Karanga people to form a new hybrid stock of 'Sutu–Ngunis'.[12]

A section of partially fused Sutoid–Nguni then made their way eastward where they appear to have divided into two groups: Mbo or Dlamini or Swazi–Nguni who moved southward towards the Swaziland–Northern Zululand area and another group who continued eastward, and mixed with the Gwamba Thonga who were also moving along the coast. This third group of 'Tonga Nguni' continued southward once they reached the coast and outflanked the Mbo on the coast. Thus Bryant is able to move the two groups more or less simultaneously from the north, their traditional point of origin, yet avoiding the tsetse fly belt along the east coast.

Finally he suggests that central and southern Zululand and the eastern Cape were populated by the original 'pure' Nguni who had moved into the south-eastern Transvaal prior to the intermixture between the Nguni and the Venda–Karanga. From the south-eastern Transvaal the 'pure' Nguni appear to have moved into Natal–Zululand via the Mzinyati or Buffalo River, where they divided into two (perhaps three) major groups, the Cape Nguni and the Ntungwa Nguni. From this region one group of the Cape Nguni, the Thembu, made their way south-eastward until they reached the coast south of Durban and then moved into the Cape; a second group, the Xhosa, kept inland, close under the Drakensberg, and went into Griqualand East before reaching the coast south of the Thembu. By having his 'pure' Nguni come into the coastal area from the south-east Transvaal, Bryant explains the 'pure' Nguni traditions about an origin 'in the west'.[13]

When considering Bryant's general theories of migration even in the restricted area south of the Limpopo, it is as well to realize that in general there is little record in the traditions of such large movements. In so far as the traditions trace migrations they appear to be of relatively small distances, at least until the Mfecane. Thus although Bryant refers to Malandela, the progenitor of Qwabe and Zulu, as the tribal Moses, who led his people to a new promised land, the total distance this chosen people travelled must have been about twenty miles—from

[12] Where I have cited Bryant's groupings of the Nguni I have followed his spelling: thus 'Sutu Nguni' and 'Tonga Nguni' rather than Sotho and Thonga. Elsewhere I have tried to conform to the current orthography.

[13] This entire section draws very heavily on Marks and Atmore op. cit. and is based on Bryant *Olden Times* pp. 3–15.

Babanango Mountain to the Hlatuze River.[14] The wider movements which Bryant talks about are clearly too far back for traditional memories except in the vaguest terms. The proof or disproof of these general theories will have to come ultimately, if it can come at all, from archaeologists and linguists.

From this point of view, indeed, even Bryant's three stream migration may already be the result of an oversimplification of earlier migrations and of spurious claims to relationships; within each of these three major groups there appear to be divisions of people who may not be organically related. The generally accepted maximum span of reliability accredited to oral tradition appears to be in the region of three hundred years, unless there are institutional modes of recollection. The Nguni as a group do not appear to have possessed these although there are some surprisingly long genealogies which appear to outrun this limit. It must also be remembered that these are the traditions of ruling families, and in this sense also represent an over-simplification.

If one posits the populating of this area by Bantu-speakers over some thousand years, which the archaeological evidence of the neighbouring Transvaal and Rhodesia certainly appears to warrant,[15] it may be that Bryant was only tapping the top layers of Bantu-speaking migration into the area. Thus amongst the thousand or so 'clans' and 'subclans' which Bryant lists at the back of his work as Nguni, some two hundred have no *thakazelo* and no parent clan or grouping in terms of the threefold classification, 'Ntungwa,' 'Mbo' and 'Tonga–Nguni'.[16] Conceivably this is because these chiefdoms and their traditions were wiped out during the Shakan wars. Alternatively these may well represent the earliest peoples of the coastlands, who were unrelated to the later 'parent-clans'.

The Later Stone Age inhabitants of most of southern Africa, including the coastlands, were the Khoisan peoples practising hunting, gathering and pastoral modes of existence. Traces of the pre-Bantu inhabitants of south-east Africa are found in their shell middens all along the coast,[17] although by the sixteenth

[14] *Olden Times* pp. 17–19.

[15] Indeed the recent Iron Age date of 410 A.D. ±60 from Swaziland, if correctly associated with the incoming Bantu-speakers, tends to push this back even farther for the south-east coast. B. Fagan 'Radiocarbon dates for sub-Saharan Africa: V' *J.A.H.* Vol. VIII No. 3 p. 525.

[16] *Olden Times* pp. 681–97.

[17] J. D. Clark *The Prehistory of Southern Africa* London 1955.

century the pastoral Khoikhoi do not appear to have lived beyond the Kei River, and by the nineteenth the San had been driven from most of their original hunting grounds into the fastnesses of the Drakensberg.

In earlier times there was considerable intermarriage between the Khoisan and the incoming Bantu-speakers. The clicks in Nguni are a well-known indication of this, although they pose a number of problems. On the whole linguists tend to think that they came into Zulu and Xhosa from Khoikhoi rather than any of the San languages. Yet while we have ample evidence of intensive contact between the Khoikhoi and the Xhosa in the Eastern Cape, we have no such evidence of contact between the Khoikhoi and the Zulu. Moreover though cognates in Zulu and Xhosa are high (about eighty per cent on two separate test lists), of the 2,400 click words in Xhosa only 375 have cognates in Zulu and there are some notable semantic differences between them; despite the fact that click words account for about one-sixth of the Xhosa vocabulary and one-seventh of Zulu. This suggests that the two languages acquired their click words, or the bulk of them, after their divergence from a common stock.[18] It still leaves open the question of where Zulu acquired them. If the Zulu click words are indeed from Khoikhoi, one has either to posit the presence of these Late Stone Age herders much farther north along the coast than their known distribution and their complete absorption by the incoming Bantu-speakers, or their similar presence in an earlier home of the Natal Nguni, which they could only have shared for a short time, if at all, with the Xhosa.

Contact between the Natal Nguni and the San hunter-gatherers is better documented. Some evidence of this is the custom, called *Ndiki*, of cutting off the final joint of the little finger, which certain Bantu-speaking groups known to have been in close contact with the San, have adopted. It is practised by a section at least of the Thembu in the Cape, and the Bomvu, Lata, Belesi, Tuli and Ncamu people in Natal.[19] Bryant, who tends to think of the San as being confined from time immemorial to the mountains, is somewhat hard put to explain how the Tuli

[18] L. W. Lanham 'The Proliferation and Extension of Bantu Phonemic Systems influenced by Bushman and Hottentot' *Proc. Ninth Int. Congress of Linguistics* Cambridge Mass. 1962 (The Hague 1964) pp. 383–4. I am grateful to Mr Gerrit Harinck for the reference. I am also extremely grateful to Prof. Lanham for written and oral communications since his paper was written, elucidating several additional points.

[19] Bryant *Olden Times* p. 517. G. W. Stow *Native Races of South Africa* London 1905 p. 129.

people, whose traditional migrations have taken them from the coast around the Tugela, to the coast around Durban, could have acquired the habit. At Durban Bluff, however, two types of pottery associated with Bantu-speakers, NC_2 and NC_3, have been found closely associated with Later Stone Age shell middens, which may help solve the difficulty.[20]

Archaeological evidence tells us most about these Later Stone Age people. Nevertheless in an article in the *South African Archaeological Bulletin* in 1960,[21] Desmond Clark used Portuguese shipwreck material to show that there were still non-Bantu, click-speaking peoples on the south-east African coast between latitudes 28° and 33° south in the late sixteenth century and that it was not unlikely 'that there were still enclaves of pure or hybrid groups on the intervening coastline'. As Desmond Clark points out almost all the survivors of sixteenth- and seventeenth-century shipwrecks along the coast were able to purchase fish from the local inhabitants. This is generally taken to mean that they could not have been Bantu-speaking, as the present-day Nguni display, according to Murdock, 'an almost Cushitic aversion to fish'.[22] Further examination of the sources, however, reveals the frequent association of fish with millet and cattle, which suggests that these were not pure Khoisan groups.[23] Nor does Murdock's dictum rule out the possibility that earlier Bantu-speakers were responsible for the fishing practices found in the Portuguese shipwreck material and depicted in San rock-paintings.

Desmond Clark himself quotes Junod on the types of boats made by the Delagoa Bay Thonga, and shows pictures of bark boats made both by the Lala–Lamba peoples of Zambia and the Delagoa Bay Thonga.[24] These boats resemble those in the San paintings of fishing on the Tsoelike River, in the Mponweni Mountains and Kenegha Poort. The human figures in these paintings could depict either San or Bantu fishermen. Certainly in the nineteenth century the Tuli people did not share this 'Cushitic aversion' to fish and the Thonga of Delagoa Bay also do not appear to share it. The Tuli, however, may represent one of the

[20] J. Schoute Vanneck 'Shell middens at Durban Bluff' *S.A.A.B.* Vol. XIII No. 50 p. 1950.
[21] 'A Note on the early river-craft and fishing practises in South-East Africa' Vol. XV No. 58 pp. 77–79.
[22] G. P. Murdock *Africa, Its Peoples and their Culture History* New York 1959 p. 382.
[23] G. M. Theal *Records of South East Africa* London 1898–9 Vols. I, II and VIII.
[24] Clark 'A Note on early river-craft . . .' op. cit.

Khoisan–Bantu composite groups which existed well into the nineteenth century, if not the twentieth, all over southern Africa. By the time Bryant came to classify the Tuli, their official designation was 'Lala'.[25]

Clearly this term Lala is used very widely, especially if one follows J. H. Soga's usage. As used by Soga the term has the connotation of 'earlier inhabitant' to it.[26] It is also used by the Tswana in the sense of 'vassal' or 'serf'.[27] Soga further equates the Lala with skilled metal-workers, and it seems mainly for this reason that he suggested a Karanga origin for the Lala.[28] This seems to be arguing by definition.

On the other hand, in view of the association of some of the Thonga groups with the Karanga, Soga's suggestion that the Lala are connected with the Karanga is perhaps not entirely without substance. Bryant too seems to lend some weight to this as he associates the Tonga–Nguni with the Gwamba Thonga who are said to have had a Karanga origin.[29] But the supposed close association of the Lala with iron-working may be misleading. It seems that other groups such as the Cunu (Ntungwa) and the Cube (either Mbo or Ntungwa) were at least as skilled and renowned metal workers as the people listed by Bryant as Lala. Having translated the term Lala as 'skilled iron-worker' Soga tends then to lump all skilled iron-workers into this category (e.g. the Bhele, whom Bryant classifies as Mbo).

Bryant, however, regards the Lala as simply one of his three Tonga–Nguni groups together with the Debe–Nguni and the Mthethwa–Nguni.[30] He suggests that the reason for differentiation between the three Tonga–Nguni groups was the result of their admixture with slightly different groups of Thonga.

In a sense, however, this still begs the question. The term

[25] *Olden Times* pp. 686–96. Bryant thinks they are offshoots of Lutuli people who lived near the Tugela. These in turn were a branch of the 'Lala' Ngcolosi. I am a little dubious about the identification of Tuli/Lutuli which may have been a later invention to explain the similarity of the name.

[26] *The South-Eastern Bantu* pp. 395–417. In general I have preferred Bryant's version to that of J. H. Soga. As Monica Wilson once remarked the 'most that can be said of Soga's work is that he gave the version current amongst the old men in the Transkei in the 1920s'.

[27] S. M. Molema *The Bantu, Past and Present* Edinburgh 1920 p. 35.

[28] *The South-Eastern Bantu* p. 395.

[29] *Olden Times* p. 7; C. E. Fuller 'Ethnohistory in the Study of Culture Change in South East Africa' in *Continuity and Change in African Cultures* ed. W. R. Bascom and M. J. Herskowits Chicago 1959.

[30] *Olden Times* p. 7.

Thonga for the people from St Lucia Bay to the Zambezi is as unsatisfactory as the word Nguni for all the people to their south. As Junod has pointed out, it is again simply a convenient label for a group 'made up of populations of various origin which have invaded the country coming from different parts', but who today speak dialects which bear a geographical relationship to one another.[31] Over the past four to five hundred years at least these people have lived in the same geographical relationship to one another, and have formed enough of an amalgam to be categorized together. While, however, some of them, like the Gwamba/Baloyi and the Tembe Thonga, trace their origin to the north and to the Karanga—the *thakazelo* of the Tembe for example is still Nkalanga—others appear to have come from Zululand and Swaziland.[32]

Although the present day Thonga groupings have a long history, many groups record the presence of earlier peoples in their area when they arrived: thus the incoming Khosa found Ntimba and Shibambo clans on arrival, while in the Nondwane country Honwana, Mahlangwana and Nkumba were already there when the first Ronga came to the area with superior weapons and superior tactics. These earlier inhabitants were said to have been scattered, few in number and without iron weapons or oxhide shields.[33] In view of the long history of this northerly area, and the absence of any physical barriers to migration southwards, it seems reasonable to suggest a trickle of population making its way farther south from the time of the earliest entry of Bantu-speakers into the Delagoa Bay region. The dearth of archaeological work on the Iron Age in South Moçambique makes this impossible to prove one way or the other. Schofield's NC 1 pottery, which he considered to be 'undoubtedly' Ronga ware, has been classified more recently as Late Stone Age, though the two views may not necessarily be entirely incompatible.[34] Although Bryant lists the Hlanga and Nkumba amongst his Nguni 'clans and subclans',[35]—names which also appear on Junod's list of the Delagoa Bay Thonga—there appears to have been a movement of certain Thonga groups from the south, Nguni area, northward which could account for this equally well. In the

[31] H. A. Junod *Life of a South African Tribe* 2 vols. London 1927 pp. 1, 31.
[32] Ibid i pp. 22–23.
[33] Ibid pp. 1, 4, 330.
[34] J. Schofield *Primitive Pottery* Cape Town 1948 p. 151.
[35] *Olden Times* pp. 684, 693. Beyond listing them, Bryant gives no further information.

absence of conclusive proof, however, this substratum of Thonga peoples appears as likely an explanation of the resemblances between the Tonga–Nguni and the Thonga as an intermingling farther north.

A final clue to Lala origins may be found in the fact that when the groups termed by Bryant Lala are plotted on his map of the Nguni in pre-Mfecane times they appear to have shown a predilection for settlement along rivers or right on the coast.[36] Their focus appears to have been along the banks of the Tugela River where they 'waxed fat and multiplied' and sent branch-lines off to the south. This may be as important a clue to their origins as their association with metal working.

Bryant's 'Debe–Nguni' appear to represent a more primitive population. Unfortunately representatives of this group were so shattered and scattered during the Mfecane that virtually no traditions of migrations or even genealogies appear to have been retained. It is also possible that even before the upheavals of the Mfecane, as fragmented, early groups the Debe–Nguni did not have any oral tradition of depth. Bryant places the Debe–Nguni amongst his Tonga–Nguni because of their 'facial incisions', a practice which is found amongst the Thonga people of Delagoa Bay, but not amongst either the Lala, Mbo or Ntungwa Nguni.[37] According to Bryant, hardly any specimens of Debe–Nguni speech have been retained, although he classifies it along with Lala as the *tekela* form of Nguni. The examples he gives—Lala: *Umunu*, Debe: *Umuntshu*, Ntungwa: *Umuntu*—show how it differed in pronunciation from both Lala and Ntungwa. The Debe–Nguni appear to have stretched in a kind of column in pre-Mfecane times from the Umvoti River to the Umzimkulu, at a distance of ten or twenty miles from the coast.[38] This could have been either because they found the coast already occupied by 'shell-midden man' or the Lala, or because they wished to avoid the sandy flats of the coastal strip.

The third group of Tonga–Nguni includes the important Mthethwa, Cele and Dube chiefdoms. Both the Mthethwa and the Cele trace their descent to a common ancestor, Nyambose, who is not on either of their genealogies. Surprisingly perhaps, the Mthethwa genealogy is thin and ill-preserved, although the Cele

[36] At the back of *Olden Times*. It is invaluable.
[37] *Olden Times* p. 547.
[38] See Bryant's map op. cit.

genealogy stretches back eleven generations from Magaye, who died in 1829, to Ndosi (who has given his name as *thakazelo* to the chiefdom). Even by Shaka's time, they were a chiefdom of considerable size and had split into numerous sub-chiefdoms. None of the other Mthethwa groups, however, appear to have genealogies longer than three or four generations before Shaka, and it is not at all clear what relationship they have with the main Mthethwa group. The classification strikes one as additionally unsatisfactory as there are also suggested associations between the Mthethwa and the Mbo (Mkize), and Bryant thinks that the Mthethwa originally formed one group with the Mbo, the Ngwane (of Swaziland) and the Ndwandwe, 'who all migrated at one time initially in one body'.[39] Bryant classifies them amongst the Tonga–Nguni however, because the Ntungwa Nguni refer to the Mthethwa as 'Thonga', a generic term of contempt. Their tradition of origin traces them from the neighbourhood of Mabudu (the Maputa River) south of Delagoa Bay, and they have a 'Thongaised' form of speech.[40]

If oral tradition appears to lend some support to a northerly Thonga origin for the Tonga–Nguni, the pattern of Mbo migration and settlement appears more complex. Again there appear to be two and perhaps three distinct groups of people involved, the Dlamini Mbo, whose chief groups are the Emalangeni, the Mbo (Mkize), the Natal Dlamini, the Ngwane of Swaziland, probably the Ndwandwe, and perhaps the Mpondo and their offshoots; the Hlubi and their offshoots; and the Zizi–Bhele group.[41] According to Bryant all the members of the Mbo group trace their origins back to the Komati River and the Lubombo mountains and to Dlamini I of *Langa* royal clan. Bryant maintains, although not entirely convincingly, that Dlamini I was probably responsible for leading the Mbo from the Komati River, their traditional dispersal point, to the area between the Lubombo mountains and the sea. They remained a while in the region of Delagoa Bay, where they came into close contact with the important kingdom of the Tembe Thonga.[42] He believes that the Mbo are both the Macomates and the Vambe of the sixteenth-century Portuguese sources. Macomates could be Ama-Komati—the people of the

[39] *Olden Times* pp. 85, 391. Soga op. cit. 300 suggests that the Mthethwa may have been 'Mbo'.

[40] *Olden Times* p. 83.

[41] Soga classifies both these last two as 'Lala' pp. 398–9.

[42] *Olden Times* pp. 313–17.

Komati River, which Bryant points out is the *tekela* form of the river the Ntungwa would call Komanzi. Vambe is almost unmistakably the prefix Va and Mbo.[43]

After a considerable sojourn near Delagoa Bay, Bryant pictures the Mbo moving southward *en masse*, some peopling Swaziland, some Northern Zululand, and some of the Hlubi, Bhele–Zizi and Natal Dlamini passing onwards to people Utrecht, Vryheid and northern Natal.[44] Though it is not clear what Bryant means by this movement *en masse*, nor whether he thinks these groups were already differentiated amongst the EmaLangeni at the time of the move, several of these groups do trace their origin to the Lubombo and to the Langa (or EmaLangeni) parent clan.

All the Mbo groups have long and well preserved genealogies, with the exception of the Ndwandwe people. Some of them—for example the Ngwane/Langa—go back over some twenty generations,[45] and there is other evidence to suggest that they have been in the south-east coastlands for a very long time. For this reason, Bryant's suggestion that it was Dlamini I who led them from the Komati River is open to some doubt, as is his linking of the Hlubi and Bhele–Zizi groups to this same figure. It is simplest to handle each of the three groups—Hlubi, Zizi–Bhele and the Dlamini Mbo—separately to see how far this common origin is borne out by the traditional evidence.

Perhaps the most problematical members of this group are the Zizi–Bhele peoples who occupied a large area alongside the Drakensberg mountains between Waschbank and the headwaters of the Tshezi (Bushmans) River. Bryant asserts that together with the Hlubi and the Mpondo they formed the head of the Mbo circling movement from the Transvaal to Portuguese East Africa and then round again to the uplands of Natal and Zululand.[46] The only migration route, however, in their traditions takes them from the Zinyati (Buffalo) River to their pre-Mfecane home, a few miles to the south. Moreover Bryant's linking of the Mbo (Mkize) group with the Bhele–Zizi group through the common personage of one Langa, who appears on all their genealogies,

[43] *Olden Times* pp. 288–90, 312, 314.
[44] *Olden Times* pp. 7, 313.
[45] *Olden Times* p. 314, has twenty-four generations to Mkulunkosi; Sim *History of the Zulu* p. 3. According to Hilda Kuper *An African Aristocracy* London 1947 p. 232, 'the royal genealogy (of the Swazi) goes back some thirty generations, but there is agreement on the last eight rulers only'. This was working from 1947.
[46] *Olden Times* pp. 7, 313.

seems somewhat rash in view of the frequency with which this particular name occurs and recurs on Nguni genealogies, and the relative lateness of the occurrence on the Mkize line,[47] seven generations back from Shaka.

His views are, however, to some extent strengthened by the remarks of G. W. Stow in the unpublished manuscript already cited. It seems unlikely that Bryant knew of its existence or that they drew on the same sources. In this, Stow regretted the disappearance of Zizi tradition because he felt it would have 'assisted greatly in solving the common origin of the various Bantu nations of South Africa, for not only the Amazizi themselves but native authorities belonging to other tribes assert that the Amazizi are the direct descendants of the main or original stem from which both branches of the great Bantu family (i.e. Nguni and Sotho . . .) have descended. For many generations it is said that their chiefs and people were said to represent the paramount tribe, whose precedency and supremacy were acknowledged by all the others.'[48]

That Stow should have regarded this group, who originally called themselves Amalanga after their first remembered chief, as the progenitor of both the Sotho and Nguni is not surprising in view of the intermediate position they do appear to have held between the two. Thus according to the Rev. Brownlee[49] their language was 'more nearly related to Sechoana than that of the Kaffirs'. They stacked their grain above the ground in baskets unlike the Nguni and prepared their milk in the same manner as the Sotho.

This may of course have been the result of their geographical position between the two major groupings of present day South Africa. A cogent case, however, has been made out both by Bryant and Ellenberger for tying up the Zizi and the pioneer clans of Basutoland, the Phuti, Polane and Pehla, who appear to be connected through the chiefs Langa, Mafu and Mtiti, whose names appear in the genealogies of the Natal Zizi/Bhele and amongst the Phuti and Polane.[50] While, however, both Bryant and Ellenberger appear to have had little doubt that these Zizi on both sides of the Drakensberg are Nguni, van Warmelo has made

[47] Ibid pp. 147, 354, 406.
[48] *The Intrusion of the Stronger Bantu Races* pp. 178–9.
[49] Cited in Stow op. cit. p. 179.
[50] Ibid p. 354. D. F. Ellenberger and J. C. MacGregor *History of the Basuto, Ancient and Modern* London 1912 pp. 21–26.

the interesting suggestion that the Basutoland Zizi are part of an ancient Sotho stock related to the MaPolana of Swaziland. He believes this ancient Sotho stock once inhabited the escarpment east of the Drakensberg in Natal and Swaziland.[51] Although in time the Zizi have become both 'Nguni-ized' and 'Bushmanized', it does seem possible that this ancient Sotho stock may be responsible for the Sotho elements which observers like Bryant detected in the Mbo group. Whether Nguni or Sotho, they appear to have been heavily influenced by the San people in their neighbourhood, sharing certain physical resemblances and practising the San custom of *Ndiki*; they also had a certain notoriety as cannibals, and this in the days of Shaka's father, Senzengakona, even before the Mfecane.[52]

The ties between the Dlamini Mbo and the Hlubi who trace their origin from one Dlamini may be somewhat closer than those between the Bhele–Zizi and either of these two. Even here, however, the connection seems somewhat tenuous. Like Langa, Dlamini was a particularly favoured cognomen for chiefs in this part of the world. Whereas the Dlamini I on the Natal Dlamini king list is the sixteenth (or seventeenth) generation back from 1820, and similarly on the Emalangeni/Ngwane (Swazi) king list from Ndungunya (died 1815), on the Hlubi king list he is only in the eleventh generation back from Mtimkulu (killed 1818). This Dlamini was the original founder figure of the Hlubi people. One wonders whether at this point a Dlamini was not necessary to lend respectability to the Hlubi king list. The appearance of a Hlubi as the father of Dlamini II on the Emalangeni/Ngwane king list in the third and second generation back from 1815 may conceivably have led to some contamination of the Hlubi genealogy.

On the other hand, however, the Hlubi genealogy would appear to have contracted rather than expanded over the ages: there appears to be some kind of link between the Southern Transvaal Ndebele (Manala and Ndzundza sections) and the Hlubi through the common chiefs Musi/Msi and Mhlanga. But whereas the Hlubi Musi and Mhlanga are in the ninth and tenth generation back from 1818, the Manala Ndebele list some twenty-six names back to Musi and Mhlanga, while the Ndzundza section have

[51] N. J. Van Warmelo *Preliminary Survey of the Bantu Tribes of South Africa* op. cit. Part 3 p. 98.

[52] *Olden Times* pp. 248, 348.

nineteen names back to these two founding fathers.[53] It is possible that whereas the Hlubi list represents generations, the Ndzundza and Manala Ndebele lists are simply king lists including collaterals.

While the ties between the Hlubi and the Bhele–Zizi group with the Langa parent clan are somewhat tenuous and vague, the relationship of the 'Dlamini' group—the Ngwane of Swaziland, the Mtonga, the Dlamini of Natal and the EmaLangeni—appears to be reasonably well authenticated. The case of the Ndwandwe is more complex. In his *History of the Zulu* Bryant placed the Ndwandwe amongst the Ntungwa Nguni, although in *Olden Times* the traditions of the Ngwane and the Ndwandwe appear to be very closely linked indeed.[54] Ndwandwe traditions are extremely confused, largely it would appear as a result of the Mfecane. As Shaka and Dingiswayo's chief military rivals, they were finally defeated more heavily than any other group. Their genealogy does not appear to have more than two names before Zwide, Dingiswayo's enemy.[55] For a chiefdom which was to achieve such influence and military prowess this seems curiously late. One is also left to account for the many sub-groups who trace their descent to the Ndwandwe.

On the other hand, the Ngwane, who were to achieve similar success in forging a state out of the disparate peoples in the area north of the Pongola River, also appear to have broken away from the parent Langa (EmaLangeni) stem at about the same time. Bryant makes the very interesting suggestion that the traditions of both these groups appear to take their rise at the time of the fall of the Tembe kingdom, the key trading state at Delagoa Bay, in the latter half of the eighteenth century.[56] It seems possible that, prior to their downfall, the Tembe held in check a large number of peoples on the periphery of their kingdom. It also seems possible that with the fall of the Tembe—possibly in part the result of increased pressures from the traders at Delagoa Bay at this time[57]—their role as state-builders and a trading power was taken on by their neighbours to their immediate south. This may in part account for the formation of the Ngwane and Ndwandwe kingdoms. The assertion of the Swazi King, Mbandeni,

[53] N. J. Van Warmelo *Transvaal Ndebele Texts* Native Affairs Department, Ethnological Publications No. 1 Pretoria 1930.

[54] *History of the Zulu* p. 12; *Olden Times* pp. 314, 316–7.

[55] *Olden Times* opposite p. 314, 161.

[56] *History of the Zulu* pp. 2–3, 51.

[57] An idea suggested to me by Alan Smith's chapter in this volume.

that the Ngwane were Thonga and part of the Tembe ruling family supports this hypothesis, although Bryant rejects the notion of so close a relationship between the Ngwane and the Tembe on linguistic grounds.[58]

Like the Mbo and the Tonga–Nguni, the pure Nguni can also be further subdivided into the Cape Nguni (Xhosa–Thembu and their offshoots), the Ntungwa or *abasenhla*, and the *abasezantsi*.[59] While the terms *abasenhla* and *abasezantsi* have a simply geographical connotation, that of Ntungwa is less easily explained. Included in the ranks of the Ntungwa by Bryant are the Kumalo/Mabaso, Mbata, Buthelezi, EmaNgwaneni—to be distinguished from the Swaziland Ngwane—and Cunu clans, and the term is also the *thakazelo* of the Kumalo and the EmaNgwaneni.

According to the Ntungwa group the term is 'in no wise applicable to individuals of the other members of the (Nguni) family' and there are differences in the history, traditions and to a minor extent in the speech of the two groups in Zululand. Thus only the Ntungwa 'up country' branch have the tradition of coming into Zululand from the west *ngesilulu*, 'with a grain basket' (an *isilulu* is the large conically shaped grain basket used by the Sotho, but unknown to the *abasezantsi*).[60] These differences may conceivably relate to the earlier groups found in their areas of settlement 'up country' and 'down country'.

The trail of the related Ntungwa people runs from the borders of the south-eastern Transvaal and Zululand up to Babanango mountain,[61] which appears to have been an important dispersal point for a number of the *abasezantsi*. At about the same time that Malandela, the progenitor of Zulu and Qwabe (some seven generations back from Shaka), was making his way to the Hlatuze River, Mafu of the Ngadini (*thakazelo* Gumede), Gwabini (progenitor of the Zungu and Makoba clans), Sibiya (*thakazelo* Gumede) and the Ema Dletsheni all appear to have been moving towards the coast.[62] The frequency of the *thakazelo* Gumede suggests that they may originally have stemmed from one parent

[58] *History of the Zulu* p. 3.

[59] 'Those up country' and 'those down country' are probably the nearest translations. The *abasezantsi* or *abazantsi* are the coastal section like the Qwabe, the *abasenhla* the more inland section, like the *Kumalo* and *EmaNgwaneni* otherwise known as the Ntungwa Nguni.

[60] *History of the Zulu* pp. 126–9. In *Olden Times* this division appears to have been ignored, and all the Natal 'pure' Nguni groups are labelled Ntungwa Nguni.

[61] See map at the back of *Olden Times*.

[62] *Olden Times* pp. 13, 25, 116.

group which is, however, now lost in the mists and myths of the past. The great rise to pre-eminence of the Zulu and Qwabe in the nineteenth century should not disguise the fact that they were relatively recent offshoots of this parent chiefdom, already settled in the heart of Zululand.

There seems little in the genealogical and tradition material to link the Thembu–Xhosa of the Cape with Natal Ntungwa groups. There are of course Natal Thembu who according to their traditions form part of the same group as the Cape Thembu. There are, however, curiously few chiefdoms grouped as pure Nguni south of the Tugela that would serve as some sort of linking trail to the Cape Xhosa, though Bryant labels the Nxasane on the Umzimkulu, the Wushe on the Umgeni, and possibly the neighbouring Zelemu as Ntungwa Nguni.[63]

On the other hand, it is a striking feature of the Nguni area that, unlike the Thonga area farther north, the languages do not deviate from a single parent stem in a purely geographical fashion. Thus Natal Lala is closer to Thonga than Ntungwa Nguni (Zulu) is to either, and Ntungwa Nguni is closer to Xhosa than either Xhosa or Zulu is to Lala.[64] The picture given of Mbo is even less clear, although it is classified along with Lala and present day Swazi as one of the *tekela* forms of Nguni.[65] It would be interesting to know what the relationships between the dialects spoken by the Hlubi, Bhele–Zizi and Dlamini group are within this broader classification.

This paper has been but a preliminary attempt to assess the work of A. T. Bryant. It does not claim to be an exhaustive analysis even of the published traditions. There is clearly a good deal still to be done, not least in the evaluation of Bryant's unpublished material and in the correlation of the traditions

[63] Ibid pp. 269, 369–72. See also Bryant's Map and list of clans and sub-clans in *Olden Times* pp. 681–97.

[64] See for example, W. H. I. Bleek 'Researches into the Relations between the Hottentots and Kafirs' *Cape Monthly Magazine* April 1857 p. 204 where he maintains that 'Tegeza' or the language spoken by the Africans of Natal is a third sub-group of Southern Bantu, as distinct from Xhosa–Zulu as it is from Tswana. Although knowledge of Southern Bantu was still in its infancy at the time, Bleek was one of the foremost linguists of his day and an acute observer. Moreover he was writing at a time when the differences between the sub-groups of 'Nguni' languages were far more marked than at the present. He also maintained that the habits and customs of the Zulu were similar to those of the Xhosa whilst those of the 'Tegeza' speakers were not.

[65] *History of the Zulu* pp. 54–55. See also D. Ziervogel *A Grammar of Northern Transvaal Ndebele* Pretoria 1959 p. 13 for a table showing the relationship of the various Nguni sub-groups.

he has recorded with those recorded by that other great authority on Nguni and Zulu history, James Stuart[66]; despite the havoc wrought by the Mfecane, field research on groups such as the Hlubi—which is in fact in progress at the University of Cape Town—and other similar groups, can be expected to yield results on both the linguistic and historical level which will help confirm or disprove Bryant's hypotheses. Nevertheless it is equally clear that the only way in which Bryant's work can finally be tested will be through the achievements of other disciplines—through archaeological and linguistic research as well as through archival work on the Portuguese and Dutch records of the sixteenth to eighteenth centuries. A complete reclassification of Bryant's work, however, would give us all a starting-point.

[66] James Stuart, for long a civil servant in Natal and author of a semi-official history of the Zulu rebellion of 1906, collected a considerable amount of material from informants at the turn of the century. In many important respects his work appears to confirm Bryant's, although no exhaustive examination of his vernacular histories nor of his large collection of unpublished material in the Killie Campbell Library (University of Natal, Durban) has yet been undertaken.

7. *Interaction between Xhosa and Khoi: emphasis on the period 1620–1750*

GERRIT HARINCK

HISTORICAL AND CULTURAL BACKGROUND AND SCOPE

At the beginning of the seventeenth century the present day Cape Province of the Republic of South Africa was inhabited by San, Khoi, Southern Nguni (of whom the Xhosa are a branch), and acculturated peoples of mixed descent resulting from interaction among these groups.[1] The San and the Khoi were the most ancient dwellers of the region. The San in foraging bands populated the more inaccessible areas in the interior. The Khoi pastoralists occupied defined, watered regions along the Orange River, the Atlantic and Indian Ocean seaboards, and inland along rivers as far as at least the Keiskama River.[2] The forerunners of the pastoral-hoe-agriculturalist Southern Nguni, the Xhosa and Thembu, probably entered the eastern regions of Cape Province

[1] In the literature San, Khoi, Xhosa and the Southern Nguni generally, are respectively referred to as 'Bushmen', 'Hottentots' and 'Kaffirs', and varied spellings of these words. These names are of non-African origin and presently they have derogatory connotations attached to them. Bitter controversy has raged over the word 'Hottentot' among South African scholars. For the most recent summation see G. S. Nienaber *Hottentots* Pretoria 1963 pp. 32–58. In this paper the names are those used by the peoples under discussion, with the exception of the San. The Xhosa referred to themselves eponymously. The Cape Khoi called themselves 'Khoina' i.e. 'human beings'; see Nienaber op. cit. pp. 310–11. 'Sana' was the word used by the Khoi to refer to the San.

[2] For the early San and Khoi see R. R. Inskeep 'The Late Stone Age in Southern Africa' in *Background to Evolution in Africa* ed. W. W. Bishop and J. D. Clark Chicago 1967 pp. 557–82. Migrations of the Khoi into the Cape region are discussed in C. K. Cooke 'Evidence of Human Migration from the Rock Art of Southern Rhodesia' *Africa* XXXV No. 3 July 1965; A. R. Willcox 'Sheep and Sheepherders in South Africa' *Africa* XXXVI No. 4 October 1966; E. O. J. Westphal 'The Linguistic Prehistory of Southern Africa: Bush, Kwadi, Hottentot and Bantu Linguistic Relationships' *Africa* XXXIII No. 3 July 1963; Westphal's migration route formulated on the basis of linguistic analysis of the various Khoi groups is radically different from that of Cooke and Willcox. See further A. J. H. Goodwin 'Metal Working Among the Early Hottentots' *S.A.A.B.* XI No. 42 1956. L. F. Maingard has attempted to place the Khoi chiefdoms in their proper geographical location based on contemporary work of D.E.I. Company officials, and travel accounts of the sixteenth, seventeenth and eighteenth centuries in L. F. Maingard 'The Lost Tribes of the Cape' *S.A.J.S.* XXVIII November 1931 pp. 487–504 map.

(Transkei) by the end of the fourteenth century. Xhosa were living at the Bashee River in the 1620s.[3] Acculturated peoples of mixed descent, such as the Ubiqua (Khoi–San) and Gonaqua (Khoi–Xhosa) lived to the north-east of the Table Bay peninsula and west of the Xhosa respectively. Peoples of European descent permanently settled in the area in 1652. In that year the Dutch East India Company established a fort at Table Bay for the purpose of supplying fresh produce to scurvy-ridden crews of ships sailing to and from the East Indies.

The demography of Cape Province was quite different by the 1800s. The Khoi and San became gradually extinct during the eighteenth century as a result of inequities in barter, susceptibility to European maladies such as venereal diseases and smallpox, eastern expansion of stock-farmers of European descent, and south-western advancement of offshoots of the nuclear Xhosa royal Tshawe chiefdom. The forward movement of the 'whites' was characterized by the destruction of San and Khoi social structures, considerable extermination of San, and amalgamation of Khoi in the form of clientship into a 'white' dominated plural frontier society.[4] Xhosa expansion to the detriment of Khoi and San was also accompanied by violence. San were eradicated and dispersed.

In this chapter we will discuss a network of reciprocal relations established between Khoi and Xhosa chiefdoms during the process of incorporation of Xhosa groups into Khoi chiefdoms. An attempt is made to reveal the manner in which Khoi and Khoi–Xhosa groups were aligned within Xhosa polities, and how the status of these groups fluctuated in the course of Xhosa expansion from about 1620 to the mid-1700s.

[3] C. R. Boxer (ed.) *The Tragic History of the Sea, 1589–1622* Cambridge 1959 pp. 217, 223. This work contains a narrative of Portuguese sailors of the *Sao Joao Baptista* which was wrecked near the mouth of the Keiskama River in 1622. The inhabitants near this river were Khoi according to description of their physical and cultural characteristics. Near the Bashee the sailors encountered a Bantu-speaking group who were pastoralists and agriculturalists. This evidence leads one to suggest that Xhosa occupied that region. Monica Wilson has illustrated from secondary sources that Bantu-speaking people resided in the north-eastern Cape long before the seventeenth century. See M. Wilson 'The Early History of the Transkei and Ciskei' *African Studies* XVIII No. 4 1959.

[4] See, for example, the classics by P. J. Van Der Merwe *Die Trekboer in die Geskiedenis van die Kaapkolonie (1657–1842)* Cape Town 1938; J. S. Marais *The Cape Coloured People, 1652–1937* Johannesburg 1937; and I. D. Macrone *Race Attitudes in South Africa* Johannesburg 1937. The most recent work is M. Whiting Spilhaus *South Africa in the Making, 1652–1806* Cape Town 1966.

The Xhosa and Khoi were culturally compatible.[5] They differed in physical make-up, language and mode of exploiting the land. Both had a high value orientation towards pastoralism which was expressed in an elaborate cattle-cult associated with the veneration of ancestors, and at times of great stress, a supreme being.[6] Unlike the Khoi, the Xhosa also practised slash-and-burn agriculture. Consequently, their division of labour differed. Khoi women were allowed to milk cattle, but in Xhosa society females were separated from the cattle sphere by ritual and taboo which restricted them to domestic and agricultural pursuits. The Xhosa and Khoi were also hunters, but the Xhosa never adopted the bow and arrow as the Khoi may have done from the San. Both made use of animal skin shields and a series of specialized assegais.[7]

Contact and interaction between Xhosa and Khoi was facilitated by the fissiparous tendency in the Xhosa social structure and by similarities in their respective social organization.[8] The Khoi were organized in patrilineal extended families, ideally polygynous, with initial uxorilocal residence. These basic social units formed part of a patrilineage. A number of patrilineages which traced descent to a common ancestor constituted a localized, exogamous patriclan. The Khoi 'chiefdoms' consisted of a series of shifting patriclan communities. These were loosely linked through the judicial and executive council which met periodically at the residence of the paramount chief, head of the senior lineage within the senior patriclan. The patriclan communities were hierarchically ranked according to their genealogical status. This was derived from the differentiation of time depths

[5] The ethnography of the Xhosa and Khoi is vast and varies in quality. For the Xhosa, the well-known works are J. H. Soga *Ama–Xosa: Life and Customs* Johannesburg 1930; T. B. Soga *Intlalo ka Xosa* Lovedale n.d. 1929; A. Kropf *Das Volk der Xosa–Kaffern im Ostlichen Sudafrika* Berlin 1889; and I. Schapera (ed.) *The Bantu Speaking Tribes of South Africa* London 1937. Khoi are described in I. Schapera *The Khoisan Peoples of South Africa* London 1930. I have also relied on relevant travel accounts, especially those in E. C. Godée-Molsbergen (ed.) *Reizen in Zuid–Afrika in de Hollandse Tijd* The Hague 4 vols. 1916–32.

[6] J. H. Soga op cit. pp. 145–82; Schapera *The Khoisan. . . .* Ch. III *passim*

[7] On the weaponry of the Khoi and Xhosa, see L. F. Maingard 'History of the Distribution of the Bow and Arrow in South Africa' *S.A.J.S.* XXIX 1932.

[8] The splitting of Xhosa chiefdoms has been analysed by Professor Hammond-Tooke. See W. D. Hammond-Tooke 'Segmentation and Fission in Cape Nguni Political Units' *Africa* XXXV No. 2 April 1965.

allocated to the act of splitting off from the most senior patriclan by a clan founder.[9]

The Xhosa were similarly organized in terms of family, lineage and clanship. Family residence, however, was strictly patrilocal. A Xhosa chiefdom consisted of a cluster of localized patriclan communities characterized by superordinate-subordinate status as determined by genealogical connections to the senior royal patriclan. Collectively they formed a single jural community with a degree of centralization enacted by local and national councils. Each community was expressed by the terms *ilizwe* (country) and *isizwe* (nation).[10]

Particularly among the Xhosa, and to a lesser degree among the Khoi, fission gave rise to a congeries of chiefdoms which acknowledged ranking similar to that within each chiefdom.[11] The nuclear chiefdom was recognized as the senior one in which the paramount chieftainship was embedded. Each chiefdom, however, remained independent of the senior one in terms of the regulation of public affairs. The complexity of the Xhosa polity is further evidenced by the principle of duality which permeated the entire structure. This principle in fact gave rise to the fission in Xhosa chiefdoms and segmentation in Xhosa patriclans and lineages and families. All Xhosa political and socio-economic units and the military organization consisted of two differentiated sections.[12] Specifically, all patriclans within a chiefdom were divided into so-called Right Hand lineages and Great House lineages. Each

[9] Insight into the structure of the extinct Cape Khoi chiefdoms may be derived from contemporary accounts. See, for example, P. Kolbe *The Present State of the Cape of Good Hope: Containing a Particular Account of the Several Nations of the Hottentots* second ed. London 1738; J. Schreyer 'Reise nach dem Kaplande und Beschreibung der Hottentotten 1669–1677' in *Reisebeschreibungen von Deutschen Beamten, und Kriegsleuten im Dienst der Niederlandischen West und Ost–Indischen Kompagnien 1602–1797* ed. S. L. l'Honoré Naber The Hague 1931; I. Schapera (ed.) *The Early Cape Hottentots, Described in the Writings of Dapper (1668) Willem ten Rhyne (1686) and Johannes Gulielmus de Grevenbroek (1695)* Cape Town 1933. Of special value for its detail is the journal of Jan van Riebeeck, Commander of the Dutch fort at Table Bay 1652–1662. Extracts from this journal which pertain to San, Khoi and Bantu-speaking peoples are in D. Moodie (ed.) *The Record, Or a Series of Official Papers Relative to the Condition and Treatment of the Native Tribes of South Africa* fasc. repr., Amsterdam 1960. For the ranking and splitting of Cape Khoi chiefdoms see ibid. pp. 215–16. A more detailed account is in J. van Riebeeck *Dagverhael* 3 vols. The Hague 1884–93 III (1649–62) pp. 401–4.

[10] Hammond-Tooke op. cit. pp. 155–7; G. P. Lestrade 'Some Notes on the Political Organization of Certain Xhosa-Speaking Tribes in the Transkeian Territories' *T.R.S.S.A.* XXIV No. 4 (1937) pp. 288–91.

[11] Hammond-Tooke loc. cit.

[12] Ibid. For the military organization see J. H. Soga op. cit. pp. 68–69.

lineage, whether Right Hand or Great House, was in turn composed of segmentary Right Hand and Great House lineages. Sons in families belonging to either the Right Hand or Great House segmentary lineages founded their own lineages. In time these were similarly ranked and segmented.

The Great House sections were supreme in status, and the heir to the chieftainship or clanheadmanship was produced by the most senior Great House lineage. In terms of succession to chieftainship the eldest representative of the senior lineage and clan of the Right Hand section acted as regent when a Great House heir had not yet attained his majority. The sections were politically co-equal at the local and national levels. Members of these juxtaposed divisions jointly formulated national and local policy and administered it. When a Right Hand section opposed a policy, or did not wish to relinquish a regency, fission occurred. Right Hand sections thereupon established a new chiefdom and acknowledged the parent chiefdom as superior in genealogical status only.[13]

Xhosa expansion initiated by fission brought about contact with Khoi chiefdoms. Moreover, the juxtaposition of the two divisions in Xhosa society had a bearing on the character of clientship of incorporated Khoi and Khoi–Xhosa, and the emergence of dependent chiefdoms composed of Khoi–Xhosa clients.

In addition to establishing the reciprocal relations created between the Xhosa and Khoi in geographically contiguous chiefdoms, and incorporation of Xhosa and Khoi, an attempt is also made in this chapter to indicate the connections between Khoi and Xhosa chiefdoms distantly removed. Moreover, linguistic evidence has been utilized to establish a category of relations between Khoi and Xhosa within Xhosa society. This is done to indicate Xhosa–Khoi contact prior to the 1600s, and to substantiate conclusions about the period under consideration reached from data derived from oral recorded traditions, official documents, and travellers' accounts. In the course of reconstructing the evidence, erroneous dating of the reigns of Xhosa chiefs has been partly revised. It is hoped that this paper will contribute to analyses of South African frontier zones, and that it will demolish some hoary myths about Xhosa and Khoi history.

[13] These were the underlying conditions as expressed in the oral traditions recorded by J. H. Soga. See his *The South-Eastern Bantu* Johannesburg 1931.

LINGUISTIC EVIDENCE

Comparative analyses of Khoi and Xhosa linguistic interrelationships indicate that interaction between Khoi and Xhosa peoples was intimate and of long duration.[14] The contact profoundly affected the phonemic system of the Xhosa language, one of the Nguni sub-group of Bantu languages. The influence of the Khoi phonemic system was largely confined to Xhosa consonants. Of some fifty-five consonants (matched by about twenty-eight Proto–Nguni consonants) of the Xhosa phonemic stock, twenty-one are primarily traceable to the Khoi sound system. Fifteen of these twenty-one are so-called 'click consonants'. As C. Meinhof first proved, they are of non-Nguni origin, for Proto–Bantu, Proto–Nguni and genetically related Bantu languages uninfluenced by Khoi (or San) do not contain such speech sounds.[15] The magnitude of the impact of Khoi–Xhosa contact is thus evident linguistically. The Khoi consonantal system converged with the Proto–Nguni consonantal system of the ancestors of the Xhosa, and produced a much more extensive third phonemic system which is contained in the Xhosa language of the present.[16]

About one-sixth of the Xhosa vocabulary is composed of words with clicks. A smaller section has non-click consonants also of Khoi origin. Many of these words are cognates of Khoi words, and they may be traced back into such Khoi languages as Kora and Nama.[17] The Khoi words 'borrowed' by Xhosa are significant from the historian's point of view. In addition to providing topographical information, they also point to socio-economic relationships between Khoi and Xhosa peoples. They cover both material and non-material aspects of Xhosa culture. Pettman[18]

[14] Carl Meinhof produced the first extensive linguistic analysis which showed that Xhosa contained much Khoi lexical material. See C. Meinhof 'Hottentotische Laute und Lehnworte im Kaffir' *Zeitschrift der Deutschen Morgenlandischen Gesellschaft* LVIII (1904); LIX (1905). A more recent attempt which takes into consideration the influence of San is L. W. Lanham 'The Proliferation and Extension of Bantu Phonemic Systems Influenced by Bushman and Hottentot' *Proc. Ninth Int. Congr. Ling., Cambridge, Mass., 1962* The Hague 1964.

[15] Ibid. 383; see p. 387 for charts of the Nguni phonemic system before Khoi contact and the system which emerged during contact. Meinhof op. cit. pp. 752–3, 759, tables and charts.

[16] Lanham op. cit. pp. 382, 388–9.

[17] Meinhof op. cit. pp. 54–69, 76–88; H. D. Anders 'Some Observations on Certain Sound Changes in Xhosa Derivatives of Khoisa' *S.A.J.S.* XXXIII pp. 921–5; Lanham loc. cit. Westphal op. cit. pp. 254–5.

[18] C. Pettman 'Hottentot Place Names' *S.A.J.S.* XVI (1920) pp. 334–52; XVIII (1922) pp. 372–82.

analysed European travellers' renditions of Xhosa and Khoi place names with clicks and concluded that at one time Khoi (and San) inhabited the Transkei as far as the Mzimvubu River. In a count from a Xhosa dictionary Meinhof found about fifty river names and six mountain names commencing with clicks. Several of the roots of these names have cognates in Nama.[19]

Khoi word roots and phonetic elements exist in Xhosa nomenclature denoting aspects of the socio-economic and ritual spheres. The 'cattle group'[20] contains terms for the variegated colour combinations of cattle which are derived from Khoi. The Xhosa word *inkomo* 'head of cattle' was derived from Khoi *goma-b* 'head of cattle'. It replaced the older form *inombe* (P-B. *-yombe; ngombe*) which has been retained in the *hlonipha* language of Xhosa women.[21] Some other Khoi derivatives are: K. *bi-b*, 'milk', Xh. *ubisi* 'milk'; K. */ga-b* 'grass', Xh. *inca* 'grass'; K. *gu-s* 'merino sheep', Xh. *igusha* having the same meaning.

The Xhosa 'religious group' contains numerous semantic correspondences of Khoi words. A few examples: K. *!gei-xa*, 'magic', Xh. *iqgira*, 'diviner'; K. *thui// koa-b*, 'supreme being', Xh. *uthixo*, 'supreme being'. A considerable number of Xhosa terms for diseases, calling upon the ancestors (K. */nuru*, 'to shout, call out', Xh. *uku-nqulu*), and procedures of animal sacrifice are of Khoi origin.[22]

Several deductions may be made from this linguistic evidence. Meinhof's and Lanham's hypotheses concerning the absence of clicks in Ur–Bantu and Proto–Nguni, respectively, permit us to state that terms for geographical features were in fact 'borrowed' from Khoi (and San) by the Xhosa as they and other Southern Nguni invaded the Khoi territories in the Transkei. By extension, Khoi and San occupied the regions between the Fish and the Mzimvubu Rivers prior to the entry of the Southern Nguni. Since

[19] Meinhof op. cit. pp. 85–86.

[20] L. F. Maingard first used this category. See L. F. Maingard 'The Linguistic Approach to South African Prehistory and Ethnology' *S.A.J.S.* XXXI (1934) pp. 132–4.

[21] J. A. Louw 'The Nomenclature of Cattle in S.E. Bantu Languages' *Com. Univ. South Afr.* C2 (1957) pp. 4–5; Westphal op. cit. pp. 253–6. The hlonipha vocabulary of Nguni married women consists of words in which phonemes are substituted systematically in order to avoid alliteration with the names of senior male affines, especially the father-in-law (HuFa). Many of the words are archaic.

[22] The words have been taken from Meinhof, Maingard, and Lanham. The orthography of Khoi differs from that of Xhosa in reference to clicks and other elements. K. ≠ : X. none; K. / : X. c; K. // : X. x; K. ! : X. q; K.kx? : X. r (i.e. glottalized affricative).

place names with clicks are scarce north-east of the Mzimvubu and in Natal, we may deduce that this area was occupied by the ancestors of the southern Nguni for a much longer period of time than the region south-west of that river. The extensive period of contact in the Transkei must have been intermittently violent. 'Xhosa' is derived from the Khoi verb stem meaning 'to destroy'. Trading relations between Xhosa and Khoi chiefdoms are suggested by the Xhosa and Khoi common word borrowing from Arabic for 'exchange article' and the intoxicating plant, 'dagga'.[23]

The Xhosa retained many Bantu forms for all religious institutions and ritual practices also denoted by Khoi 'borrowings', which indicates that these institutions and practices existed prior to contact with Khoi, and were not wholly adopted from Khoi culture.[24] Moreover, these retentions imply that, although the the Xhosa incorporated Khoi peoples, they remained in control of the regulation of public affairs. The Khoi-derived cognates in the Xhosa 'cattle group' suggest that Khoi were relegated to a socially inferior position in a patron–client relationship—the Xhosa being the patrons, and the Khoi their clients as cattle herders, messengers, envoys and so forth.[25] Important functions carried out by male Xhosa, such as cattle milking, must have remained the Xhosa's prerogative. The term *uku-senga*, 'to milk' was not replaced by a Khoi equivalent.[26] Indeed, the restriction

[23] Maingard op. cit. p. 138. He uses Kora vocabulary and states that the Khoi referred to the Xhosa as *//kosa*, 'angry men', 'the men who do damage'. Meinhof shows that the Nama employed the same term as the Kora for the Xhosa, but he does not elaborate further. See Meinhof op. cit. p. 85. That the term 'Xhosa' may be a Khoi derivative must not be dismissed, however. H. Lichtenstein who travelled through the Cape in the beginning of the nineteenth century alludes to the fact that 'Xhosa' is, indeed, a Khoi cognate. See H. Lichtenstein 'Bemerkungen uber die Sprachen der Sudafrikanische wilden Völkerstamme' *Allgemeines Archiv fur Ethnograpie und Linguistik* I (1808) p. 291 n. See also Nienaber op. cit. p. 537. In reference to trade, Meinhof gives the following Nama terms and corresponding Xhosa words; K. mari-b, valuable, money—X. imali, valuable, money (from the Arabic word for wealth); k. dakx?a–b—X. ukudakwa, to be in an intoxicated state; cf. Sotho: matakwane, hemp; (possibly from the Arabic word for tobacco). See Meinhof op. cit. pp. 61 ff.

[24] Maingard op. cit. pp. 137–8.

[25] Since the original Bantu stem is retained in the Xhosa *hlonipha* vocabulary, the ancestors of the Xhosa may have employed it prior to contact with Khoi. Moreover, the Nguni must have had cattle when entering South Africa from the north of the Limpopo river where 'inkomo' or other Khoi derivatives are not found. The Xhosa may have altered their terminology for cattle in the process of inter-action with Khoi in the form of a patron-client relationship, see Louw, op. cit. pp. 12, 15.

[26] C. Ehret has discussed Khoi–Bantu linguistic interrelationships pertaining to milking and cattle for Southern Africa in 'Cattle-keeping and Milking in Eastern and Southern

of Khoi-derived Xhosa words to socio-economic and ritual spheres of Xhosa culture expresses that Khoi participation was limited to that extent in Xhosa society.

We may infer further that the inferior social status of Khoi was balanced by their function in Xhosa religious institutions referred to by 'borrowed nomenclature'. The Xhosa must have attributed high status to what they believed to be the Khoi's ability to protect the land originally their own. The Khoi must therefore have participated in Xhosa society as diviners to prevent natural destruction, witchcraft and sorcery, to heal the sick, bring rain in times of drought, and to maintain the general welfare of the Xhosa chiefdoms.[27]

Linguistic evidence by itself is not sufficient to prove all the Xhosa–Khoi relations described. These aspects of interaction between Khoi and Xhosa arose from a process of incorporation of Khoi by Xhosa. Linguistic data does not show how this process took place, nor does it indicate the possibility of assimilation of Xhosa peoples by Khoi. It is difficult to determine the date of initial interaction from available data. On the basis of glottochronology, contact between Xhosa and Khoi first took place five to seven centuries ago, which seems probable as far as contact in the Transkei is concerned.[28] Dating the incorporation of Khoi at different periods of time at least prior to the 1600s is not possible at this stage. This would require the chronicling of sound shifts in Xhosa during its evolution from Proto–Nguni and this has not yet been attempted by linguists. When this is done, these sound shifts could be employed as measuring sticks to indicate at what period a Khoi word entered Xhosa—before or after any number of Xhosa sound shifts.

RECORDED ORAL TRADITIONS

A valuable source for data concerning seventeenth-century Xhosa–Khoi relations is the oral tradition imparted by John Knox

[27] Maingard op. cit. p. 135.

[28] Lanham op. cit. p. 383. He suggests that contact between Khoi and a probably homogeneous Nguni group took place for the first time between five and seven centuries ago, and that the ancestors of the Xhosa split off from the ancestors of the present-day Zulu speakers between five and six centuries from the present. His first assertion perhaps will not hold up to awaited archaeological evidence.

African History: Linguistic Evidence' *J.A.H.* VIII No. 1 (1967) pp. 4–17. The term *u(lu)bisi* may also be related to the common Bantu root **-viki*—'fresh'. Ibid. 14. See also Westphal op. cit. p. 135.

Bokwe to the German missionary, A. Kropf, in the late nineteenth century.[29] Intermarriage between the Xhosa paramountcy lineage of the royal Tshawe clan and a royal lineage or clan of a Khoi chiefdom occurred in the reign of paramount chief Togu.[30]

[29] Kropf op. cit. pp. 1–14. J. K. Bokwe and J. H. Soga have been the subjects of brief biographical studies. See D. P. Kunene and R. A. Kirsch *The Beginning of South African Vernacular Literature: A Historical Study and a Series of Biographies* Los Angeles 1967 pp. 12, 16–17.

[30] Togu appears sixth in the line of descent from Xhosa in J. H. Soga's genealogy of the Xhosa royal descent group. See J. H. Soga *S.E. Bantu* Xhosa genealogy facing ch. IX. The Sogas place Togu's death at 1687. Considering that an average reign lasted twenty-five years, they take this date as the starting point for dating the reigns of Xhosa paramount chiefs as far back as Xhosa. See T. B. Soga op. cit. p. 31; J. H. Soga op. cit. *passim*. Accordingly, Sikomo, father of Togu began his reign in 1650, but Ngcwangu, Sikomo's predecessor, commenced his in 1635 which makes his reign only fifteen years in duration. All reigns up to Xhosa are placed at twenty-five year intervals so that Xhosa supposedly ruled by 1535. The reigns of the chiefs Ngconde and Tshiwo who ruled after Togu are chronicled in a dissimilar manner. The dates of deaths are indicated as 1696 and 1702, but their births and beginning of their reigns are not shown. See T. B. Soga loc. cit. The Sogas base their figure of Togu's death on Theal's statement that Togu was alive in 1686. See G. M. Theal *History of South Africa, 1691–1795* London 1888 p. 214; T. B. Soga op. cit. p. 53; J. H. Soga op. cit. p. 95 f. T. B. Soga used this date and the ten reigns which followed after Togu in figuring the average length of a reign. See T. B. Soga loc. cit. 1686 has been a crucial date for the formulation of the chronology of Xhosa political history, but I cast doubt on its validity. Apparently, Theal assumed the date from data obtained from the accounts of Dutch shipwrecked sailors of the *Stavenisse* (1686) and the work of J. H. Grevenbroeck. (Grevenbroeck, in Schapera op. cit. pp. 121–3.) These are informative sources, for the sailors resided among the Xhosa for about twenty-two months and Grevenbroeck recorded their declarations. However, I found no mention of Togu in the accounts of the *Stavenisse* sailors. (Extracts of Log Book kept in the *Hooker Centaur* (1688), in Moodie, op. cit. pp. 424–28; Extracts of a Despatch of Simon van der Stel and Council to the Chamber XVII ibid. pp. 430–3. Extracts of Declaration of Capt. W. Knyff, . . . 25 March 1687, in ibid. pp. 415–16. Extract of Declaration of Ten Officers and Sailors . . . of the ship *Stavenisse* 2 March 1687 in ibid. pp. 417–18. For the complete versions in Dutch, see Godée-Molsbergen op. cit. III pp. 50–96.) The only reference to a chief whose name appears to resemble 'Togu' was made by G. Chenut, a French youth who was 'rescued' along with nineteen *Stavenisse* sailors by the *Centaur* in 1688. He was a member of the *Bode*, an English ship, and had been attacked by an Nguni group while he and some of the crew members were searching for a suitable landing place along the coast. 'Tokhe' a paramount chief who was also referred to as 'Sotopa' and 'Sesse', adopted him. (Grevenbroeck loc. cit.) After residing there for some time, he travelled to the sailors of the *Stavenisse* among the Xhosa. Theal assumed without question that 'Tokhe' was the equivalent of 'Togu'. I suggest that 'Tokhe' stands for 'Tahle', an Mpondo paramount chief (see J. H. Soga *South Eastern Bantu* Mpondo genealogy). It is possible that Tahle reigned during the 1680s. Tahle is shown as the great-grandfather of Faku on the genealogy. Faku must have been born about 1770, for he died in his nineties in 1867 (G. Calloway *Pioneers in Pondoland* p. 27). If we take an average reign of thirty years for the Mpondo chiefs who ruled during the time between Faku and Tahle, the latter's reign falls between about 1680–1710. On the basis of the evidence reconsidered here, I suggest that the dating of the reigns of Xhosa paramount chiefs should be

Bokwe states that Togu took the daughter of 'Ngosini (Nqosoro)', chief of 'the Lawo', as one of his minor wives, subsidiary to the Great Wife.[31] The son of this union was Ntinde who founded the Ntinde clan.[32]

From Togu's reign onward, reciprocally advantageous and disadvantageous connections were established between Khoi chiefdoms and Xhosa chiefdoms. The source of contact resulted from the fissiparous tendency in the Xhosa social structure. Togu begot Ziko, or Gandowentshaba, which was his praise name meaning 'Stamper-into-the-ground-of-the-enemy', as his Right Hand son, and Ngconde as the heir in the Great House. Ngconde's Great House heir for the paramount chieftainship was Tshiwo who was born after Ngconde's death. Mdange, who was Ngconde's Right Hand son, and Ntinde, hid Tshiwo and kept his birth a secret, for Gando (Ziko) had taken over the paramountcy.[33]

After Tshiwo's circumcision ceremony, Ntinde and Mdange proclaimed Tshiwo the legitimate paramount chief. Gando defeated Tshiwo in battle, and with his followers and captured cattle moved south-west from the Bashee River 'until the land of Nqobokazi was reached. Having arrived he built homesteads there beyond the Nxuba (Great Fish River)'.[34]

Pursuit of Gando brought Tshiwo further inland 'near Hinsati, the Khoi chief, near the Bushmen (San)'.[35] Plagued by the San,

[31] Kropf op. cit. 4. [32] Ibid. [33] Ibid.
[34] Ibid. [35] Ibid.

revised. The conflicting versions of the traditions provided by J. H. Soga and Bokwe are another reason for revision. According to Soga, Palo was born in 1702, the year of paramount Tshiwo's death. Tshiwo's father, Ngconde, son of Togu, supposedly died in 1695. Xhosa law of succession regulates that a G.H. heir succeeds to the paramountcy after the paramount's death. Tshiwo's reign must have been short indeed, especially when we take into consideration Bokwe's traditions which inform that Tshiwo was born *after* Ngconde's death. (Kropf op. cit. p. 8.) The reason for the discrepancy may be that the traditions of the Sogas are those of the Xhosa royal descent group, in which the paramount office was obtained. The ambiguity surrounding Tshiwo's birth and the dispute between Tshiwo and usurper Gandowentshaba, head of the R.H. section, may therefore have been deleted. Instead, the details of the dispute as found in Bokwe's traditions are transferred to the conflict between Palo and Gwali, son of Tshiwo. (J. H. Soga op. cit. 121 f.) Bokwe, on the other hand, reveals that Gwali was the R.H. son of Togu, and that he supported Ntinde and Gando against Tshiwo (Kropf op. cit. 9). The date of 1686 for Togu may have been acceptable to the Sogas, and the year of his death may have been manufactured by them in order to upgrade the reigns of Ngconde and Tshiwo so that they overlap and include the period of Gando's reign. A revised version of the reigns at thirty years per reign for the Xhosa chiefs in the seventeenth century would be: Togu *c.* 1590–1620; Ngconde *c.* 1620–1650 (Gandowentshaba *c.* 1650–1670); Tshiwo *c.* 1670–1701/2. (Xhosa's period would be *c.* 1420–1450.)

Tshiwo was forced to subdue Gando in battle. Gando's army was dispersed at the Fish on account of Tshiwo's military innovations, by dividing his army into the Left Hand and Right Hand sections and hand-to-hand combat. Gando was forced to flee into 'Hinsati's territory near the present day Somerset region'.[36] With Hinsati he created a military and political alliance, and gave his daughter in marriage to the Khoi chief. In return, Hinsati granted Gando part of his pasture grounds where he was permitted to establish his own chiefdom.[37]

Tshiwo had returned beyond the Bashee, but he experienced defection of his people to Gando. He decided to compel his rival to return by force of arms. This led to another migratory movement to Hinsati's country:

> Many rivers were crossed, until they came to Hinsati's country, where they found Gando revered as a chief with a large army. The entire country from there to Kobanqaba was dotted with many homesteads of the people of Gando.[38]

Negotiations between Tshiwo and Gando on the one hand, and with Hinsati on the other, led to carnage. Hinsati secretly wished the removal of the Xhosa from his land, while Gando's people no longer yearned for Tshiwo's country. Nevertheless, Gando and Tshiwo resolved their differences, and combined their forces to acquire Hinsati's immense herds. The agreement with the Khoi chief was breached by the abduction of his Xhosa wife, who, in the meantime, had given birth to Hinsati's heir Cwama. Hinsati was killed and his residence burnt. Cwama and his brother Sukwini retaliated with Khoi warriors. Violent battles followed as the Xhosa went into 'the heart of the country, where most of Hinsati's people lived, pillaged, destroyed, and burned until darkness fell over the land'.[39]

From this account may be discerned two processes by which Khoi–Xhosa interaction took place under varied conditions. During Togu's reign, a Xhosa lineage was the recipient in a marriage transaction with one or more Khoi chiefdoms around the Bashee River. Since the Xhosa in this case were the wife-takers and no information is given on marriage exchange, we may

[36] Ibid. [37] Ibid.

[38] Ibid. p. 9. The exact location is difficult to determine. 'Kobanqaba' may be *ikhobonqaba*, the Xhosa term for the Koonap River, a tributary of the Great Fish River; see A. Kropf *A Kaffir–English Dictionary* Lovedale 1899 p. 180.

[39] Kropf op. cit. p. 10.

assume that during Togu's reign these Khoi were in a dependent position. Conversely, Khoi royal lineages were recipients of Xhosa princesses when Xhosa were given sanction in Khoi territory.

Because Cwama came out in battle, Gando must have resided in Hinsati's territory for at least two decades. Gando's acknowledgement of Hinsati's ownership of the land occupied by his Xhosa refugees was assured through the practice of Xhosa wife-giving. Xhosa were not politically assimilated by the Khoi as indicated by Gando's right to maintain his chieftainship over his people in assigned Khoi territory. The reference to the countryside being 'dotted' with homesteads of 'the people of Gando' suggests territorial separation between the two peoples. This, however, does not necessarily imply a lack of social cross-cutting ties by intermarriage between the two peoples.

Assimilation of Xhosa by Khoi occurred when leaderless Xhosa refugees entered Khoi chiefdoms. This is exemplified by the incorporation of Xhosa refugees into Hinsati's chiefdom, initially caused by the political developments in Xhosaland after the return of Gando and Tshiwo. The paramount chief extended the political power of the Great House section of his Tshawe royal clan by stripping the Right Hand section under Gando from its noble status through inter-clan marriage. Tshiwo married Gando's sister, and this breach of the exogamous clan marriage rule rendered Gando's lineage and clan Kwayi, or Commoners. In response to this decline in social status many of the Kwayi clan abandoned Gando and returned to Hinsati's land to rejoin the Xhosa who had remained.[40]

From the union of these Xhosa with Khoi emerged the Gonaqua chiefdom under Cwama. The Xhosa refugees were physiologically and culturally assimilated into Cwama's chiefdom. Subsequent generations spoke a mixture of Khoi and Xhosa, with Khoi predominating.[41] This hydridization can only be

[40] Ibid. p. 9; J. H. Soga op. cit. p. 141.

[41] Travellers who visited the Gonaqua in the eighteenth century point this out. See, for example, A. Sparrman *A Voyage to the Cape of Good Hope . . . Chiefly into the Country of the Hottentots and Caffres . . . 1772 to 1776* tr. G. Forster 2 vols. London 1785 II pp. 6–7; F. Le Vaillant *Travels from the Cape of Good Hope into the Interior Parts of Africa* 2 vols. London 1790 II pp. 1–3. The presence of bilingualism in Gonaqua society may have influenced the Gonaqua Khoi dialect. Sparrman especially refers to the presence of Xhosa and persons of mixed descent among the Gonaqua (Sparrman op. cit. pp. 7, 27).

accounted for by reciprocal marriage between the incoming Xhosa and Cwama's Khoi. The children of polygenous marriages between Khoi males and Xhosa females learned Xhosa from their mothers and incorporated it into the Khoi language while participating in Khoi society external to the immediate family. Khoi prevailed as the predominating element of the Gonaqua's language because the Xhosa language was not incorporated as much by offspring of marriages between Khoi women and Xhosa men.[42]

The Gonaqua retained their Khoi culture. They remained exclusively pastoral. They did not adopt the Xhosa practice of circumcision in the initiation ceremonies of young men, and continued to employ the traditional Khoi bow and arrow, weapons which were never used by the Xhosa.[43]

Members of the Gonaqua chiefdom located between the Kei and Keiskama were incorporated by the expanding Xhosa chiefdoms during the early 1700s. The Mndange, Ntinde, and several other clans split from the Tshawe nuclear chiefdom, and crossed the Kei River. They were followed by the Tshawe under Palo, Tshiwo's successor.[44] By the middle of the eighteenth century all of these chiefdoms were located between the Kei and the Keiskama Rivers.[45] In the process, the Gonaqua chiefdom was subjected. Remnant Gonaqua clans regrouped themselves between the

[42] Dr Lanham refers to the polygynous family and bilingualism as elements which gave rise to the incorporation of Khoi consonants into Xhosa. He does not deal with Gonaqua or other Khoi groups strongly influenced by Xhosa. Since the Gonaqua remained predominantly Khoi in culture, I assume, at this stage that the Xhosa who were assimilated into the Gonaqua's ancestors' social structure were outnumbered. See Lanham op. cit.

[43] Ibid. 159; Vaillant pp. 40–118.

[44] J. H. Soga op. cit. p. 120 f.

[45] The royal residence of the Ntinde chiefdom was situated in an area east of the Keiskama River, between the Immozani River and the Keiskama estuary. Gwali, chief of the Gwali chiefdom, which had split from the Tshawe chiefdom in the early 1700s lived north of the Ntinde on the Twecu River, a tributary of the Chalumna River; the residence of Gcaleka, heir to Palo, was on the Kwenurha River and its tributaries. Farther inland from the coast than these chiefdoms were the Mdange, under chief 'Machola', situated on the Nahoon River and its tributary, the Cabongo. Paramount chief Palo resided at the sources of the Chalumna River, and near the Izeli River. See C. A. Haupt 'Journal Gehouden . . . op de togt door den Vaandrig August Frederick Beutler (1752)' in Godée Molsbergen op. cit. Vol. III *passim*. See also V. S. Forbes *Pioneer Travellers of South Africa. A Geographical Commentary upon Routes, Records, Observations and Opinions of Travellers at the Cape 1750–1800* Cape Town 1965 p. 146, Maps No. 5 6a b p 7; *idem* 'Beutler's Expedition into the Eastern Cape, 1752' *Archives Year Book for South African History* 1953 16th year, No. 1 pp. 297–303 and maps facing pp. 298, 300.

Keiskama and the Fish Rivers.[46] Those who remained were placed in a subservient relationship to the Xhosa. They served as cattle herders and servants of Mndange and Ntinde soldiers in military cattle outposts along the Keiskama.[47] In times of war, they functioned as soldiers and envoys of the Xhosa chiefs.[48] The Gonaqua clients did not constitute a caste, for reciprocal intermarriage was frequent.[49]

Furthermore, outstanding Gonaqua personalities acquired administrative positions by rendering military services to the juxtaposed Great House and Right Hand sections of the Xhosa chiefdom. Apparently, Xhosa chiefs effectively mobilized the support of Gonaqua lineage groups by allowing them to be separately administered by Gonaqua headmen and personal Gonaqua servants at royal residences. During the succession struggles between Tshiwo and Gando, Palo and Gwali (1720?), and between Gcaleka and Rarabe a generation later (1740?), personal officials of the paramount chiefs were bestowed with chieftainship offices over Gonaqua and related Xhosa clans.[50]

Out of this development emerged the Gqunukwebe chiefdom which was structured similarly to Xhosa chiefdoms proper. It separated itself from the Xhosa chiefdom clusters, as did other Xhosa chiefdoms. After the defeat of Gwali, the Gqunukwebe chief Zaka fled with his followers.[51] By the 1760s the Gqunukwebe reached the 'Hoengeiqua' chiefdom between the Bushman and the Fish Rivers. There they were granted territory by the Hoengeiqua in exchange for cattle.[52]

[46] Haupt op. cit.
[47] Ibid. p. 310.
[48] Ibid.
[49] Ibid. p. 311.
[50] J. H. Soga op. cit. pp. 93–95, 116–19. Soga relates that Kwane, a commoner counsellor appointed by Tshiwo, gained autonomy from the paramount chief by acquiring Xhosa clients who had been accused of witchcraft. Kwane hid them among the Gonaqua. In time the offspring of these Xhosa and Gonaqua women increased his following. Tshiwo recognized Kwane's growing influence and gained his allegiance as a client through patronage expressed by his legitimization of Kwane's leadership over his clients. These came to be called Gqunukwebe. The tradition was taken verbatim from the work of Cowper Rose who visited the Gqunukwebe in the 1820s. See C. Rose *Four Years in South Africa* London 1829 pp. 148–50. For the subsequent formation of the Gqunukwebe and their role in the dispute over the paramount chiefship between Palo and Gwali, see Col. Richard Collins, 'Supplement to the Relations of a Journey into the Country of the . . . Caffre People (1809)' in Moodie op. cit. part V, pp. 9, 10.
[51] Ibid.; Soga *Ama-Xosa* . . . p. 24.
[52] Soga op. cit. p. 119; Collins loc. cit.

DOCUMENTARY EVIDENCE: KHOI–XHOSA RELATIONS IN CAPE TRADE NETWORKS

Prior to the arrival of the Dutch at Table Bay in 1652, the coastal Khoi chiefdoms of the western Cape acquired metals and glass beads from crews of European ships and shipwrecks.[53] Such goods may also have been obtained in the interior. The information gathered by J. van Riebeeck suggests that the Chochoqua received iron, copper, and beads via the Nama Khoi from the Bantu-speaking Tlhaping Tswana. Moreover, the Chochoqua apparently were the middlemen in a barter trade in these metals and cattle, which they conducted with their eastern Khoi neighbours. The reliance of Khoi chiefdoms east of the Cape periphery on the Tswana metal producers and Chochoqua middlemen was clearly evident in the 1650s. An envoy of the Chainouqua chiefdom located thirty days inland in an easterly direction from Table Bay, informed the Dutch about:

> . . . a certain great Lord, Emperor or King, who is the Ruler over all those Cape Tribes, whom they [Khoi]call Chobona, living, very far off in the interior, rich in gold, which they [Khoi] call Chory, and say that they find [it] in the sand—and coin into money as large as the palm of the hand and larger . . .[54]

The Chainouqua indicated that the Chochoqua maintained an

[53] Goodwin op. cit.

[54] Van Riebeeck. Entry for 31 October 1657 in Moodie op. cit. p. 110. The personification may be an indication of the difficulties encountered by Khoi interpreters in translating Khoi expression for polities and groups into Dutch. 'Chobona' (*kowona*) was one of the Nama and Cape Khoi terms for Bantu-speaking people (Nienaber op. cit. pp. 212–13). 'Chobona' were definitely Bantu. They were also described as 'planting several kinds of garden stuff, . . . speaking a language different from that spoken by the tribes nearer this Cape' and 'living in stone houses with beams'. (Van Riebeeck, in Moodie loc. cit.) 'Chori' (*|ori–b* or *|uri–b*), the Cape Khoi collective term for 'metal' (Nienaber op. cit. pp. 537–8) was erroneously interpreted as 'gold'. This may be attributed to van Riebeeck's association of gold with Bantu-speaking peoples. He arrived at this view from the descriptions of the Empire of Mwenemwetapa in the journals of the J. van Linschoten East India expedition (1596). The journals of P. Cruythoff and P. van Meerhoff (1661) inform that the Nama were visited at intervals by the 'Brigoudy' or 'Brickje' who were also referred to as 'Chobona'. They brought iron, copper, and beads which they in turn had obtained from the 'real Chaboners' called the 'Chori–Eyqua'. Since *|ori-* means 'metal' and ‡ *ei–s* means 'ore' we may infer that they were the 'metal ore people'. (See the relevant extracts in Moodie op. cit. pp. 230–4, 235–6, 236–7. The Dutch versions are in Godée-Molsbergen op. cit. I, see especially pp. 63–64, 93). 'Brigoudy' and 'Brickje' may stand for 'Brikwa' (goat people), the Cape Khoi and Nama term for the Tlhaping. See, for example L. F. Maingard, 'Brikwa and the Ethnic Origins of the Bathlaping' *S.A.J.S.* XXX (1927) pp. 597–621; Nienaber op. cit. pp. 219–20, 224. The Tlhaping chiefdom dates back to the beginning of the seventeenth century. See F. J. Language 'Herkoms en Geskiedenis van die Tlhaping' *African Studies* I No. 1 (1942) pp. 116–18.

intermediary position in the Tswana–Khoi trade diffusion network by force:

This Chobona has . . . a General (Veltheer) over these tribes [those in the Cape peninsula] to keep them in subjection, and to oblige them always to acknowledge Chobona for their sovereign, and to punish the rebellious by making war upon them. The Veltheer is the same as the Saldanhars [Dutch term for the Chochoqua at that time] in dress and language, and is called *Kochoqua* [Chochoqua], consisting of two powerful armies (*heyrlegers*) or hordes, second of which is named Gorona [!*gora-na*: Kora] and both have no other employment than making war upon the rebellious for the purpose stated. . . .[55]

The Dutch became the alternative source of copper, brass, and beads for the Chochoqua and Chainouqua. The latter particularly took advantage of the Netherlanders' desire to reach Khoi and Bantu chiefdoms in the hinterland for cattle and precious metals.[56] On several occasions the Chainouqua paramount chief, Sousoa, in the early 1660s proclaimed that he was well acquainted with 'Chobona'. To make himself the middleman, a politically and economically subordinate relationship was established between his chiefdom and the 'Hamcunqua'. They constituted one of the most populous, and cattle-rich chiefdoms in the eastern interior of the Cape, and provided the Chainouqua and other more western Khoi chiefdoms with dagga.[57] Through the Hamcunqua the Chainouqua also established a connection with the Chobona, for the Hamcunqua resided to the north-west of these people and were their close allies.[58] These Chobona had struck a reciprocal alliance with the Chainouqua by the process of 'bride-giving'.

[55] Van Riebeeck. Entry for 31 October 1657, in Moodie op. cit. p. 110.

[56] Ibid. Entries for 21–22 September 1660, pp. 214–18; 1–26 October 1660, pp. 219–20; 16 December 1660, pp. 224–5.

[57] Ibid. 215. By the early 1660s the Chainouqua received tribute from the Chochoqua and other western Cape Khoi chiefdoms. This was done in order 'to show the respect which they owe to the neighbour and representative [Sousoa, paramount of the Chainouqua] of the highest king, said to be the Hancumquar, who, indeed, also resides in mat huts, but never migrates from place to place, and whose subjects subsist, independently of breeding cattle, by the cultivation of the valuable plant Dacha, which stupefies the brain . . .; and of which these tribes [western Cape Khoi] are consequently very fond. Ibid. The chief of the 'Hancumquas' was termed the 'khoebaha' [*khuba-ha*]. According to Van Riebeeck's interpreters: 'he is the chief lord of all the kings and potentates, for such is the signification of the word; for *khoe* means a high mountain, rich, fortunate, a king; and *baha*, the superlative, the highest of all, to whom all must show submission'. (Ibid.) See also Nienaber op. cit. p. 410.

[58] Van Riebeeck *Dagverhael* Entry for 10 November 1660 pp. 440–1; A. J. Böeseken (ed.) *Resolusies van die Politieke Raad, Deel I. 1651–1669* Cape Town 1957 p. 248.

A Khoi woman, who had been obtained by the Chief of the Chobona from a Khoi chiefdom, had been presented to Sousoa's envoy.[59]

The Chobona with whom the Chainouqua were affiliated in the 1660s via the Hamcunqua were not Tswana. They may be identified through a comparison of information on 'Hamcunqua' and 'Chobona' imparted by Chainouqua to the Dutch with accounts of travellers and shipwrecked sailors who traversed the eastern Cape two decades later.

In 1687 one 'Inqua Kamsaku' sent envoys to the Dutch at Table Bay for purposes of opening up a trade in cattle and sheep.[60] An expedition found this Khoi chief and his people residing at the foot of the Camdeboo and Sneeuwberg, and along the upper reaches of the Kariega River.[61] The locality of the Inqua corresponds with Van Riebeeck's geographical data on the 'Hamcunqua'. The Kariega is situated north-east of the Cape periphery. From that area the river indeed does appear to be 'far in the interior, half-way betwixt the two seas' which was the position of the Hamcunqua according to Van Riebeeck's Chainouqua informants.[62]

The Inqua may further be identified as the 'Hamcunqua' by a brief analysis of the Dutch rendition of the names of the Khoi

[59] Van Riebeeck. Entry for 31 October 1657, Entry for 1 November 1657 in Moodie op. cit. pp. 110, 111. The envoy was Chainhantima. He had '. . . a wife who was brought up in the house of Chobona, and was therefore a great friend of his; and he said, that his wife wore ornaments of gold in her ear and upon her neck and fingers'. (Ibid. p. 110.) The process of the establishment of a politically economic dependent relationship between the 'Chobona' and the Chainouqua is cast in this light: '. . . the frequently mentioned wife of this chief of the Chaynouquas [Chainhantima] was no native of the country of the Choboners, but had been taken from these tribes [Cape Khoi] by Chobona, and she was a great lady, brought up in his house as a child, and given to the chief as a wife, which seems to be esteemed extraordinary, as it is a mark of great favour when any one gets a wife out of Chobona's house; it is thus he attaches these tribes to his interest'. (Ibid. p. 111.) She was killed by the Chochoqua who attacked Chainhantima and a party of Chainouqua as they were escorting her on the way to the Dutch fort to open up trade relations with the Bantu-speaking people. (Ibid. Entry for 31 November 1660 p. 152.)

[60] Commander Simon van der Stel, Journal entry, 4 February 1687 in Moodie op. cit. p. 415; A. J. Böeseken *Resolusies van die Politieke Raad, Deel III, 1681–1707* Cape Town 1961 pp. 198–9.

[61] Ensign Isaq Schrijver 'Dagh-register, gehouden bij den Vaandrig Isaq Schrijver op sijn landtogt na de Inquahase Hottentots, beginnende den 4 January en eijndigende den 10 April 1689' in Godée-Molsbergen op. cit. III pp. 108–10. E. E. Mossop (ed.) *Journals of the Expedition of the Honourable Ensign Olof Bergh (1682–1683) and the Ensign Isaq Schrijver (1689)* Cape Town 1931 map and pp. 230–1.

[62] Van Riebeeck. Entry for 21 September 1660 in Moodie op. cit. p. 215.

chiefdom and its chief. 'Hamcunqua' was Van Riebeeck's transliteration of *≠am-!khukwa*. '*≠am-*' means 'upper, above'; '*!khu-*' is the word stem for 'rich, wealthy, fortunate chief'; and '*-kwa*' is a common plural suffix of a noun denoting a group of people.[63] 'Chief' and 'wealth' were coterminous. The *≠am-!khukwa* were therefore 'the people of the superior chief, or greater wealth' and the word was a collective term applied to the *≠am-!khukwa* chiefdom. The chief of the Inqua was referred to as 'Hijkon' by the Dutch.[64] The proper spelling should be *Gei!khu(b)* in extinct Western Cape Khoi.[65] *//kai !khu(b)* means 'great chief'. Thus, the *≠am !khukwa* (Hamcunqua), 'people of the superior chief, or greater wealth' and the *!khukwa* [Inqua?] or *//kai !khukwa* (people of Hijkon) are synonymous. The Chainouqua and Western Cape Khoi chiefdoms considered the *≠am !khukwa* to be greater in wealth, and therefore attributed prestige to them which was expressed by referring to them in the superlative.[66]

The 'Chobona' referred to by the Chainouqua in connection with the 'Hamcunqua' were the Xhosa. The Hamcunqua were described as residing north-west of the Chobona. This was correct for 'Inqua' (*!khukwa*), pointing in a south-south-eastern direction, told members of the expedition that the 'Kobuqua' dwelled along the seacoast.[67] Both -na and -kwa are plural prefixes in Khoi, and the Dutch used 'Ch-' and 'K-' indiscriminately. Hence, the 'Chobona' and 'Kobuqua' are equivalent in meaning, denoting a Bantu-speaking people. Moreover, this 'Inqua' related that the Gonaqua, from whom his people obtained dagga, bordered the 'Kobuqua'.[68] The shipwrecked sailors of the *Stavenisse* (1686) who resided among the Xhosa for several years confirm the validity of the Inqua's information. In their endeavours to reach Table Bay, they left Xhosaland and entered the Gonaqua chiefdom under Cwama (Gamma).[69] They report that the Gonaqua

[63] Nienaber op. cit. pp. 330, 349–50.
[64] Schrijver op. cit. *passim*. Variants are Heykon, Hencon, and others.
[65] Nienaber op. cit. p. 291.
[66] See note 57 on page 161.
[67] Schrijver op. cit. p. 110. See also, M. W. D. Jeffreys 'The Cabonas' *African Studies XVI* No. 2 1967.
[68] Ibid. p. 11.
[69] A. J. Kind van Maaslandsluys *et al.* 'Relaas over de gestrande fluyt *Stavenesse*' in Godée-Molsbergen op. cit. p. 61. These shipwrecked sailors contacted Gonaqua traders in Xhosaland, '. . . and having obtained permission from them to journey in their accompaniment to the land of the Maghanen [X. amaGona (Gonaqua)], their [the Gonaqua traders'] king being called Gamma [Cwama], bordering on the Inquase Hottentots and known at the Cape as being the most distant.' (Ibid.)

obtained dagga for the Xhosa in exchange for copper rings and beads. The Gonaqua in turn bartered the dagga with the Inqua.[70] From these accounts it is thus clearly evident that the Kobuqua were the Xhosa. The Chainouqua related that the Hamcunqua (who have been identified as the Inqua i.e. *!khukwa*) were in affiliation with the 'Chobona', and, on the basis of the evidence above, we are permitted to state that the Xhosa were implied.

This evidence suggests that there existed in the mid-seventeenth century a trade connection coupled with a political alliance between the Xhosa and the Chainouqua Cape Khoi chiefdom. This reciprocal relationship reflects attempts by Khoi and Xhosa to regulate the flow of goods in their trading system. Collectively, the Xhosa, the intermediary Khoi chiefdoms and the Chainouqua, formed what may be termed the Xhosa–Khoi trade diffusion network. The Table Bay region functioned as the centre of diffusion of Dutch copper, brass, beads, and other products that ranked high in Khoi and Xhosa values. At the other end of the network the Xhosa provided the diffusion centre of dagga. Between these two centres the Inqua (Hamcunqua) chiefdom was located. This chiefdom was vital in the western flow of dagga and the eastern flow of metal and beads. The Inqua obtained copper plates from the Khoi Orange River chiefdoms and possibly from the Tswana.[71] They exchanged these articles with the Gonaqua and Xhosa for the Xhosa grown dagga.[72] The latter filtered via the Inqua through the successively contiguous chiefdoms between them and the Cape peninsula.[73]

In the east, up to the eighteenth century, barter between the Inqua, Gonaqua and Xhosa was well regulated. Both Gonaqua and Xhosa periodically visited the Inqua on barter expeditions.[74]

[70] Ibid.; Schrijver loc. cit.

[71] Ibid.; Schrijver was informed by the 'Inqua' that 'towards the N[orth] lie yet three other nations called Glij, Brij, and Blij, from whom the Inqua barter flat and thin copper plates, which they again trade off to the Kubuquas and Namaquas; finally there is yet another type of people known to them called Briqua, who are man-eaters'.

[72] Ibid. pp. 110, 111; Haupt op. cit. p. 308.

[73] The Khoi chiefdoms located between the ≠ am !khukwa (Inqua) and the Chainouqua in the late seventeenth century were the 'Hessequa' 'Gouriqua' and 'Attaqua'. The Hessequa who resided east of the Chainouqua were believed to be '. . . the ones [who procure?] real dacha from the Hamcunquas'. (Van Riebeeck. Entry for 27 September 1660, in Moodie op. cit. p. 217.) J. Cruse 'Dagverheal . . .' in Godée Molsbergen op. cit. VI p. 128 f. Cruse travelled through the lands of the Gouriqua and Hessequa in 1668. The Gouriqua told him that the Attaqua had copper and iron. Dagga seems to have been the primary article of exchange in the metal and cattle barter trade.

[74] Schrijver loc. cit.

Barter between the Gonaqua and Xhosa was arranged at regular intervals. From fifty to one hundred Gonaqua men, women, and children periodically visited the Xhosa at a specific market place. There they exchanged copper and beads, obtained from the Inqua, for dagga.[75] The Xhosa apparently benefited from this barter system, for an abundance of beads and copper (and iron) was found among them by the shipwrecked sailors. The Xhosa chiefs, however, did not have a monopoly over these goods. Even in times of war conducted against the Gonaqua and Inqua the chief's prerogative was the cattle that were robbed, whereas the soldiers were allowed to retain their loot of copper, beads, and iron.[76]

The Xhosa–Khoi trade diffusion network diminished in size in proportion to European stock-farmers' expansion into the eastern Cape during the eighteenth century. The stock-farmers supplanted the Dutch officials at the fort in barter trade with Khoi chiefdoms in the interior, although the Company prohibited such activity by proclamation.[77] In the first two decades of the eighteenth century they established direct contact with the Gonaqua and Xhosa. Periodically, robbing bands of European stock-farmers, their 'mixed' sons and Khoi guides entered Gonaqua and Xhosa domains, shot people at random, collected their booty and returned.[78] However, during the following four decades as the stock-farmers crossed the Gamtoos Rivers and reached the Camdeboo, trading expeditions to the Xhosa were regulated by Xhosa chiefs and cattle were obtained in return for copper, iron, and beads.[79]

[75] Kind van Maaslandsluys loc. cit.

[76] Extracts of Log Book kept in the *Hooker Centaur*. Entry for 11 February 1668, in Moodie op. cit. p. 427; the *Stavenisse* sailors were picked up by the *Centaurus* near the Kei River on 8 January 1688.

[77] Spilhaus op. cit. A. J. Böeseken 'Die Nederlandse Kommissarisse en die 18de Eeuse Samelewing aan die Kaap' *Archives Year Book for South African History* 1944, 7th Year pp. 73–80.

[78] See, for example, Böeseken op. cit. III p. 390. In 1700 the D.E.I. Company's Political Council issued a proclamation which lifted the ban on trade between free burghers and Khoi with the stipulation that the burghers were not to take the Khoi's cattle by force. It is evident that some of the frontier cattle-farmers did not comply to the Council's restrictions. Repeatedly it was brought to the Council's attention that burgher parties 'of the worst kind' travelled 'more than 100 miles' beyond the established boundaries, '. . . and that in the far distant nations', such as the 'Horisons', 'Genocquaas', and 'Great Kaffers' they 'rob cattle, murder, and beat to death, steal and disperse'. (Ibid.). See also Böeseken op. cit. p. 75.

[79] See, for example, Report of Landdrosts and Commissioned Heemraden of Stellenbosch and Swellendam 7 February 1770, in Moodie op. cit. III pp. 1–4; Extract of Resolution of Council 13 February 1770, in ibid. pp. 5–6; Proclamation, 26 April

The disintegration of Khoi chiefdoms in response to 'European' expansion has been attributed to smallpox, spirits, and the stock-farmers' monopoly of fire-arms.[80] The inequities inherent in the barter trade should also be emphasized. In exchange for metals, beads, tobacco, and other goods the intermediary Khoi chiefdom submitted its cattle.[81] These were not replaced in sufficient numbers in a similar trade with other Khoi chiefdoms farther in the interior. Dagga seems to have been the most important exchange commodity for metals and beads between Khoi.[82] As a result the pastoral economy was undermined, and the Khoi social structure, which was based upon it, crumbled.

Members of Khoi patriclans either entered stock-farmer society as servants or joined the San. This stage of decay created repercussions among the interior Khoi chiefdoms, as roaming bands of Khoi and San plundered their cattle stock.[83] Khoi chiefdoms such as the Gouriqua and Attaqua retreated farther north to the sources of the Gouritz and Olifants Rivers.[84]

As the stock-farmers and Xhosa advanced from opposite directions during the first half of the eighteenth century, the process of disruption and retreat repeated itself. A member of the D.E.I. Company's official expedition which journeyed through the eastern Cape in 1752 gave a revealing summation of the chaos between the Gamtoos and the Bushman Rivers. He states that Khoi:

With the exception of the Damaqua, Damasonqua, and Hoengeiqua ... whom we met on the way, did not know of what nation they were, they merely called themselves by the names of rivers along which the same resided and also at times land Khoi ['land men']. All of these Khoi who prior to this time [1752] were rich in cattle have been

[80] For the most recent summation, see Spilhaus op. cit.
[81] The best detailed account of Dutch–Khoi trade in the 1650s and 1660s is in Goodwin op. cit. pp. 8–13, 17–20f. For the following century see the edited works of Moodie and Böeseken.
[82] Schrijver op. cit. *passim*. Cruse op. cit. p. 128f.
[83] Schrijver op. cit. pp. 112–17. From this account it is evident that the 'Inqua' 'Hessequa' and 'Attaqua' suffered from continuous cattle-raiding by San and Khoi bands during the 1680s. See also Haupt op. cit. p. 290f. *passim*.
[84] Haupt op. cit. p. 291.

1770, in ibid. pp. 6–7. These documents pertain to the curtailment of cattle-farmers west of the Gamtoos River and the prohibition of trade with Khoi and Xhosa. They contain relevant historical background of trading relations between the whites, Khoi and Xhosa during the half-century previous to that time.

robbed of all of them by the San. Through wars which they fought with each other and against the Caffers [Xhosa] they were partly decimated or otherwise dispersed by another. . . .[85]

In response remnant clans joined together as hunting and gathering bands.[86]

Chiefdoms which were located between the Bushman and Keiskama, such as the Damaqua and Gonaqua, established interdependent alliances with each other through intermarriage between royal lineages to combat the San, and at times, the Xhosa.[87] The most powerful among this 'loose confederacy' was the Hoengeiqua [!khugeikwa?] chiefdom which was formed from Khoi clan remnants by Dorha (or Ruyter), a runaway Cape slave.[88] In spite of the intermittent animosity shown by this confederacy to the Xhosa, their perpetuation as a separate entity was nevertheless dependent on the Xhosa. Attacks by San rendered their position insecure and they had no recourse but to send many of their herds to the Xhosa for protection.[89]

CONCLUSION

Interaction between the differentially ranked components of the Xhosa chiefdoms and Khoi patriclan communities was characterized by patterns of varied relationships. These relationships were formed in the process of the pursuit of political and economic interests shared by the Xhosa and Khoi royal agnatic descent groups. The highest office-holders of the Xhosa and Khoi descent groups seem to have been linked by affinal ties, especially during the first half of the seventeenth century. The practice of bride-giving was the mode by which the descent groups concluded political and military alliances, regulated trade, and allocated territory. I was unable to uncover data from the limited available sources to stipulate the conditions under which group, Xhosa or

[85] Ibid. p. 292.

[86] Ibid.

[87] Ibid. p. 286.

[88] Ibid. pp. 287–8; the account of Ruyter's efforts in joining together various Khoi remnant groups is in Sparrman op. cit. 158f.

[89] Ruyter seems to have been in close contact with Bange, chief of the Ntinde, see Haupt op. cit. His followers informed the expedition that '. . . they were not Gonaquas but that they were of the Hoengeyquas nation, and that all of the first mentioned resided among the Caffers and served them, further that he Ruyter had placed his cattle among the Caffers in order to save them from being robbed by the Bushmen, and lastly that his country reached from Damasonqua land up to the Chys Chamma'. (Ibid.)

Khoi, enjoyed both superior status and a favourable position in regulating similar interests during the reigns of Togu and Ngconde. However, there is sufficient evidence which shows that a Xhosa group entered into an initially symbiotic relationship with a Khoi chieftain after fission occurred in the Tshawe chiefdom.

The case of Gando and Hinsati provides the example. Territory was granted by the Hinsati Khoi and a military alliance was concluded. Gando submitted a Xhosa bride to the accommodating Khoi chief, and, apparently, he was allowed to maintain an autonomous chiefdom. Thus under conditions of fission of the Tshawe chiefdom at that time, Xhosa groups apparently attributed higher status to the leaders of a Khoi chiefdom because they were dependent on them for land and defence. At least at the level of the royal lineages the two peoples were tied by kinship and both seemed to have persisted as separate entities. Assimilation of Xhosa into Khoi society occurred as a consequence of political change in the Tshawe chiefdom. They appear to have voluntarily entered Khoi society as outcasts and refugees.

By the middle of the seventeenth century, Khoi chiefdoms were dependent on Xhosa chiefdoms. Their dependency resulted from the rapid westward expansion of the Xhosa offshoots and the Tshawe chiefdom and the encroachment of cattle-farmers from the east. During this period contact between Xhosa and Khoi chiefdoms seems to have been accompanied by conquest and incorporation of Khoi and 'mixed' Gonaqua into Xhosa society. As in the case of the Khoi's assimilation of Xhosa, more evidence is needed to analyse in detail the manner in which Khoi and Gonaqua obtained membership into the Xhosa lineage structure. Perhaps they attached themselves to the lineage of their captors and as clients owed allegiance to the captor's clan head and chief. The Xhosa patrons may have formed a separate set of lineages, subordinate in status, composed of offspring of their Gonaqua and Khoi wives.

The system of patron-clientship seems to have played an important role in the competition for the paramount chiefship office among the members of the differentiated segments of the Xhosa Great House royal lineage. Xhosa chiefs and their lineage mates sought to patronize Gonaqua clients to increase their following. Indeed, the fissiparous tendencies allowed social mobility in Xhosa society—a condition advantageous to the clients. By switching allegiance to the competing royal descent groups, they may have accelerated fission. This is indicated by the support of the Gqunukwebe to the Right Hand section during Palo's reign.

We cannot properly speak of a 'frontier' between Xhosa and Khoi societies. Territorial separation was cross-cut by trade, kinship ties between ruling lineages, and activities which affected the regulation of public affairs. Both Xhosa and Khoi societies had facilities which provided means of incorporation of aliens. They were not completely autonomous corporate groups existing independently. Political processes within Xhosa society and Xhosa expansion cannot be fully analysed without taking into consideration relations between the inter-acting of Xhosa and Khoi royal descent groups and the system of patron-clientship in Xhosa society.

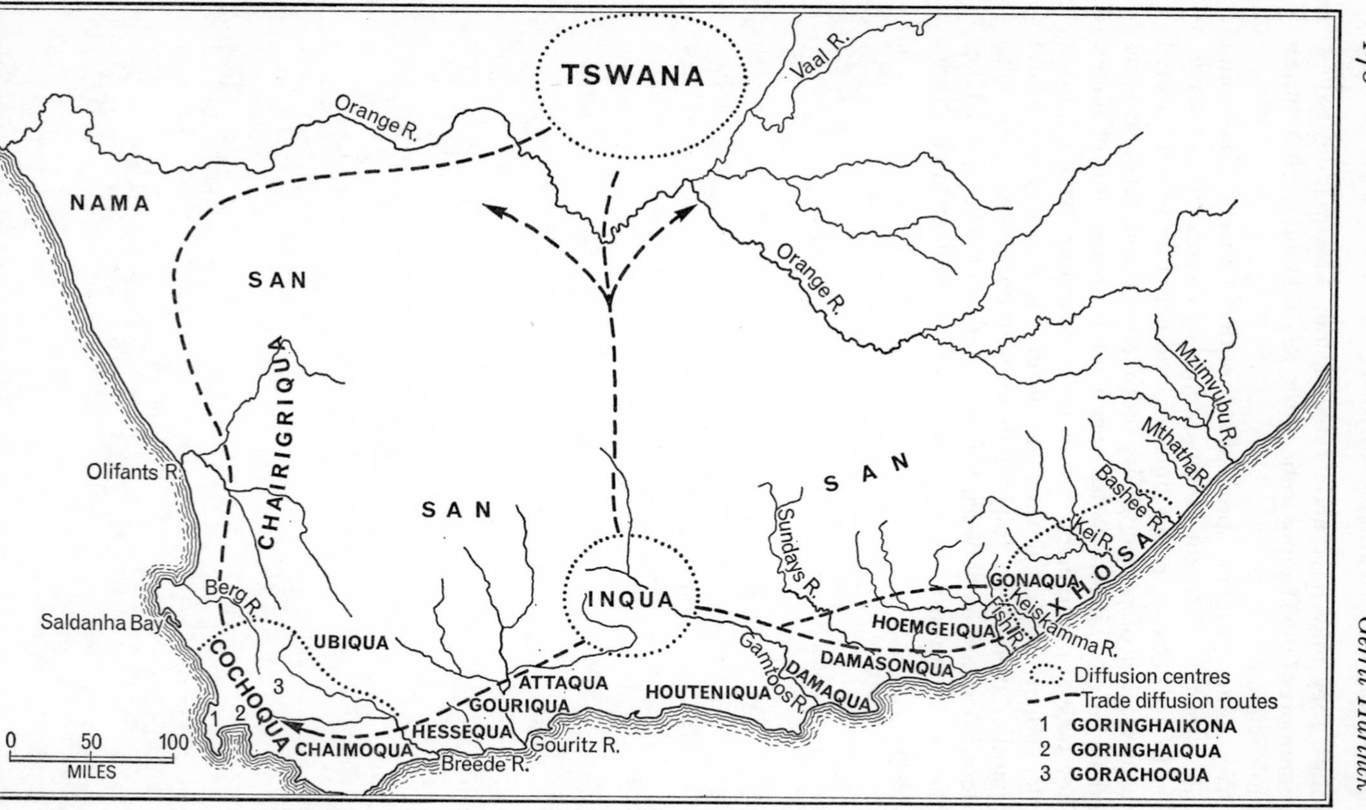

7. *Approximate locations of Khoikhoi and Bantu chiefdoms about 1650–1700*

8. *The trade of Delagoa Bay as a factor in Nguni politics 1750–1835*

ALAN SMITH

Historians concerned with the development of the Zulu 'nation' have thus far tended to rely on a mono-causal interpretation. In their view, 'the main cause of imperial developments was the shortage of land . . . by the eighteenth century the population increase had produced a land crisis. The old process of recurrent tribal splitting could no longer solve the problem.'[1] Despite its widespread acceptance, historians have been unable, as yet, to resolve many of the inconsistencies created by the use of 'population pressure' as virtually the only factor involved in the development of the larger chiefdoms among the Nguni of northern Natal. For although the effects of a burgeoning population and the resultant shortage of land are clearly visible in events such as the Mfecane, the explanation of how these pressures affected other processes, such as the simultaneous consolidation among several chiefdoms in northern Natal, remains less clear or perhaps even beyond the range of the population theory.[2] Thus far, however, other lines of inquiry, which may serve either to devalue or to complement the population theory, have not been fully examined.

The suggestion that trade with Delagoa Bay was a factor in Nguni politics is just such a possibility.[3] Although it has been admitted that trade may have been of secondary importance,[4] very little attention has been devoted to the development of the trade of the northern Nguni. By focusing on this overlooked

[1] Max Gluckman 'The Rise of the Zulu Empire' *Scientific American* Vol. 202 April 1960 p. 166.

[2] See J. D. Omer-Cooper *The Zulu Aftermath* London 1966, chapter 12. He mentions that there appears still to have been vacant land in Natal and that the normal reaction of south-eastern Bantu-speaking peoples under pressure was towards fission. The most perplexing question is why the reaction did not occur among the Xhosa who, of all the peoples, were the most pressured.

[3] First suggested by Monica Wilson 'The Early History of the Transkei and Ciskei' *African Studies* Vol. 18 No. 4 September 1958 p. 172.

[4] Gluckman 'Zulu' *Scientific American* Vol. 202 April 1960 p. 166.

aspect of Nguni history, this essay seeks to help fill that void. It will investigate the growth of the export trade from Delagoa Bay, the development of the trading connections between Delagoa Bay and Natal, and how the trade with the north may have influenced developments and been of importance to the Nguni chiefdoms.

The published source material for a study of the trade of Delagoa Bay and Natal is limited and not of easy access. For the growth of the export trade from Delagoa Bay, the accounts of European travellers, who passed through the bay between the sixteenth and the nineteenth century, provide the principal source of information.[5] In addition to these primary accounts, there are several valuable works, whose authors have made use of unpublished archival records.[6] For the interior of Natal, information can only be obtained from the records of the survivors of the sixteenth- and seventeenth-century Portuguese shipwrecks, from Europeans who penetrated inland after the consolidation of the Zulu nation,[7] and from traditional evidence.[8]

The essential characteristic of these sources, however, is that they are not primarily concerned with or fully aware of the developments in northern Natal. The Europeans, whether based at Port Natal or Delagoa Bay, remained essentially ignorant of events in northern Natal and the connections between it and Delagoa Bay. In the same manner, the published traditions tend to concentrate on the Mthethwa and Zulu and to a large degree inadequately represent the historical developments among the northern chiefdoms. Thus the obfuscation of the 'northern factor'

[5] G. M. Theal *Records of Southeastern Africa* 9 vols. Cape Town 1898–1903; E. C. Godée-Molsbergen (ed.) *Reizen in Zuid-Afrika in de Hollandse Tijd, Part 3, 1670–1752* The Hague 1922; William White *Journal of A Voyage . . . to Africa* London 1800; William Owen *Narrative of A Voyage . . .* 2 vols. London 1833; Thomas Boteler *Narrative of A Voyage of Discovery . . .* 2 vols. London 1835.

[6] Caetona Montez *Descobrimento e Fundação de Lourenço Marques* Lisbon 1948; Three works by Alexandre Lobato *Quatro Estudos e Uma Evocação Para A História de Lourenço Marques* Lisbon 1961, *História da Fundação de Lourenço Marques* Lisbon 1948, *História do Presídio de Lourenço Marques,* 2 vols. Lisbon 1949 and 1960; Colin Coetzee 'Die Kompanjie se Besetting van Delagoa-Baai' *Archives Yearbook for South African History* 1948 Part 2.

[7] Henry Francis Fynn *The Diary of Henry Francis Fynn* Pietermaritzburg 1950; Nathaniel Isaacs *Travels and Adventures in Eastern Africa,* 2 vols. Van Riebeeck Society Nos. 16 and 17; Allen Gardiner *Narrative of A Journey to the Zoolu Country In South Africa* London 1836; also John Bird (ed.), *The Annals of Natal* 2 vols. Cape Town 1965.

[8] A. T. Bryant *Olden Times in Zululand and Natal* London 1929; A. T. Bryant *A History of the Zulu* Cape Town 1964; Henri A. Junod *The Life of A South African Tribe* 2 vols. New York 1962; Cecil Cowley *Kwa Zulu* Cape Town 1966; Hilda Kuper *The Swazi* London 1952.

in Nguni history has largely been determined by the nature of the source material. Even though the combining of the diverse sources can at times result in a clear reconstruction of events and processes, the fact that the source material is mainly derived from the periphery of the area of central concern, requires that some of the conclusions presented here be speculative and suggestive.

The middle years of the eighteenth century marked a watershed in the development and evolution of the trade of Delagoa Bay. By the early years of the eighteenth century, the Portuguese and English had been superseded by the Dutch, who, lured by its possibilities as both a trading site and a base from which to reach the interior, occupied Delagoa from 1721 to 1730. From the evidence provided by these merchants, it would appear that although traders occasionally had made lucrative profits, goods for export at times had been available only in limited quantities. Compared with other ports along the south-eastern coast, Delagoa remained of secondary importance. By the second half of the eighteenth century, however, both the intensity of trade and the export capacity of Delagoa seem to have increased. European traders frequented the bay with more regularity and with greater assurances of carrying away profitable cargoes.[9]

Since no European power was established in Delagoa Bay at the mid-century, traders from several nations were induced to trade there because of the absence of commercial restrictions. Both the Dutch from the Cape and the Portuguese from Moçambique converged on the bay. Although the Portuguese ships reported that trade at Delagoa was brisk, neither they nor the Dutch were as successful as the English from Bombay, who pursued the most continuous and profitable trade. With the aid of inexpensive trading goods from Bombay and Surat, between the 1750s and the 1770s the English almost cornered the market. They established a semi-permanent trading factory, stationed boats on all of the rivers, and manufactured their own copper bracelets on the spot. According to the Portuguese, the English traders were doing 'big business'.[10]

[9] For the trade of Delagoa Bay before 1750, see Alan Smith 'Delagoa Bay and the Trade of South-Eastern Africa' Richard Gray and David Birmingham (eds.) *Pre-colonial African Trade* London 1969.

[10] Antonio de Andrade *Relações de Moçambique Setecentista* Lisbon 1955 pp. 53, 157–8; Pereira do Lago 'Instrucção Que . . .' Andrade *Relações* p. 318; Joao Montaury 'Moçambique' Andrade *Relações* p. 372.

In 1777, Delagoa Bay was occupied by the Austrian Asiatic Company of Trieste, which was under the directorship of William Bolts, a former servant of the English East India Company. Following his dismissal from the India service, Bolts, who had evidently learned of the value of Delagoa Bay while in India, proceeded directly to Europe to secure funds for the establishment of a trading settlement. Upon receiving the necessary financing from the court at Vienna, Bolts and his new company began a trading establishment, which proved to be most lucrative. With adequate financial backing and a large store of trading goods, the 'Austrians' began a brisk trade. The market was soon flooded with trading goods, and the price of ivory soared to double that of Moçambique. Alexandre Lobato has described the quantity of goods exported by the 'Austrians' as 'extremely voluminous'.[11]

The Portuguese soon ousted the 'Austrians' from their control of the trade of Delagoa Bay and attempted to monopolize the trade for themselves. Evidence for the volume of trade during this period is meagre and very contradictory. Most Portuguese sources complain that not only could they not match the achievements of the Austrians, but that there was hardly any profit obtained from their Delagoa settlement.[12] On the other hand, there are several factors which indicate that even if exports did not reach the proportions attained after 1750, the trade never came to a halt. The first is that despite the attempt of the Moçambique government to exercise a monopoly, there are reports of French, English, Indian, and Dutch vessels which visited the bay during the latter part of the eighteenth century. Although many of these ships were primarily interested in whaling, they did enter the rivers and traded with both the Portuguese and the local African population.[13] Aside from the 'illicit' trade conducted by 'foreigners', officially sponsored Portuguese also shared in the trade. In addition to the ships sent from Moçambique, the merchants of Inhambane apparently conducted an overland

[11] Lobato *Fundação* p. 27. Lobato has made use of the set of records kept by the Austrian company; these documents are extremely important because they represent the most systematic recording of the trade in Delagoa Bay during the latter half of the eighteenth century.

[12] Arquivo Histórico Ultramarino, Mozambique, Códice 1370 p. 4.

[13] Lobato *Presídio* Vol. 1 p. 142; Nogueira de Andrade 'Descripção ... 1794' ibid. p. 178; also de Mattos to Gov. General of Moçambique, 16 May 1793, A. H. U., Moz., Caixa, 28.

trade in the vicinity of the bay.[14] Therefore, it would seem safe to conclude that in the closing years of the eighteenth century, movements of trading goods in and around the Delagoa Bay area continued.

Despite certain alterations in the trading patterns which had developed during the late eighteenth century, the evidence indicates that in the first thirty years of the nineteenth century, there was no cessation of the trade. Between 1800 and the early 1820s the commerce remained the virtual monopoly of the Portuguese at Delagoa Bay, who, it was observed, concerned themselves with little else. Despite the absence of statistics for the volume of goods exported, this observation and the fact that these years witnessed the zenith of the penetration of the trade routes from Delagoa into the interior of southern Africa, suggest that the trade did not come to a halt.[15] By the middle years of the 1820s, English traders, induced by the activities of Captain Owen, had once again entered the field. Although their first attempts were vigorously opposed by the local Portuguese, the decision of the Moçambique government to take the commerce out of the hands of the garrison at Delagoa Bay and give exclusive privileges to a trading company based on Moçambique island,[16] served the purpose of inviting foreign competition. With the full complicity of the Portuguese garrison, which was being denied the right to participate in the trade, foreign vessels again began to make frequent voyages to Delagoa Bay.[17] Thus, as late as the 1830s, Delagoa Bay continued to be a point of call for foreign ships, as well as a Portuguese trading site.

From this brief outline of the development of European trade in Delagoa Bay, it can be seen that during the period 1750 to 1830 Delagoa Bay was consistently frequented by European traders and that unlike the ports to the north, whose commerce decreased during much of the eighteenth century, the trade of Delagoa Bay seems to have been maintained at high levels. Moreover, during most of this period the commerce of Delagoa Bay was competitive

[14] A. H. U., Moz., Codice 1349, p. 76; Lobato *Presídio* Vol. 2, p. 408.

[15] P. R. O., Adm. 1–2269 'The Portuguese Settlements and Dominions of the Eastern Coast of Africa'. Also see, Alan Smith 'Delagoa Bay and the Trade of South-East Africa', Richard Gray and David Birmingham (eds.) *Pre-colonial African Trade* London 1969.

[16] A. H. U., Moz., Caixa 75.

[17] dos Santos to Gov. General of Moçambique, 10 February 1832, Francisco Santana (ed.), *Documentação Avulsa Moçambique do Arquivo Histórico Ultramarino* Vol. 1 p. 204; Alexandre Lobato 'Lourenço Marques, 1830' Stúdia Vol. 17 (April 1966) pp. 26–30.

among the nationals of several European powers and not just another commercial backwater of Moçambique. Thus, as a first step in the consideration of the trade hypothesis, it would seem safe to conclude that during the period of significant political developments in northern Natal, the commerce of Delagoa Bay was sufficiently consistent and sizeable to have had influences on those who took part in it.

The very proximity of Delagoa Bay to Natal suggests that the trading relations between the two areas may have been intense. Yet before such an assumption can be made, it is necessary to know what the Europeans exported from Delagoa Bay, to determine, if possible, the origin of these exports, and to find out what goods Africans received in exchange. Could these exports have originated from Natal? It is only after we have gained some knowledge of these questions and a direct trading connection between the two has been established, that some attempts can be made to assess the influence of the trade on the internal politics of the northern Nguni chiefdoms.

Until the second or third decade of the nineteenth century, ivory was the most sought after, consistent, and important commodity to be exported from Delagoa Bay. All extant English and Portuguese documents from the sixteenth and seventeenth centuries state that the trading ships went to Delagoa Bay to procure ivory. Although the Dutch, unlike their predecessors, seemed more interested in securing metal goods, and in fact did obtain some gold and tin, these commodities were usually irregular in arrival and of less significance than the ivory trade. During the 'Austrian' occupation the same phenomenon continued to hold true. Some supplies of gold and copper were available, but the major portion of the commerce continued to be in ivory.[18] In the period following the expulsion of the Austrians from the bay, all evidence continues to confirm that this remained the order of importance of goods exported from the bay. Thus, the most important product to be exported from Delagoa Bay was a product which could have been supplied from Natal.

During the eighteenth and preceding centuries, the slave trade appears not to have been of major consequence. Of the Europeans who traded in Delagoa Bay, only during the Dutch occupation does there appear to have been a consistent effort to obtain slaves.

[18] Lobato *Presídio* Vol. 1 p. 231.

This trade survived, however, only between the years 1721 to 1730. After their factory was abandoned, the Dutch found it easier to procure slaves in Madagascar.[19] As the eighteenth century neared its end, increasing numbers of European slavers entered the Indian ocean. These slavers, however, avoided Delagoa Bay because it was not equipped to handle a large supply of slaves and at other ports to the north slaves could be obtained more easily.[20]

During the early years of the nineteenth century, the pattern of trade in Delagoa Bay changed to some degree. After 1810, the first French and Brazilian slave traders began to buy slaves from the Portuguese garrison.[21] By the 1820s the extent of this trade had increased greatly, as the Portuguese took advantage of the devastations of the various Nguni groups, which were fleeing from Shaka, and disputes among the local Thonga chiefdoms, to procure large supplies of slaves.[22] Since the Zulu are known not to have traded in slaves, this incipient slave trade may have obscured the visions of historians, many of whom have probably assumed that the trade was of older vintage. However, since this trade did not reach significant proportions until after the consolidation of the Zulu nation and was confined to the immediate area of the bay even in the 1820s and 1830s, it can be seen that it has little relevance for a consideration of the trade hypothesis and the development of the Zulu nation.

Since Delagoa Bay served as a trading centre for a vast interior, it is difficult to determine with precision the percentage of goods which originated from Natal. There are several indications, however, which suggest that Natal's share in the ivory trade was indeed significant. One of the most important considerations is a matter of geography. Since the currents along the coast of Natal were notoriously treacherous and the coastline did not possess adequate harbours,[23] if at all possible European ships tended to avoid it. As a result, Delagoa Bay was the southernmost location which European traders regularly visited. Therefore, in order to obtain European goods, the people of Natal naturally would have traded their ivory towards Delagoa Bay in the north.

Another factor which suggests that Natal's share in the ivory

[19] Henri Dehérain *Le Cap de Bonne-Espérance au VIIIe Siècle* Paris 1909 pp. 200–2.
[20] Lobato *Fundação* p. 7.
[21] Alexandre Lobato 'Lourenço Marques, 1830' *Studia* Vol. 17 1966 p. 21.
[22] Owen *Narrative* Vol. 2 p. 213; Owen to Boteler 10 May 1825 *Accounts and Papers* Vol. LXXXIII 1875 p. 156.
[23] Farewell to Somerset 1 May 1824, Bird *Annals* Vol. 1 p. 72.

trade was significant is that almost all Europeans who commented on the subject agreed that those chiefdoms on the southern side of the bay, that is, those whose immediate hinterland led towards northern Natal, were the best places to trade. Originally, the chiefdom of Nyaka, which some observers felt extended almost as far as St Lucia Bay, was considered to be the best area for trade.[24] As Nyaka's power was gradually diminished by its neighbour and rival, Tembe, the major share of the trade was observed to come from Tembe, whose chief considered himself 'the most eminent vendor of amber and ivory' in the bay.[25] Although Tembe was able to maintain this supremacy throughout most of the eighteenth century, the nineteenth century saw the upper hand pass to the chiefdom of Maputo, from which the largest supplies of ivory came to be exported.[26]

The predominance of the southern chiefdoms in matters of trade gains additional significance since it was observed that almost all goods which reached the export market came from the interior.[27] It is probable that the major share of the ivory exported from Nyaka, Tembe and Maputo came from the Natal area. As early as the sixteenth century, Portuguese travellers saw people who were carrying ivory from Natal to exchange in Nyaka, and met others who claimed to have been there.[28] Trading goods, whose origin was probably in Delagoa Bay, were found to be common as far south as the Umzimvubu River.[29] Further confirmation of the connections between Natal and Delagoa Bay is given in two Portuguese documents of the 1780s. A Portuguese friar noted that large quantities of ivory came along the Maputo River, from Nguni-speaking peoples.[30] Another source of about the same period, indicates that the chief of Tembe had 'a large quantity of ivory, which comes from the south'.[31] By the beginning of the nineteenth century a European traveller indicated that some goods came from as far away as the eastern frontier of the

[24] Henri A. Junod 'The Condition of the Natives of South-East Africa in the Sixteenth Century . . .' *S.A.J.S.* Vol. 10 (1914) p. 153.

[25] Jacob Francken 'Naarstigheid' *RSEA* Vol. 6, p. 477.

[26] See below p. 186.

[27] 'Mr. Penwell's Account of Delagoa Bay, Given by Himself' *RSEA* Vol. 2 p. 462.

[28] Lavanha 'Narrative . . . Santo Alberto' Boxer *The Tragic History Of the Sea* Cambridge 1959 pp. 173, 156.

[29] Ibid. p. 133.

[30] Santa Thereza 'Plano e Relação da bahia denominada por Lourenço Marques' Montez *Descobrimento* p. 164.

[31] Anonymous *Accounts and Papers* (1875) p. 105.

Cape Colony.[32] The correctness of this observation is substantiated by the testimony of another traveller, who met Thonga traders from Delagoa Bay at the kraal of the Xhosa chief, Gaika.[33] Thus observers at both ends confirm that the trade routes from Delagoa Bay passed through the whole length of Natal.

A survey of the goods imported inland from Delagoa Bay also indicates that there was a close connection between the two. The principal items brought by Europeans to exchange at the bay were cloth, brass, and beads. Europeans who passed through Natal make no mention of exotic cloth, a phenomenon which seems to be confirmed by information from the bay. For most of the cloth seems to have been traded to the chiefdoms in the north.[34] On the other hand, there is ample evidence that beads and brass were highly valued articles in Natal. The Portuguese who travelled through Natal found beads, which they identified as of Indian manufacture, to be common among the people they encountered.[35] They also mentioned that the people wore brass ornaments, which seemed to have been introduced by English traders.[36] The first English traders to penetrate inland to the Natal area in the nineteenth century found that these products, which they identified as of Delagoa Bay origin, were still quite common.[37] Despite the absence of primary information during a period of more than a century and a half, it would seem safe to conclude that these products, which were continuously imported into Delagoa Bay, must have been part of a continuous interchange between the bay and the northern Nguni.

Finally, since the commerce of Delagoa during these years has been described as 'big business' and 'extremely voluminous', mention should be made of the assessment of some Europeans, who give evidence to further substantiate that the largest percentage of the Delagoa exports came from Natal. During the years 1750 to 1770, when the commerce of Delagoa reached significant

[32] Report of Colonel Collins in Donald Moodie (ed.) *The Record* Amsterdam 1960 p. 43.

[33] Louis Alberti *Description Physique et Historique des Cafres, Sur La Côte Meridionale de l'Afrique* Amsterdam 1811 pp. 4–14.

[34] See for example, Jacob Bucquoy 'Zestinjarige Reize . . .' in Charles Walckenaer *Histoire des Voyages* Vol. 21 Paris 1842 p. 415; and William White 'Voyage . . .' in Walckanaer *Histoire* p. 465.

[35] Perestrello 'Saint Benedict' *RSEA* Vol. 1, p. 225, and Lavanha 'Narrative . . . Santo Alberto' Boxer *Tragic* p. 133.

[36] d'Almeida 'São João Baptista' Boxer *Tragic History* pp. 239, 241, 248.

[37] Gardiner *Zoolu Country* pp. 59–60.

proportions, the Portuguese maintained that goods from the area immediately to the north of Delagoa Bay travelled not to the bay, but to the Portuguese settlement at Inhambane.[38] Since the trading connections of Delagoa Bay and the highveld of South Africa remained underdeveloped at this time, it must be assumed that the Delagoa commerce was dependent on Natal. In the 1820s, British traders who passed through Delagoa Bay observed that 'the whole' of the Delagoa market depended on the Zulu nation.[39] Although this latter comment oversimplified the trading patterns, the combination of this testimony with the other factors indicates beyond question that most of the ivory exported during this period of extensive commerce was derived from Natal.

It is indeed more simple to point out a continuity of trade in Delagoa Bay and to establish connections between it and Natal than to show how this commerce affected the history of the Natal Nguni. Yet, upon the realization that the northern Nguni appear to have been involved in more than an insignificant trade with the north, one must proceed to a re-examination of some of the most important events and processes in the history of the area to see if trading motives can be found. Although the conclusions and suggestions presented below are not offered as a complete explanation of Nguni history, it will be seen that trade may have been an important factor in many of the developments leading to the emergence and consolidation of what came to be the Zulu nation.

It is generally accepted that among the northern Nguni, the Hlubi, Ngwane and Ndwandwe, all of which descended from the parent Dlamini group, were among the earliest Nguni chiefdoms to begin the process of state construction.[40] There are several indications that trade had a long history among these groups. Traditional evidence indicates a 'close' and 'intimate' connection between the Dlamini Nguni and the Tembe of Delagoa Bay.[41] The 'intimate' relations taken together with the geographical contiguity and the fact that most of the ivory exported from the southern side of Delagoa came from or passed through northern Natal, suggest that the Dlamini had a significant role in the

[38] 'Memórias da Costa da Africa Oriental . . .' Andrade *Relações* p. 212.
[39] Fynn *Diary* p. 52.
[40] Shula Marks 'The Nguni, the Natalians, and Their History' *J.A.H.* Vol. 8 No. 2 (1968) p. 532.
[41] Bryant *Olden Times* p. 313; Caetano Montez 'Os Indígenas de Moçambique . . .' *Moçambique* No. 30 p. 26; Kuper *Swazi* p. 2.

ivory trade. It should also be noted that according to A. T. Bryant, the Dlamini were part of the Mbo group. He equates vaMbo with the group the Portuguese called 'Vambe'.[42] If this equation has any substance, further confirmation would be given to the idea that trade had a long history among these chiefdoms, because in the sixteenth century it was reported that the Portuguese 'occasionally' traded with the kingdom of Vambe.[43]

The economic and political relations between the Tembe of Delagoa Bay on the one hand, and especially the Ngwane and Ndwandwe on the other, may have had significant consequences both at Delagoa Bay and in the interior of northern Natal. During the eighteenth century the Tembe dominated the whole of the southern littoral of Delagoa Bay and thus exercised a monopoly of the export trade.[44] It is also quite possible that Tembe influence may have been exerted over a significant portion of northern Natal, perhaps including the Ngwane and Ndwandwe.[45] One European traveller at Delagoa reported that Tembe extended two hundred miles into the interior.[46] If in fact Tembe's influence stretched over a wide area of northern Natal, then a root cause of the eighteenth-century wars in this area may have been the attempt of the Ngwane and Ndwandwe to free themselves from Tembe control. This attempt, it would seem, was not completely successful until Tembe was disrupted by internal strife. In 1794 civil war broke out in Tembe, and although the Portuguese intervened and reinstated the ruling chief, the fissure could not be healed.[47] For a significant portion of the Tembe broke away, and to the east of the river which came to be known by that name established the independent chiefdom of Maputo. It is significant that the traditions of the Ngwane and Ndwandwe as independent entities also arose in this period.[48] Thus it appears quite possible that the strife which led to the bifurcation of Tembe also helped in the foundation of the Ngwane and Ndwandwe.

The question of trade may have been an important consideration in these wars in northern Natal. Judging from the hostile

[42] Bryant *Olden Times* pp. 314–15.
[43] do Couto 'São Thomé' Boxer *Tragic* p. 70.
[44] See Francken 'Naarstigheid' *RSEA*; and William White *Journal*.
[45] Shula Marks 'The traditions of the Natal "Nguni": a second look at the work of A. T. Bryant' *supra* p. 141.
[46] White *Journal* p. 41.
[47] Lobato *Presídio* Vol. 2 pp. 120–1.
[48] Bryant *Zulu History* pp. 2–3, 51.

relations which existed between the Tembe and the Nguni, it could be suggested that the conduct, control, and monopolization of trade was an important factor. For the Tembe, as well as the other Thonga of Delagoa Bay, sought to protect their position as middlemen and preserve their monopoly. As early as the end of the sixteenth century it was observed that a chief in the mountains near Tembe, 'never under any circumstances descends from the mountains or holds any communication with his neighbours, for they are all alike very great thieves . . . he never wants to trade with the Portuguese fearing that if he sent them down from the mountains they would be stolen by his neighbours'.[49] During the Dutch period it was observed that all of the Thonga were concerned with preserving their monopoly and often went to war to prevent 'inlanders' from dealing directly with the Europeans.[50] By the middle years of the eighteenth century, relations with the 'inlanders' do not seem to have improved. In the 1750s, it was observed that the people of Tembe would not attempt to pass through the lands of the Nguni.[51] In the 1780s, it was noted that the Thonga 'would not dare go to trade with them (Nguni), in order to avoid being robbed'.[52] Thus it appears that the struggle over trade was a constant phenomenon in the relations between the coastal Thonga and 'inlanders' in general, and more particularly between the Tembe and the Nguni.

At the conclusion of these eighteenth century wars, the geographical positions and relationships between these chiefdoms had been significantly altered. One of the most important results was that the trading monopoly of Tembe was brought to an end. By consolidating their position to the east of the river, the Maputo opened an alternate line of communication from the interior to the bay. It should also be noted that both the Ngwane and Ndwandwe came to settle along the Pongola, a major tributary of the Maputo. Thus the beginning of the nineteenth century found the Ndwandwe, the Maputo and the Ngwane all clustered along a major artery of commerce to Delagoa Bay.[53]

During these years, the northern Nguni chiefdoms were also experiencing a period of internal growth and consolidation. It

[49] do Couto 'São Thomé' Boxer *Tragic* p. 74.
[50] Jan Van de Cappellen 'Rapport . . . aan den Goveneur van de Kaap Kolonie' *RSEA* Vol. 6 p. 414.
[51] Francken 'Naarstigheid' *RSEA* Vol. 6 p. 479.
[52] Santa Thereza 'Plano' Montez *Descobrimento* p. 164.
[53] See Bryant *Zulu History* pp. 3–4.

might be suggested that trade also influenced these developments. For if, in fact, these were wars fought over matters of trade, then the increased militarism and consolidation which resulted could be viewed as a logical response to the necessities of the prosecution of trade. Secondly, the accumulation of wealth derived from trade would have helped in the process of the consolidation of the state. By distributing goods obtained from the long-distance trade, a chief could command increased loyalty from both within and without the normal lineage structure. Whether chiefs exchanged these goods for commodities, service, or merely to ensure loyalty, European travellers testified to the fact that the imported goods were widely diffused through Nguni society. In later years, a concrete example of this phenomenon was provided when Dingane informed the British traders that he was anxious to have trade goods in order to reward his followers.[54] Since the ivory trade came to be a royal monopoly among the northern Nguni, trade would seem to have been an important factor in the consolidation of chiefly power. In fact, monopoly of trade may have been the crucial differentiating factor between the northern Nguni chiefdoms and the neighbouring groups. For it appears that in the areas to the south as well as among the Thonga of Delagoa Bay the chiefs never exercised this right.[55]

The early career of Dingiswayo gives support to the idea that trade of the northern Nguni chiefdoms with Delagoa Bay was important and that control of the ivory trade was a tool for the strengthening of the state. During his enforced exile from his Mthethwa homeland, Dingiswayo sought shelter among the Hlubi. From here he may have travelled to Delagoa Bay[56] and may even have travelled with a party of Thonga porters on a trading expedition to the Buffalo River.[57] Upon his return to take control of the Mthethwa chieftaincy, Dingiswayo instituted two important reforms in matters of trade. He first organized a caravan of one hundred porters, who took ivory and cattle to trade at Delagoa Bay. Thereafter, the exchange of goods with the north remained

[54] Isaacs *Travels* Vol. 2, p. 32.

[55] Cowley *Kwa Zulu* p. 39; When Fynn travelled southward towards Pondoland, he found that elephant tusks belonged to the man who threw the first assegai, Fynn *Diary* p. 104. Thonga law seems also to have required that only one tusk be given to the chief. In fact, the civil war of 1794 may have resulted from the attempt of the chief of Tembe to institute a monopoly of the ivory trade. For the dispute arose when 'Capella' tried to monopolize the trade goods. Lobato *Presídio* Vol. 2 p. 121.

[56] Bryant *Olden Times* pp. 87–88.

[57] Cowley *Kwa Zulu* p. 46.

a matter of high priority.[58] Whereas prior to his assumption of control of the Mthethwa, institutional control of trade had been very limited, Dingiswayo made all trade exclusively his prerogative. Those who transgressed his order were to be put to death.[59] Probably of greater significance than his alleged desire 'to improve the habits of his people' by showing them articles of European manufacture, was his use of these manufactured articles to win allegiances and consolidate a following. Although it is possible that these reforms were of his own independent invention, the fact that they were instituted immediately following his sojourn in the north suggests that these were operational devices he had witnessed and which he felt had helped to strengthen the northern chiefdoms.

There are other indications that Dingiswayo gained some intimate knowledge of the politics of the north. When he returned to Mthethwa, one of his primary tasks was to deal with the Qwabe, who had refused to surrender a pretender to the Mthethwa chieftaincy. Perhaps uncertain of his own power, Dingiswayo concluded an alliance with the Maputo. In return for the aid of musket-carrying soldiers, Dingiswayo agreed to exchange all of his goods through Maputo.[60] With the support of the soldiers and firearms from Maputo, the Mthethwa were easily able to overcome the Qwabe. Dingiswayo had found another way to turn the trade and politics of Delagoa Bay to his own advantage.

The standard explanation of Mthethwa expansion under Dingiswayo is that he sought to 'replace fifty discordant foreign policies with one'. Yet if one takes a closer look at the pattern of Mthethwa expansion it is observed that the only attack made to the south was at the expense of the Qwabe, with whom Dingiswayo had matters of state to settle. According to Bryant there is no evidence of Dingiswayo ever moving against the Ngocobes, Cubes, Cunus, Tembus and other clans along the Tukela and Mzinyati valleys.[61] Unless there were reasons of geography which prevented the Mthethwa from securing the allegiance of the aforementioned group, one wonders why these peoples, who were closer to the Mthethwa than many of those who were forced to submit to Mthethwa 'suzerainty', did not have their foreign policies

[58] Fynn *Diary* p. 10.
[59] Ibid. p. 7.
[60] Ibid. p. 7.
[61] Bryant *Olden Times* p. 98.

changed. For when Mthethwa expansion (according to Bryant) is charted, it is found that the groups he conquered, the elaTenjeni, Tembu, Zulu, emaMtabeni, Dhlamini, Kumalo, Dube, Cambini and Mvele,[62] were more or less located on an axis which ran from the coast in the south-east towards the west and north. This lateral expansion could be interpreted as part of Dingiswayo's continued preoccupation with trade. Since the long distance trade with the south was gaining increasing intensity, this pattern of expansion would have afforded him greater control of the trade to the north. In this connection, it should be noted that Fynn commented that during his lifetime Dingiswayo sought to monopolize the whole of the Delagoa market.[63]

Another point of interest is to seek the causes of the Ngwane–Ndwandwe–Mthethwa conflict. While Dingiswayo was proceeding with his conquests in the south, the Ngwane, who were located to the south of Tembe, were assuming control of the northern bank of the Pongola. At the same time, Zwide and the Ndwandwe were expanding along the southern bank of the Pongola. When the expansion of the Ndwandwe is charted, it is found that it proceeded from the coast in the east to the mountains in the west.[64] Only after securing this territory did Zwide embark on new campaigns, and these were directed against the Ngwane and perhaps even against the Tembe of Delagoa Bay.[65] As in the case of Dingiswayo, there is no evidence of Zwide ever attempting to move southward and apparently the battles fought with the Mthethwa were instigated by Dingiswayo. Since the Mthethwa and the Maputo had apparently conspired to exclude the Ndwandwe from the Delagoa market,[66] a motive for the direction of Ndwandwe expansion may have been to cut off the trade with the south and by attacking Tembe to seek another outlet for trade.

The chiefdom of Maputo remained a focus for the attentions of the major powers in Natal. While Dingiswayo lived and the Mthethwa–Maputo alliance remained intact, the Maputo remained free from attack. Soon after Zwide had disposed of

[62] Ibid. pp. 100–6.
[63] Fynn *Diary* p. 47.
[64] Bryant *Olden Times* p. 137.
[65] Not long after 1800, Tembe was overrun by a group from the interior. However, neither the exact date nor the group which attacked Tembe is specified. See the report of Fynn *RSEA* Vol. 2 p. 487.
[66] According to Fynn, Ndwandwe trade with Maputo began only after Dingiswayo's death. Fynn *Diary* p. 47.

Dingiswayo, however, he attacked and brought Maputo under Ndwandwe control.[67] The Ndwandwe thereafter used Maputo as an outlet for their ivory.[68] The fortunes of the inland struggle soon brought a new change to Maputo. Following Shaka's defeat of the Ndwandwe and their flight away from the southern banks of the Pongola, Maputo was brought under Zulu control. In 1823 Fynn found that there were Vatwahs in the kingdom of Maputo, whose chief was Shaka.[69] The missionary, William Threlfall, also met many 'Vatwahs', all of whom came to Maputo from the 'great king, Shaka'.[70]

An interesting aspect of the struggle for control of Maputo is that both Zwide and Shaka allowed the people to remain unmolested.[71] After his initial defeat of Maputo, Zwide's relations with them appear to have been good. According to Owen, crops and industries were improved and the country came to enjoy great abundance.[72] In Maputo, Shaka's envoys interacted peacefully, and concerned themselves almost exclusively with matters of trade and apparently only resorted to force in cases of disagreement over trade.[73] While the other chiefdoms of the bay, especially Tembe, were being desolated, Maputo remained well cultivated, populous, and continued to do a brisk trade.[74] The reason that the Maputo were granted virtual independence by Shaka was that they had gained a reputation for being shrewd traders.[75]

Delagoa Bay also became a focus of attention for the major splinter groups caused by Shaka's wars. For both the Shangane and the Ngoni for a time settled in the neighbourhood of Delagoa Bay. Unlike the Zulu, however, these groups abandoned the 'traditional' Nguni policy of refusing to sell slaves. Perhaps resulting from the exigencies of their hazardous position, both groups raided in the area of the bay and sold a large number of slaves directly to the Portuguese.[76] According to one observer, the

[67] Fynn *Diary* p. 47.
[68] William Owen 'Delagoa Bay' *RSEA* Vol. 2 p. 470.
[69] Fynn *Diary* p. 42.
[70] Extracts from the diary of William Threlfall, printed in Samuel Broadbent *The Missionary Martyr of Namaqualand* London 1860 p. 83.
[71] Fynn *Diary* p. 48.
[72] Owen 'Delagoa Bay' *RSEA* Vol. 2 pp. 468–9.
[73] Threlfall in Broadbent *Martyr* p. 84.
[74] Ibid. p. 85.
[75] Fynn *Diary* p. 48.
[76] Owen *Narrative* Vol. 1 pp. 123–4, 141–2; Vol. 2 p. 218.

Shangane found this trade so profitable that they wanted to establish themselves at the bay and gain 'a window on the sea'.[77] Judging from the astonishing increase in the slave trade during these years, it seems that these groups were able to make significant profits.

During the early years of Shaka's rule, the export of ivory to Delagoa Bay seems to have been an important concern of the king. By this time, the trade appears to have become highly organized. For the goods obtained in Zululand appear to have been transported to a narrow strip of land on the borders of Zululand and Maputo. From here it is likely that Maputo porters carried the goods, which had been collected, northward to the Portuguese factory.[78] The extent of this trade is suggested by a report of Captain William Owen. According to him, in 1823 a caravan of one thousand porters, bringing between three hundred and four hundred elephant tusks and a large quantity of cattle, arrived at the bay. Although Owen neglects to mention the source, it is improbable that this caravan could have originated in any place other than Zululand.[79] The systematic way in which trade was now prosecuted and the size of the caravans suggest that trade continued to be a matter of major concern during Shaka's reign.

At this time, European traders were becoming more interested in the trade of Zululand. Perhaps in an attempt to cut out the middlemen of Maputo, the Portuguese sought entry into Zululand. They proposed the establishment of a factory in the north of Zululand, which they assured Shaka would hasten the delivery of his ivory to the bay. Although Shaka refused this overture,[80] it seems likely that the Portuguese emissary Isaacs met at Shaka's kraal had come for a similar purpose.[81] By this time, however, Shaka had decided that he would rather have an establishment of British traders at Port Natal than Portuguese in Zululand.[82] The reason for his preference for the British seems to have been that they brought trading goods which at the time were far superior to those that were procured from the Portuguese at

[77] P.R.O. Adm. 1/2269 'Cap. O' No. 30a, 'Description of the People of Delagoa Bay by Mr. Alick Osbornne'.

[78] P.R.O. Adm. 1/2269 'Cap. O' No. 60, Owen to Crocker 19 June 1824.

[79] Owen *Narrative* Vol. 2 p. 20.

[80] P.R.O. Adm. 1/2269 'Cap. O' No. 60, Owen to Crocker 19 June 1824.

[81] Isaacs *Travels* Vol. 1 pp. 58–59.

[82] Farewell to Somerset, 1 May 1824 Bird *Annals* Vol. 1 p. 72.

Delagoa Bay.[83] A secondary factor may have been the contempt with which the Zulu viewed the Portuguese because of their slave dealing at the bay.[84]

Although the Delagoa market was probably never completely closed down, the latter years of Shaka's reign witnessed a shift in emphasis in the direction of the flow of ivory. For by 1827, Shaka seems to have become obsessed with obtaining macassar oil, with which to turn 'white hairs black'. To this end he ordered his 'whole force' to hunt elephants and in private assured the British traders that they need not bring any other trading goods but the cherished oil.[85] When the traders failed to obtain this article, Shaka no longer had any use for them and let it be known that their presence at Port Natal was no longer desired.[86] Although many interesting questions are raised by his dealings with the British,[87] for our purposes perhaps the most significant factor is that in order to obtain European goods, Shaka was willing to employ his entire military establishment in the hunting of the elephant.

During the reign of Dingane the trading emphasis seems to have shifted back to Delagoa Bay. As early as 1828 and 1829, it was reported that Dingane pursued no other trade than that of Delagoa Bay.[88] Between 1828 and 1835 the British traders at Dingane's capital continually referred to Thonga traders and Portuguese soldiers that they met in Zululand. By 1834, Fynn commented that Zululand was 'glutted' with beads obtained from Delagoa Bay and that the Zulu received 'immense' quantities of beads and brass from that source.[89] The economics of the trade had been reversed and it was now the Portuguese who supplied the better bead more inexpensively.[90] In 1835, Dingane held out the promise that he would switch the major portion of his commerce to Port Natal, if he could be assured that he would obtain as much brass from the English as he did from the Portuguese.[91]

Dingane, like Shaka before him, sought to acquire more than just beads and brass through the prosecution of trade. By the 1830s, firearms had become a highly desired commodity. Perhaps resulting from the fact that the British traders at Port Natal

[83] Fynn *Diary* p. 77. [84] Ibid. p. 299. [85] Ibid. p. 143.

[86] See Felix Okoye 'Shaka and the British Traders' (unpublished seminar paper, UCLA, April 1964) p. 26.

[87] Ibid. [88] Fynn *Diary* p. 175. [89] Ibid. p. 230.

[90] Ibid. p. 230. [91] Gardiner *Narrative* p. 105.

refused to sell firearms, Dingane turned to British missionaries, whom he allowed to enter Zululand. The missionaries, however, soon complained that Dingane and his principal indunas were interested only in learning the use of the musket. Captain Allen Gardiner, the mission pioneer, however, soon joined the traders in refusing to supply firearms, powder, and balls, to the Zulu.[92] British traders had previously noted musket-carrying Portuguese soldiers in Dingane's service,[93] but Gardiner may not have been fully aware of the fact that Dingane also received firearms and powder from Delagoa Bay.[94] Although the Portuguese were probably equally unhappy to supply the Zulu monarch with guns, Dingane had brought the entire area of Delagoa Bay under his control, and in 1833 had executed the governor of the fort at Lourenço Marques, who had refused to supply him with the goods he wanted.[95] Since Dingane was in a position to pressure the Portuguese into selling whatever supplies of firearms and powder they could obtain, the refusal of the British to supply him with this increasingly important commodity may have forced him into a continued dependence on the market at Delagoa Bay.

[92] Francis Owen *The Diary of the Reverend Francis Owen* Cape Town 1926 p. 65.

[93] Isaacs *Travels* Vol. 2 p. 113; Fynn *Diary* p. 198.

[94] See 'A Guerra dos Reis Vatuas Vizinhos do Presídio de Lourenço Marques em 1833' in *Documentação Avulsa Moçambicana do Arquivo Histórico Ultramarino*; also Lobato *Quatro* p. 138.

[95] Fynn *Diary* pp. 231–2.

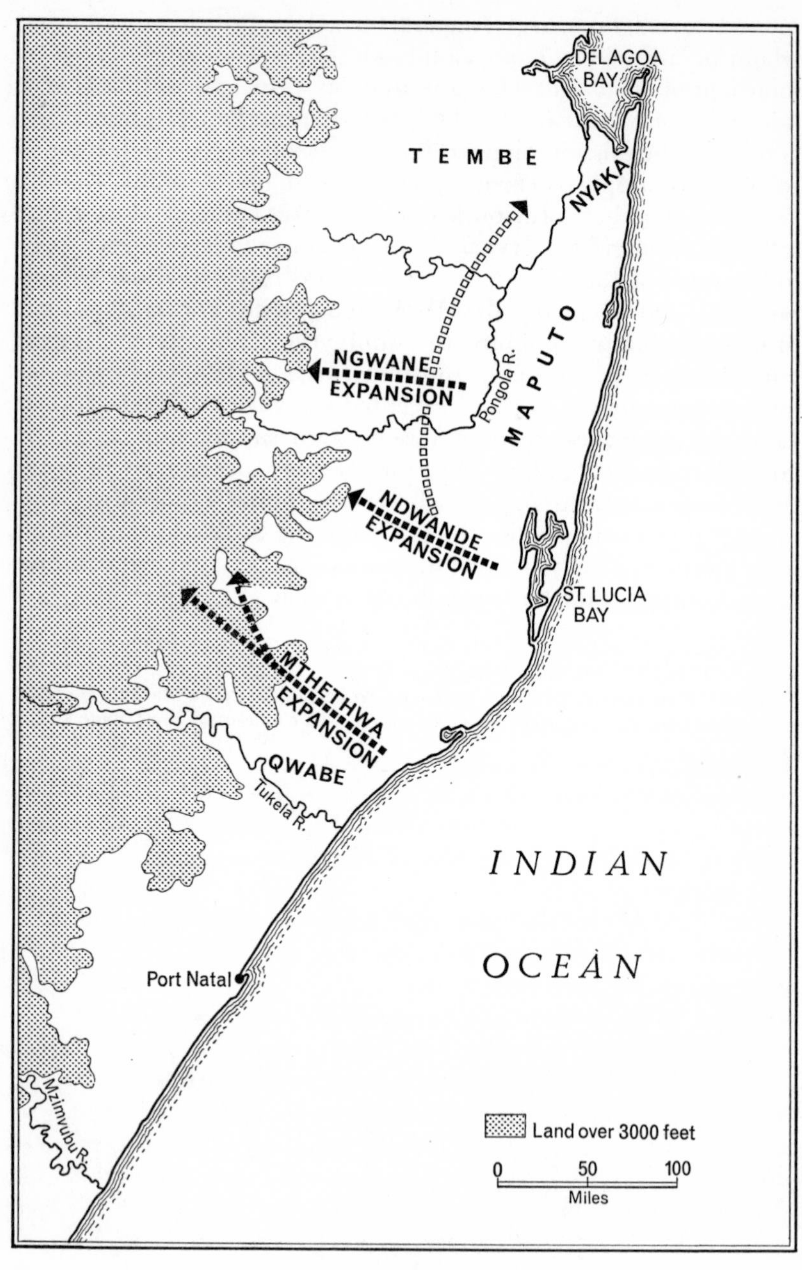

8. *Delagoa Bay*

9. *The distribution of the Sotho peoples after the Difaqane*

WILLIAM LYE

By the early years of the nineteenth century the Sotho people of South Africa had occupied most of the arable lands of the interior high veld to a considerable distance south of the Vaal River. Their political system consisted of autonomous chiefdoms comprised largely of related agnatic kinsmen. By means of continual fission, each chiefdom split in separate communities generation after generation, with no political control over the segmentary units. This dispersion assured the widest possible occupation of the arable lands within the area, and the maximum freedom for each community but, at the same time, rendered the Sotho vulnerable to potential enemies.

During the period after 1822 a succession of invaders, Nguni, Sotho, Kora and Griqua, preyed on the Sotho in the last great event in the traditional history of the southern Bantu before white intrusion. These wars, called the Difaqane, brought the traditional peoples of southern Africa in direct conflict and resulted in the weakening of Sotho society, the alteration in their settlement pattern, and a further weakening of their resistance to invasion at the moment of white intrusion.

So completely was the settlement pattern changed, many immigrants who entered from the Cape Colony were convinced that the land was vacant. Ruined kraals and heaps of bones attested to the former occupancy of the low lands, but the ruins alone remained. Actually, the result was more complex and variable and requires further explanation. This paper will discuss the effects of the wars on the Sotho to show how, in addition to the destruction of kraals and the depopulation of the exposed lands, many Sotho survived redistributed in less exposed areas.

At the beginning of the wars the Sotho were still expanding southward, though the force of their expansion had been blunted by counter pressures by pastoralist Griqua and Kora in the vicinity of the junction of the Vaal and Orange Rivers. The southern Sotho had expanded farthest south. They, and small Nguni communities associated with them, occupied the lands along the Caledon River to the foothills of the Maluti Mountains. Various Kwena chiefdoms formed the heart as they settled in autonomous communities along the Upper Caledon. South of them were settled the Phetla, Polane and Phuthi chiefdoms of Nguni origin. The Taung dwelt to the west of the Caledon along the Vet and Sand Rivers as far north as the Vaal. East of these, along the Drakensberg foothills, were the Sia, Tlokwa and Phuthing chiefdoms. Amidst all the others lived scattered kraals of the Fokeng. North of the Vaal in the east were several peoples who lived under the general paramountcy of the Pedi. These Pedi occupied the lands along the Steelpoort River. West of these two clusters lived the numerous Tswana peoples. They had spread from the Kalahari in the west and Kuruman on the south-west to the lands adjacent to the other clusters mentioned above, and north as far as the Limpopo River. All three Sotho peoples had some interconnecting lineages and traditions, but local distinctions had already developed as a result of separate development.

To this setting came the wars. The effect of the Difaqane on the Sotho peoples has been widely discussed. Theal referred to twenty-eight chiefdoms which 'disappeared, leaving not so much as a trace of their former existence', but this appears to have originated in a statement by John Centlivres Chase, an early Cape author, who cited an unnamed missionary who listed the names, locations and population of twenty-eight communities. An examination of the list, however, reveals that many were merely branches or individual kraals of the major Tswana chiefdoms which still survive.[1] That some chiefdoms did cease to exist is probably true, but, more frequently, they were temporarily uprooted and resettled in more secure areas.

A few Sotho communities on the margins of the Tswana area remained intact in their traditional lands. The best example of this was the Tlhaping, who lived at Dithakong, and their neighbours, the Tlharo and Kgalagadi. The Tlhaping avoided a direct

[1] George McCall Theal *History of South Africa, 1795–1834* London 1891 p. 303; John Centlivres Chase *The Cape of Good Hope and the Eastern Province of Algoa Bay* London 1843 p. 12. These are the twenty-eight names Chase lists: Bamangwato, Basmyreli, Bachazeli, Bawaukelzi, Bakutta, Bagachu, Bagasitze, Bamslile, Bamagase, Bamauyana, Bamokaluki, Bapeere, Barolong, Barumisana Bafoku, Barisana Bafoka, Bagoking, Basoking, Baropogate, Bapito, Battopeen, Bafoku, Baralota, Bamaraki, Bamaguade, Bagoyo, Baguin, Balouri, Basituana.

attack by the nomadic hordes thanks to the Griqua commando of 1823, and they also escaped any raid by Mzilikazi's impi, probably because of Moffat's presence. But they did suffer several attacks by the Bergenaar, rebel Griqua. In order to protect himself, one Tlhaping chief, Mothibe, took a portion of the people to land adjacent to Griquatown, and Lepui, one of his sub-chiefs, moved farther east to Bethulie under the French missionaries, but the main community remained under Mahura in their traditional area until they, too, moved to Taung.[2]

At the other extreme, the Kololo, though able to retain their corporate identity, were so completely dislocated by the wars that they abandoned their country permanently in favour of a new land beyond the Zambezi River. They began as a minor Fokeng chiefdom on the south side of the Vaal River. When they were attacked by MaNthatisi, the Tlokwa regent, they fled across the Vaal, gathered up their followers and proceeded on a career as a plundering horde. Finding that that also lacked security their chief, Sebetwane, directed his people to a land entirely removed from the disorders.[3]

Other chiefs assembled plundering bands, such as MaNthatisi, Moletsane and his Taung, Nkgarahanye of the Hlakwana and Tshane of the Phuthing, but each of these remained in the general Sotho area, and ultimately settled back in their country. Before they did so, however, each of these chiefs roamed considerable distances, and left many of their followers strewn along the way. MaNthatisi travelled the entire length of the Caledon, and Moletsane, Tshane and Nkgarahanye crossed into the Tswana country and fought their way to the borders of the Kalahari Desert before they returned.[4]

Not all dispossessed communities organized plundering expeditions. Chiefs who were driven from their lands, but sought out temporary havens, were much more numerous than those who went on the war path. Sekwati, chief of the Pedi, saw his father and all his brothers killed by the Ndebele of Mzilikazi. He alone escaped to lead his followers north to the Soutpansberg. There he lived by hiding out in the Woodbush Mountains

[2] John Melvill, Griqua Town, 17 October 1825 in L.M.S. Archives 9/4/A: F. J. Language 'Herkoms en Geskiedenis van die Tlhaping' *African Studies* I p. 126.

[3] For the career of Sebetwane see Edwin W. Smith 'Sebetwane and the Makololo' *African Studies* XV pp. 49–74.

[4] William F. Lye 'The *Difaqane*, The *Mfecane* in the Southern Sotho Area' *J.A.H.* VIII p. 122f.

whenever Mzilikazi's impis arrived to gather tribute. When Mzilikazi moved west to his new kraals on the Apies River, Sekwati returned to the Steelpoort River where he rebuilt the paramountcy temporarily vacated by his migration.[5] Among the Tswana, numerous chiefs were driven from their lands. The Ngwato, far to the north, found necessary a move from the Shoshong Hills because of the Kololo band of Sebetwane.[6] Sehunelo, chief of the Seleka-Rolong, fled from his kraal at Ga Thaba in 1823 when the first wave of marauders crossed the Vaal only to return and attempt to rebuild. After several more attacks, mostly by Moletsane's Taung, he became a nomadic drifter until he felt secure enough to settle at Platberg, farther down the Vaal.[7]

The major disturber of the Tswana chiefs was Mzilikazi. When he settled on the Olifants he drove away the Pedi, when he moved to the Apies the many Kgatla and Kwena communities fled or were captured, when he occupied the Marico River country the Hurutshe, the Ngwaketse and the Rolong of Tawane fled to the west and south in search of a refuge.[8]

Among the Southern Sotho, those who did not turn to plunder also had to flee. The Hoja formed a major part of the population on the west of the Vaal. Some of their chiefs led their people to the Griqua country in search of protection.[9] Others escaped by crossing the Orange River.[10]

A different sort of reaction concerns those who never left their country, just retreating to more defensible positions. In some instances this entailed not only creating new homesteads but also developing different ways to subsist. In general this migration was from the low and open plains, where garden plots and grazing lands abounded, in favour of narrowly constricted, but defensible, *Qhobosheane*, flat-topped hills, or ravines, where they could hide. If cattle were spared they had to be grazed under guard and

[5] Pedi tradition is recorded in J. A. Winters 'The Tradition of Ra' Lolo' *S.A.J.S.* IX [1913] pp. 87–100; and 'The History of Sekwati' Ibid. pp. 329–32; A. Merensky 'Beitrage zur Geschichte der Bapeli' *Berliner Missionsberichte* 20 pp. 327–42; D. R. Hunt 'An Account of the BaPedi' *Bantu Studies* V pp. 275–326.

[6] M. Legassick 'The Ngwato Under Sekgoma I, 1835–1875' unpublished seminar paper.

[7] C. R. Kotzé 'Die Geskiedenis van die Barolong Veral die Baseleka–Barolong, tot 1851'. Unpublished M.A. Thesis, University of the Orange Free State.

[8] William F. Lye 'The Ndebele Kingdom South of the Limpopo' *J.A.H.* X pp. 88–93.

[9] Thomas Hodgson Plaatberg (on the Vaal), 3 November 1826 in WMMS Archives, Cape, Box IV, 1826/51.

[10] Descriptions of the people who fled across the Orange destitute do not identify chiefdoms. See Charles Somerset, Cape of Good Hope, to Earl Bathurst, 30 July 1825 in Theal *Records of the Cape Colony* 36 Vols. London 1898–1905 XXII p. 419.

driven back into hiding at an instant. Little farming was possible for fear of wandering bands. The occupants were forced to revert to hunting and gathering, or thieving, and, in some instances, even to cannibalism. Dr. Andrew Smith, the Cape explorer who travelled throughout the Southern Sotho and Tswana lands in 1834 and 1835 reported numerous instances of this sort. In the vicinity of Likhuele he found a community hidden in a narrow wooded glen, fearful that they might be spotted.[11] Describing the Upper Caledon he stated:

But few natives were seen during this part of our journey and if we except a small village which belonged to an uncle of the Mantatee King [Sekonyela], we cannot say we passed any thing like a regular establishment. Many small hordes were dispersed over the mountain sides but these had neither fixed nor regular abode. They sought their shelter in the crevices of the rocks and wandered from place to place as the game migrated.
Though the country might therefore be said to be almost depopulated such, we had sufficient evidence before us, had not always been its condition. The ruins of several large villages were passed the environs of which were thickly strewed with human bones and even the appearances around the remains of the huts showed that numerous lives must have been sacrificed even at the very doors of the houses.[12]

One such community, the Ramokhele branch of the Taung, lived under Chief Moseme at Thaba Nchu near the Modder River. Moseme met missionaries of the Wesleyan and Paris Societies in 1833. Both described his situation as being destitute, as he had recently suffered the theft of cattle and children by Kora. The lands at the base of the hill lay vacant and the people eked out an existence hiding on the hill top.[13]

In the north-east, where Mzilikazi remained strong until 1837, Dr. Smith observed similar remnant Tswana communities (unidentified) who had remained in their traditional lands subsisting on the dregs of hunting and thieving, knowing that the impi of Mzilikazi would search them out.[14]

Not only weak chiefs resorted to hill-top retreats, however. Four of the strongest chiefdoms to survive the wars did the same

[11] Andrew Smith ms. *Journal* I p. 105.
[12] Ibid. p. 203.
[13] John Edwards, Boetsap 3 July 1933, WMMS Box V, Albany 1833/22; James Archbell, Platberg 2 September 1833, WMMS Box V, Albany 1833/28; Thomas Arbousset 17 July 1833, in *Journal Des Missions Evangeliques* X p. 42.
[14] *Journal* II p. 196.

and thereby preserved and extended their strength: Sekwati, Sekonyela, Moorosi and Moshweshwe. Sekwati followed something like this technique while living in the Soutpansberg where he retreated to the Woodbush Hills. On his return to the Steelpoort he established his people permanently on the hill known as Thaba Mosiu. From this hill the Pedi successfully defended themselves against the Zulu, the Swazi and the Boers until late in the century.[15]

Sekonyela was probably the strongest and most successful chief during the Difaqane. Though his Tlokwa were the first Sotho chiefdom to be dispossessed, MaNthatisi, Sekonyela's mother, held her Tlokwa together successfully until she had built a formidable fighting band capable of resisting the strongest intruders. Even this band found desirable a permanent retreat where a normal life could be resumed. Rather than return to the exposed lands near the Drakensberg passes, Sekonyela chose a mountain on the banks of the Caledon, where the Monaheng, the senior branch of the Kwena had lived. He conquered the hill Thaba Khurutlele in 1824 and gathered his following from all the Tlokwa chiefdoms, the Sia and from other communities whom he had either conquered or recruited. Ultimately, by the time the first Europeans described his situation, Sekonyela was reputed to have turned his retreat into the most defensible hill in Lesotho. He was then ruling about twenty-five thousand people over a country fifty miles to the north and east.[16] Sekonyela adopted the device of both of his Nguni adversaries, Matiwane and Mpangazita. During their stay along the Caledon, Mpangazita's people settled at Mabolela and Matiwane's people settled at Senyotong and then at Mekwatleng.[17]

Of more lasting importance, Moshweshwe, a victim of all three of these plunderers, and a minor Kwena headman, also experimented with mountain retreats at Butha Buthe, where he could not survive the protracted siege of Sekonyela, and at Thaba Bosiu, the most famous *Qhobosheane* of the Sotho people. Sekonyela had

[15] Winter 'Sekwati' p. 329; Hunt p. 288.

[16] Thomas Jenkins, Makuatling, 24 December 1833, WMMS Box V, Albany 1833/43; Thomas Arbousset *Narrative of an Exploratory Tour to the North-East of the Colony of the Cape of Good Hope* trans. John Croumbie Brown London 1852 pp. 58–9; A. Smith *Journal* I 175f.

[17] Moloja 'The Story of the Fetcani Horde' written by J. M. Orpen *Cape Quarterly Review* I pp. 267–75; D. F. Ellenberger *History of the Basuto; Ancient and Modern* written in English by J. C. MacGregor London 1912 p. 154.

already developed his power as a fighting chief. Moshweshwe gained his by developing his defences as a refuge from the wars. At Thaba Bosiu Moshweshwe tried to avoid direct fights by paying tribute to potential attackers, or by inducing a stronger chief to come to his aid. When his attackers persisted, Moshweshwe defended his people by rolling stones down the slopes of his retreat to drive off his enemies. By these means Moshweshwe gained a reputation as a successful survivor amid the ruins of the Difaqane. His successes in surviving attracted other chiefs who sought protection. Because he saved many of his cattle and could defend his lands he was able to supply what was wanted and thereby he became the paramount chief over all the Southern Sotho. He loaned his cattle out to other chiefs to herd under the *mafisa* system, whereby he retained the ownership of the cattle but the use of the milk was assigned to the chief who received them.[18] By 1833 when the first missionaries reached Thaba Bosiu, Moshweshwe had wide repute as '*the man* of the mountain', among all those who had adopted a similar means of defence. Though Moshweshwe used many circumstances and techniques to assure the continued loyalty of his subjects, his first steps to the paramountcy over the Southern Sotho were those which took him to the top of Thaba Bosiu.

Lesser chiefs who took up a similar defence on the hill tops often accepted a formal relationship with a major ruler over their area, such as Moshweshwe, Sekonyela and Mzilikazi. Those broken fragments of former chiefdoms were allowed to occupy land which a superior chief claimed because they served a useful purpose. Moshweshwe allowed such paupers to occupy land to the west of the Caledon in order to secure his title to the territory and to keep potential competitors from establishing themselves there.[19] Sekonyela had such people scattered over the territory north of his permanent settlements towards the Vaal River for the purpose of providing information regarding the approach of enemies.[20] Mzilikazi and the Tswana chiefs used people in the

[18] A. Smith *Journal* I p. 142 gives the best description of the defences at Thaba Bosiu. The *mafisa* system is described in Azariele Sekese *Mekwa le Maele a Bosotho* (Morija 1962; in Lesotho orthography originally published 1944). Moshweshwe's use of it is illustrated in Nehemiah Moshesh 'A Little Light From Basutoland' *Cape Monthly Magazine* 3rd Series II p. 232. I am indebted to Peter Sanders of Oxford for drawing this point to my attention.

[19] A. Smith *Journal* I pp. 226–7.

[20] Ibid. p. 187.

same way. The description of these paupers recalls the role of the Lala amongst the Tswana. Perhaps their function was determined by this traditional practice, but in each case cited the individuals were recognized as belonging to the former owners of the lands, such as the Rolong, the Tlharo and 'the remains of the Bituana tribe which formerly occupied the country now possessed by Musulacatzi.'[21] The people chose to accept that role in preference to being more intimately involved in the regular communities because they preferred the freedom of their poverty to the subjection to a stronger chief.

The desire for an independent existence reveals one of the most significant facts of pre-Difaqane Sotho society. Fission amongst the junior descendants of chiefs constantly divided the communities and contributed not a little to their inability to resist the wars. Prior to the wars only the Pedi had successfully united a collective group of chiefdoms into an effective paramountcy. Among the other Sotho such attempts failed. The Rolong under Tau achieved some influence over their neighbours in the eighteenth century, but in the succeeding generation the Rolong themselves split into several factions.[22]

The Difaqane altered that circumstance for the Southern Sotho. Prior to the wars they, too, had numerous autonomous segments. Tradition tells about a chief of the Monaheng Kwena named Mohlomi who was regarded as a unifier of the people, but he appears not to have influenced the political distinctions but rather to have been a spiritual leader and diplomat bringing together chiefdoms as allies through his numerous marriage alliances.[23] In the sustained conflict along the Caledon no traditional community survived in its original location. Only by uniting could they have resisted, and this they did not achieve. Moshweshwe brought unity by creating a focus of peace and stability to which the broken chiefs could submit.

The presence of the military conquest state of the Ndebele prevented any indigenous chief from developing a similar paramountcy among the Tswana, though the Tswana were also

[21] Ibid. II pp. 194–5. Smith recognized the difference between these people who were temporarily deprived of their lands and the Lala, or Kgalagadi, whom Smith also met. See Ibid. II p. 152.

[22] Z. K. Matthews 'A Short History of the Tshidi Barolong' *Fort Hare Papers* I 1 pp. 12–13.

[23] D. F. Ellenberger *History* pp. 90–8; J. C. Macgregor *Basuto Traditions* Cape Town 1905; reprinted 1957 p. 13.

handicapped by the lack of defensible hills on which to reorganize. In a sense, however, Mzilikazi created a Sotho state under his Nguni élite. The majority of his subjects were recognized as Sotho, and, apparently, the proportions of Sotho exceeded those of Nguni even after the expulsion of the Ndebele to the Trans-Limpopo country in 1837. Though his circumstances differed, Mzilikazi had analogous relationships with his subjects to those of Moshweshwe: some he absorbed directly as individuals from the chiefdoms he destroyed; others he absorbed as integral units in a subordinate vassal relationship that was not unlike the *mafisa* relationship, in that they retained their own village organization and herded cattle of the king; others he controlled by treaty or a tributary exactment, especially those on his borders. Though his system did not survive in the area, its existence prevented the development of a Tswana paramountcy which might have countered the encroachments of the Trekboers, thus it contributed to the distribution of the Sotho after the wars.[24]

A different influence was achieved through the mission societies. The London, Wesleyan and Paris Evangelical Societies all contributed to the resistance of Sotho chiefs to warring bands and, less often, they also influenced the nature of Sotho society.

The London Missionary Society arrived before the wars. They established stations among the Tlhaping at Kuruman and among the Griqua. By the time of the wars they were joined by Wesleyans who settled among the Seleka-Rolong after they had convinced their charges to settle down from several years of wandering. Later they founded a station amongst the Tlokwa of Sekonyela. Among the Tswana, the Paris Evangelical missionaries served the Hurutshe at Mosega and refugees from there and elsewhere at Mothitho. They also founded a station for Tlhaping and other unsettled Tswana at Bethulie on the Caledon River. Their most extensive work was among the people of Moshweshwe and his allies, Moletsane and Moorosi.[25]

The extent to which missionaries influenced the Sotho people that early is difficult to assess. In the case of the Tlhaping, the London Society encountered resistance and the chief, Mothibe, refused to remain with them preferring to live under the protection

[24] W. F. Lye 'The Ndebele Kingdom South of the Limpopo' *J.A.H.* X pp. 96–103.

[25] J. Duplessis *A History of Christian Missions in South Africa* London 1911; reprinted Cape Town 1965. This is the best single source for general information about all the societies in South Africa.

of the Griqua. However, Mahura, his brother, chose to remain with a portion of the Tlhaping at Dithakong, and then he, too, migrated to Taung in 1835. Only the remnants of broken communities lived at the mission station at Kuruman, but it became a magnet for the dispossessed people. The remnants were identified as Tlharo, Tau, Kwena, Rolong, and 'Bashutas'.[26]

Neither Sekonyela nor Moshweshwe permitted the missionaries to dominate their lands, though Moshweshwe successfully used them to further his control over outlying communities. The missionaries who taught in individual stations were subordinate to their leaders at Thaba Bosiu, and the missionaries at Thaba Bosiu were clearly subordinate to Moshweshwe. A further area of influence which Moshweshwe's missionaries had was as his diplomatic correspondents. They provided the most knowledgeable link with and interpreted Moshweshwe's interests to the colonial government.[27] Sekonyela, conversely, distrusted the missionaries and even threatened to attack the mission stations in his area.[28]

Probably the Wesleyans had the most far-reaching influence on any Sotho society up to the end of the wars. The Reverends Samuel Broadbent and Thomas Hodgson met their Seleka-Rolong people in 1823. From that date they remained intimately related to the community even though throughout the wars the Seleka suffered repeated attacks which caused them to become a homeless band of wanderers for a period. Hodgson and James Archbell, Broadbent's successor, applied directly to Moletsane, who at the time was still characterized as a plundering warrior, to induce him to refrain from attacking the Rolong. In this the missionaries failed, not because of Moletsane, but because their own charges sought revenge. They also interceded with the Griqua to redress a misunderstanding between Sehunelo, the Rolong chief, and Andries Waterboer, the Griqua Captain at Griqua

[26] R. Moffat and R. Hamilton 'Lattakoo' 20 August 1827, LMS Archives, 10/3/A; R. Moffat 'Lattakoo' 7 April 1828, LMS 11/1/B; R. Hamilton and R. Moffat 'New Lattakoo' 6 March 1829, LMS 11/3/B; A. Smith *Journal* II pp. 75–6; Language 'Herkoms' p. 126.

[27] Moshweshwe's diplomatic skill and his use of the missionaries for that purpose can best be seen in the extensive correspondence between himself and the Colonial Government printed in George M. Theal *Basutoland Records* 3 vols. Cape Town 1883; reprinted 1964.

[28] A. Smith *Journal* I p. 189; John Cameron, Platberg (Caledon), to H. Dugmore 17 December 1841, in Una Long *An Index to Authors of Unofficial, Privately-Owned Manuscripts Relating to the History of South Africa 1812–1920* (1947) pp. 79–81.

town. When their influence appeared to wane completely, the missionaries settled on the banks of the Vaal and induced a small fragment of Sehunelo's people to join them. When their settlement began to flourish the chief joined them and soon his scattered subjects also settled down. By 1833 they had built Platberg into a community of ten thousand. By then the chief had died and Moroka succeeded him. At that time the Wesleyans achieved nearly a complete mastery over the Seleka. Platberg proved unsuitable for such a large population so the missionaries sought out a better fountain along the Modder River. The entire community followed the missionaries to the new land of Thaba Nchu which they acquired by treaty from Moseme, the Ramokhele chief, and Moshweshwe, his master. By this device even the land on which the Rolong resided was held by the Mission Society. Thereafter the Seleka became the subjects of a missionary polity and obtained their political influence only through the leadership of the Wesleyans.[29] This case is exceptional among the Sotho; the only similar example was the role of the London Missionary Society among the Griqua in 1820 when they persuaded the people to select a Christian convert in place of their regular chief.

Thus far the concern has been for organized chiefdoms. Another influence of major significance in the redistribution of the Sotho during the Difaqane was the impact of disorganized refugees who spread indiscriminately over the entire Sotho country and beyond.

The refugees contributed to the disorganization of the countryside. Though many chiefdoms remained intact, stragglers dropped back as they were uprooted from their settlements. Plundering hordes often incorporated such stragglers, but, in turn, would slough off those who failed to maintain the pace. Their influence was felt through the manner in which they recast the nature of individual chiefdoms, strengthening one in relation to its neighbours, and altering the ethnic composition.

The extent to which refugees influenced the plundering hordes can be shown through the descriptions of them. Describing Moletsane's followers in 1826, the Reverend Thomas Hodgson recognized their mixed origins by their diversity in weapons, ornaments, dress, colour and dialect.[30] Concerning the Tlokwa,

[29] C. R. Kotzé 'Geskiedenis' 23f; I. S. J. Venter 'Die Ruilkontrakte in 1833–34 Aangegaan Tussen Mosjesj en die Wesleyane' *Communications of the University of South Africa* c20.

[30] T. Hodgson, Platberg (Vaal), 23 June 1827, WMMS Cape Box 4, 1827/21.

after they had settled down, Dr Andrew Smith noted that the nuclear Tlokwa constituted a small portion of the whole community and that the rest became subject to Sekonyela so long as it suited their needs.[31]

How many Sotho actually became refugees varied with place and time. Of the Southern Sotho virtually every community was driven from its lands. Eugene Casalis, a French missionary, estimated that two-thirds of all those who should have been subjects of Moshweshwe, that is, those designated Southern Sotho, were absent as refugees in the Cape Colony.[32] That proportion would be impossible to substantiate and difficult to believe. Moshweshwe stated that 'Most of their people [speaking of the independent chiefs of the upper Caledon] and part of mine had sought a temporary refuge in the Colony, in Griqua land, and other places.'[33] Other evidence supports this more general scattering. The missionaries at Kuruman reported 'Bashutas' among their communicants and identified them as refugees from the wars.[34] The missionaries at Griqua Town and Philippolis indicated that a large proportion of the residents in Griqua country were of the Tswana and Southern Sotho chiefdoms who lived in separate villages surrounding the Griqua settlements.[35] Even Mzilikazi acquired captives from the refugees, as did the Pedi who received some from the horde broken up at Dithakong in 1823.[36]

The refugees who reached the Colony were usually identified as 'Mantatees', 'Makatees' or 'Goes', the latter being either the San word for Black people or a corruption of the name Hoja, a numerous group of chiefdoms to the west of the Caledon. These refugees began arriving about the time of the battle of Dithakong, some brought there by James Melvill, the Government Agent at Griqua Town, others drifting in across the Orange River in a state of destitution. By 1826 George Thompson, the traveller from the Cape, reported that one thousand refugees were then living in the Colony. In the district of Graaff Reinet alone the Landdrost

[31] A. Smith *Journal* I p. 187.

[32] Eugene Casalis *The Basutos* London 1861; reprinted Cape Town 1965 p. 71.

[33] Moshweshwe, Thaba Bosiu, to Government Secretary, 15 May 1845, in ms *Letter-book*, PEMS Archives, Lesotho.

[34] R. Hamilton and R. Moffat 'Lattakoo' 20 August 1827, in LMS 10/3/A.

[35] James Melvill, Griqua Town, 17 October 1825, LMS 9/4/A; Melvill, Philippolis, 2 April 1827, LMS 10/2/B; Melvill, Philippolis, 1 July 1828, LMS 11/1/C.

[36] Robert Moffat *The Matabele Journals of Robert Moffat, 1829–60* (2 vols. London 1945) I pp. 9, 16. For the Pedi see A. Merensky p. 332.

reported forty-nine who had been apprenticed and over three hundred who drifted in unofficially.[37]

To discover some indication of the extent of the refugee migrations statistical references of the Paris Mission to Moshweshwe indicate that in 1833 he had a following of about 25,000. By 1848 this had increased to 80,000, and most of the growth was attributed to the return of refugees.[38] This is affirmed in principle by other evidence.

The Beerseba mission station, located on the south-western approaches to the Caledon River, served as a focal point for returning refugees. Speaking of that station, the missionaries reported that it was populated almost entirely by people who had returned from the Colony, and that it continued to grow despite the fact that these people successively moved on into the Sotho country once they settled.[39] The marriage register of Beerseba, which listed the birth dates and places of the candidates, confirms the impression of the large numbers of migrant refugees returning to Lesotho at the close of the Difaqane. Between the years 1842 and 1867, 231 marriages were solemnized of which the birth places for over four hundred were recorded. 132 people were born in the Cape Colony, seventy-five in Griqua country, sixty-two in lands now in the Free State, eleven from Botswana and six from Natal, more than two-thirds from places excluded from contemporary Lesotho.

[37] George Thompson *Travels and Adventures in Southern Africa* ed. Vernon S. Forbes First ed. London 1827 Part I Cape Town 1967 p. 186; Thomas Pringle *Narrative of a Residence in South Africa* London 1851 p. 76; A. Stockenstrom, Graaff Reinet, to Sir Richard Plasket, Sec. to Govt., 1 June 1825, in G. M. Theal *Records of the Cape Colony* XXIV p. 293.

As used in the Colony, the terms Mantatee, Makatee and Goe are general designations for the refugees from the trans-Orange to distinguish from the 'Kaffirs', the Nguni people of the Eastern Cape. Specific identifications are virtually impossible to discover because of this. It is known that Moorosi's Phuthi, Moletsane's Taung and various of Moshweshwe's people went to the Colony where they took the general names mentioned. See 'Statement Drawn up at the Request of Chief Moletsane, Mekuatling, 28 January 1852, in G. M. Theal *Basutoland Records* 3 vols. Cape Town 1883; reprinted 1964 I pp. 517–20; Justice of the Peace of Craddock to Colonel Somerset, 13 August 1834, in Orpen Correspondence with D. F. Ellenberger, in Papers of Paul Ellenberger, Masitisi, Lesotho. (Original unseen); Moshweshwe to Govt. Secretary, 15 May 1845, in PEMS File, Lesotho.

[38] Figures cited from Peter Sanders 'Moshoeshoe and the Creation of the Sotho Nation' unpublished seminar paper School of Oriental and African Studies London February 1967.

[39] Samuel Rolland, Beerseba, nd, in *Journal des Missions* pp. 12, 23; '4th Report of the Conference of Missionaries in Africa' Thaba Bosiu, 10 November 1838, in *Journal des Missions* pp. 14, 175; Prosper Lemue, Motito, 21 September 1839, in ibid. pp. 15, 45.

Individual case histories show the pattern of the migrations. The Moeletsi family recorded birth places for six individuals. The first two were born in Ramokhele's country, a third, in 1832, at Cradock, another from a second wife at Colesberg the same year, a fifth at Graaff Reinet in 1837 and a sixth at Beerseba in 1842. The Masuetsa family recorded births at Ramokhele's country in 1827, in Maseteli [Bastard=Griqua] country in 1832, Makhoeng [White man's land] in 1833, and Beerseba in 1834.[40]

The return of refugees was observed by Dr Smith in 1834 on his journey to the interior. They had made a temporary settlement near the Orange River twenty-one miles from Philippolis. They had worked for the colonists until they had earned cattle by which to support themselves again and then returned to find peace among their people.[41]

Moshweshwe was not the only recipient of refugees. Sekonyela received many from the north, but Moshweshwe had the advantage of being in the line of the return of those among the Griqua and the colonists. The entire Tswana complex of chiefdoms also received refugees. Moffat noted that his station consisted almost entirely of 'strangers', few Tlhaping being amongst them.[42] The communities of Lala, 'Poor Bechuanas', were also swelled above their normal complement of Kgalagadi by refugees who made their living from the *veld kos*. Professor Isaac Schapera has made a definitive study of the chiefdoms of modern Botswana which shows that every Tswana chiefdom is composed of wards and individuals within wards of alien peoples differing from the nuclear community. Lists identifying the ethnic origins of these aliens and statistical information show the degree of mixing that has taken place. His historical notes show that while some mixing occurred at an earlier period, a major part derived from the period of the Difaqane.[43]

When the wars ended many Sotho communities attempted to return to their original country. Several Tswana chiefs succeeded in this because the Boers who drove away Mzilikazi were too few to claim extensive tracts so far from their base at Thaba Nchu.[44] Others, however, found their lands claimed by other chiefs or by the Trekkers. Moletsane, for example, temporarily settled among

[40] *Marriage Register*, Beerseba Mission Station, 1842–1867, in PEMS Archives, Lesotho.
[41] A. Smith *Journal* I pp. 42, 44.
[42] See note 26 on page 200.
[43] Isaac Schapera *The Ethnic Composition of Tswana Tribes* London 1952.
[44] Prosper Lemue, Motito, 21 September 1839, in *Journal des Missions* pp. 15, 48.

the Griqua when his marauding days had ended. Then he returned to the Caledon when the missionaries founded Beerseba. He moved on to the Mekwatleng area to lands granted him by Moshweshwe. He planned to return to his original country on the Sand River, but the Trekkers occupied the area first.[45] The greatest redistribution occurred in the trans-Orange and eastern Transvaal areas where the Trekkers forestalled a return to the traditional pattern.

The Sotho people suffered their most cathartic period of history in the wars of the Difaqane and their sequels. The combination of attacks by dispossessed plunderers, small but powerful bands of Griqua and Korana, and by impis of the military state of Mzilikazi assured that the entire area was disrupted for fifteen years until the coming of the white settlers. By these wars the distribution of the Sotho peoples was drastically altered. In the first instance, entire communities were uprooted and had to find new lands to settle. In the second place, individuals had to seek refuge within and beyond the Sotho area.

One Sotho chiefdom found its way to the Zambezi River where it created a sub-imperialism of its own. Others, united with the Ndebele of Mzilikazi, did similarly in the trans-Limpopo country.

Of those who remained in the general area of the Sotho, the Ngwato had to move farther north than their traditional home, the Seleka and, for a time, other Rolong settled to the south and east at Thaba Nchu, the Tlokwa migrated west from their original lands to occupy those which had belonged to the Monaheng Kwena. All the numerous Southern Sotho chiefdoms found themselves crowded into the area to the south and east of the Caledon where they united in a different kind of polity. Relatively few Sotho communities were restored or remained at their original homes.

Within the lands which remained occupied by the Sotho, generally the open and fertile lowlands were vacated. The surviving remnant communities fled to near-by *Qhobosheane* or secluded ravines where they developed temporarily a different way of life.

Additional to the movements of communities, the migration of refugees who thus combined with other peoples altered significantly the composition of individual chiefdoms. Even less than before the wars, the terms clan or tribe describe the Sotho

[45] 'Statement Drawn up at the Request of Moletsane' op. cit.

chiefdoms which had by then become entirely composite societies. The impact of the Europeanization of the refugees who served in the colony must have contributed further, but the arrival of missionaries and settlers assured that European influence would directly impinge itself on the Sotho shortly.

The context of all these changes was what faced the white intruders in 1837 and what the Sotho people had created to face the new challenge.

10. Aspects of political change in the nineteenth-century Mfecane

JOHN OMER-COOPER

The violent upheaval amongst the Bantu-speaking peoples of nineteenth-century South, Central and East Africa, known as the Mfecane, is clearly of major importance in pre-colonial African history. Its interest and significance lie not only in its colossal scale, in the fearful destruction and loss of life which it produced or the far-reaching changes in the demographic pattern of large areas of the continent to which it gave rise, but even more in the fact that, far from being a mere matter of whirling bands of barbarians wandering and clashing with one another in a blind orgy of destructive fury, it was essentially a process of positive political change.

At the centre of the whole vast chain of disturbances was the sudden emergence of a new type of state in Zululand. From amongst a congeries of tribes organized on segmentary lines, small in size and frequently fragmenting, ruled by chiefs whose authority was severely limited by the need to win the support of segment heads and the people as a whole, emerged the large multi-tribal militarist Zulu kingdom; an extreme example of military despotism, where the youth of the state lived permanently under arms and the King ruled absolutely through military commanders who owed their position and authority to his will. In the turmoil associated with the birth and growth of this new political system, the military and political principles on which it was based were spread far from the original centre.

The Swazi kingdom, coming into existence at a stage before the process in Zululand had reached its full development, but later influenced by the example of the fully developed Zulu kingdom,[1] embodied some of the principles of its militarist neighbour in a unique synthesis of its own. The Ngoni states, taking their rise from the break-up of the Ndwandwe empire on

[1] On this see H. Beemer, 'The Development of the Military Organisation in Swaziland' *Africa* Vol. X 1937 pp. 55–74, 176–204.

its defeat by the Zulu, took over many of the techniques of their conquerors and carried Zulu battle tactics and principles of organization to southern Moçambique and across the Zambezi to far-flung areas of Central and East Africa. Under Mzilikazi, a section of the Zulu state broke away from the parent body. After a period on the Transvaal high veld, where the original nucleus grew into a powerful kingdom, Mzilikazi, under pressure from the Zulu and the Boers of the great Trek, led his regiments across the Limpopo and built the Ndebele kingdom largely on Zulu lines in modern Rhodesia. Thus, a whole series of states came into existence with recognizably common features, all owing much to the example of the Zulu kingdom, yet each possessing different characteristics of its own and developing along different lines, dictated both by initial organizational differences and by the variety of the environments and circumstances in which they grew. It is with the broad outlines of the political development of these related yet different states, which afford a unique opportunity for the comparative study of one type of state formation and development in sub-Saharan Africa, that this paper is concerned.

Before the beginning of the process of political change, which culminated in the emergence of the Zulu kingdom under Shaka, Zululand and Natal were the home of a large number of relatively small tribes belonging to the Nguni-speaking group of the Southern Bantu-speaking peoples. They had been in occupation of most of the coastal corridor between the Drakensberg range and the sea for several centuries and population in parts of the northern end of this corridor had been relatively dense from at least as early as the seventeenth century.[2] Though the Nguni-speakers of the coastal area could be distinguished from the Sotho–Tswana group of the interior plateau, the two groups were not entirely separate from one another. There were tribes of Nguni origin living on the Transvaal high veld and in parts of modern Lesotho, while on the edges of the Drakensberg and particularly in the north-east corner of the coastal corridor, in the neighbourhood of modern Swaziland, Sotho and Nguni peoples were in close contact with one another.[3]

[2] This is clear from accounts of persons shipwrecked on the coast, see for example the accounts of the wrecks of the *Santo Alberto* (wrecked near Umtata river in 1593) and *São João Baptista* (wrecked just south of the Umzimvubu in 1622) in Boxer *The Tragic History of the Sea* Hakluyt Society 1957.

[3] The terms Sotho/Tswana and Nguni are omnibus terms used to refer to broad groups of peoples. Each of these broad groups is probably made up of peoples of widely

In the tribes of the pre-Mfecane period, the chief held a pre-eminent position as the political, judicial, military and spiritual head of his people. He was ultimately responsible for taking all major political decisions affecting his people as a whole. His court, apart from being a court of first instance for those living near his residence and under his immediate authority, was a court of appeal to which cases from the courts of all subordinate authorities could be referred.[4] He was the living link between the community and its departed ancestors and as such regulated the ritual life of his community. His influence extended to the fertility of the soil and the reproduction of his people. He regulated the agricultural cycle and on his death his subjects abstained from sexual intercourse with their wives for a ritual mourning period.[5]

To provide for effective governance of the whole community, however, the tribal territory was divided into territorial segments under the immediate authority of the relatives of the chief (usually his uncles, brothers and sons). As royals, these subordinate rulers shared some of the charisma of the supreme ruler. Because of their royal descent they were potentially capable of becoming independent rulers; often they were open rivals for the throne. Each of them, while under the over-riding authority of the supreme chief, exercised authority over the people living in his territorial segment, had a court which to a great extent mirrored that of the supreme ruler and could call on his followers for military support.

For this reason, the effective power of a tribal ruler was severely limited. If he antagonized the heads of important territorial segments or lost the support of public opinion in the community generally, he would be likely to be replaced by one of his powerful rivals or to see his community split and one or more of the territorial segments hive off as an independent tribe. Government was thus conducted by consultation. A small group of

[4] In spite of the argument in the chapter by Dr. Hammond-Tooke in this volume, the custom of referring cases from lower to higher courts does seem to have been practised in the past. It was noted by the survivors of the *Stavenisse* wrecked on the Transkei coast in 1686: see J. Bird *The Annals of Natal* Pietermaritzburg 1888 Vol. I pp. 44–48.

[5] This point was also noted by the survivors of the *Stavenisse: Annals of Natal* Vol. I pp. 30–32. Alberti maintains that his prohibition was observed during the illness of a chief by those living in his vicinity: L. Alberti *Description Physique et Historique des Cafres* Amsterdam 1811 p. 171.

differing origins. The chapters by Shula Marks and Martin Legassick in this volume deal with this problem.

intimate councillors (*ama pagati*) advised the chief on all day-to-day matters. On occasions where decisions affecting the whole community were to be considered, a wider council involving all the territorial segment heads would be assembled. Among the Nguni, where dispersed patterns of settlements made mass meetings of the people at large difficult to assemble, the process of consultation was confined to politically important royals and a few influential commoners, but among the Sotho and Tswana who lived in relatively large villages and towns, the public at large attended assemblies (known as *pitso*) when matters of vital importance for the whole community were to be discussed. Though the chief was ultimately responsible for taking the final decision on all matters, the delicate balance of power between himself and his potential rivals ensured that he would normally seek to act in accordance with the general spirit of the views expressed by the participants at the various meetings. The chief's role, though it undoubtedly varied considerably from individual to individual, according to his age and experience, how recently he had come to power, and the strength of his personality, was, in general, to give expression to the consensus view of the leading men and the public at large.

A further effect of the division of the community into territorial segments headed by royals was the tendency to repeated division of the political unit. Political rivalry amongst members of the royal group was endemic and frequently came to a head on the death of a ruler. The likelihood of such disputes was positively increased by the laws governing succession. In addition to the normal households established by influential persons, a chief was expected to establish a 'great house', headed by a 'great wife', whose marriage dowry was paid by contributions from the tribe as a whole. The 'great wife' was thus an official state bride and only her children, or those of other wives affiliated to the 'great house', could theoretically succeed to the chieftainship. As a chief could only marry his 'great wife' and establish his 'great house' after his own accession to the chieftainship, he would almost certainly have sons by other wives married earlier in life who would be older than the official heir. These sons, not unnaturally, frequently disputed the succession on their father's death.

A most common result of these succession disputes was division of the community, with one or more territorial segments under the leadership of a disappointed claimant to the throne breaking away to form an independent political community. These secessions were so frequent that they can almost be said to have taken place with every generation and among the Nguni it has been argued that the head of the 'right-hand-house' had a prescriptive right to break away on the death of its founder. Through the repeated process of tribal cleavage, one original tribe would in time give rise to a whole cluster of independent political communities, which would continue to recognize their common origin and the seniority of the tribe headed by descendants of the original 'great house', but would otherwise be completely independent and often hostile to one another.

This process of tribal cleavage was not merely a product of the political system, but a functional adaptation of society to a situation in which a rapidly-expanding population was engaged in the active colonization of extensive areas of land sparsely inhabited by a previous population of San hunters and food-gatherers and Khoikhoi pastoralists. The difficulties of herding large troops of cattle together in the relatively arid environment of South Africa and the problems of communication made relatively small political units advantageous. The absence of any enemy organized on a massive scale made the assembly of large armies, with the large-scale political organization that this requires, unnecessary, while the need for rapid retaliation against small raids by San or Khoikhoi enemies dictated political decentralization.

Though the system of territorial segments, headed by royals, had the effect of encouraging tribal division and restricting the power of chiefs to the expression of the common consensus, there were features of the political organization of pre-Mfecane tribes which tended in the opposite direction. The unique position of the chief, though compatible with some restrictions on his capacity for independent action, could provide the basis for the exercise of virtually despotic power. The commoner officials, known as indunas, whom chiefs wisely employed in positions of especial trust (notably as their personal deputies) in preference to royals, constituted a nascent appointive bureaucracy which could be used to increase centralization and liberate the ruler from dependence on his potentially rebellious relatives. The system of manhood initiation created bonds of loyalty between persons who had been initiated at the same time which long outlasted the actual initiation period. There thus came into existence a system of age-grades which to some extent cut across the vertical lines of loyalty of the segmentary territorial system. The age-grade system was exploited by the Sotho peoples for military purposes. In their case, initiation schools were set up on the initiative of chiefs when they had sons of age to be initiated. Young men from the whole tribe, or a large part of it, would all attend the central initiation school and after its conclusion would retain a corporate identity as an age-regiment with a distinctive regimental name. Members of such an age-regiment would fight together in times of war under the leadership of this age-mate prince, and they could also be called on to perform special services (such as building a new household) either for the chief of the tribe or for their own particular prince.[6] The potentialities of the age-regiment system as a means of enhancing military effectiveness and political unity and weakening the divisive tendencies of the territorial system were limited in the pre-Mfecane period by the fact that the regiments only assembled occasionally, and still more by the attachment of age-regiments to particular royals who in time became territorial segment heads and frequently rivals for the throne.

Towards the end of the eighteenth century, the circumstances favouring the continuous fissiparous multiplication of small political units had begun to change. New circumstances arose which demanded larger political units and stronger military organization. Amongst the factors making for this change, growth of population and resulting land shortage is almost certainly one of the most important.

Other possible causes for which there is a certain amount of evidence are the expansion of trade with Delagoa Bay, the desire of chiefs to establish a monopoly of the traffic, and the enhanced political power which the establishment of such a monopoly placed in their hands. A movement towards the establishment of larger political units can be discovered over a wide area in South Africa. Its earliest successful manifestation is perhaps to be seen amongst the Pedi in the neighbourhood of the Steelpoort mountains on one of the trade routes to Delagoa Bay. They made use

[6] The Pedi for example were using the age-regiment system well before the Mfecane. See D. R. Hunt 'An Account of the Bapedi' *Bantu Studies* 1937 pp. 275–326. There is some evidence to suggest that some Nguni peoples may also have employed it in the pre-Mfecane period: see Alberti pp. 74–76, 175.

of the military advantages of the age-regiment system to build up a substantial empire.[7]

The development of this process amongst Sotho peoples of the interior plateau was soon eclipsed and disrupted by the consequences of a similar process near the northern end of the eastern coastal corridor. Zululand was a centre of relatively dense population which was virtually hemmed in between the mountains and the sea and had no outlet to the as yet unoccupied or sparsely inhabited lands to the south except by forcing a way through the numerous tribes of Natal. It was within easy reach of Delagoa Bay and participated in the expanding ivory trade of the port. In the late eighteenth century a movement towards the formation of tribal empires began and three main groups, the Ngwane (later known as Swazi) of Sobhuza, the Ndwandwe of Zwide and the Mthethwa of Dingiswayo emerged. By their competition with one another, they enhanced still further the need for larger political units and stronger military organization and so accelerated the pace of political change.

The first stage, which can be defined as that of the three leaders above mentioned, involved the attempt to build expanded political units by conquering surrounding peoples and reducing previously independent chiefs to the position of segment heads in an expanded chiefdom. This was accompanied by an increase in the scale and frequency of wars and by a need for improved military organization. As the frequency of wars made the circumcision rituals extremely dangerous, the traditional system of initiation was abandoned. Instead, young men of the age for initiation were grouped together in a regiment as in the Sotho system and military service took the place of the traditional circumcision and ritual seclusion.[8] The regiments included young men of like age from every segment of the chiefdom, including

[7] Hunt 'An Account of the Bapedi'. Alberti makes the interesting remark that the attempt to establish authority over a number of different tribes is a frequent aim of powerful chiefs and a main cause of wars: see *Description* p. 186.

[8] This change was ascribed by Fynn to an order of Dingiswayo 'History of Godongwana (Dingizwayo) and (in part) of Chaka' *Annals of Natal* pp. 60–61. It is is much more likely however that it was a development taking place more or less simultaneously among a number of different groups in response to circumstances. Though it seems at first difficult to believe that a change of such magnitude from the cultural and psychological point of view could have come about in his way it can be noted that the Mpondo are known to have abandoned initiation ceremonies in the disturbed circumstances of the Mfecane. M. Hunter *Reaction to Conquest* London 1961 p. 165.

those of recently conquered tribes. Each regiment was assigned to one or other of the royal households as its rallying point.

By this means, Dingiswayo and other leaders of the period were able to place larger and better organized armies in the field, and at the same time had found a way to build up a sense of common identity in the multi-tribal communities over which they ruled far more effective and thorough-going than the mere grafting of a conquered tribe on to the segmentary territorial system of its conquerors. The effectiveness of these new developments, whether as a means of increasing military power, or as a means of state building, was limited, however, by the fact that the regiments assembled only for specific campaigns and their members lived for most of the time in their various territorial areas under the authority of their segment heads. The multi-tribal kingdoms of this period, notably that of Dingiswayo, were fragile agglomerations easily broken up again into their constituent parts.

The next phase in the process of political change arose out of the competitive struggle between the rival kingdoms and was initiated by Shaka.

The essential changes which he introduced were the replacement of the throwing spear by the short-handled stabbing spear and the introduction of the tactics of close formation fighting involving prolonged drilling; the introduction of continuous military service for prolonged periods and the establishment of the age-regiments in military towns where the soldiers lived and drilled between campaigns, and finally, the development of the concept of total war aimed at the total submission or total obliteration of hostile communities. As a result of these innovations, Shaka was able to defeat the forces of Zwide (who had previously driven the Ngwane to seek refuge in Swaziland and procured the death of Dingiswayo) in a fateful battle on the Mhlatuse river in 1818. Thereafter, Shaka was able to destroy all opposition to his authority in Zululand and Natal and to build up a kingdom made up of very many original tribes.

In Shaka's kingdom, young men of like age from the many different tribes under his authority were gathered together in age-regiments barracked in a series of special military towns in a military area near the centre of the kingdom and commanded by an induna appointed by the ruler. Each military town was a royal household presided over by a senior woman and a senior induna.[9] A special herd of cattle was attached to each regiment, the cattle for each such herd being chosen for their skin colour and markings which corresponded with those of the shields used by the members of the corresponding regiment. These herds were maintained and augmented as a consequence of successful warfare against surrounding peoples. Meat for the members of a regiment was supplied from the cattle of the corresponding herd and the shields of the warriors were made from their hides.[10] All the regimental herds belonged to the king and the warriors thus had a direct interest in the success of campaigns by which the royal herds were augmented.

In addition to the male regiments stationed at the royal households, there were also female regiments made up of young unmarried women of like age. These young women, who must have constituted a large proportion of the unmarried girls in the kingdom, were legally wards of the king and when a male regiment was dissolved after completing its period of active service, the corresponding female regiment was also dissolved and its members given as wives to the warriors (who, during their period of active service, were expected to live lives of strict celibacy under pain of death).[11]

Through this extraordinary system, Shaka developed a military machine that was quite unbeatable in terms of traditional Bantu military tactics. He had also developed a method of integrating members of different tribes into a single political community and developing in them a sense of common identity and loyalty far more thorough-going than anything that had been known before. At the same time, power had become centralized in the hands of the king to a degree quite foreign to the traditional political systems. The territorial chiefs, whose power traditionally balanced and limited that of the supreme ruler, were deprived of their key position when the young men of fighting age were drawn away from their authority into the age-regiments of the king's army.[12] Power had shifted from the traditional chiefs to the

[9] See, for example, J. Stuart and D. M. Malcolm, editors *The Diary of Henry Francis Fynn* Pietermaritzburg 1950 pp. 283–4; P. R. Kirby, editor *Andrew Smith and Natal* Van Riebeeck Society Cape Town 1955 p. 42.

[10] Fynn p. 283; N. Isaacs *Travels and Adventures in Eastern Africa* Van Riebeeck Society Cape Town 1936 Vol. I p. 99.

[11] Isaacs Vol. I pp. 100, 129–33; Fynn p. 30.

[12] This is brought out very clearly in Isaacs' account of Zihlando in *Travels and Adventures* Vol. I p. 149.

military indunas who commanded the age-regiments and who alone possessed the force to restrain the will of the king. The indunas, however, were in a far weaker position in the new system than the territorial chiefs in the old. They lacked the charisma of royal descent and could never become rulers themselves. They owed their positions to the will of the king and could be dismissed and replaced at will. What is more, the whole way that the army was organized tended to focus loyalty on the king rather than on the individual commander. Shaka was thus able to escape to a very great extent from the traditional restraints on the will of a ruler and to exercise an almost absolute authority.

In the Zulu kingdom under Shaka, compared with the previous patterns of tribal government, an extraordinary transformation had been brought about. There had emerged a large, multi-tribal kingdom organized as an absolute military despotism.

The state had become a vast military machine, completely under the control of the king, who exercised his authority through agents who were his own creatures and had no other basis for their position than the favour of the king. This had been achieved, not through any process of radical innovation, but rather through the development of the potentialities of existing institutions in a certain direction, a process, moreover, which though it may have owed much to individual initiative and originality at certain stages, had begun and had its rationale as a functional adaptation of society to changed conditions.

Concentration of attention on the central government and military organization of the Zulu kingdom, however, tends to obscure the total pattern of political organization in the kingdom at large and to exaggerate the extent of the changes that had taken place, for the Zulu kingdom under Shaka could be said to have contained within itself two different systems of organization —virtually two different states.

In the central military area was the army, made up of the youth of many different tribes organized into age-regiments, barracked at the royal households and commanded by officers appointed by the king. Outside this area, however, the rest of the population lived in traditional fashion under the authority of territorial chiefs. Many of these were chiefs of tribes who had been subdued by the Zulu and though Shaka sometimes removed the ruling chiefs of tribes he conquered and chose others in their place, he normally chose them from the royal line of the tribe concerned.[13] Thus, leaving the organization of the army apart, the Zulu kingdom did not destroy the traditional segmentary pattern of political organization. It was, apart from the army, an agglomeration of tribes under the paramountcy of the Zulu king, in which chiefs of previously independent tribes, while retaining authority over their own people, were reduced to the status of subordinate territorial rulers in the wider political system. In spite of the great changes involved in the growth of the Zulu kingdom, therefore, the older pattern remained very much alive and was bound to react on the new aspects of political organization. The members of the age-regiments were still members of their tribes of origin and would go back to live under their traditional chiefs on completion of their period of military service. Under Shaka, moreover, the centralization of the military organization was less than perfect. Some tribal chiefs were allowed to command age-regiments made up predominantly of their own tribesmen. This made possible the secession of the Khumalo under Mzilikazi and later of the Qwabe under Nqeto (in the reign of Dingane). In spite of the changes in favour of centralization, therefore, the traditional segmentary pattern had not been destroyed and the possibility of cleavage along traditional segmentary lines remained very much in existence.

Furthermore, the concentration of military power, while it diminished the danger of territorial rulers breaking away, opened the way for a different kind of cleavage. The indunas, not being of chiefly descent, could not secede with their regiments to found independent kingdoms, but they could express their dissatisfaction or their rivalries with one another by transferring their loyalty from the ruling king to other members of the royal family. In 1828 both the new and the old decentralizing tendencies came together. The fall of Shaka was brought about by the Induna Mbopha who transferred his allegiance to Dingane and Mhlangane and helped them to assassinate the king, yet the underlying mood of popular resentment against Shaka which made this action possible was based on dislike of the rigours of the military system, the never-ending wars, the concentration of power in royal hands, and the general desire for a return to traditional ways.[14]

[13] Thus, in the case of the Mthethwa, Shaka got rid of Dingiswayo's heir Mondise and replaced him with another royal, Mlandela. Bryant *Olden Times in Zululand and Natal* London 1929 pp. 202–4.

[14] This is brought out very clearly in the speech ascribed by Isaacs to Shaka's assassins in Isaacs Vol. I p. 259.

Dingane, coming to power in this way, tried at first to relax the military system, but this merely brought the centrifugal tendencies of the traditional segmentary system into the open with the secession of the Qwabe and forced him to revive the regimental system and keep the young men occupied in external wars to prevent the break-up of the kingdom into its tribal constituents. After the defeat of Dingane by the Boers at Blood River, the new type of segmentation emerged again with the secession of Mpande, backed by a number of regimental commanders. For a short time, indeed, before the battle of Umgongo, two Zulu kingdoms, organized on similar lines, were in existence. Thereafter, and particularly in the period following the overthrow of Cetshwayo, at Ulundi, the two forms of segmentation became increasingly intertwined and entangled, but the development of the Zulu kingdom was so powerfully influenced by European intervention after Blood River that it is difficult to distinguish developments arising from the inherent nature of the Zulu political system from those imposed on it by deliberate intervention from without.

Of the states which arose at the time of the Mfecane, based on principles similar to those of the Zulu, the Ndebele kingdom of Mzilikazi was much the closest to the Zulu pattern. It began, indeed, as the result of the breakaway of part of the Zulu army, mainly composed of members of the Khumalo tribe who fled under Mzilikazi into the Transvaal high veld, thus constituting themselves an independent kingdom. In Mzilikazi's kingdom, the characteristic features of Zulu political organization, which distinguished it from pre-existing systems, were at first more strikingly apparent even than in the Zulu kingdom itself.

In Shaka's kingdom, the army, with its highly centralized organization, was still a state within a state and was surrounded by a much more traditionally organized penumbra. In Mzilikazi's kingdom at the outset the army was the state and there was no penumbra organized on traditional segmentary lines. Mzilikazi's followers were organized into age-regiments commanded by indunas appointed by him. As in Shaka's kingdom, the regiments were barracked in a series of military towns. The regiments were maintained in meat supplies from the royal herds, which were constantly augmented by successful warfare.[15] Though there is no

[15] Though Mzilikazi was by no means the sole owner of cattle in his kingdom he appears to have exercised control over all slaughter of beasts including those in private hands.

mention of female regiments in Mzilikazi's kingdom, a large proportion of the unmarried women appear to have been regarded as his wards and were given by him in marriage to his warriors when they were permitted to adopt the insignia of manhood.[16] The whole kingdom was intensely centralized. Messengers constantly came to Mzilikazi, bringing detailed reports of events in every part of his kingdom. The whole structure and organization of the state focused the loyalty and attention of its members on the person of their king to an extraordinary degree.[17]

The Ndebele had fled from their homeland on to the high veld as a relatively small group. Their survival and the expansion of their power depended on their capacity to absorb members of the tribes they encountered into their political system and imbue them with a sense of loyalty to their new community. Whereas the Zulu only faced the problem of absorbing members of other Nguni-speaking tribes who shared the same language and culture as their conquerors, the Ndebele on the high veld and, still more pronouncedly after their flight to modern Rhodesia, had to devise methods of assimilating peoples of different language and culture from their own. The primary method adopted by the Ndebele to this end was the incorporation of captives from conquered tribes in the regimental system. Through fighting alongside members of the original nucleus they came in time to identify themselves with their new community and to feel themselves Ndebele. At the same time, however, members of the original nucleus and their descendants retained a higher social prestige than newly-assimilated captives and ultimately a three-tier system of social classes emerged.[18] The members of the original nucleus and their descendants constituted the highest prestige group, assimilated

[16] Thus Pelissier remarks that none of the young warriors were allowed to marry until a new generation was ready to replace them. Then Mzilikazi would assemble all the young women and after choosing for himself distribute the rest to the young warriors, each according to his merits. *Journal des Missions Evangéliques de Paris* Vol. 8 1833 p. 10. See also Moffat *Matabele Journals* Vol. I p. 26.

[17] Thus Archbell who encountered Mzilikazi in October 1829 remarked that '. . . he has obtained such authority among his people that their very senses are influenced by him; so that nothing delights his people that does not delight him and if he is well pleased his people are in exstacy.' Archbell to Secretaries Wesleyan Missionary Society, Platberg, 31 December 1829 M.M.S. 1829/31.

[18] On this question see A. J. B. Hughes *Kin Caste and Nation among the Rhodesian Ndebele* Manchester 1956.

R. Moffat *The Matabele Journals of Robert Moffat* edited by J. P. R. Wallis 2 vols. London 1945 Vol. I p. 25.

captives belonging to the Sotho/Tswana peoples of the high veld the second, and members of the latest group to be assimilated, the Shona peoples of Rhodesia, the third and lowest. The emergence of these social classes and the limitations on inter-marriage between them served to preserve the original Nguni language and culture and maintain their prestige.

If assimilation of conquered peoples, through incorporation of captives in the age-regiments, remained the primary and most thorough method of attaching new members to the Ndebele kingdom, it did not long remain the only one. At least as early as the settlement of Mzilikazi at Mosega, he had begun to tolerate alien peoples living within his kingdom under local authorities of their own, without being incorporated in the regimental system.[19] After the movement of the Ndebele kingdom to Rhodesia, this took place on a greatly increased scale and the Ndebele kingdom took on a highly-complex character. There was the central core, consisting of the members of the regiments and who included members of the original nucleus, together with assimilated captives at different levels; there were villages of Shona people living in the vicinity of the regimental towns under close political control; there were Shona chiefs, ruling their own peoples, who clearly recognized the paramountcy of Mzilikazi; finally, there were chiefs who were virtually independent but from whom tribute could be extracted from time to time by the age-regiments. At this point, the kingdom merged into a sphere of influence and government into foreign policy.[20] The Ndebele kingdom thus developed by accretion much the same kind of penumbra that the Zulu kingdom had had from the start.

Because in its early days the Ndebele kingdom was no more than the army, the organization of the army was the organization of society and the regiments into which the army was divided were the units of social and political life. For this reason, the Ndebele regiments took on a permanent identity which they did not have in the Zulu kingdom. When a regiment had completed its period of full-time active service and its members were given permission to wear the head ring (the insignia of manhood) and to marry, they retained their corporate identity, remained living around their regimental headquarters and could still be mobilized as a

[19] See e.g. Moffat *Matabele Journals* Vol. I p. 70.

[20] On the complex patterns of Ndebele foreign relations see the chapter by Richard Brown in this volume.

regiment in times of war.[21] In course of time, the process went further. The sons of the members of a particular regiment would enter the regiment of their fathers, and though new regiments were still formed from time to time on the original age-regiment basis, the established regimental towns became permanent and hereditary politico-military units, embracing members of very different ages. The regimental towns thus took on some of the characteristics of territorial chieftaincies in the pre-Mfecane tribal systems.[22] As the regiments evolved away from their original age basis into territorial segments of the community, so the possibility of political divisions, based on rivalries between the regiments, developed. Since, however, the commanders of regiments were indunas who lacked the charisma of royal descent, the centrifugal forces generated by regimental differences had to express themselves through dynastic divisions within the Ndebele royal family. The first event of this kind was forced on the community by the circumstances of the migration from the Transvaal to Rhodesia. For ease of travel and safety, the community was divided into two sections, one accompanied by Mzilikazi himself, while the other went with many of the royal wives and children, under the command of an induna named Gundwane Ndiwene. As the two sections subsequently lost contact with one another, there were for a time two separate Ndebele states. This division was on the point of being legalized, as the indunas of the section which had travelled without the king began to despair of seeing him again and were about to install his heir, Nkulumane, in his place. The re-establishment of contact between the two sections and the execution of the indunas responsible for contemplating this act of treason prevented permanent division along regimental lines from taking place at this time.[23] On the death of Mzilikazi, however, the centrifugal tendencies of the regiments revealed themselves again in the dispute over the succession. The refusal of the Zwangendaba regiment to accept the succession of Lobengula must inevitably have led to division of the community, had

[21] On occasions of acute danger, as when faced with attack by Dingane, the regiments of adult men (*madoda*) took part in the fighting along with those of the youths (*majaha*). When one of the adult regiments broke in face of the Zulu attack, Mzilikazi punished its members by separating them from their wives and reducing them temporarily to the status of youths. *The Diary of Dr. Andrew Smith* edited by P. R. Kirby 2 vols. Van Riebeeck Society Cape Town 1939–40 Vol. I p. 87.

[22] See A. J. B. Hughes *Kin, Caste, and Nation.*

[23] On this see N. Jones (Mhlagazanhlansi) *My Friend Kumalo* Salisbury 1945.

Lobengula's forces not succeeded in completely destroying and breaking up the opposing camp.[24]

With the evolution of the Ndebele kingdom, therefore, the rigidity, logical simplicity and high degree of centralization of its original political system were progressively modified. The central core of the kingdom, organized on a regimental basis, acquired an ever-growing penumbra of adherents who were outside the regimental organization and administered by their own leaders. Furthermore, as the regiments acquired a permanent identity, segmentary tendencies grew up within the central core itself. Before Mzilikazi's death, these two developments were already beginning to interact on one another. New regiments were being formed which were made up of youths almost exclusively from the conquered Shona tribes, though they were placed under the command of Ndebele indunas.[25] As in the case of the Zulu kingdom, the initial development of the Ndebele state was cut short by European intervention which had already begun to influence the course of events at the time of the succession dispute which followed Mzilikazi's death in 1868. Nevertheless, and in spite of this truncation, a general trend away from a simple, highly centralized pattern towards a complex pattern of segmentation along two different but inter-related lines is clearly apparent.

The Ngoni of Zwangendaba and the Maseko Ngoni were original sections of Zwide's Ndwandwe kingdom. After the defeat of the Ndwandwe forces on the Mhlatuse river, they fled into Moçambique and later across the Zambezi into east Africa. They took with them the age-regiment system of military organization and the battle tactics based on the use of the stabbing spear that were typical of the Zulu.[26] To a far greater extent even than the Ndebele, they faced the problem of assimilating large numbers of persons of very different cultures to a relatively small nucleus of Nguni speech and culture. To achieve this, they made use of two different institutions which interacted on one another, the quasi-lineage territorial system and the age-regiment system.

In accordance with the traditional principles of Nguni tribal organization, the members of the Ngoni nuclear groups were

[24] See R. Brown 'The Ndebele Succession Crisis 1868–1877' in *Historians in Tropical Africa* Salisbury (Cyclostyled) 1962.

[25] An interesting account of the formation of new regiments of this type is given by J. Mackenzie *Ten Years North of the Orange River* Edinburgh 1871 pp. 327–9.

[26] See, for example, R. F. Burton *The Lake Regions of Central Africa* London 1860 Vol. II p. 77.

divided into territorial sections under the authority of the chief or his close relatives. Followers of the chief were allocated to one or other of the royal households founded for the numerous royal wives. The Ngoni moved vast distances but they did not keep moving all the time. Rather, their movements took the form of long, rapid journeys interspersed with fairly prolonged periods of fixed settlement.[27] Wherever such a settlement was made, the territorial relationships between the various sections were preserved and the villages of the different royal households, each of which contained a bevy of royal wives, were built in a fixed territorial relationship to one another.[28] Similarly, within each village, the particular position in which an individual built his hut was fixed by his social position within the village community. In the course of their migrations, the Ngoni acquired large numbers of captives from the peoples they encountered. When such captives were acquired, they were given by the ruler to their captors or other people in his favour. The captive who was thus assigned to a lord was regarded as a kind of dependent relative. He and his lord were bound together by the same kind of reciprocal rights and duties as members of a single family (except that the prohibition of intermarriage within normal families did not apply to these artificial family systems). As the process of acquiring captives continued, a relatively humble member of the original Ngoni nucleus could acquire increasing numbers of dependants and break away from his original village to found a village of his own, though he would still remain affiliated to his original superior and his new village would be built in a territorial relationship to that of his overlord which reflected his social position in relation to him. Still later, as the erstwhile commoner's following increased, and he acquired more wives, he would divide them up into a number of households.

Not only could originally humble members of the Ngoni nucleus behave in this way, but so could an original captive. In addition to being assigned to the household of his captors, a captive was expected to serve in the age-regiment appropriate to his apparent age. Through distinguishing himself in battle, he could acquire captives of his own who formed the nucleus of a

[27] This is clear from accounts of the migration, for example, see Chibambo *My Ngoni of Nyasaland* Africa's Own Library 3 London 1942.

[28] The account given here is mainly based on J. A. Barnes *Politics in a Changing Society* London 1954.

personal following which could eventually expand into a number of household villages. As the Ngoni continued amassing more and more captives, the territorial quasi-lineage system constantly proliferated until the original royal households and those of other close members of the royal lineage became the centres of large territorial chieftaincies. The age-regiments continued to be constituted on a state-wide basis from the youths of like age from all territorial segments. On the occasion of major campaigns, the whole force of a kingdom would be assembled in age-regiments. In contrast to the Zulu and Ndebele systems, however, the Ngoni regiments did not live permanently in separate regimental towns, but when not engaged on a major campaign, they resided in their appropriate territorial segment. Each major territorial segment thus contained a section of all the age-regiments, constituting a territorial army which could be used by the head of that particular segment for military enterprises independent of the central authority.[29]

As the territorial system proliferated and the size of the community grew too large to be effectively governed, it would inevitably split along the lines of division in the territorial system. In the case of the main Ngoni community, the Ngoni of Zwangendaba, this took place on the death of their leader which was followed by succession disputes resulting in the division of the community into a series of separate Ngoni states. Each of these, as it continued to grow, developed internal segmentation, presaging further divisions.

As in the case of the Ndebele, concentration on the methods by which the Ngoni attempted the complete assimilation of captives into their political systems would give an over-simplified picture of the development of their kingdoms. If outright incorporation of captives into the territorial and regimental systems was ever the only means by which the Ngoni augmented the population of their kingdoms, it did not continue to remain so. To differing degrees, the different Ngoni kingdoms acquired dependants who were not part of the regimental organization. The ways that this happened and the results which it produced varied from kingdom to kingdom in accordance with a variety of

[29] Thus Wiese remarks national campaigns including the whole kingdom should be distinguished from local raids undertaken at district level and not involving the authority of the King. C. Wiese 'Expedição Portugueza a M'Pesene' *Boletim da Sociedada de Geographia de Lisboa* X 1891 and XI 1892.

factors. A striking contrast has been seen in this regard between the kingdoms of Mbelwa and Mpezeni which may thus perhaps be taken as examples.

The kingdom of Mbelwa contained a large number of powerful segments, including notably that of Mbelwa's brother (and possibly senior), Mtwaro, and that of another of his brothers, Mperembe, who had originally gone with Mpezeni but later broke away from him to join Mbelwa. The kingdom established itself in the very rugged country of the Vipya plateau where the nature of the terrain and the difficulties of communication reinforced the centrifugal tendencies inherent in the segmentary system. In these circumstances, it is not surprising that Mbelwa was unable to exercise close control over other segment heads, who conducted themselves almost like independent rulers and undertook numerous campaigns without reference to the central authority. Arising out of this situation, captives belonging to a particular tribe tended to accumulate in the territorial segment bordering their area of occupation, instead of being evenly distributed throughout the whole kingdom. What is more, in addition to acquiring captives who were incorporated in the territorial and regimental system, the chiefs of Mbelwa's kingdom encouraged members of alien tribes, notably the Tonga, to settle near them in a tributary relationship, without being fully incorporated in the Ngoni polity. In this way, the sense of tribal identity amongst conquered peoples within the kingdom was preserved and between 1875 and 1880 the kingdom was shaken by a series of attempted secessions by conquered tribes. Of these, the Tonga succeeded in maintaining their independence, while the Kamanga, Henga and Tumbuka were crushed. Thereafter the centrifugal tendencies of the territorial system militated against effective action to crush the Tonga and facilitated the infiltration of missionary influence into the kingdom. In Mbelwa's kingdom, two forms of segmentation, one based on pre-Ngoni tribal affiliation and the other on the logic of the Ngoni system itself, can thus be seen operating at the same time and interacting on one another.

In Mpezeni's kingdom, particularly after the secession of Mperembe, the king was not faced with serious rivalry from the heads of other territorial segments. His power was consolidated in the long and precarious struggle with the Bemba and the subsequent prolonged period of migration. The area in which the kingdom finally established itself was open country, making for easy communications. As a result, the kingdom did not suffer from serious rebellions by conquered tribes or from a marked tendency to internal division along the lines of the territorial system. This contrast between the two kingdoms, however, is probably more apparent than real and stands out so clearly only because the development of Mpezeni's kingdom was abruptly cut short by European conquest. Though the centrifugal forces in Mpezeni's kingdom had not developed to the same extent by the time of the European conquest as they had in Mbelwa's, a tendency towards development along the same lines is already clearly apparent. Not only did the growth of the territorial system inevitably generate divisive forces which were already coming into the open in the last days of Mpezeni's rule,[30] but Mpezeni's kingdom, like Mbelwa's, was developing a penumbra of unassimilated subject peoples.

Some Chewa and Nsenga chiefs were left in isolated fortified villages and expected to pay tribute, a recognition that although possible it was difficult to conquer them.[31] Others settled under Mpezeni and were permitted to continue ruling their own people who were not incorporated in the regiments but paid tribute in agricultural goods.[32] Finally on the fringes of Mpezeni's kingdom and lying between him and Mbelwa was the Chewa chief Mwase Kasungu who paid tribute to both Ngoni kings while maintaining effective independence of either.

The Swazi kingdom of the Ngwane was the only one of the Zulu-type kingdoms to be established during the first phase of political change in Zululand before the emergence of the fully fledged Zulu system under Shaka. It was, however, subsequently influenced by the Zulu kingdom and its organization modified into something between that of the period of Dingiswayo and that of Shaka. In the Swazi kingdom, the youth of the whole community were formed into age-regiments but the majority of the members of the regiments remained at home under the immediate authority of territorial chiefs, some of whom belonged to the Swazi royal lineage, others to the royal families of tribes conquered by the Swazi when they moved into the area. Considerable numbers

[30] It is clear from a number of accounts that in the period immediately preceding the conflict with colonial forces Mpezeni was losing control over many of his indunas who were lending their support to Nsingu.

[31] For example, Chiefs Msoro, Sandwe, Kathumba and Chananda.

[32] These included Chiefs Mafuta, Kawaza and a number of others.

of more adventurous or ambitious boys, however, went to the capital where they remained continuously in barracks, constituting a standing royal army made up of sections of the total age-regiments. In the event of a major campaign, the youths from the countryside would be summoned to the capital where they would link up with their age-mates already established there, to form the full age-regiment army. In addition, the Swazi developed a system of personal clientage under which individuals of humble birth attached themselves to important persons in the Swazi political order in return for their protection and support. These persons might, in some cases, be the territorial chiefs of the people concerned, but would not necessarily be so. The power of the Swazi king to take arbitrary action was limited by the divisions of political authority between himself and the Queen Mother, who was the ritual head of State, and by the practice of wide consultation, involving the holding of public assemblies similar to the Sotho *pitso* as well as narrower councils of notables.[33]

The changes in the political systems of Nguni-speaking people which led to the emergence of the Zulu kingdom and a series of other states with certain basic features in common with that of the Zulu amounted to a revolution in the character of political organization.

These far-reaching changes did not, however, involve the adoption of new institutions and principles of organization; rather they arose as a result of the modification of existing institutions step by step in a logical process dictated by the pressure of circumstances. However striking the differences between the multi-tribal military despotism of Shaka and the pre-existing state system may be, the organizational bricks out of which the Zulu kingdom was constructed were traditional ones. The new features of political organization which expressed themselves in the Zulu kingdom and in the other related kingdoms of the Mfecane period, moreover, did not imply the total elimination of traditional forms of organizations. In the Zulu kingdom itself the territorial sections of the kingdom continued along very traditional lines. Conquered tribes continued to be ruled by chiefs belonging to their traditional royal dynasties, even though the authority of these chiefs was profoundly modified by the overriding power of the king and the incorporation of young men from subject chiefdoms in the royal

[33] The account given here is mainly based on H. Kuper *An African Aristocracy* London 1947 and H. Beemer op. cit.

army. In the Swazi kingdom the situation in this respect was similar to that in the Zulu, while in the Ndebele and Ngoni kingdoms a penumbra of peoples governed by their own chiefs but subject to the overriding authority of the king grew up by accretion.

In most of the kingdoms moreover the distinctive new features of high centralization, increased royal power, universal militarism and thoroughgoing acculturation of conquered tribes or captives aimed at cultural homogeneity tended to give way in time to a much more complex and flexible arrangement, with the emergence of segmentation within the central core together with the centrifugal forces of traditional tribal identities. The Zulu kingdom and those of the Ndebele, Ngoni and Swazi can, in fact, be regarded as responses to emergency conditions; they were born in conditions of military crises and as they established themselves more securely so their organization began to change away from a simple highly-centralized pattern to a more complex, decentralized segmentary one. This process of change cannot be adequately understood by looking at political and military factors only. Economic factors were undoubtedly important in the generation of the crisis out of which the new type of states emerged, and the maintenance of the militarist organization which they displayed was probably dependent on the economic parasitism of neighbouring peoples. Almost continuous predacious warfare was the price which had to be paid for the concentration of population in settlements that were too large to be economically efficient and for the diversion of energy and effort from agricultural and pastoral pursuits to military activities. Constant raiding for cattle is a well-known aspect of the activities of the militant kingdoms; less well known is how provisions of agricultural foodstuffs which must have formed the bulk of the diet were secured. Did the girls who made up the female regiments at Shaka's military towns undertake agricultural work to provide food for the male regiments? Were the young men sustained by food supplied by their families? Were grainstores a major object of plundering raids as well as cattle? Did tributary rulers pay tribute in cereals as well as other commodities?[34]

[34] In the case of the Ngoni, it is clear that regular tribute in agricultural goods was levied from some subject peoples. The agricultural practices of the Matengo between Songa and Lake Malawi for example were modified under his pressure to provide for a substantial annual surplus to meet the Ngoni demands. See Allan *The African Husbandman* London and New York 1965 p. 47.

Economic parasitism in the extreme form of armed plunder must inevitably suffer from the law of diminishing returns. This can be seen in the devastation of Natal and the need as time went by for Zulu armies to go even farther from their home to find suitable raiding areas. In the case of the Ngoni the pattern of repeated migration which led them to cover such vast distances can probably be at least partially explained by the exhaustion of raiding grounds around their successive centres of settlement. Ultimately, however, raiding must give way to a more stable pattern of relationships if the economic support of the community is to be permanently secured, and this largely explains the evolution towards a greater complexity which can be observed in the Ndebele and Ngoni kingdoms.

The Zulu kingdom and the related militarist states which arose at the time of the Mfecane were the result of the adaptation and modification of existing institutions to emergency conditions, and as the emergency faded we can see changes taking place which to some extent represent a return to pre-existing forms. Yet, as in all historical processes, there could be no simple return to the starting-point. The events of the heroic period in the life of the states had left an indelible impression. Old loyalties had been disrupted and new identifications had been established. New patterns of organization had emerged and vested interests in them grown up.

11. The 'other side' of frontier history: a model of Cape Nguni political process

DAVID HAMMOND-TOOKE

The contribution of an anthropologist, whose professional interest and area of data-collection have typically involved the synchronic study of present day societies, to an historical volume presents problems. The emphasis on change over time, central to the historian's interest, involves the deployment of archaeological, linguistic and ethnographic data in the posing and confirming of hypotheses (in the earlier periods) and exhaustive archival research (in the later). This, especially the latter, appeared to me to exceed the 'limits of my naïveté'[1] and raised the question as to what specific contribution I could make.

In the event I have attempted a reconstruction of the system of government of the Cape Nguni chiefdoms, those congeries of Xhosa-speaking peoples who waged a hundred years war with the expanding white power on the Cape Frontier. It seemed to me that a thorough understanding of these polities, faced with the threat of survival throughout this period, especially the process by which collective decisions were made, would shed important light on the historical processes that preceded and followed the confrontation and subsequent incorporation of these chiefdoms into the plural society of South Africa. Mindful of the comparative neglect of the African point of view among most South African historians (as opposed to the position north of the Limpopo), I have called this study the 'other side' of Frontier history.

The Cape Nguni system of government, unlike that of those societies called by Omer-Cooper in his contribution to this volume, 'Zulu-type states', remained small-scale and based on the independent chiefdom. There is no recorded instance of the large scale incorporation of alien chiefdoms into an expanding, militarized kingdom: rather there was a segmentation process that tended to split chiefdoms after an optimum size had been reached. The reasons for this are difficult to determine. Professor Monica

[1] The quotation is from M. Gluckman and J. Devons *Closed Systems and Open Minds*.

Wilson (p. 73) has suggested that the clue lies in the failure of Cape Nguni chiefs to gain control of the extensive external trade that occurred between the Xhosa-speaking tribes and the Khoikhoi (see Chapter 7) and, later, the whites. Certainly, as Omer-Cooper has stressed,[2] the adoption of the Sotho age-regiment system (for whatever reason) was an important contributory factor in the expansionist history of the Zulu and their offshoots. Be this as it may, there is a strong supposition that the type of polity here described characterized the Natal chiefdoms before the Shakan period and can thus provide a 'base-line' model against which the important changes involved in North Nguni nation-building can be assessed.

The analysis also has relevance to a wider problem on which I am currently engaged—the reconstruction of the political life of the Mpondomise of the Transkei, Republic of South Africa, prior to annexation, and the changes that subsequently occurred within it.

THE PROBLEM

The problem arises out of an attempt to trace the changes in the political system of the Mpondomise from the pre-1874 period of independence, through the appointment of white political officers and the imposition of Cape Colonial control, through the introduction of a system of district councils, to the Bantu Authorities system of indirect rule, introduced in 1956. Fieldwork was done at various times during 1961–5 on the present-day relations between chief, headmen and people, the presence of pressure groups, attitudes to the white bureaucracy, the traditional ideas of 'good' government, and so on. Most of this research was in the classical social anthropological tradition—collection of cases, participant observation, interviews—in fact a study of the society as it functions today. The emphasis was all along not so much on structures as on *process*, in this context the decision-making process (on both the administrative and judicial level) by which local government in the Transkei is currently carried on.

Even this investigation was not easy. In addition to the 'delicate' nature of research in a Transkei which had recently seen the *Poqo* movement, a state of emergency and considerable opposition to the Bantu authorities system, there is a problem common to all

[2] See J. D. Omer-Cooper *Zulu Aftermath* London 1966 and his contribution to this volume.

studies of political process, the fact that political decision-making is not easily observed. It is the product of lobbying and confidential interaction between those in power. Power and influence, unlike authority, are not institutionalized[3] and depend on factors of personality, subtle pressures and the marshalling of support that, as often as not, take place behind the scenes and are thus not susceptible to observation. For instance, the relevant section of the Bantu Authorities Act might state that the chief or headman rules in conjunction with his council—but what does this mean in practice? How much 'authority' has he got to enforce his decision, who does make the decisions, are there pressure groups and, if so, how do they make their wishes felt?

The problem is exacerbated when an attempt is made to see the material against an historical background, in an endeavour to answer the question: how has the governmental *process* changed over the years from annexation to the present? It is fairly easy to reconstruct the *structure* of tribal government (chiefs, sub-chiefs, councils, and so on), but any reconstruction on these lines alone tends to be formalized and static. What we want to know is how it worked. There is also the difficulty of making certain that one's description is objectively 'true'.

The anthropologist faced with these problems has at his disposal three main sources of evidence, namely oral tradition, contemporary records of white administrators, missionaries and others who visited the area when the system was still working, and comparative material from other closely-related tribes. In the research project discussed above, the historical base-line can be set at 1865, when the first missionary, Bransby Key, settled on the Inxu River and founded the Anglican mission of St Augustine among the Mpondomise. Before this time one is entirely dependent on oral tradition and comparative ethnographic data. The period 1865–74 is sketchily illuminated by Key in his evidence before the Cape Native Laws and Customs Commission of 1883 and in the writings of his successor, Godfrey Callaway.[4] From 1874 onwards the Cape Colony Blue Books on Native Affairs appear, containing the annual reports of successive magistrates, as well as significant

[3] See M. G. Smith 'On segmentary lineage systems' *Jnl. Royal Anthrop. Inst.* 86 2 (1956) for a discussion of these concepts. They are also referred to below.

[4] Especially his biography of Key *A Shepherd of the Veld* London 1911. Even here Bishop A. G. S. Gibson, in his Introduction, regrets 'The absence of material for a fuller account of the first years in Pondomise-land, especially 1865–1868' (p. xi). Key's letters seem to have been lost or destroyed.

correspondence and telegrams concerning alarms and excursions, particularly during the Langalibalele campaign (1873–4) and the Mpondomise Rebellion (1880–1). The position is much the same for the other Transkei tribes.

The main source of information is oral tradition—what the people themselves remember. This can be obtained by fieldwork among the tribes, supplemented, for the south-eastern Bantu generally, by two published sources which are themselves, in essence, records of oral tradition, namely the tribal histories of Bryant[5] and Soga.[6] They do not always agree on details. Recording from present-day informants raises problems. Firstly, one must be continually on guard against sectional or political interpretations, designed to support a political 'cause'. Secondly, there is the 'feedback' that results from the publication of books and articles: while investigating certain aspects of Thembu history I have had had one of my own books quoted to me as an authoritative source! Thirdly, the oldest informant during the 1960s is likely to be not more than 70 years of age, with an effective memory of between 55 and 60 years. He himself, therefore, is not likely to have personal recollection of events before 1900. It is true that he will have known personally men who were adults before this, and listened to their accounts of the past, but these accounts would tend to be idealized and biased and, in any event, would not provide the rich personal material (especially case histories and details of personality clashes) which are essential for this type of reconstruction.

One method of attacking this essentially historical problem is by building a model—a representation or description of a structure, an analogue. Basic to the model concept is a belief that social systems (in this case, the political system) are indeed *systems*, are not mere agglomerations of elements fortuitously brought together by historical accident, but form meaningful patterns of interrelationship between the constituent units. The model, then, is an idealized and subjective construct of the pattern. As aids to intellectual understanding models are, strictly speaking, neither true nor false: they are merely more or less useful for the task in hand. It is true that their adequacy rests on the degree to which they reflect objective reality and, to that end, every effort must be made to

[5] A. T. Bryant *Olden Times in Zululand and Natal* London 1929.

[6] J. H. Soga *The South-Eastern Bantu* University of Witwatersrand Press Johannesburg 1930.

achieve accuracy. For the historian, presumably, the accuracy of the model is all-important. Much of his professional activity is directed towards establishing historical 'fact',[7] through inference modified by internal and external criticism. For the anthropologist a model of pre-annexation tribal government would not have to be necessarily objectively 'true' in this sense. It is possible to treat a model, built up from oral tradition and the memories of informants, as a myth (in the technical sense), as a charter or blue-print, in the minds of present-day tribesmen, which colours their attitude to the present and by which they gauge the adequacy or otherwise of the governmental system under which they live. Such a model would comprise, then, the 'political philosophy' of present-day tribesmen, by which they judged, for instance, whether a chief under a system of indirect rule had exceeded his authority, or whether decisions emanating from his council were legitimate or not or, indeed, whether his accession to office was valid.

But for historians the 'truth' of the ethnographic model is all-important for, in the interpretation of historical events, the traditional system was synchronous with the events themselves, influencing them directly and not, as in the anthropological model just discussed, as a different epistemological order. Events during the years immediately preceding and following on annexation were directly influenced by the actual pattern of inter-relationships within tribal systems and adequate interpretation of these events must be based on a thorough understanding of traditional systems. A classic example of failure to understand the realities of a situation is the totally inadequate model of inter-tribal relations operated by successive governors of the Cape, who sought to hold a paramount chief responsible for the actions of minor chiefs in his cluster.[8] The death of the Xhosa paramount, Hintsa, is indirectly attributable to ignorance of the relationship of a paramount to his brother chiefs.

It was thus necessary for my essentially anthropological purposes to devise a model which would allow me to assess the main changes in the governmental system of the Transkeian

[7] See S. Stebbing *A Modern Introduction to Logic* fourth edition London 1945 pp. 382–8, for a discussion of this aspect of the historian's task. For a full discussion on the method of history see W. H. Dray *Philosophy of History* New Jersey 1964 and *Laws and Explanation in History* London 1957.

[8] See W. D. Hammond-Tooke 'Segmentation and fission in Cape Nguni political units' *Africa* 35 2 (1965) pp. 143–66 for a full discussion of these 'tribal clusters'.

tribes and also give me an insight into how the people themselves conceived the way in which they should be governed. It seemed to me that my efforts might perhaps be of use to historians concerned with the interpretation of events during the period of political incorporation in the eastern Cape, during the latter half of the nineteenth century. They might also have a wider relevance through a spelling out of the type of question that can be asked of the data. It should be noted that the model is not a 'process model' as described by Vansina,[9] but aims at being dynamic rather than static. Although I shall take the Mpondomise as a case study, and explicitly build the model upon their system, I should stress that the Cape Nguni, of whom they form a part, exhibit a picture of considerable cultural homogeneity, and the model will be generally valid for this whole congeries of tribes. I shall therefore deploy recorded material on other tribes where necessary. Here we are fortunate in the presence in the area of a number of sympathetic and perceptive observers—men of the calibre of the missionaries William Shaw, William Boyce, Henry Dugmore, and administrators like Maclear, Stanford and Blyth.

SOME ELEMENTS OF A DYNAMIC MODEL

By isolating the political or governmental system for special study one is, of course, arbitrarily abstracting a series of event-sequences from the on-going flux of social life. In building a model of this type one is concerned, first of all, with the hierarchy of political roles, and the relationship between them, as we are dealing here with established state-type societies in which this type of role is well developed. The political system can be broadly defined as the system of power-distribution in a society and political roles are those that enjoy the socially-acknowledged right to exercise this power. In a sense, of course, as Leach has pointed out,[10] power is an aspect of all social relations, but political power can be distinguished by the extent of its fiat and on its reliance on physical force.[11] But although recourse to force is an ultimate sanction in all political systems, it lies rather at the subliminal level—latent, and ready for ultimate mobilization, but not normally resorted to.

[9] J. Vansina 'The use of process-models in African history' in J. Vansina, L. V. Thomas and R. Mauny (eds.) *The Historian in Tropical Africa* London 1964.

[10] E. R. Leach *Political Systems of Highland Burma: A Study of Katchin Social Structure* London 1954.

[11] A. R. Radcliffe-Brown 'Preface' in M. Fortes and E. Evans-Pritchard (ed.) *African Political Systems* London 1940 xiv.

The power associated with political roles is much more consciously involved with the acknowledged right to make decisions for the society. No matter how small the group, decisions have to be taken on such matters of public concern as the waging of war, the commencement of planting and harvesting, the organization of the ritual cycle, the allocation of fields and residential sites, and so on. These are administrative decisions. Then, too, in all societies men and women come into conflict, get involved in disputes, and mechanisms for solving these must be institutionalized. Judicial decision-making is the obverse of administrative decision-making. When we speak of the power inherent in political roles it is the power to make both administrative and judicial decisions, as well as the power to enforce them, that is meant.

But the concept of power itself needs explanation. What do we mean by power in this sense? Is the power of, say, a cabinet minister, operating in the debating chamber, or at the hustings, the same as the power he has over members of his civil service department? Obviously there is a difference here, and M. G. Smith has suggested[12] that a distinction be made between *political power*, i.e. the ability to determine the course of events by influencing public opinion and marshalling support for a policy decision, and *administrative authority*, i.e. the acknowledged right to command. Political (power) relations occur between contraposed, equal units in a system, and is essentially alegal ('no holds are barred'—although there are broadly-stated norms that define limits to action); administrative authority is legally defined, is hierarchical and always involves superordination and subordintion. We shall build these concepts into our model. Do we find 'politics' (in Smith's sense) in Nguni states, and, if so where? Do the chiefs and subordinate political officers have authority and, if so, what are its limits and where is the basis of its legitimation?

Political power and administration authority have another attribute. They are always territorial. In Cape Nguni systems (as in most primitive states) there is another authority structure that operates *pari passu* with the political, namely the kinship. Families are embedded in the larger descent groups of lineage and clan and the genealogically senior heads of these groups have 'authority' over their kin members. Governmental authority differs from the kinship authority in that it extends over all who live in

[12] M. G. Smith op. cit.

the tribal territory, irrespective of relationship. This distinction will be important in our model-building when local government is discussed, for always there is a delegation of authority on territorial lines, an attempt to control areas far from the capital by placing them under the control of subordinate political officers. Many of these areas were settled by concentrations of descent group members, under their own kinship heads, and the linking of these areas into the state could involve either the recognition, or non-recognition, of these kin-group leaders into the political structure.

The above model is a static one. When we have described it we have described the structure of the political system. We shall have defined the political roles, the rules of recruitment to them, the territorial extent of the authority inhering in them and the normative system legitimizing and defining its limits. To understand how the structure works we need a dynamic element—the element of *process*. This is not the same thing as a process model as conceived by Smith[13] and Vansina,[14] which is designed to illuminate *structural* change. The process here is contained within the system and involves rather the cybernetic properties of input, oscillation, feedback and compensation.[15] In practice this involves a study of the relationship between the terms of the model, in particular that between the holders of political office themselves and between them and their subjects, in fact, the 'balance of power', the pressures of public opinion, the resolution of the conflict that accompanies all decision-making. Only if we can incorporate this type of information into our model will it be truly dynamic and 'useful' in historical interpretation.

THE POLITICAL PROCESS AMONG THE MPONDOMISE—AND OTHERS

The Mpondomise, numbering about 40,000 and occupying the Transkeian districts of Tsolo and Qumbu, are Xhosa-speaking pastoral-hoe-culturalists belonging to the congeries of southern Bantu peoples known collectively as Cape Nguni.[16] They are divided into two chiefdoms, occupying parts of the above-mentioned districts, and culturally appear to stand midway

[13] M. G. Smith *Government in Zazzau* London 1960.
[14] J. Vansina 1964 *op. cit.*
[15] N. Wiener *Cybernetics* New York 1948.
[16] For a discussion of the Cape Nguni from a political point of view see Hammond-Tooke 1965 op. cit.

between their two most important and numerous neighbours, the Mpondo and Thembu. After the Mpondomise Rebellion of 1880–1, part of their country was confiscated, to be given to other, smaller, tribal groups and today they also border on Hlubi, Tolo and Sotho (Monaheng, Tlôkwa, Kwena) chiefdoms. They have also long been neighbours of the Bhaca.

Although the Mpondomise today form two tribes, named after the two chiefs reigning at the time of annexation (*amaMpondomise akwaMhlontlo* and *amaMpondomise akwaMditshwa*), in the past they were one. The segmentation and fission of political units was an intrinsic feature of Cape Nguni society, assisted by the institutionalized right of the righthand house[17] of a chief to break away and form a separate chieftainship. Theoretically a tribe could split into two independent chiefdoms with each generation: in practice this did not, of course, always occur. All Nguni tribes have undergone this process, however, the fission being precipitated by usurpation, succession disputes and the like.[18]

Although, in theory, rules of succession were clear (the heir should always be the eldest son in the great house) in practice there was frequently uncertainty. The marriage of a great wife was a diplomatic move, linking unrelated tribes, and was usually contracted when a chief was getting on in years. He might die before the great wife was appointed, raising the problem of the ranking of other wives, the great house might be childless or, as frequently happened, the heir might be a minor on his father's death necessitating the appointment of a regent with all its possibilities of usurpation.

The Mpondomise have come off lightly. There have been two cases of usurpation of the ruling line, but only one new chieftainship has been created. Other tribes were not so fortunate. The Xhosa commenced a period of accelerated fission towards the end of the seventeenth century which, in six generations, resulted in the original tribe splitting into ten different chiefdoms. The causes of this proliferation were various and were probably correlated with rapid expansion into relatively unoccupied territory. It resulted in the establishment of four new chiefdoms between 1800 and 1830 (Ndlambe 1804, Mdushane about 1818, Gasela 1820,

[17] Nguni wives are ranked into two main houses (the Great house and the righthand house), and all other wives are allocated as 'supports' to these two. Allocation took place after the marriage of the Great Wife.

[18] For a discussion of some of these causes of fission see Hammond-Tooke 1965 op. cit.

Mqhayi about 1830). The rate of Thembu fission was not as rapid, yet during the 200 years between about 1650 and about 1850, six new chiefdoms broke away.[19] These tribes were united by the fact of common origin and their chiefs were members of the same royal lineage, but each was entirely independent of the other. They form what I have called elsewhere a *tribal cluster*, the genealogically senior chief being paramount and enjoying ritual pre-eminence (only he could initiate the annual first fruit rituals, which were then performed by the minor chiefs).

The paramount chief had no *political* authority over the other chiefs in his cluster. He did not, for instance, hear appeals from their courts, nor was political fealty symbolized in the payment of tribute or the *isizi* death dues, nor could he control them in their relations with other tribes. William Shaw describes graphically the hesitancy of the Xhosa paramount Hintsa to take responsibility for accepting a missionary, until he had heard the views and decisions of his fellow cluster chiefs.[20] Stephen Kay comments, 'But what tended finally to establish the name of this pagan despot [Ngqika], was the manner in which he was publicly recognized in the year 1817 as sole representative of the Kaffir [Xhosa] tribes; a measure the most injudicious and unwise that could possibly be adopted. Not only was it repugnant to the feelings of every other chief but, as might have been expected, naturally calculated to excite a spirit of jealousy, seeing that each was as independent of him as he was of them. . . .'[21] And Thompson: 'Another arrangement proposed by the Colonial Government on this occasion was, to make Gaika [Ngqika] responsible for the conduct of the Caffre nation, and that the government should treat with only him, and have nothing to do with any of the other chiefs. This gave Gaika some consequence but gained him no respectability; for the plan proposed was repugnant to the feelings of the other Caffres, as every chief considers himself a King in his own kraal, and altogether irresponsible to any superior.'[22]

There is obviously a resemblance here to the early mediaeval

[19] Op. cit. 1965 pp. 159–61.

[20] W. Shaw *The Story of My Mission in South-eastern Africa* London 1860 pp. 482–3. In his *My Mission* Shaw 'gathered' that this was partly 'as a mark of respect to them' and partly a 'tacit reproof for their not having consulted him in so important a matter'. My interpretation is backed by Shaw's account in his unpublished *Journal* in the Albany Museum, Grahamstown. In any event, consultations did not mean obtaining approval for action.

[21] S. Kay *Travels and Researches in Caffraria* London 1833 p. 53.

[22] G. Thompson *Travels in Southern Africa* London 1829 p. 343.

kingdoms and principalities of north-western Europe. The Capetian kings, for instance, 'took no steps whatever to maintain order, restrict bloodshed or protect the rights of persons within the fiefs of the feudatories. The counts fought amongst themselves, usurping and annexing, without any control from above'[23] and, according to Joliffe, in Anglo-Saxon England there was no king's peace, 'but only innumerable local peaces, no rigidly defined territorial boundaries and no enforcement of authority from the centre, except *in extremis*'.[24] Chilver classifies the Capetian monarchy as a 'multiple state' and describes the Kingdom of France in the early part of the twelfth century as 'a group of small feudal states under hereditary rulers who were the final judicial, fiscal and military authorities within them, each in nominal dependence on a king (himself the ruler of a small state) whose paramount authority was undefined and largely moral'.[25] There is an obvious resemblance to a tribal cluster here, but even 'nominal dependence' on the paramount seems to be missing in the Cape Nguni context and it seems closer to the facts to regard each chiefdom as an independent state and not part of a 'multiple state' in Chilver's sense.[26] The crucial difference would appear to be in the concept of Sovereignty. There was no idea of a territory 'owned' by the paramount, other than his own particular chiefdom, and no obligation on the part of the cluster chiefs to provide military aid to him. Constituent chiefs were in no way vassals of the paramount and no tribute was paid. In other words, there was no political theory which acknowledged the sovereignty of the paramount over the territories of the junior chiefs, nor, significantly, was there an obligation for chiefdoms in a cluster to unite in defence of one another.

Relations between these states, both related and unrelated, seem to have been characterized by naked power within a system of equal, competing units, each attempting to maximize its own advantage relatively unaffected by restricting norms—political relations, in Smith's sense. The limits of the jural community

[23] A. Southall *Alur Society* London 1956 pp. 252–63. Dr T. R. Davenport has commented (personal communication) that fissiparous tendencies among Nguni tribes, encouraged by the polygynous family structure, reflect the Merovingian Franks rather than the Capetians.

[24] J. E. A. Joliffe *Constitutional History of England* London 1948 p. 255.

[25] E. M. Chilver 'Feudalism in the Interlacustrine kingdoms' in A. Richards (ed.) *East African Chiefs* London and New York 1960 p. 381.

[26] Southall op. cit. describes the analogous Alur syste as a 'segmentary state'.

coincided with the chiefdom and it was only within its confines that the rule of law operated, that disputes were settled by due process in the courts and that the obligations of co-operation and loyalty were laid on members. Distance between chiefdoms varied along two co-ordinates, the geographical and the social. Geographical separation meant that, typically, chiefdoms situated far from one another seldom interacted, positively or negatively: on the other hand there was a tendency for neighbouring chiefdoms to be in a perpetual state of mutual enmity. Intra-cluster feuds were just as likely as those between clusters. Relations between the two Mpondomise chiefdoms appear to have been permanently strained, and rivalry was particularly strong between Mhlontlo and Mditshwa during the twenty-year period immediately preceding annexation. Evidence for frequent clashes between the two chiefdoms comes from oral tradition and official reports in the Cape Blue Books, as annexation occurred during the reign of the two chiefs (Mhlontlo died in 1912; Mditshwa in 1886). In 1860 Mditshwa was defeated by Mhlontlo[27] and in 1872 the latter again commenced hostilities against his kinsman. In August, Mditshwa and the West Mpondo chief, Ndamase, attacked Mhlontlo. Numbers of horses and cattle were taken, but the nature of the conflict can be seen from the casualty list—two men killed on Mhlontlo's side and eleven on Mditshwa's.[28] J. M. Orpen, newly-appointed British Resident, reports that most of the fighting was done by Mhlontlo himself 'with a small party, varying from twelve to thirty men, good shots, and armed with Winchester and other rifles'.[29] Other clashes were certainly occasionally on a somewhat larger scale. As the co-operation between Mditshwa and Ndamase indicates, alliances between unrelated chiefdoms could occur and, indeed, they were fairly common. There is no doubt that chiefs were in frequent contact with one another, exchanging views and information, during the whole period of the frontier wars. In many cases they were related to one another through dynastic marriages.

But conflict was more evident than *ententes*. Fighting between the contiguous Thembu and Mpondo was so frequent that a buffer strip of land was granted along the banks of the Mthatha River to certain white settlers in about 1869, by both Ngangelizwe

[27] J. H. Soga *The South-Eastern Bantu* pp. 480–1.

[28] Cape of Good Hope *Blue Book on Native Affairs* G.27–'74 1874 72.

[29] Idem. p. 73.

of the Thembu and the Mpondo chief, Nqwiliso. Bransby Key speaks of wide strips of open veld that divided some tribes. He writes that between the territory of Mpondomise and Mpondo there was 'a belt of unoccupied country some twenty miles across waving with grass, intersected by no roads. There were only one or two little narrow footpaths, hardly visible in the long grass, worn by a few travellers that passed from tribe to tribe.'[30] This neutral zone was the haunt of game and was said to be still tenanted by lions. As Callaway observes: 'In those days [*c.* 1865] such a belt of unoccupied country between tribe and tribe was felt to be necessary as a protection. It would have been quite impossible for the Mpondomise to have built their kraals within measurable distance of the kraals of the Tembus. At any moment the war-cry might be shouted from hill to hill, and the cattle swept away by raiders.'[31] That this neutral zone was not always present, however, is indicated by the Rev. H. H. Dugmore's comment: 'One general remark is applicable to the whole of the above tribes [Thembu, Mpondo, Bhaca]. The limits of their respective territories are not clearly defined, and hence their 'Borderers' are frequently intermingled; which has been the occasion of many feuds, and in some cases has involved whole tribes.'[32] Possibly this was due to increasing pressure on the land.

Our model of intertribal relations has an obvious relevance for frontier history. The folly of overstressing the powers of a paramount chief has already been alluded to. There also seems no doubt that alliances were contracted between chiefs: certainly they exchanged information and discussed strategy in the face of white encroachment on their land. But it does not necessarily follow that they were 'responsible' for one another's actions. During the earlier frontier wars, as we have seen, the southernmost Xhosa tribes (Ngqika, Ndlambe, Ntinde, Gqunukhwebe) reacted individually and situationally to the threat. It is possible that, during the cattle killing of 1857, Moshweshwe, the Sotho chief, was in contact with his Xhosa opposite numbers,[33] but he could not have been 'responsible' for the decisions taken. Even the chiefs themselves seldom, if ever, made the decisions, as we shall see.

[30] Quoted in G. Callaway op. cit. 1911 p. 28.
[31] Idem.
[32] In J. Maclean (ed.) *Compendium of Kaffir Laws and Customs* Mount Coke 1858 p. 8.
[33] See, for instance, F. Brownlee *Reminiscences of Kaffir Life and History* Lovedale 1896 p. 169 and J. Rutherford *Sir George Grey* London 1961 pp. 349–50, 353.

It is possible to build a fairly adequate model of intertribal relations before the imposition of the *Pax Capensis*. The events were dramatic and were certainly worthy of enshrinement in tribal memory and official file. Reconstruction of the political system of individual chiefdoms, however, is not quite so easy. Here we have a traditional process going on quietly and, in a sense, obviously, with little to arouse the analytic curiosity of missionary or political agent. As far as white observers were concerned, the concept 'chief' was assimilated to that of 'king' or 'monarch', on the Western model, although the more perceptive observers realized that it was not an absolute monarchy and involved the active participation of the people themselves. Apart from limiting the chief's right to wage war and inflict the death penalty, little modification of his powers was deemed necessary.[34] But positive action had to be taken on the local administrative level and a rational bureaucratic system devised. This was done by dividing the annexed territory into districts, and the districts themselves into locations over which were placed district headmen. Two questions immediately arise: what was the original form of *local* government, and to what extent was it used as a basis for the new location system? Did the authorities work on the traditional model, or was it ignored in the new system?

Informants are quite explicit that the present system of location headmen bears little resemblance to that of the past. The name of this official (*isibonda*) is itself a neologism, coined for this new type of office. It means literally a supporting pole for a hut roof and, apparently, was something less than complimentary—although now it is an accepted part of the language. Older informants told me: 'The name *isibonda* is a despising word given by the people to the Government-appointed headmen. To them the headman was not a chief but merely placed, like a pole, to look after a certain area. It is a new thing.' Key comments: 'The natives so far [1883] do not readily accept new men—Government made chiefs—unless men of acknowledged power and influence.'[35]

[34] Subsequent events were to show that, in fact, the whole nature of the chieftainship had been deeply affected—see W. D. Hammond-Tooke 'Chieftainship in Transkeian political development' *Journal of Modern African Studies* 2 4 (1964) pp. 513–29.

[35] B. L. Key, Minutes of Evidence in Report of the Cape Native Laws and Customs Commission, 1883 p. 188. Bransby Key's short account of the Mpondomise system in the 1883 Commission Report is not always clear. For instance, he speaks of 'villages" of related kraals and his description of the 'headman' of these villages tallies with what

The Mpondomise state was under a chief (*inkosi*), theoretically the senior member of the senior lineage of the royal Majola clan. The dispersed settlement pattern characteristic of the Cape Nguni, however, made decentralization of control essential and the tribal territory was divided into large tracts or 'districts' (*imihlaba*), each under a sub-chief (*inkosana*, plural *iinkosana*). These sub-chiefs were usually royal princes, typically sons, brothers and other close agnates of the reigning chief, placed as 'eyes' in strategic areas on the outer marches of the country. During the 1870s, in the years immediately prior to annexation, the tribe under Mditshwa was divided into six districts, under Mandela (Tsitsa), Same (between Xokonxa and Sidwadweni), Matshanda (Mjika), Ranuga (country lying west, towards the present Maclear), Mkhondweni (Ntywenka) and Majangaza. Of these Ranuga and Mkhondweni were half-brothers of Mditshwa in the *iqadi* (supporting) house of the great house, Majangaza was a half-brother in another supporting house (*msenge*) and Mandela was a paternal uncle.

These districts appear to have been comparatively large and were divided for administrative purposes into smaller areas called *izithile* (sing. *isithile*), which I translate as 'ward', each under a headman called an *isiduna* (plural *iziduna*) not to be confused with *induna*, a chief councillor. Wards were fairly well-defined areas of settlement, usually named after some prominent geographical feature such as a river or mountain, and appear to have been settled in the past mainly by patrikinsmen. The ward head was normally the senior male agnate, but the office was essentially a political one and the incumbent was an appointee of the chief who could supplant him if unsatisfactory. All informants stress the importance of personal factors in the recognition of a ward head, especially the possession of wealth. '*Iziduna* were great men in the nation' and were expected to be intelligent, loyal and courageous in battle, for they were responsible for leading the company of warriors from their ward when the army was mobilized. War was the crucial test of a ward head's fitness for office, and cases are still remembered of *iziduna* being deposed for cowardice.

---

informants remember of the *iziduna*. These 'villages' could be merely extended families, or they could be neighbourhood units (Hammond-Tooke 1962 pp. 53–7). In neither case is the term 'headman' for the controlling authority appropriate.

The ward headship was essentially a political office in that its authority extended over all who lived within the confines of the ward, irrespective of kinship alliance. Although wards tended to be settled by clansmen, it soon happened that others, in groups and families, applied for permission to settle, and the ward head's authority extended to them. Over the years the process continued. In Zingcuka location, Tsolo, the 249 homesteads contain members of no less than fifty-one different clans. Ward heads, like the sub-chiefs, were chiefs in miniature and were addressed as such. They had specific administrative and political functions, the extent of which was territorially defined. In fact their most important administrative function was the allocation of residential and arable land. Rights to a portion of the tribal land were a reciprocal of allegiance to a chief and the position was similar to the 'estates of administration' system described by Gluckman for Lozi, Tswana and Zulu.[36] Sub-chiefs and ward heads had oversight of areas which they sub-divided among their followers. Each member of the political hierarchy had the obligation to see that all within his area were provided for with arable land, in particular. The ward head was assisted in the administration of his area by a council of all adult men. Among the Mpondomise, and perhaps all other Cape Nguni, he was also helped by the leaders of quasi-kinship groups, the *izithebe* (singular *isithebe*), an institution standing structurally between the political system, represented by the ward head, and the kin-based descent groups. These *izithebe*, which I translate as 'hospitality groups', were (and are) associations of family heads with a lineage segment as their core, but also including non-kin, the main function of which is to receive and allocate meat and beer at feasts but which were also used to provide communal labour. They were probably also segments in the tribal army.[37]

The subordination of ward heads (and possibly also the sub-chiefs) to the chief was expressed in the rule that a portion of all court fines be sent to the chief's court, that death dues on the demise of a family head be forwarded via the lower authority to the chief and the reservation of the death penalty to the chief's court itself. In fact there is strong evidence that lower courts were

[36] M. Gluckman *Essays in Lozi Land and Royal Property* Rhodes-Livingston Paper No. 10 1943 p. 28f.

[37] W. D. Hammond-Tooke 'Kinship, locality and association: hospitality groups among the Cape Nguni' *Ethnology* 2 3 (1963) pp. 302–19.

in fact courts of arbitration as they had no force at their disposal. Bransby Key, in his evidence to the Cape Native Laws and Customs Commission of 1883 states: 'These headmen or petty chiefs [he does not clearly distinguish them] can settle cases, and send out messengers of courts "umsila"[38] to execute judgements, but they cannot use force. Anyone, in fact, who called out an armed force is liable to a heavy penalty.'[39] In theory, too, appeals lay from the lower courts to that of the chief, but it is extremely doubtful whether this was so in reality. A text by ex-regent I. Matiwane gives an interesting insight into the working of the system: 'Subjects of an *isiduna* were allowed to take their cases on appeal to the chief if they were not satisfied with the isiduna's judgement. But such cases were very rare. In fact this was not encouraged. There were various ways of discouraging such appeals. The chief's court did not, in most cases, go against the decision of the *isiduna's* court. If the appellant lost the appeal, it only meant that the fine went up. Even if he did not lose the case, it meant that he would have his life made miserable by the *isiduna* and the people of his ward. They took the view that an appeal to the chief's court undermined the integrity of the *isiduna's* court' [of which they were all, of course, participating members—see below]. Matiwane also stressed the duty of the ward head to support the chief, if occasion arose, against the sub-chiefs (*iinkosana*), who had a tendency to try and usurp the chieftainship, or become independent. It will be remembered that these were typically royal brothers, some of whom (particularly he of the righthand house of the former chief) had a pre-emptive right to secede and split the Mpondomise state. The ward heads, owing their position to the chief himself, acted as a stabilizing force in the political system.

It is extremely difficult to trace the evolution from *isiduna* and *iinkosana* areas to the locations of today. According to informants some of the ward heads were appointed headmen, or, in some areas, the sub-chief was so confirmed, but they maintain that relatively few were thus recognized. The position among the Mpondomise was complicated by the 1880 rebellion and the alienation of some of the tribal land as punishment. When the East Griqualand Lands Commission (the 'Vacant Lands Com-

[38] Lit. a 'tail', from the leopard tail, attached to an assegai, that was his symbol of office (see below).

[39] B. L. Key *1883 Commission Report* p. 188.

mission') met in September 1883, they found it expedient to divide the Tsolo district into nine locations, on a tribal basis, one for the Mpondomise (under the regent Mabasa; Mditshwa had been deposed), one Tolo, one Bhele, one Mfengu and four locations of mixed origin under headmen appointed by the magistrate for their loyalty during the war. These original nine locations were subsequently further subdivided into smaller areas, also called locations, by Government Notice 647 dated 29 September 1910. Informants state that the ward areas were usually bigger than the present locations 'for the *isiduna* was expected to support an *impi* (regiment)'. The new system increased, in a sense, the control of the chief over his people. Under the traditional system the chief usually confirmed the head of the predominant clan in the area as ward head. The rebellion caused considerable interdistrict movement and, when the locations were demarcated, there was a strong tendency for chiefs to appoint close relatives as *izibonda*. Today seventeen of the twenty-four Mpondomise headmen in the Tsolo chiefdom belong to the royal clan. This would indicate that it was the sub-chiefs, rather than the *iziduna*, who were appointed and that the *iziduna* lost their authority. On the other hand we do not know how many *iziduna* there were, so the number thus affected may not have been very great.

This model of the administration hierarchy is based almost exclusively on Mpondomise material. The main structure is similar for Mpondo,[40] Bomvana[41] and Bhaca[42] and there is no reason to doubt that the 'dynamics' of the system was not the same among them. The aim of the model-building will have been served, however, if it sensitizes historians to the working of a society of this type.

One of the main problems was to determine how the tribe was originally governed. In particular, it was important to determine the nature of the authority of the chief, especially its limits. Were the chiefs absolute monarchs (as was Shaka) or did the administration of the tribe proceed on more 'democratic' lines? In fact, how and by whom, were decisions made? Satisfactory answers to these questions were central to the study, as it was felt that

[40] M. Hunter *Reaction to Conquest* London 1936 pp. 378–82.
[41] P. A. W. Cook *The Social Organization and Ceremonial Institution of the Bomvana* Cape Town 1930.
[42] W. D. Hammond-Tooke *Bhaca Society* Cape Town 1962 pp. 204–24.

traditional concepts of the relationship between chief and people were basic to the present-day 'political philosophy' of tribesmen: in them were enshrined the ideals of 'good government' by which the people judge the administration to which they have been subsequently subjected. This is particularly important when trying to assess the impact of a system of indirect rule, such as the Bantu Authorities structure that has been established in the Transkei since 1956.[43] The problem also has relevance for historians attempting to understand the relationship between black and white in the nineteenth century.

The relationship between chief and subject was, and is, conceptualized in the idea of *khonza*. *Khonza*, from the point of view of the subject, means faithful service: from the point of the chief it involves authority, the right to command both respect and obedience. But this authority differed in certain important respects from the authority of bureaucratic systems as classically defined by Max Weber[44] in that there was no clear separation of the authority role from other (e.g. kinship) roles, no specialized training for office, and relations between office-bearer and subject tended to be particularistic and diffuse. But, more importantly, the authority of the chief lacked what may be termed continuity of definition. There was a generalized acknowledgement that the chief's imprimatur was necessary for a decision to be valid, but the decision-making itself was not the prerogative of the chief alone. He did not normally enjoy a continuing unquestioned right to command but his authority had to be continually recreated situationally, in specific contexts. This is expressed in the formula that chiefs could not rule on their own, but only in constant consultation with their councillors and people. Indeed, it was the group of councillors and adult tribesmen which made decisions in the chief's name.

'There were always people at the great place. These people were called the *abagcini bomzi*' (keepers of the homestead). They were men who had left their kraals to be present at the Great Place to serve the chief. Some were poor, some well-to-do. The chief did not solve tribal matters by himself. Their homes, while they were away, were looked after by the Great Place. These men were

[43] W. D. Hammond-Tooke 'Chieftainship in Transkeian political development' *Journal of Modern African Studies* 2 4 (1964) pp. 513–29.

[44] M. Weber *Wirtschaft und Gesellschaft* Tübingen 1922, tr. and repr. in H. H. Gerth and C. Wright Mills, from Max Weber *Essays in Sociology* New York 1958 pp. 196–244.

sometimes referred to as the *izinja zakomkhulu* ('the dogs of the Great Place'). The organization of the capital was in their hands, including the ploughing of the chief's fields and care of his herds. They also received visitors and messengers from other chiefs, and the *isizi* (death dues) beast. These councillors, or *amaphakathi* (lit. 'those inside'), attained their position through personal qualities of loyalty and intelligence. One or two may have been councillors of the late chief; others, boyhood friends of the present chief, whose advice and probity had been found valuable. They were sometimes referred to as *abahluzi*, 'sifters', stressing their function of sifting and evaluating evidence. Formerly they tasted the chief's food to guard against poisoning. They were not necessarily relatives or brothers of the chief, in fact royal brothers did not trust one another. Sibling rivalry was well recognized in the society, as the expression '*Nithanda ukulwa ngathi niyezana*' ('You like to fight like brothers') indicates. The fruits of office being very desirable, this applies *a fortiori* to royal brothers. Informants stated: 'The chief is never on friendly terms with his brothers. Sometimes the rivalry comes from half-brothers of the *umsulandaka* (first wife married: never heir-bearing) who always feel that they deserve status as their mother was the first to come to the Great Place. The chief does not favour the idea of brothers settling near him as they are the first to criticize him if he makes a mistake.' 'A chief's brothers may easily influence the people against him because they are very near to his position.' We have seen that the *iziduna* were expected to support the chief against possible usurpation from the *iinkosana*.

Around this semi-permanent core of close councillors was a fluctuating group consisting of the more prominent tribesmen, who spent a greater or lesser part of their time at the Great Place sitting on court cases and discussing affairs of state. 'In the old days most men spent a lot of time at the Great Place. Even young men attended and learned a lot when customs were discussed.' 'When a young man came out of circumcision his father would give him a horse and he would go and live at the Great Place so that the chief could use him for messages. This is how people learnt the procedure and customs of the Great Place.' The process of becoming a councillor was not formalized. There was no specific appointment and the achievement of the role of accredited *iphakathi* depended on performance and continuous involvement in tribal affairs. Theoretically anyone could become a councillor and, in fact the 'tribal council' consisted ideally of all adult members of the tribe. It was this group which was the *de facto* decision-making body.

The actual decision-making process involved broadly two types of activity, legislative and judicial (the *execution* of decisions involved other procedures) and the chief-in-council constituted itself into two different institutions to effect this. These were the *moot*, whose function it was to decide on the day-to-day administration of the chiefdom and wards, and the *court*, which mediated in disputes between tribesmen. Cases of dispute within a ward referred to the court of the ward head (after first being discussed by the lineage court, if the quarrel was between kinsmen); appeals (in theory) lay to the court of the district chief and ultimately to the court of the chief himself although, as we have seen, this was more often honoured in the breach than in the observance. The functional distinction between the moots and the courts was reflected in different terms for the two bodies, although membership tended to be identical. The chief-in-council, sitting as a legislative or rule-making body, was called the *imbizo*, and when constituted as a court of law, the *inkundla*, from the area between the stock byre and the huts of the homestead. The activities of these two bodies were never confounded. The group convened as a moot, for instance, would refuse to hear cases until it had formally resolved itself into a court. A variation of the moot was the tribal gathering also called an *imbizo* (from *ukubiza*, 'to call') at which matters of national importance were placed before the people as a whole.

Legislation, the primary function of the moot, must be viewed very widely. The term is used here to cover both formal law-making and ordinary administrative decisions. Informants found it difficult to cite cases of true law-making (i.e. specific changes of custom) from the past, and this is not unexpected in a relatively static society in which the rate of social change was slow.[45] Examples given usually refer to what should more correctly be termed administrative modifications.

An educated informant's text points up clearly the balance of power between chief and people as reflected in the decision-making process:

[45] The Cape Nguni differ in this respect from the Tswana, among whom formal legislation appears to have been fairly common, see Schapera *Tribal Legislation among the Tswana of the Bechuanaland Protectorate* London 1943.

Even strong chiefs like Mhlontlo never made laws that went against the wishes of the people. Even in the past a chief always had his councillors. These men were his advisers on matters of law and order. Even during times of crisis a chief would have to listen to their advice on what action to take. They would refuse to sanction tactics which they regarded as dangerous.

In making a new law a chief had to consult his close advisers and discuss the intended law with them. Then a meeting of the whole tribe would be called and the matter laid before them. Influential men would have the chance of airing their views and, after thorough discussion, the chief and his advisers would have the feeling of the meeting. Opponents of the plan were encouraged to speak out because people should not be like a stream that flows only in one direction. After full discussion, the chief and his councillors would withdraw so that the councillors could voice their opinion as to whether they felt that the majority were in favour of the matter or not, and whether modifications should not perhaps be made.

The chief would then return to the *ibandla*, with his advisers, and formally pronounce the new law. If the people were obviously unhappy about it, it was withdrawn (*roxiswa*). A chief who dared to go against the wishes of his people ran the risk of losing their support, and perhaps his chieftainship.

Whatever the actual position in the past, the above text reflects the folk-myth which informs present day attitudes to chiefly power. It is significant that, according to the text, the main aspect discussed by the chief and his confidants in private was whether the people were happy about the decision and not, apparently, the decision itself. Consensus was all important. Informants cite the case of the chief Dosini as an example of the dangers of unpopular and unilateral action on the part of a chief. Legend relates that Dosini arbitrarily attempted to close certain waterholes to his people: before he knew what was happening the major part of his tribe had left him and joined his brother Cira. It is clear that chiefs relied on their councillors to prevent them acting contrary to popular will: on their part the people trusted the councillors not to give bad advice or lead the chief astray:

It was in the meetings of the *ibandla* that the chief was able to test the loyalty of the people to him. If he found that the opinion of the councillors was rejected on many occasions, then he had to do something about the composition of his council. It meant they were no longer a yardstick by which he could test the loyalty of his people.

This brake on the power of the chief was noted by many early visitors to the Cape Nguni.[46] The missionary W. B. Boyce, commenting in 1839 on D'Urban's treaty system, wrote:

. . . that the chiefs are generally unable to enforce provisions of a treaty disagreeable to their people, is a fact well known to all acquainted with the state of Kaffirland; and is the natural result of the position of the Chief in reference to his people. His power depends upon the number of his fighting men, and as from the subdivision of power among the junior and collateral branches of the great families, the number of Chiefs is continually on the increase, every Chief is compelled by a sense of his entire dependence upon the willing services of his people to avoid doing anything which will offend them, lest they should desert to other Chiefs, and thus add to the power of their rivals. The evils resulting from this state of things are increased in proportion to the small number attached to a chief; for if his men are but few, he is the more anxious to avoid offending even one of them.[47]

Another influential Methodist missionary, H. H. Dugmore, has this to say: 'In the case of a Kaffir chief, the principal checks to the despotic inclinations which the possession of power always induces are, first, the division of the tribes, and secondly, the existence of a very influential council.'[48]

Further support comes from the five Ngqika councillors from Victoria East who gave evidence before the 1883 Cape Native Laws and Customs Commission:

1197 Is the chief above the law? No, before a chief can talk on a matter he must call all his councillors together.

1198 A chief can't kill anyone whom he chooses; if he wishes to have anyone killed he must call the councillors together, and say what must I do with so-and-so, who has been troubling me very much. In that case, also, the chief would be guided by what the councillors said.

1199 Yes; a chief can do wrong, and it often happens that when a chief does wrong he would be interfered with, and punished, by having his favourite councillor, or prime minister, eaten up. The man who would be eaten up would be the leading councillor, or

[46] See for instance 'Justus' [M. Beverly] *Wrongs of the Caffre Nation* 1837 p. 53; C. Rose *Four Years in Southern Africa* 1829 p. 79; J. Sutherland *Original Matter . . . in Lieut. Col. Sutherland's Memoirs . . .* 1845–6 p. 87; A. Steedman *Wanderings and Adventures in the Interior of Southern Africa* 1835 p. 255; E. E. Hapier *Excursions in Southern Africa* 1849 Vol. 2 p. 127; C. J. F. Bunbury *The Cape of Good Hope* 1848 p. 69; G. Thompson *Travels in Southern Africa* 1829 p. 348 and W. Shaw *The Story of My Mission in South-Eastern Africa* 1860 pp. 440–1.

[47] W. B. Boyce *Notes on South-African Affairs* London 1839.

[48] Quoted in J. Maclean op. cit. p. 24.

the man who had been appointed to office on the day the chief was circumcised.

1200 The prime minister is the chief's mouthpiece, and the other councillors say, as a reason for eating him up, that it must have been by his advice that the chief did wrong.[49]

This last comment stresses the main effect of this bounding of the chief's effective authority. The chiefship is sacred and, as such, must be above criticism and reproach. This is achieved by effectively withdrawing the chief from the decision-making process. All decision-making involves the possibility of error and the Cape Nguni avoid this by making their chiefs constitutional monarchs. It is perhaps because they do not 'rule', i.e. make administrative decisions, but rather 'reign', that Cape Nguni chiefs (except the Bhaca) are not subject to the institutionalized criticism found in the Zulu and Swazi 'rituals of rebellion' analysed by Gluckman.[50]

The same process characterized decision-making in the court. Cases were discussed by those present, each one giving his views and cross-examining witnesses, and the function of the chief was merely to pronounce the verdict. In fact, it was not strictly necessary for the chief to be actually present during the proceedings.

It should be stressed, however, that this was the ideal. In actual fact a particular chief could sometimes act, by sheer force of personality, in an autocratic manner. Mpondomise informants stated that it sometimes happens that the chief is a man of strong will and people are thus afraid to oppose him, 'but one thing clear is that an unpopular law made by him will die with him'. There is some evidence that the chief had a relatively free hand in the organization of the army and, apparently among the Mpondo, 'Old men say that the chief always wanted to fight and often the people did not want it, but the order for war lay with the chief alone, and if the army were called out men could not refuse to go.'[51] It is obvious that in time of national danger the running of affairs could not be left entirely to a 'committee'.

The relationship between the chief and his people was not static

[49] Minutes of evidence, Nos. 1197–2200 *Report of the Commission* G4–'83 Cape Town. The expression 'eating up' refers to the political confiscation of all stock. See also following evidence.

[50] M. Gluckman *Rituals of Rebellion in South-east Africa* 1963.

[51] M. Hunter *Reaction to Conquest* London 1936 p. 395.

and tended to change during his reign. Here again we are indebted for insights to the perceptive Dugmore:

> The operation of the influence of the Amaphakathi in modifying the power of the chief is remarkable, as it has its periodic revolution, its waxings and wanings. . . . The result of this process is that a chief, dying in his old age, leaves a minor, often a mere child, to succeed him. What then is the position of the young chief? He finds himself surrounded by a number of grey-headed veteran associates of his father, who are strong in the possession of long continued popular influence, and insolent from their consciousness of possessing it. If he will yield himself to their sway, his course is smoothed for him; if he manifests much self-will, they do not scruple to remind him that they were the councillors and companions of his father before he was born; that his mother owed her appointment, and consequently her son his rank, to their advice and influence; and they will sometimes hint that they can unmake as well as make chiefs; and threaten him with the elevation of a brother as a rival.
>
> The rule of a young chief is thus in reality the rule of the old councillors of the tribe. The relative position of the two parties, however, gradually changes. While the young chief is advancing towards the vigour and resolution of manhood the older councillors die off and the younger councillors are appointed. One after another of the old Amaphakathi falls a victim to an accusation of witchcraft, the Kaffir state engine for the removal of the obnoxious. . . . That under such a system there should be more than enough of tyranny, might be inferred from the natural rapacity of powers. But it is not the tyranny of *one* . . . it is divided amongst many, and it is often more or less neutralized by the rival popular interests of the tyrannizers themselves.[52]

Enough has been said to indicate clearly the relationship between chief and people, and the nature of authority, both legislative and judicial. The folk myth of present day Mpondomise accords well with the reports of early writers who knew the Cape tribes intimately. It is this ideal that is used as a yardstick when contemporary tribesmen judge whether they are being governed 'well' or not. It is true of course, as Leach has pointed out[53] that the lack of formal separation of powers meant that there was a danger that the governmental process would reflect the interests of those who controlled the system, and that in primitive societies the relative lack of tyranny is due more to inefficiencies in the

[52] In J. Maclean op. cit. pp. 28–9.

[53] E. R. Leach 'Law as a condition of freedom' in D. Bidney (ed.) *The Concept of Freedom in Anthropology* The Hague 1963 pp. 80–1.

bureaucratic system than to explicit democratic ideals, but the Cape Nguni do seem to have specific mechanisms to avoid the undue concentration of power in the hands of one man.

THE ENFORCING OF DECISIONS

Once decisions had been taken they had to be enforced. In court cases fines of stock had to be attached or, rarely, a man put to death, and it is these judicial decisions that pre-eminently involved physical force to ensure compliance.

Among all the Cape Nguni there was one specific role of executive officer, one which resembled our messenger of the court or sheriff. This was the *umsila*, appointed from among the councillors, who derived his name from the leopard's tail attached to the assegai which he carried as a badge of office. After a court decision the *umsila* accompanied the litigant against whom judgement had been given to his home and waited there until the fine was handed over. If the fine was refused the *umsila* placed the assegai in front of the kraal and departed; the occupants of the homestead were bound to return it to the Great Place on the next morning on pain of being 'eaten up' i.e. having all their stock confiscated. Assaulting or obstructing the chief's *umsila* in the execution of his duty was considered a particularly serious offence and was heavily punished: it threatened the very basis of tribal administration. Informants state that if the *umsila's* summons was ignored the councillors and young men would themselves go in a body, armed, and attach the stock. They also insist that the matter would be kept, if at all possible, from the chief's ears. 'If he heard he would say that he is no longer a chief, and this would be an insult to the whole tribe.'

Fines, paid in stock, were the usual form of restitution, even in cases of murder and assault (*amatyala egazi*—'blood cases') and one head of cattle was paid over to the chief's court as a court fee (*isizi*). The death penalty was practically confined to cases of witchcraft and here the chief's authority for the execution was technically required, although in most cases public vengeance was spontaneous and swift, the diviner's accusation superseding formal judicial process. If a witch was caught red-handed e.g. naked at night in a cattle kraal, a sure indication of witch activity, he was seized and impaled on a sharpened stake (*cutha*) by the kraal owner and his neighbours, or stripped naked, pegged to the ground and covered by vicious black ants (*izaphompolo*)—but his execution had to be formally reported to the chief, as indeed all deaths had to be reported.

It will be seen that there was no separate executive body. The same group of tribesmen that constituted itself into a moot, for the management of public affairs, or into a court, for the settlement of disputes, acted, on occasion, as an enforcing body for decisions, assisted by the younger warriors. It seems probable, however, that this was only necessary in extreme cases and that the prestige of the chief and his political officers, ward heads and sub-chiefs, plus the pressure towards conformity characteristic of a small-scale community, worked towards compliance.

SUMMARY

The structural pattern of the governmental system is clear: a three-tiered hierarchy of political office with ever-narrowing spheres of authority running from the chief, through sub-chiefs, ward headmen to the heads of kraals. At each level this authority was both judicial and administrative in that the incumbent of office had the power to settle disputes and allocate tasks and goods to all within his territorial purview. The chief's authority ranged over all within the tribal territory, the ward head similarly controlled ward members and the heads of homesteads were legally responsible and had authority over all within his homestead whether related or not. Purely kinship authority structures, involving the roles of clan head, lineage head and kraal head, although occasionally coinciding with political office, belonged to a separate hierarchical system which does not immediately concern us in this context, although the political system acknowledged the duty of these kinship 'officers' to attempt settlement by arbitration in cases involving kin, before cognizance could be taken of it in the courts. At each level in the government hierarchy the functions of political officers were broadly the same, but with increasing range, both spatially and in the command over physical force.

But, as we have seen, although authority was invested in one man who was ultimately responsible, at least in theory, for decisions, the decision-making process itself was diffused over a much wider group and flowed from an interaction process that aimed at consensus. The genius of tribal government was the participation of all adult members of the relevant territorial units. It thus involved a political process, in Smith's sense. In every court case the jury or judges were a man's peers, fellow members of his ward or tribe, who sought to influence the verdict by their eloquence and power to sway opinion, and in every decision involving public policy a similar system operated. Whether the issue be the admission of refugees, or missionaries, to the chiefdom, the allocation of land, the timing of the harvest or the appointment of a tribal herbalist, the resulting decision was the product of conflicting forces, which involved the marshalling of support and the influencing of fellow-members—none of whom, even the chief or headman, had any more authority than any other. The chief or headman acted merely as chairman of the body. The composition of the court or moot was the same—all the adult, i.e. circumcised, members of the tribe who wished to be present—and each could speak and thus feel that he had had a hand in influencing policy. The legitimization of the authority of a Nguni political officer, then, rested on a generally-accepted right to pronounce, in the name of the society, decisions resulting from an essentially *political*, and democratic, process. Specific authority had to be constantly recreated situationally against the background of this general authority. Once consensus had been reached the decision could be executed and enforced with the physical backing of the moot or court or, in extreme cases, by the army.

This was the ideal. There were, of course, political officers who themselves decided on a course of action and attempted to enforce decisions, but they always ran the risk of alienating their followers and, paradoxically, undermining their authority. Also, an exception to the above was the family head, who had undisputed authority over all resident in his homestead. This was probably because of his crucial role in the socialization process: it seems that other holders of kinship authority, e.g. lineage heads, had to rely, like chiefs and headmen, on persuasion and arbitration—although their writ was backed by the fear of the ancestral wrath that could be visited on the disrespecter of a senior kinsman.

It is thus clear that political officers in the traditional system were not, in themselves, initiators of social change. They could not normally govern on their own or force their will on a reluctant public.

The only sphere in which the chief appears to have had outright authority was in the right to declare war and in the domain of religion and ritual. This latter authority inhered partly in his position in the kinship structure and partly in the mystical attributes that seem everywhere to accrete to supreme political office. As head of the royal lineage only he could approach the august spirits of his ancestors—who themselves had political authority in that their influence was wider than the members of their own descent groups. They watched over the welfare of the tribe as a whole, in some vague, undefined way. The chief's other ritual authority was vested in his control over the, basically magical, communal rituals of the strengthening of the crops, the *ulibo* first fruit ritual and the protection of the country against hail and lightning. The actual performance of the rituals was in the hands of professional herbalists, but they had to be formally commissioned by the chief and could not take place without his approval. Rainmaking was performed by the Bushmen living among the Mpondomise, but most Cape Nguni chiefdoms had their own rainmaker.

Paradoxically it was the sanctity of the chief's office that limited his effective authority. Ideally a chief could do no wrong—the chieftainship was sacred—but this illusion could only be maintained if the chief was insulated from the decision-making process with all its possibility of error and miscalculation.

It can be argued, with a large degree of truth, that this picture I have drawn is itself inadequate. It gives a formalized description of how both contemporary observers and present-day informants understood the way in which the political system should be run. This does not mean that every decision was the product of free discussion leading to consensus based on rational, impartial discussion. As in all such systems men, including chiefs and headmen, attempt to manipulate the power system by forming factions and coalitions, by promises, threats and sheer blackmail. Wealth and strong lineage following can skew the picture of interaction between 'egalitarian', contraposed units in the political system. Unfortunately we just do not have this type of detailed behavioural data for the pre-Annexation period. This model, rather, defines the institutional framework within which this competition for power operated—the parameters of expectation against which actions are judged and, as such, is presented as potentially useful for historians working on the history of contact in the Eastern Cape.

12. The external relations of the Ndebele kingdom in the pre-partition era

RICHARD BROWN

Studies of individual African 'political communities', to adopt Schapera's useful phrase,[1] have sometimes tended to foster a picture of isolated, unchanging tribal polities, each pursuing its own immediate interests relatively unconcerned by what is happening outside its own locality. Or, in the case of the more warlike peoples, attention has been focused on their military exploits to the neglect of the diplomatic conduct of external relations. There has thus been little discussion of how southern African political communities perceived and attempted to influence their position in a wider world.

Although the nineteenth century, with its explosive developments within both black and white societies, obviously increased the necessity for external awareness, we should not overlook that this need was already inherent in the social and political organization of the southern Bantu-speaking peoples. Crops and cattle had long since lifted many of the constraints of the physical environment and created the possibility, as was seen north of the Limpopo, of large heterogeneous political communities like the Mutapa and Rozwi state systems linked by trade to the world outside Africa. But even where political organization remained small in scale—despite wider cultural uniformities—and most trade was still parochial, the diminished reliance on kinship as the basis of political affiliation and the existence of specialized and complex governmental institutions helped to create competitive interactions of an 'international' kind.

Competition was for the control of people as much as land, but relations between these political communities or microstates were usually extremely fluid and tended to operate to keep the units small. The absence of fixed capital assets, the widespread availability of land, restricted trading opportunities, the open membership of political communities, weaknesses in the means of control

[1] I. Schapera *Government and Politics in Tribal Societies* London 1956.

away from the centre all maximized the opportunities for the movement of individuals and groups from one political community to another and for the emergence of new political communities. Disputes about succession and internal political competition easily became entangled in external relations and further heightened the need for political authorities to look beyond their own immediate horizons.

Nineteenth-century developments, particularly the political consolidations set in train by the rise of Shaka's Zulu kingdom and the Boer penetration of the interior by the Voortrekkers, did not so much create international relations in southern Africa as dramatically increase their scale and intensity. The new forms of state-making coupled with the changes in military organization, weapons and tactics enabled far greater resources to be deployed on external policies. Insecurities widened from their previously local level, but the rulers of the new African kingdoms were still largely concerned with competing for the control of people: increasingly for security as well as prestige. Even the rapid extensions of the white farming, trading, hunting and missionary frontiers were not wholly revolutionary before the transformations brought about by the gold and diamond discoveries in South Africa. Many aspects of the white presence could be drawn into existing patterns of interaction between political communities, but the refusal of whites, with rare exceptions, to become assimilated set them apart. For many areas, it was the widening opportunities for trade, above all for obtaining guns, which tended to have the greatest immediate impact in the sphere of external relations.

These general themes are here illustrated from the Ndebele experience with the use of published and archival material.[2] While these sources enable an impressionistic reconstruction to be attempted, it has to be recognized that the record at present is far from complete and that the exercise involves the familiar problem of interpreting African behaviour mainly from records left by a relatively small number of whites, none of whom was a trained observer. Not only was their knowledge of African societies very incomplete, but they also suffered as observers from the severe cultural ethnocentrism characteristic of nineteenth century white

[2] References are to the collections in the National Archives of Rhodesia (N.A.R.) and the Natal Archives (Natal). I am indebted to the staff of both institutions for their assistance.

society.[3] None the less, it is possible to give some indication of the general processes as well as the content of Ndebele external relations, while recognizing that much, especially where purely African interactions are concerned, remains hidden. No attempt is made to draw a sharp analytical distinction between process and content, and in the discussion which follows aspects of both are considered as seems convenient: in this way some sense of change over time is preserved.

The rulers of the Ndebele, despite their military prowess, were soon aware of the need for external relations based on more than the assegai. Mzilikazi's dramatic defiance of, and flight from, Shaka in 1822 exhibited the twin characteristics of aggression and fear which were to underlie the Ndebele approach to their external environment.

External relations comprise both spontaneous interactions between a political community and its external environment and the more purposive attempt to control these interactions which has traditionally been called foreign policy. From the moment when Mzilikazi fled from Shaka having deliberately defied his authority, he and his followers were in a position of particular dependence on the external environment while being in an unusually strong position to change it. This arose both from the immediate consequences of the flight and from the type of mobile state which eventually emerged.

Mzilikazi left Zululand with only some two or three hundred young warriors and a smaller number of women and children. Although in the context of the military revolution which had accompanied the rise of the Zulu kingdom, the soldiers were numerous enough to represent a formidable force north of the Drakensberg mountains, they were a tiny nucleus with which to build a powerful kingdom. Even though Mzilikazi benefited from the voluntary accession of later Nguni refugees fleeing from Shaka, most of the increase in manpower resulted from the raiding activities of his army. Thus by 1829 he may have controlled a population of some sixty to eighty thousand, a significant proportion of which had been directly incorporated into the Ndebele social system.[4]

[3] See H. A. C. Cairns *Prelude to Imperialism* (London 1965) for an extensive discussion of white ethnocentrism in a central African context.

[4] W. F. Lye 'The Ndebele Kingdom South of the Limpopo River' *J.A.H.* Vol. X No. 1.

The success of Mzilikazi's policies can be seen as the result of his own qualities of leadership and the new military techniques at his disposal, but it was also the product of the ability to exert an influence over the external environment through the mobility of the expanding core group. Thus the years in the Transvaal (1823–37) saw a series of relocations of the nascent state, both as a means of seeking security from enemies like the Zulu, Griqua, Tswana and Kora groups which are known to have attacked or raided it and also in order to maximize the opportunities for increasing the wealth and population of a rapidly-expanding raiding state. The foreign policy of a state with the ability to move and establish itself elsewhere must be deeply affected by this possibility. If foreign policy is defined as the attempt by those who have the authority and capacity to influence the external environment of the state in ways considered by them to benefit it, then the ability to move provides an opportunity, denied to most states, to influence the nature of the external environment by a shift in geographical location. The recent descriptions of the Transvaal period of Ndebele history make it clear how important the moves were to the survival and expansion of the original band of fugitives.[5] The significance of this factor for the 'Rhodesian' period will be considered below.

Geographical mobility was not the only purposive interaction with the external environment observable in the period before 1837, for Mzilikazi quickly perceived the significance of the use by his enemies to the west of guns, and welcomed his first contacts with white traders in 1829. Moreover, he seems to have initiated this contact just as he took the first step towards involvement with missionaries in general and Robert Moffat in particular. Interest in the remarkable personal relationship which began with their first meeting should not obscure the extent to which Mzilikazi saw the missionary in political terms. The importance Mzilikazi attached to making the contact is shown by the high standing of the deputation sent to the mission station at Kuruman. Much to Moffat's discomfort, Mzilikazi persisted in seeing him as 'the King of Kuruman' and as 'a chief of considerable power' who would be able to supply the Ndebele with guns and

[5] Ibid. and J. D. Omer-Cooper *The Zulu Aftermath* London 1966.

(1969) pp. 88, 97. This is by far the fullest and most authoritative reconstruction of the Transvaal period of Ndebele history.

ammunition.[6] This was hardly surprising since Moffat had a widespread reputation among Africans in the interior as the architect of the celebrated defensive victory over the so-called Mantatees in 1823, while Moffat's role as a go-between in attempting to moderate inter-African conflicts likely to affect the mission station was soon clear to Mzilikazi. Thus between Moffat's two visits to Mzilikazi in 1829 and 1835 many messages of a diplomatic kind passed between the two men.[7]

Nor was Moffat the only object of Mzilikazi's diplomatic policies. His readiness to accept missionaries as residents, his willingness to admit the Andrew Smith expedition to allow his envoys to return with it to Cape Town and to conclude the 1836 treaty of friendship with the British authorities can also be seen as a policy of controlling his relations with whites by diplomatic means, and as part of a strategy designed to improve security by reducing the likelihood of attacks by his other enemies. Although the presence of the American missionaries did not prevent the Boer attack of revenge on Mosega, Mzilikazi made it clear many years later that in inter-African disputes at least the presence of Moffat was a guarantee of peace.[8]

Up to 1836 Mzilikazi experienced whites mainly as a resource to be exploited in the context of his other concerns, but with the coming of the Voortrekkers this situation was drastically changed. Whether or not he realized the full implications of his first attacks on the advance party of trekkers who had entered what he considered to be his territory unannounced, he had already begun to become aware and fearful of the threat of white settlement.[9] Since the missionaries at Mosega had earlier reported rumours that Mzilikazi was contemplating a move to the north to escape further from the Zulu,[10] the conflict with the Voortrekkers was not necessarily a last ditch defence of a homeland so much as an opportunity to acquire cattle. At any rate, the series of battles

[6] Robert Moffat to Richard Moffat, 15 August 1832, N.A.R., MO 5/1/1; *The Matabele Journals of Robert Moffat 1829–60* ed. J. P. R. Wallis (2 vols. London 1945) Vol. I p. 87 (20 June 1835).

[7] References to these exchanges can be found in Moffat's letters to his brother, Richard, between 1831–34 in N.A.R., MO 5/1/1.

[8] 'Nobody will fight where you are. Do you think the Makololo do not know Moffat?' *Matabele Journals* Vol. I p. 371 (6 September 1854).

[9] *The Diary of Andrew Smith 1834–36* ed. P. R. Kirby (Cape Town 1939–40) Vol. II p. 66.

[10] *Letters of the American Missionaries* ed. D. J. Kotzé (Cape Town 1950) p. 140. Joint Letter to Anderson, 18 August 1836.

which preceded the actual beginning of the move were not conclusive and if the Ndebele had been worsted, they had not yet been vanquished. The precipitating factor seems, indeed, to have been the renewed pressure of the Zulu in mid-1837. The Ndebele were already on their way when they suffered their most serious reverse at Boer hands in the battle of eGabeni later in the same year. The Ndebele departure from the Transvaal should not therefore be seen just as an automatic consequence of the expansion of the Boers.

A related point of interest is the persistent oral tradition among the Ndebele that it was Robert Moffat who advised—or in some versions actually guided—the removal of the nation to present-day Matabeleland. This tradition has usually been treated with sceptism because at the time Moffat himself had never travelled in that region and because the suggestion was scorned by the missionary's son, John Smith Moffat. Some fifty years after the event, the younger Moffat, while on the diplomatic mission which led to the treaty that bears his name, reported to his superior:[11]

> Lobengula and his indunas have dwelt much on the statement that it was my father who advised Umsiligazi when in what is now the Marico district, to migrate northward to this country. I have heard the common people out of doors refer to the same thing. I am not aware that my father ever gave such advice. I do not recollect ever to have seen a reference to it in his voluminous letters and journals of the period in question. It is unlikely, as he would have known that such a migration would mean an extension of the career of conquest, and extermination in a vast region northwards, which he deplored as having already taken place in what is now the Transvaal.

However, notwithstanding J. S. Moffat's evidence, it is highly likely that the oral tradition contains a core of truth. There is in Robert Moffat's papers a draft in his hand of a pseudonymous letter to a missionary journal in which he gives a hostile review of Boer activities in the interior and remarks in passing: 'It has been stated on good authority that an individual in whom M. [Mzilikazi] placed almost unbounded confidence earnestly and repeatedly warned him by every means to avoid coming into collision with the Boers and rather retire into the interior than commence a warfare with the white man.'[12] The passage later

[11] J. S. Moffat to S. Shippard, 12 December 1887, N.A.R., HC 1/1/16 (Public Records).
[12] Draft letter to *British Banner*, February 1853, N.A.R., MO 5/1/1.

explains why the advice could not be acted upon and suggests that it was not so much the Boer attack on Mosega, but fear of the Zulu and rumours of further Boer attacks which finally precipitated the move. In view of the known relationship between Moffat and Mzilikazi, it can hardly be doubted that the unidentified individual who advised withdrawal was Moffat himself, while Mzilikazi's remark to the missionary in 1854 'I have not forgot the fulfilment of the warnings you gave me at Mosega' probably refers to the same incidents.[13]

The move across the Limpopo, even if not as unpremeditated nor as divorced from inter-African conflicts as is often implied, was a much more serious event for the Ndebele than earlier changes of location. It involved a marked reduction in numbers through the release of many Sotho subjects and brought about serious political strains arising from migration in two separated groups. These were not reunited under a single authority for more than two years and then only after the elimination of many indunas for having proposed the recognition of a successor to Mzilikazi.

Although the Ndebele never again effectively resumed migration, their ability to move as an organized political entity despite difficulties should be seen as a continuing influence on external relations. The issue was raised in 1866,[14] two years before the death of Mzilikazi, and again during the succession crisis which followed it,[15] but the most important occasions when relocation became a serious possibility were probably those which accompanied the pressures of the 'scramble'. Reports that the Ndebele would cross the Zambezi became widespread in the interior and were of particular concern to the Lozi.[16] Preparations included the making of canoes by Tonga tributaries of the Ndebele along the southern bank of the Zambezi 1886–88. The exceptionally heavy raid on Tonga north of the river in 1893 may well have been a further preliminary to an attempted escape from the problems created by the white occupation of Mashonaland. This

[13] *Matabele Journals* Vol. I p. 328 (8 October 1854).

[14] *The Matabele Mission of J. S. & E. Moffat 1858–78* ed. J. P. R. Wallis (London 1945) pp. 241–6, T. M. Thomas to A. Tidman, 13 August 1866.

[15] Ibid. pp. 249–50, W. Sykes to J. Mullens, 30 November 1869.

[16] Lieut. C. E. Haynes, C. 4643 (1886) p. 121; J. S. Moffat to S. Shippard, 12 December 1887, N.A.R., HC 1/1/16 (Public Records); G. W. H. Knight-Bruce to S. Shippard, 7 December 1888, Colonial Office Confidential Print *African (South)* 358, encl. in No. 96.

raid, which brought the hazard of small-pox with the returning soldiers, coincided with the 'Victoria incident', the British South Africa Company's *casus belli* for the conquest of Matabeleland; and when Lobengula with a large following fled from the smoking ruins of Bulawayo later in the same year he was following in more difficult circumstances his father's historical precedents. Lobengula's death ended what was probably a vain attempt and most of those who had accompanied him slowly returned and submitted to their white conquerors, though similar attempts were made by some Ndebele groups during the course of the 1896–7 risings.[17] By the time of the scramble the kingdom had remained stationary for some fifty years and perhaps local attachments, particularly religious ones which were tending towards an Ndebele fusion with pre-existing cultures, helped to inhibit migration until it was too late.

The effect of the possibility of migration on the handling and content of external affairs during these fifty years can only be surmised, but it seems reasonable to suppose that it might exaggerate an appearance of self-sufficiency and self-confidence. It was these characteristics which caught the immediate attention of most white observers, and historians (including the present writer) have tended to follow them and to represent the Ndebele as unchallenged lords of the interior once they had established themselves in Matabeleland. It is true that their position, if at times threatened, was never seriously weakened until the era of the scramble; yet this does not mean that they could afford to ignore their external environment. The rulers, at least, knew better and showed by their actions considerable awareness of what was happening in the more distant parts of southern Africa. Although outwardly little changed between 1840 and 1890, developments in the external environment of the Ndebele were lessening their underlying ability to control it, but these were not immediately apparent. To begin with, the pattern of external relations did not differ greatly from that observed for the Transvaal period.

The sense of insecurity was diminished, not eliminated, by the new location. Mzilikazi seems originally to have intended to withdraw even further into the interior, but was prevented from crossing the Zambezi, as Zwangendaba's Ngoni had managed a few years earlier, by the opposition of the Kololo and by tsetse

[17] T. O. Ranger *Revolt in Southern Rhodesia* (London 1967) pp. 123–4, 233, 261.

fly.[18] Instead, Mzilikazi was forced to choose the high and healthy cattle country north and west of the Matopo mountains near modern Bulawayo. This had the advantage from the Ndebele point of view of already having experienced the disruptive activities of Zwangendaba's and other migrating raiding groups, but the disadvantage of being uncomfortably close to the Boers on the other side of the Limpopo. Although the Ndebele managed to beat off Potgieter's cattle raid in 1847, the agreements negotiated with Potgieter and Pretorius in January and May 1853 respectively suggest a revival of the attempt to control relations with whites by diplomatic means.[19] Significantly, Mzilikazi had already made strenuous efforts to reopen contact with Moffat, perhaps wishing to balance his Boer alliances with a British missionary, but also because of the state of his health.[20]

Moffat's records of his 1854 and 1857 visits provide the most extensive surviving contemporary evidence during the period before the establishment of the mission station at Inyati in 1859. Settlement was highly concentrated and militarized, adapted as much for defence as aggression, for even though Moffat estimated that the population under Mzilikazi's direct control had regained its former level, he found the king still as troubled about Zulu as about Boers. Mzilikazi was therefore elated by the news of the Zulu civil war between the sons of Mpande, yet still confided 'that though he was now at so great a distance, he could not help fearing Zulus'.[21] In this respect, at least, the Ndebele appreciation of their position seems unrealistic and fear of the Zulu seems to have persisted until the British conquest of Cetshwayo in 1879. Rumours of the approach of Zulu armies, such as occurred in 1866, 1869, and 1877,[22] quickly produced panic and the whites usually had great difficulty in obtaining permission to bring

[18] *Matabele Journals* Vol. I pp. 371–2 (6 September 1854). Zwangendaba avoided these obstacles in his more easterly crossing of the Zambezi near Zumbo.

[19] For English translations and discussion of the degree of authenticity of these agreements see S. Samkange *Origins of Rhodesia* (London 1968) Chapter V. The Dutch texts are printed in G. S. Preller *Lobengula* (Johannesburg 1963) pp. 307–8. Preller's claim that Potgieter 'defeated the Matabele in the Matopos' (p. 33) is not confirmed by the firsthand accounts collected by Moffat in 1854 *Matabele Journals* Vol. I pp. 225, 243, 271–2.

[20] Ibid. Vol. I pp. 326–7 (8 October 1854).

[21] Ibid. Vol. II p. 84 (5 October 1857).

[22] *Matabele Mission of J. S. & E. Moffat* pp. 241–6, T. M. Thomas to A. Tidman, 13 August 1866; J. Swinburne to T. Shepstone, 21 May 1869, Shepstone Papers, Box 19, Natal; T. M. Thomas, unpublished journal 1874–1883, N.A.R., TH 2/1/1/ (Photocopy of original in Witwatersrand University Library), entry for 2 March 1877.

individual Zulu servants into the country for fear they turned out to be spies.

Some of Coillard's difficulties with Lobengula following his attempted mission to the Banyai in 1877 arose over his Basuto companions, members of another political community the Ndebele had earlier failed to vanquish. Interestingly enough, since it indicates the scale of the social field of which Ndebele external relations had become a part, one of the stated objections to the Basuto was that their countrymen had turned over the famous 'rebel' chief Langalibalele to the British authorities in Natal.[23]

The objection was not to foreigners as such since we hear of small groups of Mfengu, Griqua, Khoikhoi and others from far afield becoming assimilated, in addition, of course, to captives.[24] Even Kololo after their overthrow by the Lozi in Barotseland were given refuge.[25] Whatever their other reasons for being welcomed—and there is evidence to suggest that such foreigners often obtained important ritual and advisory positions—one result of their presence was to expand the volume of information on which to base external relations.[26] The Ndebele rulers clearly suffered on occasions from inadequate or inaccurate information, but this can easily be exaggerated and as time went on the amount available steadily expanded. The Mwari cult, among other things a 'secret intelligence service' stretching over a very wide area of south-central Africa, was probably of considerable importance.[27] Detailed evidence is scarce, but under both the Ndebele kings there was certainly some exchange of information between them and the cult authorities.[28]

Apart from this and information obtained from captives and during the course of raids, news was supplied and diplomacy carried on by accredited messengers and official delegations. A striking illustration of the extent of their operations were the

[23] F. Coillard *On The Threshold of Central Africa* trans. C. W. Macintosh (London 1897) pp. 35–39.

[24] *Gubulawayo and Beyond: Letters & Journals of the Early Jesuit Missionaries to Zambesia (1879–1887)* ed. M. Gelfand (London 1968) pp. 251, 264; *Diaries of the Jesuit Missionaries, 1879–81* trans. M. Lloyd (Salisbury 1961) pp. 53–54, 75–76.

[25] W. Sykes to J. Mullens, 30 November 1869, N.A.R., LO 6/1/3; Coillard *On The Threshold* pp. 40–41.

[26] See footnote 24 above.

[27] T. O. Ranger *Revolt in Southern Rhodesia* pp. 21–24.

[28] T. M. Thomas *Eleven Years in Central South Africa* (London n. d. 1872) pp. 290–1; *The Northern Goldfields Diaries of Thomas Baines 1869–72* ed. J. P. R. Wallis (3 vols. London 1946) Vol. II p. 391.

'spies', as the source refers to them, who were sent out north of the Zambezi on Lobengula's accession and returned with the report that they had found 'six different tribes of modified Zulus'.[29] Whether this reference to the Ngoni states included any in what is now Tanzania is not clear, but the information would seem to reach at least as far as northern Malawi. There were few areas of southern Africa which were not accessible to properly accredited messengers, as the extensive searches for Mzilikazi's principal heir show.

The existence of regularized forms of diplomatic interaction was particularly important in maintaining stable relations with the neighbouring Gaza kingdom. Since it too was a powerful raiding state whose sphere of influence met that of the Ndebele along the Sabi river, peaceful coexistence was essential. Apart from tensions over cattle lifting, conflict appears to have been avoided throughout the period, a considerable achievement in such disturbed times.[30] Soon after succeeding to the throne Lobengula was reported to have sent oxen to the Gaza king, Mzila;[31] and in 1879 relations were further cemented when Lobengula took the daughter of Mzila as his chief wife.[32] Arrangements for the marriage involved much diplomatic contact and the importance of the event was shown by the size of the retinue which accompanied her to Matabeleland, along with seven or more other prospective Gaza brides for Lobengula, including also a sister of the Gaza king. The retinue was liberally entertained in the months before the weddings took place. Mzila's successor subsequently returned the compliment by marrying a daughter of Lobengula, although later it was said that Lobengula was 'considered stingy' for having sent only one wife in return.[33]

If the conduct of diplomacy was facilitated by specialist messengers and envoys, the absence of literacy was a serious handicap and could lead to difficulties and disagreements as

[29] 'Memorandum on the Zulus and Matabele' by A. Bailie, N.A.R., BA 10/2/1.

[30] Cattle lifting and the stationing of soldiers are mentioned by St Vincent Erskine to T. Baines, n. d., [*c.* 1869], N.A.R., BA 7/1/1.

[31] Baines *Goldfields Diaries* Vol. III p. 623.

[32] Both the published Jesuit mission sources, footnote 24, contain many references to the marriage. Estimates of the size of the retinue varied from 600–700 to 1,000 *Gubulawayo and Beyond* pp. 142, 177.

[33] *Gold and the Gospel in Mashonaland, 1888* eds. C. E. Fripp and V. W. Hiller (London 1949) pp. 91–92 (Bishop Knight-Bruce's journal, 13 October 1888). Omer-Cooper mentions this marriage but implies it took place before Mzilikazi died *Zulu Aftermath* p. 60.

happened among an important official deputation to the Natal government.[34] Illiteracy also offered favourable opportunities to individuals and groups to use rumour as a means of influencing relations between political communities. Although whites were sometimes responsible for starting rumours to this end, there is no reason to believe them responsible for all the many false reports which disturbed the interior.[35] And some rumours, one suspects, originated within political communities as a means of bringing pressure to bear on decision-making outside the institutionalized councils.[36]

The literacy of the white missionaries and traders provided an important new channel for the conduct of external relations, but one which they continued to monopolize since the Ndebele were indifferent to the attempts of the missionaries to start schools. Although Mzilikazi made little use of the whites as intermediaries, Lobengula's reign began in a flurry of diplomatic activity and he soon relied on whites extensively to transcribe outgoing messages and to read incoming ones. One of them provided him with the famous elephant seal with which to authenticate the documents written on his behalf.[37] As most other African governments by this time also had access to scribes, Lobengula's correspondence was not confined only to communicating with white governments. His illiteracy obviously placed him to some extent at the mercy of those whites who wrote and translated for him, but it does not seem, at least until the scramble, that any serious advantage was ever taken by them. And although more than one came to think of himself as the king's exclusive agent, Lobengula appears to have deliberately avoided becoming dependent on any single individual; nor were customary methods of communication entirely superseded.

While the presence of whites helped to intensify the more distant

[34] Statements made to T. Shepstone, 16 August 1870, Natal, S.N.A. 1/7/6.

[35] White rumour-mongering for political ends was alleged against an agent of the Transvaal, J. W. Viljoen, by the missionary John Mackenzie *Accounts & Papers* 1868–9 XLIII, Wodehouse to Buckingham, 19 October 1868, and enclosures. See also E. C. Tabler *Pioneers of Rhodesia* (Cape Town 1966) p. 165.

[36] The rumours that Sir Sydney Shippard was bringing an invading army into Matabeleland on his official visit to Lobengula in 1888 may well have been connected with those Ndebele who were at the same time pressing Lobengula to abandon all negotiations with the whites and allow them to be massacred. Shippard to High Commissioner, 12–16 October 1888 *African* (*South*) 369, encl. in No. 64.

[37] The seal was made by the artist-explorer-prospector Thomas Baines *Goldfields Diaries* Vol. III p. 683 19 August 1871.

diplomatic activities of the Ndebele, a great deal of the attention paid to external matters concerned their relations with their neighbours within the Ndebele sphere of influence. The territorial area of the kingdom proper was surprisingly small, restricted to the area of concentrated military settlements within thirty to forty miles of the royal capital. By the end of Mzilikazi's reign this area was estimated to contain a fighting population alone of ten to twenty thousand men.[38] 'Greater' Matabeleland, the territorial area claimed by the Ndebele kings, was in effect a specialized part of the external environment which they sought to control for reasons of overall security and as a source of cattle, grain, and manpower.

The Ndebele do not seem to have even attempted to bring all the local peoples within the full framework of a social system whose viability rested on the tightly-controlled residential system of regiments. This system was well adapted for the effective socialization of a steady stream of mostly young captives, but would have been considerably strained by an attempt to assimilate directly large blocs of subject peoples. Unlike some of the Ngoni groups, the Ndebele were chary of attempting to do so on any large scale. The precise relationship which actually obtained depended partly on the geographical position of the groups concerned and partly on the reaction of such groups to the presence of Ndebele military power. Some of the Shona-speaking groups who were already living in the area which came to form the kingdom proper were, along with captives obtained in raids, directly incorporated into the lowest of the three 'castes' into which Ndebele society was stratified. Others outside the central area were merely placed under Ndebele indunas and left outside the regimental residence system. They did, however, herd cattle for the king, send produce to the capital and provide some conscripts and volunteers when new regiments were formed.[39] These outposts also functioned to prevent unauthorized entry and to maintain the security of the kingdom by giving warning of impending danger.

Elsewhere the Ndebele sought to use their military strength to bring those Shona-speaking chieftaincies who could not with-

[38] Thomas estimated 20,000 in 1866 *Matabele Mission of J. S. & E. Moffat* p. 242, but Bailie's estimate ten years later was only 7,000–10,000, footnote 29 above.

[39] H. Kuper, A. J. B. Hughes, J. van Velsen *The Shona and Ndebele of Southern Rhodesia* (London 1954) pp. 68–69.

stand the impact of raiding into a tributary relationship. This colonial-type of external relations was neither uniformly warlike, nor always successful. In many cases, the Ndebele sought to extend their influence by capturing a local chief or other members of the royal lineage, keeping them in Matabeleland proper for varying periods—years if they were youths—and then returning them to their own communities to be loyal tributary chiefs or, in some cases, just influential local people.[40] But the activities of the more distant puppets could not usually be seriously supervised and the extent of Ndebele influence in many of the tributary areas fluctuated considerably. It was strongest in the south-east and east towards the Limpopo and Sabi rivers and to the west and north-west towards the Zambezi, but this latter area was thinly populated. To the south-west influence over the more distant Kalanga tended to falter, depending largely on the complexities of political conflict among the adjacent Tswana; to the north-east it was the resistance of Shona-speaking peoples themselves which was the main stumbling block to the further expansion of regularized tributary relationships.

Away from the area of concentrated power, the Ndebele were far from being the sole determinants of the situation within their claimed sphere of influence. Their raiding parties did not regularly carry all before them. Even excluding the more directly military conflicts with major rivals like the Kololo, a surprising number of the references to raiding activities indicate partial or sometimes total failure. Supply difficulties and the ease with which individual raiding parties could be cut off, as well as defensive resistance from those attacked accounted for these failures.[41] Furthermore, the ban on trading guns to the Shona from Matabeleland could not prevent them being obtained from the east coast; and with the nineteenth-century developments in trade from the west coast as well as from the south (in spite of attempted regulation by governments in South Africa) meant that there were few, if any, raided peoples who did not possess at least some firearms. However, contrary to a common misconception, the Ndebele too acquired and used guns.[42] Lobengula even went to considerable lengths to obtain cannon. Baines had hoped to consolidate his

[40] Baines *Goldfields Diaries* Vol. II p. 498; *Gold and the Gospel* p. 61 (Bishop Knight-Bruce's journal, 12 August 1888); T. O. Ranger *Revolt in Southern Rhodesia* pp. 26–31.
[41] T. Baines to E. Oliver, draft n. d., 1869/70, N.A.R., BA 8/1/2/1.
[42] E. C. Tabler *The Far Interior* (Cape Town 1955) pp. 165–6, 172–3, 221.

concession in 1870 by supplying some,[43] but when he failed to do so Lobengula solicited one from a shocked British government.[44] Eventually he obtained a pair of worthless cannon from two daring and unscrupulous traders in 1877.[45] On balance, though, it would appear that the long-term trend in the interior was undermining the military advantage of the Ndebele. In part, this reflected the ability of raided peoples to change their ways of life to counter the Ndebele threat.

If trade was gradually transforming their relations with other African states by supplying them with guns, trade was also increasing in some degree the Ndebele dependence on the outside world. Its direct effects, however, were limited since the important transactions, the trade in ivory and the issue of hunting licences, were a royal monopoly. The politically powerful benefited as recipients of royal generosity, but the mass of the population had to be content with the occasional bartering of food for small amounts of cloth and beads during the seasonal influx of whites. In fact, that the traders and hunters were white was probably more immediately important for external affairs than their commercial activities.

The Ndebele rulers were clearly aware of the ambiguous position of the whites who gained entry to Matabeleland in increasing numbers from the mid-1850s and adopted towards them a policy which was often unpopular with their subjects. The essence of the 'official' policy can be summed up as the attempt to control the implications of their presence by affording them special treatment. This did not reflect the power of numbers in Matabeleland itself, since there were probably never more than fifty in the country at any one time and these were obviously dependent on the goodwill of the Ndebele authorities for their personal safety and commercial success. Yet the whites considered themselves to be in some sense representatives of the powerful political communities from which they came and to which they were constantly returning or, in the case of the few resident missionaries, with whom they were in frequent communication. This aspect of the white presence was reinforced when they were entrusted with semi-official duties by the colonial governments to

[43] T. Baines to E. Oliver, 6 December 1870, N.A.R., BA 8/1/2/2; Baines *Goldfields Diaries* Vol. II p. 321.

[44] Lobengula to Sir H. Barkly, 14 October 1875 and Lord Carnarvon to Barkly, 14 March 1876, Conf. Pr. *African* 110, encl. in No. 9, No. 11.

[45] Tabler *Far Interior* p. 418.

the south. Moreover, whites sometimes claimed a spurious official status or banded together to make collective demands on the king. In a more general sense, the whites as a whole saw themselves as collectively upholding the prestige of the white man in southern Africa.

Even though the rulers were often aware of the significance of distinctions based on function, nationality, and individual character and were certainly not mere dupes in white hands, the treatment of any individual white man once he had been granted admission to the country had to be seen in the context of the external relations with white governments. Thus, although their small numbers forced the whites in general to adhere to the strict rules governing their activities they were not fully under customary Ndebele law and were left to judge their own disputes among themselves and also had special privileges denied to local people.

Whites constantly sought to draw attention to the wider implications of their treatment. For example, the child of a Swedish trader accidentally broke a royal dish, a serious crime in Ndebele eyes. Rather untypically, Lobengula angrily shook the child's parents with his hands. This led to a deputation of missionaries to the king whose spokesman told Lobengula 'respectfully but firmly'[46]

> that the king must never lay his hands upon a European; such an action might excite his people and lead to the massacre of all Europeans in his country. Such an occurrence would, without any doubt, bring grave retribution to the king and his people.

As this statement tends to suggest, the official policy towards the whites as a group was not shared by all Ndebele. In general, the young unmarried warriors, whose future social and economic status depended in part on maintaining the traditional raiding state intact and who were not beneficiaries from trade, resented the white intrusion most, while the older men who had already acquired dependants and cattle were more favourable. At the same time, attitudes to whites could not be divorced from the imperatives of domestic politics. The kingdom possessed many of the aspects of a segmentary state and the four major divisions (each comprising a group of regiments) into which it was split provided major bases for political competition, especially since the segments had territorial as well as military-administrative

[46] *Diaries of the Jesuit Missionaries* p. 17 (10 September 1879).

aspects. Competition among the political élite was intense, as the number of leading figures who were eliminated suggests. Even Mzilikazi was said to fear assassination,[47] and his successor's hold on the throne was for long much weaker. Major policy decisions, such as to allow the missionaries to stay in 1859, were invariably preceded by lengthy discussions, sometimes lasting for several months. The interconnection between the internal and external environments perhaps also helps to explain why the Ndebele rulers conciliated and protected the whites and, after 1837, were never responsible for launching an attack on them, yet made relatively little attempt to exploit their modernizing skills.

Attitudes to whites did not prevent them being used as resources in internal politics. This, and other points which have been made above, can be illustrated from events arising from the disputed succession following Mzilikazi's death in 1868. The dispute remained alive throughout the 1870s and since Lobengula's opponents sought outside support from both white and black, internal and external politics became closely fused.

Lobengula was not installed in his father's office until after a fifteen-month interregnum as there were doubts about the existence and whereabouts of an heir with a better claim. Nevertheless, Lobengula had the support of a majority of the powerful indunas and he was duly confirmed in office by the appropriate holders of ritual authority and by the acclamation of a majority of the people. Opposition came from within one of the four primary divisions of the kingdom. The dispute therefore represented a major cleavage inherent in the structure of the kingdom and threatened the possibility of a major secession. However, the contest remained focused on the kingship even after Lobengula had defeated his opponents militarily in the battle of Zwangendaba a few months after his accession.

His opponents included other sons of Mzilikazi who had fled the country, but who, like the group in Matabeleland, supported, nominally at least, the candidature of a man claiming to be the principal heir, the missing Kuruman. His identity has never been satisfactorily established. He had turned up as an employee of the Natal Secretary for Native Affairs, Sir Theophilus Shepstone, who eventually came to accept his bona fides. Thus the stage was set for a struggle which was to stretch over a vast geographical area and involve the Transvaal, Cape, Natal and British

[47] R. Moffat to A. Tidman, 25 December 1862, N.A.R., LO 6/1/2.

governments. Further complications arose from the fact that Mzilikazi's death coincided with attempts by whites from as far afield as Australia to exploit the newly-discovered gold deposits within 'greater' Matabeleland.

Shepstone claimed neutrality on behalf of the government of Natal, but he clearly saw himself, and was seen by others, in the traditional role of the powerful chief actively involved in the processes of succession in weaker political communities.[48] Lobengula certainly viewed him in this light and conducted an intensive diplomatic campaign to undermine Shepstone's cautious support for 'Kuruman' by trying to gain recognition of his own legitimacy and destroy that of his opponent.[49] He also attached the two leading gold companies to his cause by granting them concessions—in one case, in return for a secret pledge by the company manager 'to aid and support' Lobengula 'by public report to the British Government'. Efforts were also made to win the confidence of the missionaries. The campaign failed to stop Shepstone giving 'Kuruman' limited diplomatic and material aid to enable him to return with his small party of exiles to Matabeleland.[51]

At this point, the involvement of the Ngwato, the Tswana-speaking neighbours of the Ndebele to the south-west, illustrates a different facet of external relations. Here it is not so much the widening scale of Ndebele involvement which is striking, as the decline in Ndebele self-sufficiency and their inability to control even indirectly areas of former influence.

The Ngwato were situated on the only regular route into Matabeleland from the south. In the earlier period this was of little consequence to the Ndebele and, in any case, the Tswana

[48] 'Memorandum concerning Kuruman', n. d. [? 1869], Shepstone Papers, Box 24, Natal; Lt. Governor of Natal to Earl of Kimberley, 23 September 1870, Natal, G.H., Vol. 278; Shepstone to A. L. Levert, 18 October 1870, Natal, S.N.A. 1/1/20.

[49] Baines to D. Erskine, 10 April 1870, *Goldfields Diaries* Vol. II pp. 322–5; Lobengula to Lt. Governor of Natal, [19] and 29 August 1871, Ibid. Vol. III pp. 683–7, 697–8; Lobengula to Shepstone, 13 February 1871, Natal, S.N.A. 1/1/20.

[50] Agreement of 9 April 1870, encl. in A. L. Levert to Shepstone, 30 May 1870, Natal, S.N.A. 1/1/20, together with copy of concession. The Baines concession, *Goldfields Diaries* Vol. II p. 317ff; Vol. III pp. 695–6.

[51] Shepstone informed Lobengula that while the Natal government could not prevent 'Kuruman's' return, it would not take 'the customary step' of sending him back, letter of 27 May 1871, Baines *Goldfields Diaries* pp. 614–15. However, in spite of this assurance, the Natal government provided the 'Kuruman' party with transport and provisions and also solicited the good offices of the Transvaal government on its behalf, Shepstone to Government Secretary, Pretoria, 3 June and 22 August 1871, Natal, S.N.A. 1/1/21; memorandum by Shepstone, 15 August 1872, S.N.A. 1/1/22.

generally were unable to resist Ndebele pressures. Relations with the Ngwato largely revolved around the person of Macheng who was their chief in 1870. He had been captured by an Ndebele raiding party as a youth and carefully preserved as a valuable political commodity since he was the principal heir to the Ngwato chieftaincy. After being kept in Matabeleland for more than a decade, he was allowed to return to become the chief, but not before he had adopted Ndebele ways and been used to further the varied purposes of a string of intermediaries. In 1857 Mzilikazi had sought to gain credit with Moffat as well as increased influence over the Ngwato by handing Macheng over to the missionary. Moffat passed him on to the Kwena chief, Sechele, who in turn restored Macheng to his people.[52]

However, Mzilikazi's hopes of maintaining an influence of any significance over the Ngwato collapsed. In the short run, this was because Macheng was soon ousted from the chieftaincy after his triumphal and roundabout return from Matabeleland, for attempting, it was said, to rule in the Ndebele manner. In the long run, the decline in Ndebele informal influence was due to the expansion of interior trade which made Shoshong, the Ngwato capital, the largest, most prosperous and hence best-armed town in the interior.[53] This in turn encouraged Kalanga on the south-western borders of 'greater' Matabeleland to shift their allegiance. When Mzilikazi retaliated with a major punitive raid against Shoshong in 1863, his forces were none too successful even though Ngwato military discipline was minimal.[54]

Relations with the Ngwato worsened as a result of the succession crisis. Macheng, who had regained his position in the closing years of Mzilikazi's life, saw it as a further opportunity to pursue Ngwato independence. He defied Lobengula, asserted territorial and taxation claims over the new Tati goldfields and obstructed Ndebele traffic and personnel on what had now become the vital route to the south. Finally, the one-time captive of the Ndebele sought to turn the tables completely by supporting 'Kuruman's' attempts to unseat Lobengula. He gave 'Kuruman's' party refuge on their arrival from Natal and promised military assistance. The

[52] A. Sillery *Sechele* (Oxford 1954) pp. 118–37; *Matabele Journals passim*; R. Moffat to A. Tidman, 15 July 1857, N.A.R. LO 6/1/1.

[53] Coillard *On The Threshold* pp. 48–49.

[54] J. Mackenzie to A. Tidman, 27 April 1863, N.A.R., LO 6/1/3; *Matabele Mission of J. S. & E. Moffat* pp. 205, 220; J. Mackenzie *Ten Years North of the Orange River 1859–69* pp. 267–85.

challenge in the event was a weak one and insufficient to arouse the opposition group inside Matabeleland. However, this was because Macheng's own position at Shoshong was once again precarious. The fiasco did not prove that Lobengula was now secure, but that his opponents were weak without dependable allies.[55]

Lobengula's problem was the fear that 'Kuruman' would find white allies nearer and more adventurous than Shepstone had been. Hence he was alarmed when President Kruger gave 'Kuruman' and his followers asylum, since he could not be sure that he would not also give more practical assistance in the pursuit of Boer territorial expansion. Instead, 'Kuruman's' base in the Transvaal became a convenient refuge for malcontents and fugitives from Matabeleland.[56]

The main body of Lobengula's opponents, however, remained within Matabeleland. They had a reputation for treating whites roughly,[57] but outside Matabeleland their representatives actively sought white military assistance. 'Kuruman' offered a party of disaffected Transvaalers who were about to trek 'land to their hearts' content' if they would render him armed assistance. 'Kuruman is assured that if, by your aid he could reach his friends, such a number of them would immediately rally round him as to render further service from you unnecessary and thinks that when Lobengula hears of his approach at the head of an armed force he will flee.'[58] Forty years earlier the Voortrekkers had taken advantage of a similar conflict to gain control of much of Zululand. In this case, the proposal was turned down and the correspondence sent to Lobengula. When it was interpreted to him he 'wept tears . . . and said he had not yet turned his back from fear of Kuruman.'[59]

The very next year in 1877 the forward movement in imperial policy under Lord Carnarvon brought Shepstone to the Transvaal,

[55] Lobengula to Macheng, 2 May 1870, encl. E. and A. L. Levert to Shepstone, Natal, S.N.A. 1/1/20; Lobengula to Shepstone, 24 April 1871, S.N.A. 1/7/6; J. B. Thomson to J. Mullens, 16 January 1872, N.A.R., LO 6/1/4; Thomas *Eleven Years* pp. 410–11.
[56] Lobengula to Sir H. Barkly, 10 April 1876, enclosing Lobengula to President of South African Republic, 10 April 1876, Conf. Pr. *African* 110, encls. in No. 38; F. C. Selous, undated notes, N.A.R., SE 1/1/1.
[57] *To The Victoria Falls: Diary of Major Henry Stabb* ed. E. C. Tabler (Cape Town 1967) pp. 82–84 (27 and 28 July 1875).
[58] As translated from the Dutch originals and recorded by T. M. Thomas in his journal, 23 August [1876]. N.A.R., TH 2/1/1.
[59] Ibid.

where he became the British Administrator. As he informed the High Commissioner at Cape Town, 'the possession of the person of Kuruman gives Her Majesty's Government the means of exercising great influence over the reigning Matabele king.'[60] Shepstone sought to use this influence to get Lobengula to accept a British Resident. When this was put to him by an official emissary the king was reluctant to discuss the matter. 'But ultimately', recorded the interpreter, 'when it had been suggested to his Majesty that in view of the possibility of the Transvaal Boers leaving their country for these parts and bringing with them the supposed uKurumana it would be well for him to be on friendly terms with his next-door neighbour Sir Theophilus Shepstone he seemed to approve of the idea of a British Consul's being placed at Gubulawayo.'[61] The interpreter who knew the king well, having been one of the original group of missionaries in 1859, commented on the attempts to draw the kingdom more closely into the British sphere in a way which anticipated many of those that were to be made a decade later when the pressure finally became overwhelming. He believed that Lobengula was opposed in principle, 'but that ere imperilling his life or Kingdom he would make some efforts to meet the wishes of the English Captain [R. R. Patterson]. He was actuated by fear and not any good principle.'[62]

The whole of Patterson's party subsequently perished from drinking poisoned water while on a hunting expedition. Not all the evidence pointed to their having been murdered by order of the king as has been alleged.[63] Indeed, such an act would have been uncharacteristic of the policies pursued by Lobengula at any time of his reign. As the missionary quoted above suggested, fear was likely to make him concede ground, not invite retribution. Whether responsible or not, Lobengula must have been exceedingly concerned about the possible consequences of the deaths. Ironically, it was the forceful rejection of Lord Carnarvon's southern African policy by their old enemies the Boers and the Zulu which spared the Ndebele further pressure and prevented any

[60] Shepstone to Frere, 2 April 1878, C. 2220, encl. 2, No. 130.
[61] Thomas, journal, 10 September 1878.
[62] Ibid.
[63] L. Gann *History of Southern Rhodesia* (London 1965) p. 61. Thomas, one of whose sons was a member of the fatal party, reveals some of the difficulties involved in the evidence in later entries in the journal quoted above and in a letter to Shepstone, 19 February 1879, Shepstone Papers, Box 21, Natal.

British attempt to use the Patterson incident imperialistically. On the other hand, the eventual downfall of Cetshwayo, after initial successes which significantly had led to a period of rough treatment for the whites in Matabeleland,[64] and the recovery of their independence by the Boers of the Transvaal had a profound effect on Ndebele external policy. The Zulu defeat following their earlier triumphs was a dramatic demonstration of white power. The Boer victory over the conquerors of the Zulu not only reinforced this lesson, but also led Lobengula to make renewed conciliatory overtures to Pretoria.[65] Together Ulundi (1879) and Majuba (1881) probably played a part in stimulating within a few years Lobengula's remarkable attempt to forge an alliance against the white advance with Lewanika of Barotseland.[66] This, as far as we know, unprecedented move to seek an alliance against whites and for such a general rather than specific purpose is a clear indication of Lobengula's awareness of the changing nature and increasing scale of the external environment. The offer seems additionally to have been a characteristic move in inter-African relations, since it appears to have originated when Lewanika was in exile and was to include assistance to him to recapture his throne. As it coincided with the indications that the Ndebele were considering the possibility of moving north of the Zambezi, it is hardly surprising that Lewanika was unable to overcome his strong fears of Ndebele aggression and turned elsewhere for support. However, in so far as cooperation against the white advance was envisaged the proposed alliance was a significant turning point in intention if not in result.

The failure to reach an agreement meant that Lobengula's underlying policy towards the whites on the eve of the partition remained one of attempting to avoid an outright conflict with them. His eventual failure was not so much due to a lack of understanding of the world around him, as to the limitation on his freedom of manœuvre imposed by the Ndebele social system and to the strength and ruthlessness of his white opponents. The disputed succession and the growing ambitions of whites in his part of Africa had already involved him in nearly two decades of

[64] C. D. Helm to Whitehouse, 10 September 1879, N.A.R., microfilm register No. 53, reel 3.

[65] S. Samkange *Origins of Rhodesia* pp. 45–55; P. J. Joubert, Commandant General of the South African Republic, to Lobengula, 9 March 1882, copy in N.A.R., SE 1/1/1.

[66] G. L. Caplan 'Barotseland's Scramble for Protection' *J.A.H.* Vol. X No. 2 (1969) pp. 280–1; F. S. Arnot *Missionary Travels in Central Africa* (Bath 1914) pp. 21–22.

extensive diplomatic contact when Rhodes appeared on the scene. During this time his own internal position had been strengthening as he steadily eliminated his more dangerous opponents. Had the external pressures been stronger or his handling of them less effective during the period when the succession issue was still active and allowing the exploitation of the kingdom's segmentary characteristics, its incorporation under white rule might well have taken a different form. Instead, the Ndebele kingdom faced the crisis of the Partition with its unitary characteristics uppermost.[67] When white hopes that it would collapse from within were not fulfilled, they decided to overthrow it from without.[68] Incorporation by the sword was thought to have been achieved in the war of 1893, but white expectations again proved false when both the Ndebele and the Shona took up arms in 1896.

[67] R. Brown 'Aspects of the Scramble for Matabeleland' E. Stokes and R. Brown, eds. *The Zambesian Past* (Manchester 1966) and editors' introduction.
[68] T. O. Ranger *Revolt in Southern Rhodesia* pp. 93–7.

13. *The passing of Sotho independence 1865–70*

ANTHONY ATMORE

The years between 1868 and 1870 witnessed a situation of some complexity on the high plateaux of Lesotho. Moshweshwe and his people found themselves the centre of a power struggle between three, at least, of the political components of white South Africa: the Orange Free State, Natal, and Sir Philip Wodehouse, who was both High Commissioner and Governor of the Cape Colony, and as such could therefore be said to represent the old colony, although his relations with the Cape politicians were anything but cordial.[1] The Sotho had been defeated in war and had suffered a considerable amount of destruction from the Free State's scorched-earth policy.[2] They were certainly not in a position to determine the course of events, as they had been in the days of Moshweshwe's prime, but they were able, by devious means of the kind that infuriated the whites, to manœuvre between the white contenders. The actions of the Sotho leaders intensified the mistrust of the whites one for another, and delayed the implementation of the final settlement.

At the beginning of 1868 the Free State was intent upon pursuing the third, and undeclared, stage of the war with Lesotho which had first developed into open fighting in June 1865.[3] Its

[1] See *The Cambridge History of the British Empire* Vol. VIII South Africa Chapter XVI, C. W. de Kiewiet 'The period of transition in South African policy, 1854–1870' pp. 420–3, 426–37; P. A. Molteno *The Life and Times of Sir John Charles Molteno* London 1900 pp. 89–143.

[2] e.g. Jousse (for Moshesh) to Burnet, civil commissioner of Aliwal North 15 October 1867, in G. M. Theal *Basutoland Records* Vol. III p. 828; Moshesh to Wodehouse 26 February 1868 ibid. pp. 878–9; G(overnment) H(ouse) 10/7 (Cape Town), Orpen to Wodehouse, 16 November 1865. The most vivid descriptions of the sufferings of the Sotho during the course of the fighting are to be found in Mabille's letters and Mrs Mabille's 'Memories' quoted at length in Edwin W. Smith *The Mabilles of Basutoland* London 1939 pp. 143–75. [G. M. Theal *Basutoland Records* Vols. I to III published Cape Town 1883/1964, Vols. IV to VI unpublished MS in Cape Town archives; photostat copies in Maseru archives. Henceforth *BR*.]

[3] For the declaration of war, see proclamations of Brand and Moshweshwe *BR* Vol. III pp. 357–62, and for Free State war aims see, *inter alia*, *BR* III pp. 848–50, Brand to Wodehouse, 31 January 1868.

commandos had raided deeply into the then habitable land of Lesotho. These forces were composed of several different peoples: Afrikaans- and English-speaking Free Staters; adventurers who came illegally from the Cape; the 'native allies' of the Free State—Mfengu who had in a similar way crossed the Orange River from the Herschel Native Reserve to get their share of the plunder and who included many Tlokwa, the long-standing enemies of the Sotho—and other traditional enemies of Moshweshwe, such as Moroko's Rolong and the Monaheng of Letele, the senior branch of the Kwena group.[4] The loyalty of these allies to the Free State was questionable; C. S. Orpen (the better known Joseph Orpen's brother, and one of the 'Smithfield English'), for example, stated that 'our native allies prey upon us as well as upon the Basutos . . . whenever they are made to disgorge or divide with their commandant Webster they make our farmers pay the piper to recover their loss'.[5] When the fighting finally came to an end, many of the Monaheng and other scattered groups moved into Lesotho.[6] At times there were probably more English than Afrikaners in the Free State commandos, and certainly more Africans than whites of both groups.

Although the white commandos were not particularly efficient or well-coordinated fighting units, they bore the brunt of the fighting against the Sotho and generally succeeded in overcoming them. Their weapons were superior, as Moshweshwe pointed out: 'If (Brand) says that my people have not been able to cope with his burgers in open field, no wonder since they have the best rifles, the best powder and cannons.'[7] The Free State could buy arms and ammunition from the Cape and Natal, the Sotho could not. The excuse for this discrimination was the Bloemfontein Convention of 1854. In fact, a prohibition on the sale of arms and ammunition to the neighbouring African peoples was one of the terms of the 1852 Sand River Convention with the Transvaalers, but was *not* included in the 1854 convention. Thus one of the major factors in the defeats of the Sotho in the 1865–8 wars was

[4] The enlistment or recruitment of British subjects in the Cape was prohibited by Wodehouse in a proclamation of 27 June 1865, ibid. pp. 370–1. There is plenty of evidence to show that such enlistment and recruitment of whites and blacks was substantial. A great part of J. M. Orpen's correspondence with Wodehouse, GH 10/7 in Cape Town archives, is concerned with these illegal operations.

[5] GH 10/7 (CT), C. Orpen to Halse, 25 November 1868.

[6] *BR* V pp. 281–8, Bowker to Wodehouse, 20 and 27 August 1869.

[7] *BR* IV pp. 31–8, Moshesh to Burnet, 19 March 1868.

based upon a legal fallacy, a fact of which Wodehouse was personally aware.[8]

The commandos also perhaps showed greater fortitude on the field of battle—so at least the consensus of white opinion held to be true. But there was at least one dissenting voice, that of Joseph Orpen, who thought that 'the Boers (were) greater cowards than the Basutos . . . (they) have never attempted an attack hand to hand as the Basutos did one night at Thaba Bosiu—and if the Boers had got shot to the extent that Basutos have they would have been far *more* discouraged—when repeatedly twenty to fifty Basutos are shot down in a "great battle" in which no Boer is wounded it shows that they must have *some* courage to stand and be shot and that it does not require *much* in the Boers to stand and shoot them—and that an infinite superiority in weapons and ammunition is what makes the Boers victorious.'[9] Moshweshwe, in the letter quoted above (note 7), claimed that 'in many places a dozen or a score of Basutos have again and again withstood successfully the efforts of a whole commando of 500 or 1000 men. In one case a petty chief, Tlibelime, kept the whole camp of Mr Joubert at bay with eight men, and if it had not been for want of water he would never have been compelled to leave his little stronghold.'

By early April 1866 the Free State was able to force the treaty of Thaba Bosiu upon Moshweshwe and Letsie, and most of southern Lesotho, and all that on the west bank of the Caledon, became Free State territory, the Sotho inhabitants being given notice to quit. All that remained to the old chief and his first born son of useful land was the country around Thaba Bosiu and the Berea plateau. A few days previously Letsie's brother, Molapo, had also come to terms whereby all his country, that is the land north of the upper Phuthiatsana River, became Free State territory. Molapo became a Free State subject, as Moshweshwe and Letsie did not. He and his people were allowed to remain in Leribe district, but had to vacate their lands to the west of the Caledon.[10] Fighting subsequent to these treaties arose because the Free State alleged that the Sotho had not abided by their terms. Molapo always managed to persuade President Brand and the com-

[8] *BR* III pp. 394, Wodehouse to Cardwell, 12 July 1865; ibid. pp. 581–3, Wodehouse to Cardwell, 2 January 1866; also Orpen correspondence with Wodehouse.

[9] GH 10/7 (CT), J. M. Orpen to Wodehouse, 6 November 1865.

[10] *BR* III pp. 643–4, 647, 649–51, 654–6, Treaty of Imparani, 26 March 1866 (with Molapo) and Treaty of Thaba Bosiu 3 April 1866.

mandants on the spot that he was doing his best, and did not become involved in the renewed hostilities. These were recommenced on a small scale against Letsie in March 1867[11] and on a much larger scale against all the Sotho, with the exception of Molapo and his uncle, Paulus Mopedi, in September of that year. The object of the Free State was to clear what it called the conquered territory of Sotho. Although the commandos won spectacular victories, storming the Sotho mountain fortresses one after another[12] and carrying off enormous numbers of cattle and other stock, they were never able to achieve this object. The wretched Sotho returned from the caves and valleys deep in the mountains to their wrecked villages and devastated crops in the wake of the Free State forces. The Free State won the war but could not keep the peace.

By this time a stalemate in the war of attrition had been reached. The loot from the commando forays benefited only a certain number of Free Staters, and the economy of the country had been denuded by the expenses of the war and of the long period of insecurity. Southey, Wodehouse's colonial secretary, commented: 'the . . . success of the Boers . . . has been very much exaggerated and in reality they are now only making war on the standing crops, and making an occasional capture of a few head of cattle. The people (he meant the Free Staters) are tired and weary of the thing, and feel that it is with them and the Basutos as it is with the two Kilkenny cats—they are eating each other up, exhausting their resources, and doing no good, but ruining themselves and their fine country.'[13] The outlook for the Sotho was more serious. Nearly all the fighting was by then taking place in Lesotho, and the commandos were committed to the destruction of crops and habitations. Many tens of thousands of people might be forced by lack of food to make counter raids into the Free

[11] Ibid. pp. 748–66.

[12] Maboloka, Makwai's mountain, in December 1867 (ibid. pp. 837–8), Mathebe, on which Moshweshwe's brother and great Sotho warrior Poshudi was killed, in February 1868 (ibid. pp. 863–4), and Qeme, Letsie's fortress, in the same month. The Free State commandant claimed to have captured over 10,000 head of cattle, 8,000 sheep, and 1,500 horses on Qeme; ibid. p. 877, Pansegrouw to Brand, 23 February 1868. Moshweshwe wrote of the loss of 'a great quantity of cattle', and significantly put the blame for the defeat on defectors from the Sotho side. '(The Boers) have for servants and spies so many natives that they know all the roads and paths up to the mountains.' Moshesh to Shepstone, 21/23 February 1868, Laydevant papers, Roman Catholic presbytery, Maseru.

[13] Southey Papers (SP), Cape Town archives, Vol. 56, Southey to Currie, 23 February 1868.

State, or even to flee over the Drakensberg into the lands of the Cape Africans. The dangers to the whole of South Africa from this running sore in its heartlands was the recurring theme in the arguments used by Wodehouse to persuade a British government reluctant to sanction any further extension of British authority in South Africa to intervene between the Free State and the Sotho.[14] This the Duke of Buckingham, colonial secretary in Lord Derby's ministry, finally decided to do in December 1867.[15] Early in the new year the high commissioner was able to announce to Brand and to Moshweshwe that 'H.M. the Queen (had) been graciously pleased to accede' to the latter's request that he and his 'tribe should be received as subjects of the British Throne'.[16] Brand received this information with studied coolness, refusing to terminate hostilies against the Sotho, and telling the High Commissioner that British intervention north of the Orange was contrary to the 1854 Convention.[17] The further Free State successes subsequent to the announcement of 13 January induced Wodehouse to issue the proclamation of 12 March, declaring Lesotho to be British territory[18] and to order all available Cape troops[19] to move into Lesotho 'to bring to a close the operations which the forces of the Free State are now carrying on.'[20] Fortunately for the High Commissioner, the presence of these uniformed policemen was sufficient to curb the Free State raids, and no clash between rival white forces took place. But the Free State continued to look upon Wodehouse's activities as illegal, and Brand refused to cooperate in a general peace settlement.[21]

[14] *BR* III pp. 596–8.
[15] Ibid. p. 834, Buckingham to Wodehouse, 9 December 1867.
[16] Ibid. p. 840, Wodehouse to Moshesh, 13 January 1868. The aims of and reasons for Wodehouse's policy towards Lesotho, and for the vacillations of the British government, are considered in detail by C. W. de Kiewiet *British Colonial Policy and the South African Republics 1848–72* London 1929. See also *C.H.B.E.* op. cit. de Kiewiet, Chapter XVI, and C. F. Goodfellow *Great Britain and South African Confederation, 1870–1881* Oxford University Press (Cape Town) 1966 pp. 21–8. The period 1865–71 is surveyed from the white point of view by J. van der Poel in 'Basutoland as a Factor in South African Politics, 1858–1870' *Archives Year Book for South African History* 1941 I pp. 171–228.
[17] *BR* III pp. 848–50 Brand to Wodehouse, 31 January 1868.
[18] Ibid. p. 894. The final document in the published *Basutoland Records*.
[19] These consisted of a few hundred white soldiers, the Frontier Armed and Mounted Police (F.A.M.P.), whose commandant, Sir Walter Currie, was appointed High Commissioner's Agent in Lesotho. *BR* IV pp. 26–7, Commission of Sir Walter Currie, 16 March 1868.
[20] Ibid. pp. 40–2, Wodehouse to Currie, 14 March 1868. See also *BR* III p. 874, Wodehouse to Buckingham, 18 February 1868.
[21] *Despatches re: Recognition of Moshesh, Chief of the Basuto, and of his Tribe, as British*

By sending the F.A.M.P. to Lesotho Wodehouse was taking a calculated risk. The move was unauthorized by the Cape parliament, and any fighting between the commandos and the Cape police would have united white South African opinion against him. Wodehouse could not even be certain of the loyalty of the Cape troopers, some of whom had already deserted to the commandos.[22] Furthermore, he was well aware of the reaction of the British government to the prospect of employing British soldiers yet again in South Africa.[23] Wodehouse acted as he did for a variety of reasons, for what he considered to be the good of South Africa as a whole, and of the Cape in particular. He was also committed emotionally to the Sotho and their country. There is every reason to believe his statement, made whilst he was going 'through a great deal of trial and anxiety', that he 'intervened on behalf of these people at the time of their greatest distress . . . from what some would term a sentimental sympathy for the tribe.'[24]

Relations between Lesotho and the Free State were only part of the High Commissioner's troubles. For some time another contender had been hovering in the wings of the high veld drama. One of the first moves in the 1865 war was the pursuit of cattle from the Free State into Natal territory by Lesawana, or Ramaneella, Moshweshwe's nephew. Here this analysis of events from the white side must be interrupted to explain the relationship of this Lesawana to the other Sotho leaders. He was an important figure in the domestic policy of the establishment. His father, Makhabane, had been killed in a Sotho raid against the Thembu in 1835. Moshweshwe held himself responsible for the death of his brother, and in a sense adopted the children of the dead man, Lesawana, the first born son, being an especial favourite. He was given the eldest daughter in Moshweshwe's first house, Tswamathe, as his first wife, and thus became the brother-in-law of Letsie and Molapo. Lesawana's eldest daughter, as will be recounted later in this chapter (p. 299), was to play a crucial role in the arrangements made by Moshweshwe for the succession, not to himself, but

[22] *BR* III p. 582, Wodehouse to Cardwell, 2 January 1866; also *BR* IV pp. 353–65, Brand to Wodehouse, 8 July 1868.

[23] *Rec.* I p. 88, Buckingham to Wodehouse, 27 March 1868.

[24] *Rec.* II, 28, Wodehouse to Granville, 30 July 1869.

Subjects 1868–1869 XLIII, 4140 pp. 45–6, Brand to Wodehouse, 27 March 1868. (Henceforth *Rec.* I. *Rec.* II=1870 XLIX, C.18; *Rec.* III=1870, XLIX, C.99.)

to his son Letsie.[25] Lesawana's raid, a comparatively minor affair, produced an extreme response from Natal, which commenced as panic but soon became a desire for revenge and expansion.[26] Only the disapproval of Wodehouse prevented the Natal government from invading Lesotho—mainly with Zulu 'levies'—to enforce restitution for the raid.[27] On his part, the High Commissioner tried to use his authority to persuade the Sotho to pay the fine of 10,000 head of cattle demanded by Natal.[28] In October 1865 he sent his agent, Burnet, to negotiate with Moshweshwe, Letsie and Molapo the payment of this fine.[29] Burnet's mission was only partially successful and the Natal authorities remained unsatisfied—a feeling, however, that diminished as it became apparent that larger issues were at stake. Even before Burnet's negotiations and his peace treaty with the Free State, Molapo had turned to Shepstone for protection, fearing, he alleged, that Letsie planned to 'sacrifice' him and his people to Natal in lieu of the fine.[30] Molapo became increasingly concerned about his position as a Free State subject and again contacted Shepstone. These contacts were followed by others from Moshweshwe, during the bleak months following the treaty of Thaba Bosiu when it appeared to the old chief, and to his son, Tsekelo, who was responsible for the approach to Natal, that all appeals to Wodehouse were in vain.[31]

[25] For Moshweshwe's reactions to Makhabane's death, see his praise poem (*thoko*) in Z. D. Mangoaela *Lithoko tse marena a Basotho* Morija, 1957 p. 8. Many of the Sotho informants recount evidence about Lesawana. I found the statement of Lekhoba, Makeneng, 30 January 1966, particularly useful.

[26] *BR* III pp. 377–81, 392–4, Shepstone to Molapo, 11 July 1865. For Natal's policy towards Lesotho, see E. Axelson *Natal and the Annexation of Basutoland, 1865–70* University of Natal M.A. Thesis 1934.

[27] Ibid. pp. 410–12, Wodehouse to Maclean, 25 July 1865. Wodehouse was adamant in his refusal to sanction the use of British troops by Natal.

[28] *BR* III pp. 456–7, Wodehouse to Moshesh, 26 August 1865.

[29] Ibid. pp. 496–7, Wodehouse to Burnet, 16 October 1865. There is an interesting series of reports by Burnet about this mission in GH 20/2, Cape Town archives, which supplements the material published in *Basutoland Records*. Burnet, as civil commissioner of Aliwal North, the nearest Cape magistracy to Lesotho, had been for years a leading figure in the relations between the *sechaba* and the white men, but had seldom used his influence to the good of the Sotho people. Orpen, writing of Burnet's mission, stated that he had 'thought Mr Burnet might be moved by the misery and desolation he saw but he passes through and it excites not the slightest feeling as far as I can judge . . . He thinks solely of getting the fine out of Moshesh—perhaps he is all the better officer for having but that idea—but his utter inability to feel any sympathy with a black skinned human being certainly does this—it prevents his *understanding* them completely.' GH 10/7 (CT), J. M. Orpen to Wodehouse, 20 November 1865.

[30] *BR* III pp. 432–4, Cockburn to Shepstone, 5 August 1865.

[31] Ibid. pp. 613–14, Moshesh to Shepstone, 15 July 1866.

Wodehouse had little enthusiasm for the prospect of Natal annexing Lesotho, realizing that although Shepstone saw in it the occasion to further his own ambition to be supreme chief of the whole of south-eastern Africa, the majority of the white Natalians would demand the appropriation of land from the Sotho. Nevertheless, he dutifully forwarded the correspondence from the Natal government on the subject.[32] The arguments of Keate and Shepstone, and what appeared to be the general wish of the Sotho establishment, persuaded Buckingham to instruct the High Commissioner to make arrangements for just such an incorporation.[33] Thus it was that Keate and Shepstone accompanied Wodehouse when he visited Lesotho in April 1868, at the same time as the Free State volksraad resolved to send a deputation to London to protest against the High Commissioner's actions.[34] Since the beginning of the year the colonial press, and many of the Cape politicians, looked askance at Wodehouse's plans, and were furious that their Governor should use Cape troopers to further his policy as High Commissioner, and incidentally to further the expansionist aims of Shepstone.[35]

The almost complete disunity among the whites was mirrored by that of the Sotho people. Wodehouse's proclamation and his subsequent visit to Lesotho found the *sechaba* (nation) in a state of disarray, on the verge, apparently, of disintegration. Moshweshwe was an old man[36] whose powers were visibly declining. Mabille, a sympathetic observer, wrote early in 1866 that 'Moshesh is now so aged, his faculties are so enfeebled, that he is no longer able to watch carefully over the interests of his people,'[37] whilst Burnet reported to Wodehouse that the old chief's 'once vigorous mind' had 'partially gone, his judgment harassed and poisoned' by the 'witchdoctors and prophets . . . on Thaba Bosigo (sic), whose dreams, charms and revelations guide everything.'[38] The losses in war and the humiliating peace with the Free State had taken their toll on his prestige,[39] his authority, his

[32] See, *inter alia*, ibid. pp. 813–14, Wodehouse to Buckingham, 17 September 1867.
[33] Ibid. pp. 834–6, Buckingham to Wodehouse, 9 December 1867; *Rec.* I pp. 89–90, Buckingham to Wodehouse, 9 July 1868.
[34] Ibid. pp. 46–7, Resolution of Volksraad, 24 March 1868.
[35] See, for example, Ellenberger papers, Dyke to Ellenberger, 9 March 1868.
[36] Moshweshwe was over eighty in 1868, being born about 1785. See D. F. Ellenberger *Histori ea Basotho* Morija 1956 p. 107.
[37] Mabille to Miss Cellerier, 30 January 1866, quoted in Smith, op. cit. p. 153.
[38] *BR* III p. 568, Burnet to Wodehouse, 17 December 1865.
[39] But see Orpen's characteristically personal comments: 'weak and old and losing

wealth,[40] and his health. The same crises had done nothing to lessen the emnity between the two most powerful men in the *sechaba*, Moshweshwe's eldest sons, Letsie and Molapo, nor the jealousy between many of the younger sons who made up the Sotho establishment. The Sotho-phobe Burnet, in the report quoted above (note 38), wrote of the lack of 'proper intelligence or confidence existing between him (Moshweshwe) and his children on account of his jealousy of their interference with his authority coupled with their jealousy of each other as to the succession . . . each seeking to advance his own personal influence, and to profit by the divisions which are the curse of the country.' The young missionary Rolland, who had been born in Lesotho, stressed in a report to the High Commissioner 'the utter failure of any attempt to oppose a combined and organized resistance to the forces of the Free State'.[41]

The disunity of the *sechaba*, although intensified by the Free State incursions, was in no way the result of them. It was inherent in the political structure of the high veld peoples, which Moshweshwe had turned to his own account in the palmy days (from the point of view of the nadir of the *sechaba's* fortunes in 1865–8) of nation building but which he had not originated. The political nature of Sotho society tended to be segmentary. The economic basis of political organization was cattle wealth, which, in the dry and frequently harsh environment of the high veld, was either scattered over a wide area or concentrated in favourable localities. The Sotho were probably no more fissiparous than the Nguni. The more fertile and moister south-eastern coast lands could support a higher density of men and cattle, and expansive tendencies inherent in the southern Bantu, who are still at a migratory stage of political development, operated among the Nguni to lure segments of chiefdoms to new pastures. On the High Veld it was rather the economic pressure of even a small

[40] Wealth in cattle. Large numbers of Moshweshwe's own cattle had died during the siege of Thaba Bosiu in August 1865, whilst Letsie's and Molapo's share of *mafisa* cattle went largely untouched. (The *mafisa* system—the loaning of cattle as a means to exert political authority—cannot be examined in a paper of this length.)

[41] *BR* IV p. 125, Emile Rolland, notes on the political and social position of the Basuto tribe, 30 March 1868.

respect as he is I *know* that his people still retain a strong affection to Moshesh for what he was . . . in establishing his government on the goodwill of the people and not on fines and exactions.' GH 10/7 (CT), Orpen to Wodehouse, 18 December 1865.

increase in the numbers of men and stock which forced segments to hive off. Thus among the Nguni the environment encouraged segmentation, whilst among the Sotho it almost forced it. This pressure among the Sotho was manifested politically in the form of conflicts for power and authority among collateral kinsmen.

Moshweshwe had without doubt been a successful ruler, laboriously building up a *sechaba*, an amalgam of many groups, which, although dominated politically by one of these, the Kwena, was an extratribal entity. The *sechaba* comprised a complex system of interests and loyalties. At the focal point of this was the personality of the ruler, Moshweshwe. A man was a Mosotho because he recognized the authority of Moshweshwe, even if this focus of loyalty was at some remove. At an early stage of his rule Moshweshwe obtained the allegiance of his brothers by granting chieftainship rights over outlying districts. By the 1860s, however, Poshudi and others were acting almost independently of their brother—indeed, Moshweshwe could only retain a nominal control by letting them do what they liked. One reason for this lack of control over the peripheral districts of Lesotho was the encroachment of the white men on the high veld. Another cause of the dissatisfaction of his brothers was Moshweshwe's policy of placing his major sons on land previously their preserve. By the time Moshweshwe's sons had grown to manhood a large proportion of the land of Lesotho, and therefore of the political power in the nation, was in their hands. Moshweshwe could still count upon, even in his old age, a considerable degree of loyalty from Letsie, Molapo, Masopha, Sekhonyana, Tsekelo and the others, but none of his sons felt strong political ties to one another. The policy of these sons of Moshweshwe was to increase the political legacy that could be handed down to their own sons. Thus a pattern can be seen to emerge in the political structure of the Sotho establishment, which consisted almost entirely of the sons of Moshweshwe. In each generation a member of the establishment was linked by ties of loyalty to his father and to his own sons, but tended to be in conflict over rights to land and to cattle with his brothers and with paternal uncles and cousins. This area of conflict led to disunity and fragmentation, and political machinery operated in an attempt to obviate these dangers. The practice of preferred cross-cousin marriages was a device to mitigate the feelings of hostility between segments of the *sechaba*, but in times of crisis such bonds might not be strong enough to prevent secessions.[42]

The enmity between Letsie and Molapo dated from their youth, certainly from the time their father sent them both to Morija to watch over the newly arrived French Protestant missionaries in 1833.[43] Moshweshwe appeared to favour Molapo, at least politically,[44] thus creating a precedent which was followed by several of his successors, Letsie included. This was no doubt a political measure designed to lessen the power of the heir during the father's lifetime, examples of usurpation by heirs being only too common among the Sotho and Tswana peoples. There is no evidence that his father disapproved of Molapo becoming a Free State subject in March 1866.[45] Letsie certainly expressed himself in strong terms[46] but he subsequently attempted to obtain a similar status for himself, and for a short time did so,[47] with little regard for his father or for the *sechaba* as a whole. Others naturally followed suit. Letsie's uncle, Paulus Mopedi, made his separate peace[48] and their most influential half-brother, Sekhonyana (Nehemiah), consistently refused to offer resistance to the Free State forces, and kept Brand informed of the plans of the other Sotho leaders.[49] His mother had been Moshweshwe's favourite wife, and he was constantly at odds with Letsie and Molapo;

[42] For a much fuller treatment of some of these notions, see Ian Hamnett 'Koena chieftainship seniority in Basutoland' *Africa* xxv 1965 pp. 241–50 and G. I. Jones 'Chiefly succession in Basutoland' Cambridge papers in Social Anthropology 4 *Succession to high office* ed. Jack Goody Cambridge University Press 1966 pp. 57–81.

[43] See, *inter alia,* communication from M. Damane, 5 March 1966. Letsie was born in 1811 and Molapo in 1814. By the end of Moshweshwe's reign, therefore, Letsie was approaching his sixties.

[44] There are many instances of this biased treatment, of which perhaps the best known is Moshweshwe's treatment of Letsie after the Sotho defeat of Sekonyela and the Tlokwa at Joala-Boholo in 1853. See Letsie's *thoko* in Mangoaela, op. cit. p. 36. In his verbal statement, Chief 'Mako Moliboea Molapo (Hlotse, 26 November 1965) comments upon this, and suggests reasons for Moshweshwe's feelings towards his first-born son in Letsie's own behaviour towards his wives and children.

[45] For Molapo's motives in making the separate peace, and for Moshweshwe's reactions, see A. Sekese, article in *Leselinyana*, December 1893. Sekese, the greatest Sotho historian, became secretary to Molapo's son, Jonathane, after the Gun War.

[46] *BR* III pp. 671–3, Letsie to Wodehouse, 26 April 1866: 'Molapo greatly weakened us by coming to an understanding with the Boers . . .'

[47] Ibid. pp. 778–81, Reception of the Chief Letsie as a Free State Subject, 22 May 1867. See also comments of *Leselinyana,* December 1869.

[48] Ibid. pp. 783–4, 1 June 1867. This particular treaty remained in force, and Mopedi's people continued to occupy Witsies Hoek in the Free State and later in the Union (and Republic) of South Africa.

[49] See correspondence in Goewermentsekretaris file 1339, Bloemfontein archives.

excluded from holding any large amount of land in Lesotho, he was more concerned about acquiring territory for himself in East Griqualand than about the fate of Lesotho. Tsekelo, another half-brother, tried unsuccessfully to jump on the Free State band wagon with Molapo.[50] Moletsane, chief of the Taung, the largest group of non-Sotho in the *sechaba*, like Letsie, constantly requested to become a Free State subject. All these examples of disunity and disloyalty were the products of the pressure of war. As observers such as Shepstone and Wodehouse pointed out, the various treaties between sections of the *sechaba* and the Free State were moves in the diplomatic game played with some success by the Sotho leaders.[51] They should not be taken at their face value to imply complete disintegration. Shepstone justly noted that 'The Basutos must . . . be looked upon and treated as one people, and there is not much reliance to be placed on political differences between members of one family.'[52] Nevertheless, the imposition of white administrative control, within fixed boundaries, did put a halt to a process of segmentation which had been in evidence for several years. White overrule provided the necessary limits within which the Sotho could exercise their political talents without the danger either of internal disruption or of further intervention from the Free State.

The appearance of the Cape troopers, followed by Wodehouse (and a few days later—inexplicably—by Keate and Shepstone), greatly increased the scope for Sotho political activities. The issue that was most productive of disunity among the ranks of the protagonists was that of annexation to Natal. Wodehouse (see p. 289) preferred that Lesotho should remain under his personal control as High Commissioner or, if a choice had to be made, should be joined to the Cape. At Aliwal North, on his way up to Lesotho, he encountered strong advocacy of the Cape's case from the Wesleyan Methodist missionary John Daniel, who had a few weeks previously had 'some talk' with Tsekelo Moshweshwe.[53] From this time Tsekelo began to play an important part in Lesotho's relations with the white parties interested in Lesotho and in sowing the seeds of dissension among them. An intelligent

[50] GS 1339, Bloemfontein, Tsekelo to Brand, 25 March 1866.
[51] *BR* III pp. 721–3, Shepstone memorandum, 4 September 1866; ibid. pp. 816–7, Wodehouse to Burnet, 19 September 1867. The High Commissioner treated 'all the negotiations between the Free State and Moshesh and Letsie as . . . mere moonshine'.
[52] Ibid. p. 860, Shepstone memorandum, 4 February 1868.
[53] Ibid. p. 876, Daniel to Burnet, 21 February 1868.

young man of thirty-one, he had been sent by his father to be educated at Cape Town, and was one of the first members of the Sotho establishment to evince a restless ambition partially divorced both from his own society and from the alternative offered by the missionaries. He was also something of a playboy, with a reputation for womanizing.[54] Tsekelo had been used by his father and by his half-brother, Molapo, to make contact with Shepstone and the Natal authorities, and had pleaded for annexation by that colony. Now that the High Commissioner had again become an important factor in Lesotho affairs, Tsekelo performed a *volte face* of the kind that was to become typical of his sinuous diplomacy.

Unknown to Keate and Shepstone, Wodehouse arranged to take Daniel with him into Lesotho as interpreter. By the time the two Natalians reached Thaba Bosiu they found that Moshweshwe and Letsie, egged on by Tsekelo, had stated at the *pitso* held to welcome Wodehouse their preference for being ruled either by the High Commissioner or by the Cape, and their abhorrence for Natal. Letsie wondered 'how any (one) in his senses could ever have conceived such an idea' as union with Natal.[55] Such feelings were no doubt genuine. The Sotho had perhaps fallen under Shepstone's spell,[55a] but they also feared him and the Zulu impi he could reputedly call upon—he and Keate had an escort of Zulu with them in Lesotho—and had only turned to Natal when all else had failed. Probably Daniel let them know that this kind of attitude would be privately pleasing to Wodehouse, although they were to expect him to express surprise and displeasure in public. The Sotho had the satisfaction of witnessing an open and growing estrangement between Keate and Shepstone, on the one hand, and Wodehouse on the other,[56] and were thereby encouraged to assert their interests and give vent to their grievances. Moshweshwe pressed for protection under the High Commissioner so that he and his successor would retain the substance of power and authority, as Shepstone was quick to point out.[57] He and his sons were also vitally concerned over the land problem. This concern

[54] See, *inter alia*, statement of 'Mako Moliboea Molapo, note 44.
[55] *Rec* I p. 55, Wodehouse to Buckingham, 2 May 1868. See also ibid. pp. 56–7, Moshesh to Wodehouse, 21 April 1868; ibid. pp. 114–20, Keate to Buckingham, 6 August 1868.
[55a] Ibid. pp. 67–8, statement of Molap, 5 May 1868.
[56] Keate to Buckingham, op. cit.; Bloemfontein GS 1155 (b) pp. 267–9, Holm to Brand, 27 March 1869; *Rec.* II, pp. 47–56, Buchanan to Granville, 5 November 1869.
[57] Keate to Buckingham, op. cit.

had two aspects. One was that the boundaries should revert to the 1864 line, which included a large area of country on the west bank of the Caledon.[58] The other was the claim that, within whatever boundaries were decided upon, there should be no further alienation of land from the *sechaba*. Just before the white dignitaries left Lesotho, Tsekelo and his brothers raised, perhaps for the first time, the demand 'Basutoland for the Basutos'.[59] By the end of this transitional stage (1868–71) the Sotho had failed to retain their pre-war boundaries, and had lost all the trans-Caledon country—growing recognition that this would be so made them increasingly disenchanted with the High Commissioner and his politics[60]—but had secured the second demand. It had for long been Wodehouse's policy to establish Lesotho as a 'Native Reserve' on the lines of the Herschel reserve south of the Orange, and the Basutoland Annexation Act (August 1871), which was passed the year following his departure from South Africa, separated Lesotho from the ordinary laws of the Cape Colony.[61] This prevented land alienation, which would have required legislation from the Cape parliament, until 1879, after Moorosi's rebellion had been suppressed by the Cape forces.

The one leading Mosotho who did not join the majority in forsaking Natal was Molapo. As he had not broken his treaty with the Free State, and as a Free State agent was resident in Leribe, Wodehouse considered him still to be a Free State subject.[62] Therefore, although the March (1868) proclamation did not say so, Leribe was excluded from British protection—in spite of Molapo's earnest appeals to be reunited with the *sechaba*.[63] He had no wish to remain in his anomalous position, and as the High Commissioner could not hold out much hope for the future it was natural for him to retain close ties with Natal. Leribe was the only part of Lesotho that then abutted upon that colony, Shepstone had favoured him with advice, and he had retained, apparently

[58] See, for example, GS 1155 (b) p. 73, Bloemfontein, Molapo to John Fick, 28 March 1868; *Rec.* I, pp. 56–7, Moshesh to Wodehouse, 21 April 1868.
[59] Keate to Buckingham, op. cit.
[60] For an early example of this, see Ellenberger papers, Dyke to Ellenberger, 8 June 1868.
[61] For text of Act, see Basutoland, *High Commissioners' Proclamations and Notices* Cape Town 1909 pp. 42–3.
[62] GH 15/3 (CT), Wodehouse to Keate (private), 13 January 1868; *Rec.* I pp. 53–4, Wodehouse to Buckingham, 2 May 1868; *BR* IV pp. 395–6, Wodehouse to Keate, 7 August 1868.
[63] Ibid. p. 118, Molapo to Wodehouse, 29 March 1868.

with his father Moshweshwe's blessing, a number of 'prominent and influential natives in Natal' to act as his agents with the secretary for native affairs.[64] If the rest of Lesotho was to be administered by the High Commissioner or by the Cape, then Molapo opted for separation and annexation of Leribe to Natal. Letsie, who had no ambitions in Leribe, and had probably already written it off as a field for the exercise of his authority, did nothing to dissuade his brother from this intention.

Wodehouse, Keate and Shepstone went their separate ways at the end of April or beginning of May without settling any of Lesotho's major problems, but the maintenance of a small detachment of F.A.M.P. under James Bowker, the High Commissioner's agent, implied that Wodehouse had established a *de facto* authority in the territory. An uneasy interregnum followed, during which Sotho and Freestaters indulged in mutual raiding, with the former losing their faith in the ability or desire of the British government to prevent Free State raids or to clear the recently settled white farmers from what was considered their rightful land.[65]

After the failure of the Free State deputation to England[66] Wodehouse persuaded Brand to come to terms. He met Brand and other Free State delegates at Aliwal North and hammered out an agreement with them in February 1869. The Free State abrogated the 1866 Thaba Bosiu treaty, and agreed to take steps to release Molapo from his allegiance, but held on to all the land west of the Caledon.[67] The group most seriously affected by these boundary changes was the Taung of Moletsane, who had to remove from the Mekwatleng area where they had resided as allies of Moshweshwe since the late 1830s. For the first time in the long and bitter history of conflict between black and white on the high veld, the Sotho were excluded from the meeting which reached decisions so vital for their future. Wodehouse even gave way to Brand's objection to a French missionary being present 'to watch over the interest of the Natives'.[68] The High Commissioner then journeyed on to Lesotho to inform the *sechaba* of the terms of the

[64] Ibid. pp. 67–8, Statement of Molapo, 5 May 1868.

[65] For this period, May 1868 to February 1869, see *BR* IV and V; *Rec.* I and II; GH 10/7—correspondence of the Orpens, Halse and others; Ellenberger papers—Dyke letters.

[66] *Rec.* I pp. 92–3, Buckingham to Wodehouse, 9 November 1868.

[67] Minutes of the Aliwal North conference in *Rec.* II pp. 8–19.

[68] Ibid. p. 52, Buchanan to Granville, 5 November 1869.

Aliwal North settlement, and on this occasion he summoned the Sotho rulers and people to appear at a *pitso* before him. All the Sotho establishment, Molapo included, attended on the High Commissioner, with the exception of Moshweshwe himself. Old age and infirmity excused the great chief from setting the seal of acceptance by his presence to a transaction so inimical to the feelings of the *sechaba*. At the *pitso*, Moletsane immediately objected to the enforced removal of himself and his people, 'on the ground that the Governor had misled or deceived him, having previously promised him the restoration of his land'.[69] Letsie, who was not very concerned with the lost country to the west of the Caledon, but who did want to extend his control over the land vacated by Makwai on which Wodehouse intended to resettle the Taung, insisted that in the absence of his father he was 'incompetent to acquiesce or otherwise in said arrangements'.[70] The following day, therefore, Wodehouse climbed Thaba Bosiu to discuss the settlement with Moshweshwe, who sarcastically retorted: 'Is that peace?'[71] and who wrote a few days later, again complaining of the Moletsane move, and of the right assumed by the High Commissioner or his agent of allocating land in Lesotho.[72]

The objections of the Sotho to the Aliwal North settlement rapidly took the form of overt political action. In this they were encouraged by one at least of the missionaries,[73] Daumas, and by the Natal lawyer and newspaper editor Buchanan, who was an admirer of Shepstone and was intensely sympathetic to 'native interests', and who had attempted to champion Moshweshwe's cause since the beginning of the Free State war.[74] There can be little doubt that Shepstone was unofficially using Buchanan in a move to reassert Natal's claim to administer Lesotho, and, as in the previous year, it was Molapo who was most immediately

[69] *BR* V pp. 96–110, account of Korokoro Pitso (22 February) in the *Friend of the Free State*, 25 February 1869. Wodehouse's assurances given the previous year are substantiated by Daumas, the missionary at the old station at Mekwatleng; see *Rec.* II pp. 69–70, Daumas to Chesson, 2 November 1869.

[70] Account of Pitso op. cit. For Letsie's claim to Makwai's country, see *BR* V pp. 130–5, Bowker to Wodehouse, 28 March 1869.

[71] Daumas to Chesson op cit.

[72] PEMS archives, Morija, Wodehouse to Moshesh, 1 March 1869.

[73] Tsekelo's mission to England split the French mission—most of the missionaries in Lesotho were persuaded by Wodehouse and Bowker to support the settlement, but the Paris headquarters for a long time campaigned with Tsekelo and Daumas against it.

[74] The series of *Recognition* papers contain exhaustive material by and about Buchanan.

concerned in what Wodehouse termed 'these intrigues'.[75] Molapo and his sons stood to lose valuable land if the settlement were enforced. A *pitso* was convened on Thaba Bosiu, and, with the approval of old Moshweshwe and Molapo, if not of Letsie, Tsekelo was delegated to join Buchanan in Natal[76] and to accompany him and Daumas to England to object to Wodehouse's arrangements. Thus the situation of 1868 was reversed: then, the Free State thwarted a settlement, now it was the Sotho themselves who tried to obtain more favourable terms. In this Tsekelo's deputation was unsuccessful, though he and his white colleagues won for themselves quite impressive support, the full weight of the philanthropic machine ranged itself behind them.

The deputation, however, was able to hold up the ratification of the Aliwal North convention till March 1870.[77] The two years' delay between Wodehouse's proclamation of March 1868 and this ratification gave the Sotho a breathing space before the white administration became fully effective. The collection of hut tax was commenced in July 1870, but Cape rule did not really get under way until Charles Griffith arrived as the new High Commissioner's agent in August 1871. The intermission allowed the *sechaba* to settle down economically[78] and, to a certain extent, politically. The Taung, for example, were peaceably resettled around Maboloka,[79] and this accommodation was accepted by Letsie and the other chiefs *in situ* on their own terms and not on those of the whites. The Sotho establishment were also able to absorb the shock of Moshweshwe's death in March 1870 with the minimum of white political interference. Bowker and his handful of policemen had made such little impact on the country that they took no part in the funeral ceremony, an occasion which deeply moved the whole *sechaba* and the missionaries both Protestant and Catholic.[80] Bowker merely reported the death to

[75] *BR* V pp. 153–5, Wodehouse to Bowker, 13 April 1869.

[76] One of the best pieces of evidence for the Sotho side of this affair is a private letter in Bloemfontein, GS 1155 (b) pp. 267–9, Holm to Brand, 27 March 1869. Holm was Free State agent in Leribe. Sekhonyana was first considered as Sotho delegate, before the choice of Tsekelo; there was also talk of Orpen being involved.

[77] *Rec.* III p. 3, Wodehouse to Granville, 19 March 1870.

[78] This settling-down period coincided with the initial exploitation of the diamond deposits in Griqualand West, which greatly stimulated the economy of Lesotho.

[79] See Morena Abraham Aaron Moletsane *Autobiographical Memoir* privately printed for Capt. R. S. Webb, Paarl, 1967 pp. 3–4.

[80] For account of death and funeral of Moshweshwe, and controversy over his conversion, see Edwin W. Smith op. cit. especially quotations from Mrs Mabille's 'Memories'; letter of Théophile Jousse *J.d.M.* 1870 pp. 201–7; Journal of Fr Gerard,

Wodehouse, with no comment.[81] He had no hand in the matter of the succession to the great chief. This had long been recognized as falling to Letsie, as the eldest son, and although Molapo, Masopha and others might have resented their brother's position, there was no conflict over the succession. On 18 January 1870, less than two months before he died, Moshweshwe summoned a *pitso* and formally transferred his responsibilities as great chief to Letsie.[82]

It was at this *pitso* that Moshweshwe attempted to make arrangements for the succession after Letsie, and here again, this was a wholly Sotho affair, with no interference from the white authorities, who were not apparently informed of what had taken place, or even from the missionaries.[83] Yet this was an issue that was to have the utmost future political import. Briefly, there was no surviving male issue in Letsie's first house. Moshweshwe had married the daughter of this house, Senate, to her cousin, Molapo's eldest son Josefa, who became mad. The son of this marriage, Motswene, was considered by Moshweshwe to belong to his mother Senate's family, namely to Letsie, and not to Molapo's lineage, and, whilst still a child, he was proclaimed by his great-grandfather at this *pitso* to be Letsie's successor. This highly controversial arrangement was complicated by another previously made by the old chief, whereby Senate was considered as a male and 'married' to her cousin Maneella, Lesawana's daughter (see p. 287). Lerothodi, the eldest son in Letsie's second house, co-habited with Maneella, and he in fact succeeded his father, and sons of this union succeeded him.[84]

A further result of the hiatus in Wodehouse's efforts to bring the Sotho under white government was that Molapo was not absolved from his allegiance to the Free State until April 1870.[85] The long period of at least formal separation from the rest of the

[81] *BR* V p. 452, Bowker to Wodehouse, 17 March 1870. Wodehouse, in the briefest of notes, informed Granville that he did 'not think this event will in any way embarrass our arrangements for establishing a new order of government in *Basutoland*'. *Rec.* III p. 3, 19 March 1870.

[82] *Leselinyana*, February 1870 p. 17.

[83] Cochet diary, 20 January 1870.

[84] There is abundant evidence, both written and oral, on this controversial matter, which cannot be considered in this paper.

[85] *BR* V pp. 459–64, ceremony at Leribe, 11 April 1870.

---

quoted in *The Life of Fr. Joseph Gerard, 1831–1914* by Aimé Roche, O.M.I., n.d. pp. 203–6 (also letters Gerard to Allard) in Roman Catholic presbytery, Maseru; *Leselinyana* April 1870 pp. 25–7.

sechaba intensified the divisions between himself and Letsie, between Leribe and the rest of Lesotho, which have left their mark on much of the subsequent course of Sotho history.

When he succeeded his father, Letsie stayed at Matsieng, near Morija, and did not remove to Thaba Bosiu. This left something of a vacuum around the vicinity of the mountain, which was readily filled by Letsie's and Molapo's brother Masopha. By the time Griffith arrived in Lesotho, in August 1871, Masopha was already playing a central and critical part in the affairs of his country. It was Masopha who, until his death in 1898, remained most resistant to the attempts of the white administrators, Cape or British, to enforce their authority; and he was able to consolidate his power in the period of intermission before this authority was able to be exerted.

During the years 1868 to 1870, when the period of warfare with the Free State gradually came to an end, and before a white administration was properly established, the leading figures of the *sechaba* had ample scope for political manœuvre. The important decisions regarding their future relations with the other parts of South Africa were no longer in their hands. To a large extent Wodehouse was responsible for these decisions, and was able ultimately to enforce them upon every party concerned, white as well as black. The imposition of white overrule interrupted a process of fragmentation in Sotho political society. The kind of conflicts which otherwise might have resulted in complete secession (e.g. Molapo from Letsie) became internalized, and the Sotho had to adapt themselves to periods of crisis from which there were virtually no external escapes.[86]

Nevertheless during the years 1868 to 1870 the Sotho leaders had considerable freedom of action within their own political system, and took decisions which were to shape their own history for several decades. This kind of freedom of action was becoming rare amongst African societies in southern Africa faced with the full weight of white interference. That the Sotho maintained it was due very largely to the position of Lesotho at the heart of the inter-white conflicts at that time. That they retained it thereafter, in the face of white efforts to undermine it, was due in part to the continuation of white state rivalries,

[86] After the Gun War, several of the 'loyal' Sotho, notably George Tlali Moshweshwe and his followers, had to be found land by the Cape government outside Lesotho, in the case of George Tlali in Griqualand East.

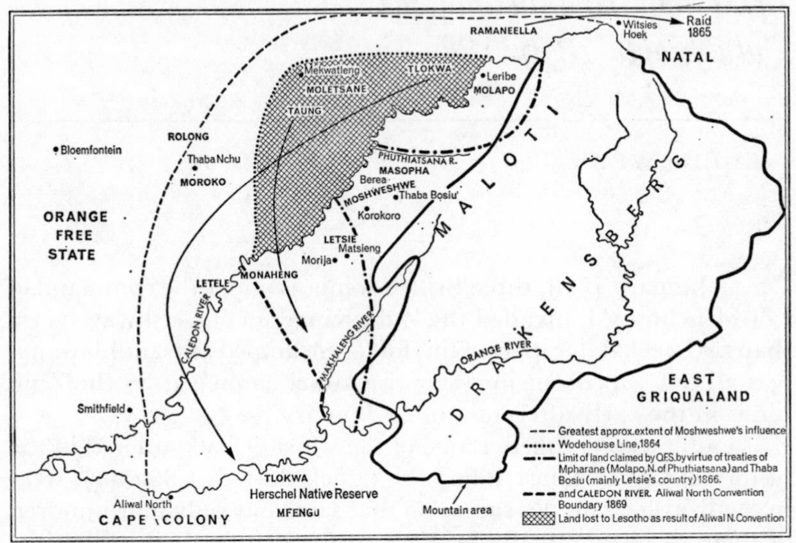

9. *Lesotho 1865–71*

but in part also to their determination to resist. The Sotho lost their independence in 1868, but under the umbrella of white control, the *sechaba* continued to function, and indeed, after a few years' recuperation, to prosper in a limited and a sober kind of way.

14. Great Britain and the Zulu people 1879–1887

COLIN WEBB

On 11 January 1879, three British columns under the command of Lord Chelmsford, invaded the Zulu Kingdom of Cetshwayo. Less than two weeks later, part of this force, encamped at Isandhlawana, was all but wiped out in a surprise attack launched by the Zulu impis in the early afternoon of 22 January.

Isandhlawana ranked as one of the worst defeats suffered in the history of British arms. When the attack started, 1,800 men were in the British camp. By sunset on that same day only four hundred of these survived. In the brief space of one afternoon's fighting, 1,400 men had lost their lives.[1]

Yet, spectacular as the Zulu success was, it was also ephemeral. In January 1879, the European giant that was stepping into Zululand had still not flexed its muscles. When it did so, its power proved irresistible, and by September 1879, the Zulu nation had gone down in hopeless defeat.

Seven-and-a-half years later, in February 1887, a strife-torn and demoralized Zulu people accepted annexation to the British Crown. By then, Cetshwayo was dead, a section of his former kingdom had slipped into European hands, the military system created by Shaka had been destroyed, and the heir to the Zulu throne had been reduced to the leader of a faction amongst the people whom his father had ruled. In eight years the most powerful of the independent African societies south of the Limpopo had lost the ethos of nationhood and disintegrated.

My purpose in this chapter is to examine the contribution of British policy to this collapse.

Mono-causal theories of imperialism no longer command the respect which once they did, for too many exceptions have been found, by far, to prove any general rule. While some empires were a source of pride and joy, others were reluctantly acquired; and in

[1] D. R. Morris *The Washing of the Spears* London and New York 1966 p. 387.

many cases, though not in all, the desire for land, raw materials and markets played little part in the calculations of the statesmen who pegged out colonial claims.

British policy in Zululand during the years 1879–87 was an expression of such a reluctance to expand. That it was so, invests it with no special virtue; for it was not altruism that inspired this diffidence, but personal, party, and national interest. For seven years British statesmen evaded the consequences of a war that had involved Britain inextricably in Zululand's affairs, and during those years the social and psychological bonds of Zulu national life collapsed.

The initial evasion was that of a Conservative Government that had been placed in a position of acute discomfort by the actions of its High Commissioner in South Africa; for the Earl of Beaconsfield and his Cabinet colleagues had not wanted war with the Zulu in 1879; hostilities had been precipitated by Sir Bartle Frere, the High Commissioner, acting in defiance of the expressed wishes of his superiors in London.[2] On 7 November 1878, Sir Michael Hicks Beach, from the Colonial Office, had written to inform Frere that 'matters in Eastern Europe and India . . . wear so serious an aspect that *we cannot now have a Zulu war*', and a telegraphic summary of this dispatch had reached the High Commissioner on 30 November. Eleven days later, without securing the approval of the government he represented, Frere had presented the Zulu King with an ultimatum so severe in its demands that war became inevitable.[3]

From the start, therefore, the Government was exposed to the charge of allowing Britain to be dragged into an unnecessary and unwanted war by failing to discipline and control its most senior South African official. To this was soon added a second charge; for as the Blue Books rolled off the presses, publishing Frere's voluminous correspondence with the Colonial Office, the evidence mounted that his insubordination had been the product, not of wilful perversity, but rather of over-enthusiastic devotion to the cause which he had been appointed to serve. His selection for South Africa had been prompted by the Conservatives' desire to federate a politically-fragmented corner of the Empire; yet South African federation, Frere argued, would remain impossible until

[2] See E. H. Brookes and C. de B. Webb *A History of Natal* Pietermaritzburg 1965 pp. 127–35.

[3] Lady Victoria Hicks Beach *Life of Sir Michael Hicks Beach* London 1932 pp. 104, 110–12.

Britain became 'master up to the Portuguese frontier'.[4] Not only would the Cape steadily refuse to link its fortunes with Natal and the Transvaal while these territories remained exposed to a militarily powerful Zulu kingdom, but the Boers of the Transvaal would remain unwilling British subjects until Britain gave them 'real security against Zulu . . . aggressions'.[5]

Thus Beaconsfield and his colleagues found themselves doubly exposed: to the charge of careless neglect and mismanagement, and to the charge of launching a South African policy which, by its own inner momentum, was leading to unwanted annexationist wars.

Whether the furore would have been any less violent if the war had not commenced with a disaster to British arms it is impossible to say. Perhaps the Government would have quietly disentangled itself from the conflict in a negotiated settlement, leaving the Zulu people their independence. Alternatively, Zululand might have been conquered and unobtrusively added to the possessions of the British Crown. However, after the shock of Isandhlawana neither of these alternatives was open, for the Government of Lord Beaconsfield found itself caught in the political cross-fire of those demanding the vindication of British arms, and those discharging their anti-expansionist volleys. During the months that followed, debates on the Zulu War consumed more parliamentary time than the affairs of the whole of South East Africa had consumed during the preceding half-century, and the animus that inspired many of these bitter exchanges was the animus that W. E. Gladstone was later to recapture when he charged the Conservatives with financial profligacy in the pursuit of 'false phantoms of glory'.[6]

The news of Isandhlawana had reached London on 11 February 1879, two days before Parliament reassembled after the Christmas recess. By early March, the fate of the Zulu people was already being decided in the councils of a Cabinet harassed by dissent and anxious to disarm its parliamentary critics.[7] To restore British prestige, the Zulu nation was to be defeated: but—to

[4] J. Martineau *The Life and Correspondence of Sir Bartle Frere* 2 vols. London 1895 II p. 259. See also *British Parliamentary Papers* Cd. 2454 p. 133, Frere to Hicks Beach, 29 June 1879.

[5] C–2222, 6, Frere to Hicks Beach, 5 November 1878. See also B. Worsfold *Sir Bartle Frere* London 1923 pp. 81, 112.

[6] P. Magnus *Gladstone* London 1954 p. 261. For debates on Zulu War see *Hansard* Third Series, Vols. CCXLIII–CCXLIX.

[7] Hicks Beach op. cit. pp. 123–4 and 129.

spike the guns of the Opposition—there was to be no annexation of Zulu territory.

In the debates that followed, these plans assumed more definite shape. Frere had acted wrongly, the speakers on the Government benches admitted, but he was not to be recalled from his post. As war had come, it was to be used to extract the maximum advantage. The Zulu were to be reduced to submission, not with the object of taking their land, but for the purpose of imposing conditions that would destroy their military power. Frere's war was to be prosecuted to a successful conclusion to make South Africa safe for federation under the British flag.[8]

It was thus in the heat of a party political struggle that the future of a nation was decided. The ground which the Opposition chose for its main assault was not the injustice of war upon a people who need not have been enemies, but the administrative incompetence of the government of the day;[9] and because party interest became the issue in the contest, the British electorate assumed a more important place in the minds of the policy-makers than did the war-scarred Zulu nation. What mattered was not a just settlement, but a successful settlement—a settlement that would bring positive advantages to Imperial Britain and restore public confidence in a shaken Government.

The details of the arrangements to be made in Zululand were left to the discretion of Sir Garnet Wolseley who, on 28 May 1879, had been issued with commissions appointing him Governor of Natal and the Transvaal and High Commissioner for the adjacent territories.[10] The fact that he was a soldier with no special knowledge of Zulu society and its traditions seems to have mattered little. On 2 September, at Ulundi, Wolseley met the leaders of the defeated Zulu nation. The next day he reported home on the settlement he had imposed.[11]

Most of the Blood River Territory—claimed by Transvaal Boers before the war, but recommended for award to the Zulu kingdom by a boundary commission in 1878[12]—was now to be

[8] *Hansard* Third Series, Vol. CCXLIV, 1606–95, 1865–1950, 1991–2090, and Vol. CCXLV, 20–123, 1573–76.

[9] For motion of censure see *Hansard* Third Series, Vol. CCXLIV, 1606.

[10] Brookes and Webb op. cit. p. 143.

[11] C–2482, 255f, Wolseley to Hicks Beach, 3 September 1879, and enclosures. See also: C.O. 879/17, African 205; and C.O. 879/17, African unnumbered, 'Report of Zululand Boundary Commission' 5 December 1879.

[12] Brookes and Webb op. cit. pp. 130–1.

ceded to the Transvaal. Beyond this, no territory was to be annexed; but the Zulu nation was to be paralysed politically. Cetshwayo was to be deposed and sent into exile, 'never to return'. With the exception of the ex-King's half-brother, Hamu, who had surrendered to the British early in the war, the members of the royal house were to be reduced to the status of commoners. Zululand was to be divided up into thirteen tiny kingdoms, each under the rule of a chief nominated by Wolseley. And, where possible, these new units were to be revivals of tribal chieftainships that had existed before the wars of Shaka.[13]

Beyond these general arrangements, specific conditions were imposed on the thirteen kinglets. They were to abandon all military organization, prohibit the importation of arms, discontinue arbitrary executions and prosecutions for witchcraft, abide by the boundaries assigned to them, and accept for certain purposes the arbitration of a British Resident, who was to have no executive power, but was to be stationed amongst the chiefs as the 'eyes and ears' of the British Government.

From the start there were critics who questioned both the justice and the wisdom of the settlement.[14] Old loyalties could not be blotted out by the ink of a British official's pen; nor could paper titles to kingship invest former nonentities with the aura of Zulu royalty. Such radical revisions of the structure of a traditionalist society required the continued presence of the enforcing power of the conqueror if they were to succeed. Yet in London enlarged territorial and administrative responsibilities had been renounced in the political hue and cry that followed Isandhlawana. Having made his settlement, Wolseley and his troops therefore withdrew, leaving behind a Resident who was to be the 'eyes and ears' but not the 'arm' of a power that had launched a revolution.

Though his main concern was for the welfare of the colonial society to which he belonged, Sir Theophilus Shepstone, Natal's former Secretary for Native Affairs, came close to the heart of the matter when he wrote:

> . . . the Zulu country has suffered the total destruction of its Government. . . ; the natural and immediate reaction must be towards anarchy of a dangerous kind, and Natal as well as Zululand will be affected by it. The destruction of this restraint has been the work of

[13] Ibid. pp. 99–100, 146–8.

[14] See, for example, C.O. 879/17, African 224, memo. by A. A. Pearson 7 May 1880 'Sir Garnet Wolseley's Settlement of Zululand' p. 4f.

our hand, and we are bound, for the safety of the people whom we have conquered . . . to replace the government we have destroyed by one less barbarous certainly, but equally strong. . . . (The Zulu headmen) . . . suddenly released from . . . bondage . . . will be beggars on horseback, and their rides are likely to be as eccentric and as fatal as those of beggars are said to be.[15]

Shepstone saw the evil in terms of the sudden removal of the Zulu king's despotic executive power. In fact the shock ran deeper, for the king's functions were more than executive; they were ritual, economic, military, legislative and judicial.[16] The system erected by Wolseley in place of the dismantled monarchy was almost certain to short-circuit wherever national sentiment remained strong.

The remarkable thing is that the settlement worked at all. In May 1880 a Colonial Office memorandum prepared for the Cabinet reported that the official communications on Zululand were all favourable, and later dispatches from the men on the spot confirmed that 'peace and quietness continue to prevail'.[17] That this was so was almost certainly due to initial misapprehension on the part of the Zulu themselves, who saw in the thirteen kinglets the chosen indunas of a new paramount authority whose power would be used to support their rule.[18]

By the middle of 1881 these illusions had been broken. For months previously disputes had been simmering between certain of the appointed chiefs and the subjects placed under them. Yet the local representatives of British authority consistently disclaimed responsibility for the settlement of such internal troubles. Deputations to the Natal Governor had been turned away. The Resident, bound by his instructions, had advised the Zulu to settle the disputes 'among themselves'; he was there 'only to hear and see whether Sir Garnet Wolseley's laws were carried out'.[19]

[15] Ibid. pp. 14–15, Appendix C, memo. by Sir T. Shepstone, 23 August 1879.

[16] See E. J. Krige *The Social System of the Zulus* London 1936 pp. 248–60 and *passim*; M. Gluckman *Custom and Conflict in Africa* Oxford 1963 p. 34; and M. Fortes and E. Evans-Pritchard (eds.) *African Political Systems* London 1962 pp. 25–55 'The Kingdom of the Zulu' by M. Gluckman.

[17] C.O. 879/17, African 224, memo. prepared for the Cabinet, 7 May 1880, p. 5; and C–2783, pp. 10–11, Colley to Kimberley, 20 November 1880, and enclosure 1.

[18] J. Y. Gibson *The Story of the Zulus* Pietermaritzburg 1903 p. 219; C.O. 879/18, African 230, No. 14916, Wood to Kimberley, 20 August 1887; C.O. 879/19, African 242, Kimberley to Bulwer, 2 February 1882; and C.O. 179/138, Natal 17210, Wood to Kimberley, 23 August 1881, minute by Kimberley.

[19] F. E. Colenso *The Ruin of Zululand* 2 vols. London 1884 I pp. 17–30; and Natal Archives, G.H. 677, Zululand Correspondence.

More significant still, when a usurper led a successful rebellion in the petty Mthethwa kingdom, it was not British power that restored Wolseley's displaced appointee, but the impis of two neighbouring kinglets.[20] The implication was clear; the conqueror of 1879 had declined to be master in the Zulu house. Questions of mastership were, therefore, to be decided by the Zulu themselves fighting it out.

In an eleventh-hour bid to prevent a major upheaval, the acting High Commissioner, Sir Evelyn Wood, was granted permission in April 1881 to arbitrate in the most threatening disputes of all: those involving the members of the former royal house and the appointed chiefs who were now their rulers.[21] Two of the petty kingdoms were particularly affected: one was the territory of Cetshwayo's distant cousin, Zibhebhu, under whom had been placed the royal heir, Dinuzulu, and two of his uncles, Ndabuko and Ziwedu; the other was the territory of the royal Judas, Hamu, who had under him the Zulu nation's chief-induna, Mnyamana, and the fiercely royalist Qulusi clan.

Those who had devised the post-war settlement had hoped to resuscitate, so far as was possible, the loyalties of pre-Shakan days. By 1881, when Wood stepped in to arbitrate, the signs of a more complex reaction were present: the nation was not simply dissolving into 'tribes', but dividing also on a supra-'tribal' level into Usutu royalists on the one hand, and, on the other, anti-traditionalists who had found some advantage in the new order, and were determined to defend it against any revival of the fortunes of the House of Shaka. The disputes involving the Princes and Umnyamana thus had an explosive content. If violence should occur, all Zululand might take up arms.

In the circumstances, Wood did the best he could. Towards the end of August 1881, after a lengthy investigation of the complaints and the countercharges, he summoned an assembly of the chiefs at Inhlazatye, to announce the results of the inquiry and to make other proposals.[22] It is clear that he hoped to make the

[20] C.O. 879/18, African 230: No. 12097, Wood to Kimberley, 8 July 1881; No. 13680. Wood to Kimberley, 1 August 1881; No. 14050, Wood to Kimberley, 7 August 1881; and No. 14916, Wood to Kimberley, 20 August 1881, and Kimberley to Wood, 20 August 1881.

[21] C.O. 179/137, Natal 6661, Wood to Kimberley, 13 April 1881; and C–3182 p. 26, Kimberley to Wood, 30 April 1881.

[22] C–3182 p. 99f, Wood to Kimberley, 31 August 1881. See also C–3182 p 34f, enclosures on Wood to Kimberley, 23 June 1881. For Colonial Office minutes see C.O. 179/138:

occasion as solemn and impressive as possible. He himself was 'in full pontificals . . . so covered in medals as to be almost indistinguishable'.[23] But the real weakness could not be concealed. Wood could only talk; he could not enforce. It was over to the kinglets to give effect to what he recommended. Yet it was precisely here that the trouble lay, for it was the relations between the appointed chiefs and their subjects that was the issue in question. The results manifested themselves within weeks in the form of a rapid plunge towards violence which the Resident, Osborn, reported in a brief, but disillusioned dispatch on 7 October:

My dear General Wood,

I shall not be able to go to Usibebu's. The country from within a mile or two of this, right on, is in such a disturbed state, that even native messengers have to make large circuits round to avoid contact with those within the pale of disturbance. I shall be able to do little if any good, even if I did go, (for) the Zulus understand now that I have no authority.[24]

Long before this despairing note was penned, a decisive change had occurred in Britain. In a snap election held early in 1880, the Liberals with superior party organization and lavish spending, had appealed successfully to a population deeply disturbed by recession, unemployment and agricultural depression.[25] The British voters on that occasion had little concern for anything beyond the affairs of their own island kingdom; yet, in returning Liberals and Radicals, they were giving five years of power to men whose outlook on empire and imperial responsibility was profoundly to influence the future history of the Zulu people.

Since the 'Empire scare' of 1869–70 Liberal spokesmen, William Gladstone amongst them, had been assiduously cultivating an improved image of their Party. The Liberals, they asserted, had never desired the dismemberment of the Empire; on the

[23] Lady Florence Dixie *In the Land of Misfortune* London 1882 pp. 378–85.

[24] C–3182 p. 139, Wood to Kimberley, 17 October 1881, enclosure Osborn to Wood, 7 October 1881.

[25] G. E. Buckle (ed.) *The Letters of Queen Victoria* Second Series, 3 vols. London 1926 III p. 79, Duke of Connaught to Queen Victoria, 11 April 1880; W. F. Monypenny and G. E. Buckle *The Life of Benjamin Disraeli, Earl of Beaconsfield* 6 vols. London 1910–20 VI pp. 523 and 526; A. Lang (ed.) *Life, Letters and Diaries of Sir Stafford Northcote* London 1891 p. 313; H. J. Hanham *Elections and Party Management* London 1959 pp. 143–5, 228–9, 361–3, and Chapters VII, XII and XIII *passim*; R. Blake *Disraeli* London 1966 pp. 697–700, 709–19.

Natal 15682, Wood to Kimberley, 31 August 1881; and Natal 17877, Wood to Kimberley, 31 August 1881.

contrary, they valued the colonies, both as a source of trade and as a means of establishing benign British institutions in other parts of the world. Their objection was to imperialism not to Empire, and their goal was the golden one of a community of self-reliant societies, reared up to freedom and independence under England's 'splendid parentage'.[26]

For all these asseverations, however, it remained true that enthusiasm for Empire beat with a less robust pulse in the breasts of Gladstone and many of his Liberal supporters than it did in the breasts of Beaconsfield and the Tories. In Beaconsfield's view, England's strength lay in the possession of a mighty Empire giving her unchallenged supremacy in the world. Gladstone, by contrast, believed that annexations by 'augmenting space ... diminish power'.[27] In his opinion:

> The root and pith and substance of the material greatness of our nation lies within the compass of these islands, and is, except in trifling particulars, independent of all and every sort of political dominion.[28]

The difference was important. When Beaconsfield talked of consolidating the Empire he thought in terms of getting 'possession of the strong places in the world'. He shared with Lord Carnarvon the desire to establish 'a more real connection' between Britain and her colonies, so that the trend towards self-government would not cause a 'loosening of the ties'.[29] For Gladstone, imperial consolidation meant something quite different. It meant limiting, so far as was humanly possible, the 'irrepressible tendency' of the Empire to expand, so that Britain's leaders could devote themselves to the more statesmanlike task of converting the existing Empire into a community of states enjoying 'perfect freedom and perfect self-government' though bound together by a 'union in heart and character'.[30]

In the debates on Afghanistan and the Zulu War these differences had sharpened. And during his great Midlothian campaign of November–December 1879, Gladstone's salvoes against the

[26] P. Knaplund *Gladstone and Britain's Imperial Policy* London 1927 pp. 145–6. For discussion of the 'Empire scare' and its repercussions see R. Koebner and H. D. Schmidt *Imperialism* Cambridge 1964 Chapter IV *passim* and *Cambridge History of the British Empire* Vol. III Cambridge 1959 pp. 18–40.
[27] Knaplund op. cit. p. 143.
[28] *C.H.B.E.* III p. 60.
[29] Buckle *Disraeli* IV p. 335 and V p. 195. See also *C.H.B.E.* III pp. 4 and 40–41.
[30] Knaplund op. cit. pp. 143–4; *C.H.B.E.* III pp. 19–20, 128.

'mischievous and ruinous misdeeds' of Beaconsfield's government had reverberated across the nation. Amongst the incendiaries that he hurled at his 'invisible antagonist' was the charge of 'ten thousand Zulus slain for no other offence than their attempt to defend . . . with their naked bodies their hearths and homes'.[31] At another meeting he reminded his audience that:

> The errors of former times are recorded for our instruction in order that we may avoid their repetition. . . . Remember the rights of the savage. . . . Remember that the happiness of his humble home . . . is as inviolable in the eye of Almighty God as can be your own.[32]

The sentiments were noble; but they were also deceptive. 'Avoiding the errors of former times' meant balancing the budget before all else. 'Remembering the rights of the savage' meant leaving distant peoples to their fate, whatever their condition might be. The import of Midlothian was not that Beaconsfield and his colleagues had failed in their duty to indigenous peoples on the fringes of the Empire; the real import was that they had failed the British electorate by squandering the nation's resources on worthless adventures overseas.

Midlothian probably affected the general election very little. But the campaign was a personal triumph for Gladstone. It re-established his leadership over the Liberal Party; and his success convinced him of the righteousness of his cause. Thus when the new Liberal administration took office, it was led by a man who was publicly committed to avoid 'forward' imperial policies and was personally convinced that the Almighty had chosen him for this cause.[33]

During its first year in office the Liberal Government's main South African preoccupation was the state of affairs in the Transvaal. Before the end of 1880, however, Zululand had already begun to press itself more and more insistently upon the attention of those responsible for colonial affairs. With the territory slipping towards anarchy, the revision of the Wolseley settlement became an unavoidable issue, and the new Secretary of State, Lord Kimberley, asked the advice of his senior officials on the British Government's rights in the territory. The reply, in the form of a

[31] J. Morley *Life of William Ewart Gladstone* 3 vols. London 1903 II p. 200.
[32] P. Magnus op. cit. p. 262.
[33] See Morley op. cit. II pp. 196, 220, 223; Magnus op. cit. pp. 256, 270; Blake op. cit. p. 711.

minute by R. G. W. Herbert, the Permanent Under-Secretary, was instructive. He wrote:

Lord Kimberley,

Sir Garnet Wolseley's settlement ... was based on the conquest of Zululand and deposition of the King by the Queen's troops. I believe the whole country thereby became vested in Her Majesty, who, declining to annex it to her own dominions, 'parcelled it out into independent chieftainships', deciding 'what territory was to be allotted to each chief'....

Whether by so 'parcelling' and 'allotting' the Territory the Queen entirely and finally divested herself of her ownership is a question which it may be better not to decide at present....[34]

For Britain it was a convenient position to adopt. As the rest of the minute made clear, by avoiding a decision on the question of sovereignty, the British Government could escape responsibility for Zululand's affairs, yet reserve for itself the right to intervene if ever it deemed it in its own interests to do so. During the next four-and-a-half years the exercise of rights without responsibility was to characterize almost every British move in Zululand.

For a time, during the disturbances of 1881, the Colonial Office toyed with the idea of appointing sub-Residents to reside with the thirteen chiefs. Significantly, however, their salaries and expenses were to be paid for by the chiefs themselves, so that there would be no charge on the British treasury.[35] At his Inhlazatye meeting of 31 August 1881, Wood put this proposal to those assembled and, of the nine kinglets present, six accepted the scheme.[36] Modest as it was, however, it began to cause uneasiness in a Government 'adverse (sic) to any unnecessary interference in the Zulu country', and by the end of the year the Colonial Office was beating a hasty retreat.[37] In a dispatch to Sir Henry Bulwer, the new Governor of Natal, Lord Kimberley explained:

... Her Majesty's Government ... have come to the conclusion that the plan is open to very serious objections ... [for the Zulus would

[34] C.O. 179/134, Natal 17262, Colley to Kimberley, 1 October 1880, minute by R. G. W. Herbert, 12 November 1880.

[35] C.O. 179/135, Natal 19893, Colley to Kimberley, 20 November 1880, minutes; C.O. 179/137, Natal 13855, Wood to Kimberley, 23 June 1881, minutes; C.O. 179/138, Natal 15682, Wood to Kimberley, 31 August 1881, minutes.

[36] C.O. 179/138, Natal 15682, Wood to Kimberley, 31 August 1881, minutes; C.O. 879/18, African 230, No. 15682, Wood to Kimberley, 31 August 1881.

[37] C.O. 179/138: Natal 15682, Wood to Kimberley, 31 August 1881, minutes; Natal 17877, Wood to Kimberley, 31 August 1881, minutes.

expect the sub-Residents to] ... exercise a real authority and afford them that effectual ... redress of grievances, of the loss of which, since the deposition of Cetywayo, they so loudly complain.[38]

For the moment, therefore, the Zulu were to be left to fight as best they could the fires that the Wolseley settlement had ignited. Privately, Kimberley admitted that he did not expect the settlement to last, but he saw in that no reason to submit to the pressures of the Resident and others, Zulu leaders included, who were urging 'direct British interference'.[39] Instead, his mind was turning to a course which, he believed, would free the British Government of the Zulu incubus and simultaneously relieve it of the embarrassment of Cetshwayo, whose continued detention at the Cape was provoking widespread criticism and becoming 'extremely distasteful to a large proportion of the supporters of Mr Gladstone's Government'.[40]

The story of Cetshwayo's return to Zululand has been told so often that it need not be retold in detail here.[41] One aspect deserves special emphasis, however, for it illuminates the nature of British policy at this time. Although Gladstone and Kimberley were both sympathetic to Cetshwayo and disliked being 'his gaolers',[42] the restoration was not primarily an attempt to right a personal wrong by allowing the ex-King to end his days amongst his own people. In its main aspect the restoration was a political move; an expression of the hope that Cetshwayo would establish order in Zululand, and so save Britain from the consequences of the ill-conceived settlement that had followed the triumph of her

[38] C.O. 879/19, African 242, Kimberley to Bulwer, 2 February 1882, p. 4.
[39] C.O. 179/138: Natal 15682, Wood to Kimberley, 31 August 1881, minute by Kimberley, 6 September 1881; Natal 19513, Wood to Kimberley, 10 October 1881, minutes. C.O. 879/19, African 243: No. 64, Wood to Kimberley, 31 August 1881; No. 65, Wood to Kimberley, 21 September 1881; No. 69, Wood to Kimberley, 13 September 1881, enclosure; No. 92, Wood to Kimberley, 15 October 1881, enclosure.
[40] C.O. 879/23, African 307, confidential memo. prepared for Cabinet by E. Fairfield, January 1886. 'General View of Zulu Affairs 1879–1885' pp. 1–2; British Museum Add. MS. 44226, Gladstone Papers, CXLI, pp. 253–4, Kimberley to Gladstone, 2 September 1881. See also C.O. 179/138: Natal 17877, draft dispatch, Kimberley to Bulwer, undated; Natal 19513, Wood to Kimberley, 10 October 1881, minutes; and C.O. 879/19, African 243, No. 66, Robinson to Kimberley, 16 September 1881, and enclosures.
[41] See C. T. Binns *The Last Zulu King* London 1963 Chapters 16 and 17; Gibson op. cit. pp. 225–67; Brookes and Webb op. cit. pp. 149–53.
[42] Br. Mus. Add. MS. 44226, Gladstone Papers, CXLI p. 253, Kimberley to Gladstone, 2 September 1881.

arms in 1879. Colonial Office memoranda described the restoration as an 'experiment' adopted 'as the only alternative to the extension of direct British authority over Zululand'.[43] It would not, I think, be beyond the bounds of historical propriety to describe it rather as a gamble; and a gamble on which the British Government staked nothing except the peace of Zululand and the welfare of the Zulu people themselves.

Long before Cetshwayo boarded the Royal Navy's *Briton* to make the journey home, the Colonial Office had been plied with warnings that there were powerful parties in Zululand that would be hostile to the ex-King's return. To accommodate this opposition the decision was taken that Cetshwayo's authority should be limited to only a portion of his former kingdom.[44] In the north, Zibhebhu was to be preserved as the ruler of an independent Mandhlakazi kingdom, while in the south, along the Natal border, a Reserve Territory was to be established, both as a military buffer and as a refuge for chiefs and clans opposed to the revival of the royal house. Further than this, however, the British government was not prepared to go. Except for the demarcation of the new frontiers, there was to be no supervision of the new settlement—no assistance to Cetshwayo in the task of re-establishing his authority; no peace-keeping operations along the new borders; no protection to individuals and clans that might find themselves placed under hostile rulers; no superintendence of the upheaval that was bound to occur if chiefs and clans uprooted themselves from their old lands and moved into the territories that best represented their loyalties and interests. Even the Reserve Territory was to be administered at no cost to the British treasury, and the term 'Protected Territory' was to be carefully avoided lest it suggest to the inhabitants of the Reserve that they could 'depend for defence not on themselves, but on British power'.[45]

Such an abdication of responsibility might pass without com-

[43] C.O. 879/23: African 304, memo. by E. Fairfield, 4 August 1885, 'Vacillation in Policy in South Africa' p. 2; African 307, 'General View of Zulu Affairs' pp. 2–3.

[44] C–3247 pp. 57–8, Bulwer to Kimberley, 20 April 1882; C–3466 pp. 197ff, Bulwer to Kimberley, 3 October 1882, and enclosures; and Br. Mus. Add. MS.44228, Gladstone Papers, CXLIII pp. 25–28, Kimberley to Gladstone, 23 November 1882.

[45] C–3466 p. 216, Kimberley to Gladstone, 30 November 1882. See also Br. Mus. Add. MS.44227, Gladstone Papers, CXLII p. 233–4, Kimberley to Gladstone, 29 September 1882; Br. Mus. Add. MS.44228, Gladstone Papers, CXLIII pp. 3, 29 and 32–35, Gladstone to Kimberley, 23 November 1882, Kimberley to Gladstone, 24 November 1882, and Kimberley to Gladstone, 22 December 1882.

ment if it had been made in ignorance of the explosive tensions which the Wolseley settlement had generated; but this was not so. In a private letter to Gladstone, Kimberley wrote of the new arrangements:

By the course we have adopted, I hope and believe we shall preserve peace on . . . (the Natal) . . . border, altho' it is useless to disguise from ourselves that the matter may . . . lead to . . . conflict amongst the Zulus. . . . But if that conflict is only postponed, we may by prudent management avoid being concerned in it.[46]

Such was the outlook on imperial responsibility early in 1883. As one of the permanent officials at the Colonial Office was subsequently to comment:

. . . the late Government (of Mr Gladstone) failed to back its own man (Cetshwayo), and allowed him to be so used . . . as to give him no chance of success.[47]

Cetshwayo was landed at Port Durnford on the Zululand coast on 10 January 1883. By early March reports were already coming in of serious disturbances along the frontier between his territory and that of his Mandhlakazi rival, Zibhebhu.[48] Those involved flung accusations and counter-accusations at one another. The traditionalist Usutu faction, royalists hoping for the revival of the old order, charged Zibhebhu and his Mandhlakazi followers with insulting and provocative behaviour. The Mandhlakazi accused the Usutu of breaches of the conditions of the new settlement. The Natal officials accused the Bishopstowe Party, Bishop Colenso and his family and friends, of stirring up Usutu ambitions. The Bishopstowe Party accused the 'official clique' of deliberately working for Cetshwayo's downfall.

The question of who incited trouble, and who caused the first 'incidents' is hardly relevant, however. As Kimberley himself was aware, the agitators would have been 'powerless' if the tensions and discontents had not already been there;[49] and Cetshwayo was

[46] Br. Mus. Add. MS.44228, Gladstone Papers, CXLIII p. 44, Kimberley to Gladstone, 7 January 1883.

[47] C.O. 879/23, African 304 'Vacillation in Policy in South Africa' p. 3.

[48] C–3616: 68, Bulwer to Derby, 6 March 1883, enclosure 1; 75, Bulwer to Derby, 10 March 1883; 78, Bulwer to Derby, 15 March 1883, enclosure 1; 88, Bulwer to Derby 21 March 1883, enclosure, and 131, Bulwer to Derby, 9 April 1883, enclosure 2.

[49] Br. Mus. Add. MS.44228, Gladstone Papers, CXLIII p. 12, Kimberley to Gladstone, 26 October 1882.

to make the same point when he bitterly complained to a European visitor:

I did not land in a dry place. I landed in the mud. . . . You speak of my coming and fighting . . . I came and found long-standing feuds and bitterly opposed enemies. There are no new feuds since I came.[50]

Perhaps the European visitor who recorded these words should be allowed his own say, for his sentiments were not those of the land-grabbing imperialist when the wrote:

The country ought to have been annexed. . . . it was iniquitous folly to restore him (Cetshwayo) to divided honours with Usibebu. There could not possibly be peace. . . . Candidly I admire Usibebu. . . . I do not blame him for worrying and harrying the Usutu Party and the King's brothers and relatives in the days of his chieftainship as one of the thirteen. He acted as most human beings would have acted under similar circumstances. But I do blame a Government that forgot that he was human. . . . I do not blame Usibebu for point-blank refusing to resign when his fellow-kinglets resigned by Imperial request. . . . but I do blame a Government so purblind as to ignore the certain outcome of this spirited refusal.[51]

The rest of Cetshwayo's story must be briefly told. At the end of March 1883 a Usutu impi, estimated by some as 5,000 strong, launched an attack against the Mandhlakazi, but was ambushed in the Msebe valley, and overwhelmed with perhaps greater loss of life than that sustained in any other battle in Zulu history.[52] Five months later, the Mandhlakazi followed up this victory with an invasion of Cethwayo's kingdom. The Usutu forces were unable to withstand the attack. Ulundi, the royal capital was razed to the ground. Cetshwayo, with other members of the royal family, was forced to flee to the Reserve for safety and there on 8 February 1884, he died.[53]

Throughout these events, the British Government firmly maintained the attitude so unselfconsciously summarized by Kimberley's successor, Lord Derby, in a telegram to the Natal

[50] W. Y. Campbell *With Cetywayo in the Inkandhla and the Present State of the Zulu Question* Durban 1883 p. 11.

[51] Ibid. pp. 37–38.

[52] See Gibson op. cit. pp. 248–50. See also C.O. 879/20, African 255: No. 6701, Bulwer to Derby, 22 April 1883; and No. 6702, Bulwer to Derby, 22 April 1883.

[53] C.O. 879/20, African 255: No. 12534, Bulwer to Derby, 23 July 1883; No. 12981, Bulwer to Derby, 29 July 1883; and C.O. 879/21, African 281, No. 2256, Bulwer to Derby, 9 February 1884.

Governor, Sir Henry Bulwer: 'We prefer, if possible, to leave (the) Zulus . . . to settle their own affairs.'[54]

For Bulwer, it was not so easy to remain complacent, for facing him was the reality that Cetshwayo's flight to the Reserve had left Central Zululand without government. In November 1883, he accordingly sent off a dispatch in which he outlined the alternative courses which, in his view, the British Government might adopt in the circumstances. The third of these—one to which Bulwer himself was strongly opposed—was that of leaving the country 'to itself' and 'to anarchy', in which event he predicted, in a secret and confidential parenthesis, it would fall into the hands of land-hungry Boers from the Transvaal. To avoid this happening, he strongly urged that the British Government should either extend the Reserve to include Cetshwayo's Central Kingdom, or install Cetshwayo's sixteen-year-old son, Dinuzulu, in the central territory, with a Resident and a Zulu Council of Regency to assist him.[55] These proposals, telegraphed by Bulwer on 16 November 1883, were circulated to the Cabinet the following day, and the issue was kept before the Cabinet during the weeks that followed.[56] Nearly six months later, however, at the end of April 1884, the decision of the Cabinet was still being awaited. For all practical purposes, therefore, Bulwer's unwanted third alternative had come into operation: the territory was being left 'to itself' and 'to anarchy'.

The result corresponded almost exactly to what the Natal Governor had predicted. In January, there were 'encounters' between Boers and Zulu in Zibhebhu's territory. By February, Transvaal subjects were entering the country in increasing numbers and, at the end of April, a large party of armed Boers rode into Zululand to open negotiations with Dinuzulu and his advisers. If the Usutu leaders did not themselves invite this intervention, they were certainly sufficiently despairing of British assistance to welcome the proffered hand that the Boers extended it to them. Negotiations were opened, and early in May a bargain was struck. The firearms of the white men were to be used to destroy Zibhebhu's power; Dinuzulu was to be placed on the

[54] C.O. 879/20, African 255, No. 19598, Derby to Bulwer, 20 November 1883.

[55] C.O. 879/20, African 255, No. 19858, Bulwer to Derby, 17 November 1883.

[56] C.O. 179/148: Natal 19598, Bulwer to Derby, 16 November 1883, minutes; Natal 21688, Bulwer to Derby, 22 November 1883, minutes; Natal 21647, Bulwer to Derby, 26 November 1883, minutes; and Natal 108, Bulwer to Derby, 30 November 1883, minutes.

throne of his father; and a Boer Protectorate was to be established over his kingdom. In return for these services, the newcomers from the Transvaal were to be allowed to remain in Zululand with farms on which to graze their cattle.[57]

At the Colonial Office the reports of these events produced a measure at least of the alarm that had been felt by Bulwer for so long. In March, a memorandum was prepared recommending the extension of the Reserves over central Zululand.[58] As the telegraph wires tapped out the latest Zululand dispatches, these items were hurried to the presses of the Stationery Office to be turned into prints for the Cabinet. But the Gladstone ministry was not easily perturbed. It took its decision at last in the second week of May, shortly after receiving the news of the entry into Zululand of the armed Boers. On 16 May, six months to the day after anxiously putting forward his alternatives, Bulwer received his long-awaited reply:

> After full consideration of recent reports and recommendations, Her Majesty's Government adhere to (the) decision not to extend British sovereignty or protection over Zululand.[59]

What this decision meant for the future of the Zulu people was clear four months later: the Boers had defeated Zibhebhu and driven him into exile in the Reserve; they had declared a Protectorate over Zululand and proclaimed Dinuzulu king. But, as the price for these services, they had expropriated some 4,000 square miles of Zulu territory, and on this a 'New' Republic had been proclaimed.[60]

Nobody in 1884 doubted that the New Boer Republic of Zululand would rapidly outgrow the 4,000 square mile cradle of its birth. However, more was needed than the plight of the Zulu people to persuade an anti-expansionist government to add to Britain's commitments in a distant corner of the globe.[61] As subsequent events were to show, even the threat of German

[57] C.O. 179/151: Natal 1610, Bulwer to Derby, 28 January 1884; and Natal 3831, Bulwer to Derby, 5 February 1884. C.O. 179/152: Natal 6661, Bulwer to Derby, 24 March 1884; and Natal 7340, Bulwer to Derby, 4 May 1884.

[58] C.O. 879/21, African 280, memo. by E. Fairfield, 4 March 1884 'Proposed Extension of the Reserve'.

[59] C.O. 879/21, African 281, No. 8149, Derby to Bulwer, 16 May 1884.

[60] C.O. 879/21, African 281: No. 8920, Bulwer to Derby, 28 May 1884; No. 10001, Bulwer to Derby, 13 June 1884; and No. 14631, Bulwer to Derby, 26 August 1884.

[61] C.O. 879/21, African 281, No. 12134, Bulwer to Derby, 16 July 1884, and Derby to Bulwer, 23 July 1884.

intervention was not enough to lead Gladstone along paths which he still associated with 'Beaconsfieldism'.

In the latter months of 1884, German agents seeking rights and concessions, had made their appearance under mysterious circumstances in the Zulu country. To Bulwer, in Natal, it seemed that Bismarck was about to repeat the trick that only a few months before had made South West Africa a German Protectorate.[62] And he was not alone in holding these views. At the Colonial Office alarm was expressed lest Britain's difficulties be 'increased tenfold' by Germany's obtaining a foothold from which to interfere in the already troubled politics of South Africa.[63] The British press, with all Bismarck's rapid colonial moves of 1884 before it, began to trumpet the cry that Britain's interests were in danger. And Derby, catching the panic—fearing a demonstration of public opinion 'which even the present government could hardly resist', demanded of his Cabinet colleagues that the whole Zululand coast be annexed.[64]

His fears were not shared by the Prime Minister, however. In what he himself called a few 'old-fashioned notes', Gladstone set out to steady his wavering Colonial Secretary. Extensions of British authority 'simply to keep the Germans out' would involve Britain in a 'scramble' for territory that would be neither 'dignified' nor 'required by any real interest'. He warned Derby that the annexation of the Zululand coast would 'tend powerfully to entail a responsibility for the country lying inland; a responsibility which he believed it would be 'impolitic to assume'.[65]

In the end, it was Gladstone who prevailed. Only St Lucia Bay was annexed, and the Zulu problem was left for others, less averse to imperial responsibility, to handle.[66]

In the latter months of 1885 it seemed at last that this might

[62] C. O. 179/154, Natal 865, Bulwer to Derby, 16 December, 1884.

[63] C.O. 179/154, Natal 21694, Bulwer to Derby, 19 December 1884, minute by A. W. L. Hemming.

[64] Br. Mus. Add. MS.44142, Gladstone Papers, LVII pp. 106–7, Derby to Gladstone 23 December 1884. See also C.O. 179/154, Natal 21566, Bulwer to Derby 18 November 1884, minutes.

[65] Br. Mus. Add. MS. 44142, Gladstone Papers LVII pp. 113–4, Gladstone to Derby 30 December 1884. See also A. Ramm (ed.) *Political Correspondence of Mr Gladstone and Lord Granville, 1876–1886* 2 vols. Oxford 1962 II p. 304, Gladstone to Granville, 28 December 1884.

[66] C.O. 879/21, African 281 : No. 20792, Derby to Bulwer, 8 December 1884; and No. 21860, Bulwer to Derby, 21 December 1884.

happen. In June of that year, Gladstone resigned, and Lord Salisbury formed a Conservative Government in which Colonel F. A. Stanley succeeded his brother, Lord Derby, at the Colonial Office. If Stanley differed from his brother in politics, he differed even more radically in temperament. Suddenly the business of the Colonial Office began to move with a brisk, military efficiency that had been unknown for years. Whereas Derby minuted urgent Zululand dispatches with the one paralysing word 'Wait', Stanley called for memoranda and documents on which to base a decision. Moreover he had with him, as his Parliamentary Under-Secretary, Lord Dunraven, whose view it was that the whole Zulu question should have been settled long before, both because of Britain's obligations to the natives, and because the disorders in the country and the activities of the New Republic were an open invitation to foreign interference.[67]

The influence of British party politics upon the affairs of Zululand had still not run its fateful course, however. Lord Salisbury had come into office at the head of a caretaker administration with minority support in the Commons. It had to tread warily, and it survived only to January 1886, too short a time for Stanley and Dunraven to implement their plans for the Zulu country.[68]

By February 1886, Gladstone and the Liberals were back in harness. The officials at the Colonial Office—anticipating hostilities between the Boers and the Zulu, and still fearing foreign interference—continued to press for a final settlement; but it was not to be. With the Irish issue dominating British politics, and with the slow-moving hand of the ageing Lord Granville directing colonial affairs, another six months went by, during which negotiations were opened with the New Republic, but nothing achieved.[69]

[67] C.O. 179/162, Natal 17291, Foreign Office to Colonial Office, 1 October 1995, minutes; C.O. 179/157, Natal 11468, Bulwer to Stanley, 1 June 1885, minutes; C.O. 179/158, Natal 13807, Bulwer to Stanley, 5 August 1885, minutes. See also: C.O. 879/22, African 300, 'Memorandum on Zulu Affairs' for use of Cabinet; C.O. 879/22, African 295, No. 13807, Stanley to Bulwer, 7 August 1885; and C.O. 879/23, African 307, memo. for use of Cabinet by E. Fairfield January 1886 'General View of Zulu Affairs 1879–1885'.

[68] For this and other Cabinet changes in the period under consideration see R. C. K. Ensor *England 1870–1914* Oxford 1936 Chapter III *passim*.

[69] C.O. 879/24: African 324, No. 1500, Granville to Havelock, 12 March 1886; African 329, No. 23, Granville to Havelock, 11 March 1886. C.O. 879/24, African 324: No. 7512, Havelock to Granville, 2 May 1886; No. 10680, Havelock to Granville, 17 June 1886; and No. 12100, Havelock to Granville, 9 July 1886.

Yet by one of those strange twists of human affairs, the Irish issue, which helped to delay a settlement, hastened the return of a Cabinet in which there were men with the will to tackle the Zulu problem and call 'halt' to the expansion of the Boers. In August 1886, after only six months in office, Gladstone was defeated on Home Rule, and when elections were held, Lord Salisbury and his supporters returned to Westminster with a composite majority of 118. Colonel Stanley did not resume his former place at the Colonial Office, but Edward Stanhope took up the negotiations which Lord Granville had commenced.[70] In return for a considerable reduction of the Boers' expanding territorial claims, Britain *de facto* recognized the New Republic's independent status.[71] And, with that issue settled, the remainder of Zululand was brought under British authority early in February 1887.[72]

Colonial rule and the Zulu reaction to it were to spawn new tensions and new troubles; but the period of dereliction—perhaps the most crucial phase in the collapse of the ethos of Zulu nationhood—had come to an end. Henceforward, the imposer of policies was itself responsible for the affairs of the Zulu country.

If this account of imperial policy in Zululand in the years 1879–87 reads like a charge-sheet, indicting Britain with sole responsibility for the destruction of Zulu nationhood, that is not its purpose. When the historian draws out one thread from the events he is studying, that thread is bound to assume an exaggerated significance; for the rest of the tangled skein is left out of account. In fact, there were many others, apart from the wielders of governmental power in London, whose actions and interests and ambitions contributed to the collapse and disintegration of Zulu national life. Land-hungry Boers, unsympathetic British officials, partisan white 'advisers'—all these shared the responsibility, as did the Zulu people themselves, for it was their rivalries and resistance that produced the conflicts which others sought to manipulate or remedy or exploit. To attribute the plight of the Zulu nation solely to the misdeeds of the conqueror is to repeat the error of those who would attribute the rise of Nazism solely to the iniquities of the Versailles settlement. Doing so denies to the Zulu

[70] C.O. 879/24, African 324, No. 12582, Stanhope to Havelock, 4 September 1886.
[71] C.O. 879/24, African 324, No. 19519, Stanhope to Havelock, 2 November 1886.
[72] C.O. 879/26, African 337, No. 2938, Havelock to Holland, 14 December 1887.

the status of responsible human beings, for it reduces them to the passive objects of other men's actions.

In isolating the one thread of British policy my purpose was not to indict, but to emphasize certain features which may be important for understanding the process by which African peoples were brought under European control during the nineteenth century.

Most obvious is the fact that, whatever role acquisitiveness might have played in general, it was not always the desire for land and resources that led European men to actions and policies that were destructive of the political independence of African societies. Even Frere's war policy of 1878 was aimed, not at depriving the Zulu people of their land, but at the quite different goal of a stable South Africa that would permit federation and self-government. And, until 1885–6, the policies that were improvised in London as a result of this unwanted war, were policies designed to avoid the acquisition of the Zulu country. Yet, paradoxically for the Zulu people, it was these anti-expansionist policies that spelt ruin.

Less obvious, but more important perhaps, is the fact that policies that seemed irresponsible when viewed from the Zulu or the South African point of view, bore a quite different aspect in London. The British policy-makers of the 1880s were no more blackguardly than other politicians and administrators at other times and in other places. In fact, Gladstone's political life was infused by an unusually high sense of moral duty. But one of the features of the imperial relationship was that it involved the politicians in a shifting system of relative responsibilities; and in the 1880s that remote corner of the globe called Zululand ranked so low on the scale of responsibilities, that the interests of its inhabitants suffered by default as much as by design.

Exacerbating this was ignorance—in particular, ignorance of the fragile structure and functioning of a society in which reverence for the royal house was the only agency short of force that could keep sectional rivalries in check, and so prevent a resort to feuding. That this ignorance existed is not a matter for blame. (The nineteenth century was not blessed with anthropologists as we are today.) But the Wolseley 'settlement' serves as a dramatic example of the chaos that could be unleashed by a paramount power searching for stability, and, in its search, heedlessly imposing a new order in disregard to the traditions of the conquered people.

Finally, there is the fact that the establishment of an imperial relationship, such as that created by Britain's military victory in 1879, exposed the Zulu people to forces and influences that were quite unrelated to the local situation. Party strife in England, agricultural depression, Irish Home Rule, Anglo–German diplomatic relations—issues such as these were as significant in determining the fate of the Zulu people as were the decisions of those specifically responsible for the framing of colonial policy.

In the history of African societies, the establishment of the imperial relationship, even in its informal guise, must rank as a development of revolutionary significance. By the last quarter of the nineteenth century, Zululand had been linked to the wider world, and the history of its people had ceased to be the story of a chrysalis society undergoing mutation in an insulated local environment. The Zulu people were exposed, not only to alien rule and extraneous cultural influences; they were exposed also to the repercussions of affairs and events of which they themselves had no direct knowledge or understanding. With the cocoon broken, a large part of their history after 1879 was the story of their buffetings by the elements to which they were now exposed.

Index

Index

Aasvogelskop, 58, 60
Abraham, D. P., 5
Acocks, J. P. H., 56
Afrikaans, 3, 8
Afrikaners: *see* Boers
age grades, 16, 18, 212 *passim*, 231
Aliwal North, 293, 296, 297, 298
Alur, 73
Amadzimba, 40, 49
Ama-Komati, 137
Amalanga, 139
Amaphakathi, 254
Amazizi, 139
Amba, 75
Anglican mission of St. Augustine, 232
Anglo-German diplomatic relations, 323
Anglo-Saxon England, 240
Angola, 2, 37–8
anthropologists and anthropology, 1–3, 5, 9–10, 33, 41, 53–4, 69, 71–86, 93–4, 111
Apies, R., 194
Arbousset, T., 89, 91, 108, 129
archaeologists and archaeology, 3–12 *passim*, 24–70, 87, 111, 118, 119
Archbell, J., 96, 200
Arend, J., 108
Ashanti, 78
Atiya, 78
Atlantic Ocean, 32, 145
Atmore, A., 21, 22–3, 126, 282–301
Attaqua chiefdom, 166
Austrian Asiatic Company, Trieste, 174 *passim*
Avongara, 78

Ba-Kgabo-Ea-Melle: *see* Kgatla
Babanango Mountain, 131, 142
Backhouse, J., 114
Bahurutsi, 64, 88
Baines, T., 272
Bakoni, 126–8
Bakwena: *see* Kwena
Bamangwato: *see* Ngwato
Bambandyanalo, 7, 8, 34, 36, 52–5, 66
Bambata, 31, 34, 40, 49
Bangwaketsi, 88
Bantu Administration and Development, 93; Authorities Act, 232; Chiefdoms, 161; dispersal, 119; fishermen, 133; populations, 64, 117, 139, 290; pottery, 68; languages, 3, 5, 8, 43–4, 82; -speaking peoples, 8, 11, 20, 43–4, 50, 51, 69, 79, 80, 83 *passim*, 112, 117, 121, 131 *passim*, 152, 160, 207, 208, 259
Banyai, 268
Barberton Nelspruit, 118
Barolong, 88
Barotseland, 268, 280
Bas-Congo, 39
Bashee, R., 146, 155, 156
'Basters' 81
Basuto, 88, 268, 283, 284, 293, 295
Basutoland, 139, 141, 295; Annexation Act, 295
Batlapin, 88
Batlaro, 88
Batoka Plateau (Zambia), 28
Beach, Sir Michael Hicks, 303
Beaconsfield, Earl of, 303, 304, 310, 311
Beaumont, 36
Bechuana, 96, 204; chiefs, 82
Beerseba mission station, 203, 204, 205
Beit Bridge, 31
Belesi, 132
Bemba, 75
Berea Plateau, 284
Bergdama, 117, 121
Bergenaar, 193
Berlin mission, 90
Bernard, F. O., 33
Bethulie, 193, 199
Bhaca, 238, 242, 247
Bhele, 134; /Zizi, 137, 138, 140, 141, 143; location, 247
Bisa, 81
Bishopstowe Party, 315
Bismarck, 319
Bland, R., 63
Bloemfontein, 4, 283
Blood, R., 218; territory, 305
Blyth, L., 235
Boers, 19, 22, 93, 196, 204, 208, 218, 260 *passim*, 278 *passim*, 304, 305, 317 *passim*
Bokwe, J. K., 153–5
Bolts, W., 174
Bomvana, 247
Bomvu, 132
Botswana, 15, 24, 34, 35, 53, 71, 94, 96, 99, 101, 105, 116, 121, 203, 204; Iron Age, 24, 34, 35, 58
Bowker, J., 296, 298
Boyce, W., 235, 252
Brand, President J. H., 22, 283, 284, 286, 292, 296
Brandberg, The, 35
Brazilian slave traders, 177
Breutz, P. L., 4, 11, 92, 94, 102, 111
British Cabinet, 22, 23, 307, 317, 318, 321; Crown, 304; East India Company, 174; Government, 22, 275–6, 312, 314, 317; Resident, 306; South Africa Company, 19, 266; traders, 180
Brits, 100, 101
Broadbent, Rev. S., 200
Brothwell, D. R., 53
Brown, J. T., 89

Brown, R., 20–1, 259–81
Brownlee, J., 139
Bryant, A. T., 3, 5, 11, 65, 70, 126–44, 181, 184, 185, 233
Buchanan, J., 297
Buckingham, Duke of, 286, 289
Buffalo (Zinyati) River, 63, 130, 138, 183, 184
Buispoort site, 36, 58, 59, 64, 66, 67
Bulawayo, 30, 33, 266, 267
Bulwer, Sir Henry, 312, 317, 319
Burnet, B., 288, 289, 290
Burundi, 38
Bushmans River, 138, 166, 167
Bushmen: *see* San
Bushveld, 56, 62
Butha Buthe, 196
Buthelezi, 142

Cala, East London, 64
Calder's Cave, Gokwe, 29, 30, 47, 49
Caledon river and valley, 15, 96, 100, 192 *passim*, 284, 294, 296, 297
Callaway, G., 232, 242
Cambini, 185
Camdeboo, 162, 165
Campbell, J., 50, 89, 91, 109
Cape, The, 1, 11, 12, 42, 66, 71, 81, 94, 96, 130, 132, 143, 160 *passim*, 173, 177, 202, 230, 234, 275, 284, 287, 292 *passim*, 304; Colony, 20, 22, 191, 202, 203, 231, 282, 295; Province, 42, 145, 146; Town, 4, 77, 85, 144, 263, 279, 294
Carnarvon, Lord, 278, 279, 310
Carolina, 114, 118
Casalis, E., 82, 89, 202
Castle Peak, Western Swaziland, 36, 47, 49
Cattle, 3, 6, 9, 10, 12, 22, 52, 64, 72, 75, 76 *passim*, 108, 118, 120, 121, 147, 151, 152, 159, 160 *passim*, 179, 187, 194, 195, 197, 199, 204, 211, 215, 228, 242, 248, 252, 254, 255, 259, 263, 267, 269, 271, 274, 285, 287 *passim*, 290, 291
Cele chiefdom, 136
Cetshwayo, 78, 218, 267, 280, 302, 306, 308, 313 *passim*
Cewa, 76
Chainouqua, 161, 162, 164; chiefdom, 160, 164
Chase, J. C., 192
Chelmsford, Lord, 302
Chewa chiefs, 226
Chibi district, 32
chiefdoms, amalgamations of, 107, 122; clusters of, 98 *passim*, 120–1, 159; origins of, 98 *passim*; paramount chiefs, 147, 148, 154–5, 157, 158 fn., 159 fn., 161 fn., 194, 197, 198, 200, 217, 234, 239; sub-chiefs, 98–9, 232, 244, 246
Chilver, E. M., 240
Chirundu, 29
Chobona, 161, 162, 163
Chochoqua, 160, 161
Chondwe group (Copperbelt), 25, 26, 27, 46, 49
Chwenyane, 58
Cira, 251
Ciskei, 51, 78
Clark, D., 73, 133
clients, 41, 71, 82
Coillard, F., 268
Colenso, Bishop, 315
Colesberg, 204
Colonial Office, 303, 307, 312, 314, 315, 319, 320, 321
Comoros, 37
Congo, 38, 39, 83; basins, 84; pedicle, 25
Conservatives, 310, 320
Cooke, C. K., 41
Copper, 6, 24, 26, 27, 28, 29, 30, 32, 35, 51, 55, 68, 69, 161, 164, 165, 176
Copperbelt, 25, 26, 75
councillors, 14, 18, 148, 210, 232, 244, 248 *passim*, 317
Cradock, Govenor, 204
Crocodile, R., 100
crops, 6, 8, 10, 65, 72, 112, 186, 258, 259, 285
Cross Upcott, A. W. R., 76
Cube, 134, 184
cultural compatibility, 3, 6, 7, 8, 10, 13, 17, 51, 54, 66, 86–7, 93, 95 *passim*, 102–3, 114, 116, 118, 120, 122, 126, 129 *passim*, 145–6
Cunu, 127, 134, 184
Cwama Gamma, 156–7, 163

D.E.I. Co., 166
Dama, 80
Damaqua, 166, 167
Damasonqua, 166
Dambwa group (Zambezi valley), 25, 29, 30, 34, 43, 47, 49
Daniel, J., 293, 294
Dar es Salaam, 2
Daumas, 297, 298
Debe, Nguni, 134, 136
Delagoa, 108, 173, 174, 179, 180, 181, 185, 188; Bay, 14, 68, 96, 108, 118, 127, 133 *passim*, 141, 171, 212, 213; Thonga, 135
Derby, Lord, 286, 316, 319, 320
decisions: making of, 18, 20, 210, 230–2, 236–7, 239, 242, 250–8, 275; enforcing of, 246, 250, 252–7
descent, systems of, 75 *passim*, 116, 131–69 *passim*, 210, 217, 221, 236, 237
Difagane, 13 *passim*, 58, 59, 67, 102, 111 *passim*, 191–206. *See also* Mfecane
Dighoya, 112, 115
Dingane, 14, 183, 188, 189, 217, 218
Dingiswayo, 16, 20, 141, 183 *passim*, 213, 214, 226
Dinuzulu, 308, 317, 318
diplomacy, 21, 198, 200, 238, 259–81, 293, 294, 323
Dirolong (Rustenburg District), 103
Dithakong, 192, 200, 202
Dlamini, 78, 130, 143, 180, 185; I, 137, 138, 140; II, 140; Mbo, 137; Nguni 180
Dombozanga, 31, 34, 40, 41, 47, 49
Dorha (or Ruyter), 167
Dosini, Chief, 251
Drakensberg mountains, 60, 104, 105, 130, 132, 138, 139, 140, 192, 196, 208, 261, 286
Dube, 185; chiefdoms, 136
Dugmore, H. H., 235, 242, 252, 254

Dundo Airfield, 38, 47, 49
Dunn, J., 78
Dunraven, Lord, 320
D'Urban's treaty system, 252
Durban, 63, 133
Dutch (people), 12, 81, 90, 144, 160, 162, 173, 174, 176, 177
Dutch East India Company, 144, 146, 174

Early Iron Age (and early iron-using peoples), 24–49; agriculture, 24, 28, 33, 40, 41, 44; animal husbandry, 24, 26, 27, 28, 32, 42 *passim*; contact with Late Stone Age, 40–2; copper, 26, 27, 28, 29, 33, 32, 33, 36; correlation with speakers of Bantu-language, 43–4; economy, 24, 28, 35; gold, 24, 33; human skeletal remains, 33, 43; Angola, 37–8; Botswana, 24, 35; Burundi, 38, 39; Congo Republic, 38; Kenya, 39; Malawi, 24, 37; Moçambique, 28, 37; Rhodesia, 24, 29, 30–5, 37, 39, 40, 41; Rwanda, 38, 39, 40; South Africa, 35–7; Swaziland, 35–6; Tanzania, 39; Transvaal, 24, 35–7; Zambia, 24, 25–30, 34, 37, 40, 41; iron-working, 24, 26, 27, 28, 29, 32, 33, 36, 38, 39, 40, 45; origin and spread, 42–5; pole and *daga* constructions, 27, 29, 32; pottery, 24, 25, 26, 27, 28, 29, 30–1, 32 *passim*; rock paintings, 24, 37, 41; stone walling, 32, 33; trade, 32, 35, 41–2
East Africa, 28
East African coast, 6
East Indies, 146
economy, 24, 28, 35, 83, 85, 228
eGabeni, 264
Ehret, C., 44, 83
elaTenjeni, 185
Elizabethville, 84
Ellenberger, D. F., 3–4, 5, 11, 70, 88, 92, 102, 111, 139
Ema Dletsheni, 142
Emalangeni, 137, 138; Ngwane king list, 140
emaMtabeni, 185
EmaNgwaneni, 142
'Empire scare', 309–10
English-speaking peoples, 3, 283
Equator, 13, 39
Ermelo, 105, 114
ethnography, 87, 95, 230, 232, 234
Ethnological section of the Native Affairs Department (*see* Bantu Administration and Development)
ethnology, 1, 3, 4, 18, 93–4, 201, 204, 260
European commercial activity, 14, 171–90 *passim*
Europeans, *see* white people in African Kingdoms

F.A.M.P., 287, 296
Fagan, B. M., 7, 8, 28
farmers and farming, 17, 35, 40, 41, 69, 166, 283
fertility, 72
Feti la Choya, 38, 47, 49
fire, 72
fire-arms, 14, 166, 184, 188, 189, 260, 262–3, 272–3, 283, 306, 317
fish: taboo on eating of, 84–5, 133
Fish River, 3, 11, 12, 151, 159
fission and fissiparous societies, 12, 13, 18, 19, 99, 107, 110, 147–9, 155, 168, 169, 171, 191, 198, 212, 217, 228, 238
Fokeng, 64, 65, 67, 92, 102, 112, 114, 122, 192, 193; ba ga Motlatka, 102; ba Thekwane, 102, 113; culture, 114, 116, 118; groups, 113; language, 117
food-producing peoples, 7, 8, 9, 24, 40, 44
food-taboos, 84–5, 133
France, 4
Frankfort, Orange Free State, 100
Frazer, D., 81
French vessels, 174; slave traders, 177
Frere, Sir Bartle, 303, 305, 322
frontier zones, 3, 11, 147, 230 *passim*, 260
Funa, 46, 49
Furi Mine, 38, 47, 49
Fynn, H. F., 185, 186, 188

Ga Thaba, 194
Gaika (Ngqika) Chief, 179
Galloway, A., 53
Gamtoos Rivers, 42, 165, 166; valley, 42
Gando (Gandowentshaba), 155–6, 157, 159, 168
Gardner, G. A., 52, 53, 54, 67
Gasela chiefdom, 239
Gaubert, P., 78
Gaza, 14; king, 269
Gcaleka, 159
Germans and Germany, 4, 17, 90, 154, 319
Ghoya, 60, 66, 68, 102, 114
Gladstone, W. E., 304, 309, 310–11, 313, 315, 318, 320, 321, 322
Gluckman, M., 245, 253
Gokomere, Rhodesia, 29, 30, 31, 32, 33, 34, 46, 49, 57, 66, 67
Gokwe, 29
gold, 3, 6, 55, 160, 176, 260, 276, 277
Gonaqua, 146, 158, 163–5, 168; chiefdom, 157, 158, 163; language, 158
Gouriqua chiefdom, 166
Gouritz, R., 166
Gqunukwebe chiefdom, 12, 159, 169, 242
Graaf Reinet, 202, 204
Granville, Lord, 320, 321
Great Britain, 4, 17, 302–23
Great Trek, 208
Greefswald Farm, 51, 67
Griffith, C., 298
Griqua (people), 191, 193, 199, 200, 201, 204, 205, 262, 268; commando, 193; country, 194, 202, 203, 204, 293
Griquatown, 95, 193, 202
Gumede, 142
Gundu, 28, 46, 49
Gundwane Ndiwene, 221
guns: *see* fire-arms
Guthrie, M., 82, 83, 86
Gwali, 159
Gwamba Baloyi, 135
Gwanba Tonga, 130, 134

Hamcunqua, 161, 162–4

Hammond-Tooke, D., 19, 20, 230–58
Hamu, 306, 308
Hancock, Prof. Sir Keith, 17
Hanover, 90
Happy Rest Farm, 36, 49, 57, 66
Harinck, G., 11–13, 17
Heidelberg district, 102
Hekpoort, 57
Henga people, 225
Henry, L., 78
Herbert, R. G. W., 312
Herero, 76
Hermanns borg mission, 90
Herschel Native Reserve, 283, 295
High Commissioner, British, 279, 287, 289, 290, 293, 294, 295, 296, 297, 298, 303
Highveld, 50, 56, 62, 68, 69, 80, 100, 101, 104, 105, 108, 111, 119, 121, 122
Hima, 84
Hinsati, 155–68
Hintsa, Chief, 234, 239
historical evidence, 1, 3–4, 6, 10, 12, 13, 16, 23, 92–122 *passim*; for Sotho-Tswana history, 87 *passim*, 191 *passim*, 282 *passim*; for Khoi and Xhosa history, 145–69; for Nguni history, 126 *passim*, 171 *passim*; for Mpondomisi history, 20, 231 *passim*; for Ndebele history, 104–11, 140–1, 259–81
Hlakwana people, 193
Hlanga, 135
Hlatuze, R., 131, 142
Hlubi, 65, 105, 137, 138, 140–1, 143, 144, 180, 183; chiefdoms, 238
Hodgson, Rev. T., 200, 201
'Hoengeiqua' chiefdom, 149, 167; people, 166
Hoepen, E. C. N. van, 60
Hoja, 194, 202
Honwana, 135
Hottentots, *see* Khoikhoi (Khoi)
human skeletal remains, 7, 33, 53
hunting and collecting peoples, 8, 12, 13, 24, 28, 35, 41, 69 *passim*, 71, 73, 79, 81 *passim*, 119, 120, 167, 195, 260
Hurutshe, 60, 67, 100, 109, 113, 116, 194, 199; Bakgatla-Ba-Bagolo, 103 pottery, 60, 68
Hurutshe-Kwena clans, 129
Hutu, 84

Ibadan, 2
Ila-Tonga peoples, 119
Ile des Mimosas, 46, 49
illegitimacy, 76, 77
immigration: *see* migration
incorporation, processes, modes and results of, 11, 102, 107, 118, 122, 146, 153, 157, 168, 219 *passim*
Indonesia, 37
Inhambane, 110, 180
inheritance, 75, 76, 77, 78
'Inqua', 162–5. *See also* Hamcunqua
Inskeep, R. R., 28, 29
(In)Ucomati R., 138
Inxu R., 232
Inyanga, 30, 31, 43, 49, 65
Irish Home Rule, 320, 321, 323
Iron Age, 8, 11, 23. *See also* Early Iron Age and Later Iron Age
iron and iron-working peoples, 3, 6–10 *passim*, 24, 51, 53, 54, 55, 57, 61 *passim*, 87, 104, 109, 116, 119, 121, 134, 135, 160, 165, 176, 177, 178, 180, 183, 186, 187, 188, 213
Isaacs, 187
Isamu Pati, 30
Isandhlawana (battle), 302, 304, 306
Ituri forest, 71, 75
ivory, 14, 15, 55, 72, 107, 108, 109, 122, 174–8 *passim*, 213, 273

Joliffe, J. E. A., 240
Josefa, 299
Junod, 133, 135

Kaffir, chiefs, 82, 252; state, 254; (Xhosa) tribes, 239
Kafue, 26
Kalahari, 38, 86, 96, 100, 101, 108, 110, 116, 117, 119, 120, 192, 193
Kalaka, 110
Kalanga people, 225, 272
Kalambo, 25, 26; Falls site, 25, 46, 49; material, 39; pottery, 26
Kalomo culture, 28, 29, 30
Kalundu group, 25, 29; site, 28, 30, 47, 49
Kangonga, 27, 46, 49
Kamanga, 225
Kanye, 101
Kapula Vlei, Wankie Game Reserve, 29, 47, 49
Kapwirimbwe group, 25, 27, 28; site, 27, 46, 49
Karanga, 32, 134, 135
Kariega, River, 162
Karridene, 62, 65
Kasai, 39
Katanga, 82
Kattea, 117, 121
Kavirondo, 39, 49
Kay, S., 239
Kazembe, 82 fn.
Keate, J., 289, 293, 294, 296
Kei, R., 132, 158
Keiskama, R., 145, 158–9, 167
Kenegha Poort, 133
Kenya, 3, 38, 39, 83
Key, B., 232, 243, 246
Kgalagadi, 110, 111, 116, 117, 192, 204; chiefdoms, 122
Kgari, Chief, 110
Kgatla, 103, 104, 106, 108, 114, 117, 120; -Kgafela, 103; ba-Kgabo-Ea-Melle, 103; chiefdoms, 122; communities, 112, 194; lineage clusters, 105, 111, 121
Kgopolwe, 33, 47, 54
Khami, 34
Khoikhoi (Khoi): chiefdoms, 155, 156, 161, 164; cultures and wares, 35, 42, 59, 63, 65, 68, 81, 83, 132; -Xhosa trade network, 160–7; relations with Xhose, 145–69; social organization, 145 *passim*
Khoisan, 53, 54, 69, 112, 116 *passim*, 131, 132
Kholokoe, 103
Khosa, 135
Khumalo, 217, 218
Khurutshe, 101
Kikuyu, 75
Killi Campbell collection, Natal University, 4

Kimberley, Lord, 312–13, 315
kingdoms, origins of, 16, 18, 72, 73, 78; *see also* under Ndebele, Ngoni, southern Sotho, Swazi and Zulu
Kinshasa Province, 38
kinship, 74, 75, 77, 78, 85, 156 *passim*
Klein Letaba, 68
Kobanqaba, 156
'Kobuqua', 164
Kolobe, 115
Kolobeng, 84
Kololo, 14, 193, 194, 266, 268, 272
Komati, River, 137, 138
Koni, 106
Kora (lang.) 150, 152 fn.; (people), 191, 195, 262
Korana people, 152 fn., 205
Kropf, A., 154
Kruger, President, 278
Kubung, 115
Kudu, 115
Kukwe, 80
Kumadzulo, 29, 46, 49
Kumalo people, 142, 185
Kumalo-Mabaso, 142
Kunene, 38
Kuruman, 192, 199, 200, 202, 262
Kuruman (Ndebele Pretender), 275 *passim*
Kutswe, 118
Kwale, 39, 46, 49
Kwayi clan, 157
Kwena, 88, 89, 102 *passim*, 120, 129, 196, 283; Monaheng, 205; chiefdoms, 101, 102, 115, 122, 192, 238
Kyungu, 73

Laidler, P. W., 50, 60, 65
Laka, 105
Lala, 68, 116, 134, 136, 143, 198, 204
Lala-Lamba, 133
Langa, Cape Town, 77; clan, 137 *passim*
Langalibalele, Chief, 233, 268
Laslett, P., 78
Lata, 132
Late Stone Age, 24, 28, 29, 31 *passim*; contact with Early Iron Age, 24, 26, 28
Later Iron Age, 50–70; pottery, 53–60, 63–8; iron-working, 51 *passim*; copper, 51; human skeletons, 53
Lavanha, 64
Law, 72, 83
'Lawo' people, 155
Leach, E. R., 235, 254
Lebombo mountains, 108 fn.
Legassick, M., 9, 11, 15, 16
Leopard's Kopje culture, 30–1, 33, 34, 35, 47, 55, 58
Lepui, Chief, 193
Leribe, 295, 296, 300
Lerothodi, 299
Lesawana (or Ramaneela), 287–8, 299
Lesotho, 22, 84, 88, 196, 203, 208, 282 *passim*
Lete, 106; chiefdom, 105
Letele, 283
Letsie, 22, 284 *passim*
levirate, 77
Lewanika, Chief, 81, 280
Leydsdorp, 110
Likhuele, 195
Limpopo River and valley, 2, 7, 34, 37, 50, 51, 54, 55, 56, 66, 68, 69, 119, 129, 130, 208, 265, 272, 302
lineage clusters: *see* chiefdoms, clusters of
lineages, 10 *passim*, 98, 99, 110, 120, 121, 147 *passim*, 167–9, 245
linguists and linguistic evidence, 3, 5, 9, 10, 11, 44–5, 73, 74, 80 *passim*, 97, 111, 131, 132, 142, 144, 149, 150, 151, 153, 154, 163, 230
Linyati, 82 fn.
liquor and liquor trade, 19, 166
Livingstone (town), 29
Livingstone, D., 84, 89
Lobato, A., 174
Lobedu, 71, 110, 117, 118; culture complex, 111, 118
Lobengula, 21, 221–2, 264 *passim*
London Missionary Society 201
Loolekop, 36, 54
Lourenço Marques, 62, 189
Lovedale, 81
Lowe, 116, 121
Lowe, C. van Riet, 50, 60
Lozi (people), 81, 245, 265, 268
Luangwa, R., 25; valley, 81
Lubombo mountains, 137, 138; people, 138
Lubumbashi, 84
Lukuzulu, 30
Lulu mountains, 103
Lunda, 79, 82 fn.
Lusaka, 6, 25, 27, 30
Lydenburg district, 60, 106
Lye, W., 14, 15, 16, 191–206

Mabasa, 247
Mabille, 289
Mabjaba-Matswane, 100
Mabjuba (1881), 280
Mabolela, 196
Maboloka, 298
Mabveni, 32, 49, 80
MacCalman, H. R., 35
Macgregor, J. C., 4, 11, 88–9
MacIver, R., 33
Machadodorp, 60
Macheng, Chief, 277, 278
Madiliyangwa, 34, 40, 49
Mackenzie, J., 96
Maclear, H., 235
Macomates, 137
Madagascar, 37, 177
Mafu, Chief, 139, 142
Magaliesberg, 57, 60, 68, 80, 109
Magaye, 137
Maggs, T., 59
Mahlangwana, 135
Mahura, Chief, 193
Majangaza, 244
Majola clan, 244
Majura, 200
Makalanga, 88
Makhabane, 287
Makhoeng, 204
Makoba, 142
Makonde, 76
Makwai, 297
Makwana, Chief, 114
Makwe rockshelter, 28, 49
Malandela, 130, 142
Malapati type ware, 31, 34, 35, 36, 47, 49, 57
Malawi, 24, 28, 37, 43, 269; Early Iron Age, 24, 28, 43; Lake, 78
Malope, 100, 109
Maluti mountains, 192
Mambova, 29

Manala, 104
Manala section, 140; Ndebele, 140–1
Mandau, 34, 49
Mandela, 244
Mandhlakazi, 315, 316
Maneella, 299
Mantatee (king), 195; (people), 202
MaNthatisi, 193, 196
Maokagani Hill, Botswana, 34
MaPolana, 140
Mapungubwe, 7, 50, 52, 54, 55
Maputa (Mabudu), R., 137
Maputo chiefdom, 178, 181, 182 *passim*; River, 178
Maquaina nation, 108
Marico, R., 96, 100, 109, 194; district, 104, 264
Marks, Shula, 11, 126–44
marriage, 74 *passim*, 118 *passim*, 156 *passim*
Maseteli country, 204
Mashonaland, 265
Masilo, Chief, 100, 109
Mason, R., 51, 54, 57, 59, 60–1, 66
Masopha, 22, 291, 299, 300
Masuetsa family, 204
Matabele king, 279
Matabeleland, 34, 41, 53, 264, 266, 270 *passim*
Matiwane, 196, 246
Matlekas, 108
Matopos (Hills), 34, 40, 49, 267
Matrilineal descent, 75 *passim*, 119
Matshanda, 244
Matsieng, 300
Mbande Hill, 73
Mbandeni, King, 141
Mbata, 142
Mbelwa, 225, 226
Mbo, 11, 64, 65, 105, 127, 130, 131, 134, 135, 136; Mkize, 137 *passim*, 181; Nguni, 95; Dlamini, 137, 140
Mbopha, Induna, 217
Mdange, 155
Mditshwa, 241, 247
Mdushane chiefdom, 238
Meinhof, C., 150–1
Mekwatleng, 196, 205, 296
Melvill, J., 95, 202
Melville Koppies, 57, 58, 212
Merwe, N. J. van der, 36, 54
Messina, 51
Mfecane, 13 *passim*, 58, 59, 67, 102, 111, 113, 114, 122, 127, 128, 130, 136, 141, 191–206, 207–29
Mfengu, 18, 77, 268, 283; location, 247
Mhlanga, Chief, 140
Mhlangane, 217
Mhlatuse, 214
Mhlontlo, Chief, 241, 251
migration, 8, 9, 10, 11, 24, 67, 93, 112, 129–33, 136, 137, 138, 156, 203–5, 220 *passim*, 266
military organization: *see under* Ndebele, Ngoni, southern Sotho, Swazi, Zulu
missionaries, 3, 4, 17 *passim*, 89 *passim*, 186, 189, 232, 235, 252, 257, 260, 262–70, 273 *passim*, 292, 294, 298, 299
Mkhondweni, 244
Mkize line, 139. *See also* Mbo Mkize
Mmanaana-Kgatla, 104
Mndange clan, 158, 159
Mnyamana, 308
Moçambique, 2, 3, 28, 37, 84, 118, 119, 135, 173, 174, 208, 222
Modder, R., 195, 201
Moeletsi family, 204
Moffat, J. S., 264–5
Moffat, R., 50, 89, 91, 96, 129, 193, 204, 262 *passim*, 267, 277
Mohalesberg: *see* Magaliesberg
Mohlomi, Chief, 111, 198
Molapo, 22, 284 *passim*
Molema, S. M., 4, 89
Moletlane, 105
Moletsane, 22, 111, 193, 194, 199, 200, 201, 204, 293, 296, 297
Molopo, 110
Monaheng, 196, 283; chiefdoms, 238
Mondise, 217 fn.
Moorosi, 15, 22, 196, 199, 295
Mopedi, Paulus, 285, 292
Morija, 292, 300
Moroka, 15, 201, 283
Morolong, 115, 116
Mosega, 115, 116, 199, 220, 263, 265
Moseme, Chief, 195, 201
Moshweshwe, 15, 21, 22, 97, 196 *passim*, 242, 281 *passim*
Mothibe, 193, 199
Mothitho, 199
Mpande, 218, 267
Mpangazita, 196
Mperembe, 225
Mpezeni, 220, 225
Mphetla, 64
Mphunthi, 64
Mpolane, 64
Mpondo, 19, 65, 77, 137, 138, 238, 241, 242, 247, 253
Mpondomise, 231 *passim*, 242, 245, 247, 253, 254; chiefdoms, 20, 241; Rebellion (1880–1), 233, 238
Mponweni Mountains, 133
Mqhayi chiefdom, 239
Msane, 127
Mthatha, R., 65
Mthethwa, 13, 14, 136, 172, 184, 185, 213
Mtimkulu, 140
Mtiti, Chief, 139
Mtonga, 141
Mtwaro, 225
Murdock, 75, 133
Mutapa state system, 259
Musi/Msi, 140
Mvele, 185
Mwari cult, 55, 268
Mwase Kasung, 226
Mzila, King, 269
Mzilikazi, 17, 21, 59, 105, 111, 193 *passim*, 217 *passim*, 261 *passim*
Mzimbuvu, R., 12, 151
Mzinyati River and valley: *see* Buffalo River

Nakapapula rockshelter, Serenje, 26, 40, 46, 49
Nama (lang.), 150, 151; (people), 86
Namaqualand, 80
Natal, 3, 8, 15, 20, 22, 62, 63, 65, 67, 127, 128 *passim*, 171 *passim*, 203, 208, 214, 268, 275, 282, 283, 287, 289, 293, 294, 295, 296, 304, 305, 306, 307, 314 *passim*; coast, 7, 62–6, 68, 69, 70, 80
Ncamu, 132

Ncwangeni, 127
Ndabuko, 308
Ndamba, 75
Ndamase, 241
Ndau, 119
Ndebele, 17, 19, 65, 117, 193 *passim*, 219 *passim*, 229; Kingdom, 14–16, 20–1, 218, 222, 228, 259–81; military organization, 261 *passim*
Ndlambe, chiefdom, 238, 242
Ndonde sub-group, 75
Ndosi, 137
Ndungunya, 140
Ndwandwe, 14, 127, 137, 138, 141, 180, 181, 186, 213; chiefdoms, 13; empire, 207; kingdom, 222
Ndzundza, 104, 140–1
Negroid peoples, 3, 8, 33, 41, 42, 43, 54, 86
Nenquin, J., 38
Nfwane, 213
Ngadini, 142
Ngami, Lake, 110
Ngangelizwe, 241
Ngconde, 155, 168
Ngindo, 76
Ngocobes, 184
Ngosini (Nqosoro), Chief, 155
Ngqika, 139, 242, 252
Nguni, the term Nguni, 126–7; historical evidence, 126–44, 171 *passim*
Ngwaketse, 89, 109, 110, 118, 194
Ngwane, 142, 180, 181, 182, 214, 226; chiefdoms, 13; Ngwane-Ndwandwe-Mthethwa conflict, 185
Ngwato, 89, 109, 110, 116, 194, 205, 276, 277; pottery, 55
Nkalanga, 135
Nkgarahanye chief, 193
Nkulumane, 221
Nkumba, 135
Nogeng, 115
Nondwane, 135
Noto, 115
Notwani, R., 109
Nqeto, 217
Nqobokazi, 155
Nqwiliso, Chief, 242
Nsenga Chiefs, 226
Ntimba, 135
Ntinde, 155, 158, 159, 242
Ntsuanatsasti, 64, 100, 102, 113
Ntungwa, 131, 134, 143; Nguni, 136, 137, 141
Ntusi, 82 fn.
Nuanetsi, R., 34
Numas entrance shelter, 47, 49
Nyasa, 81
Nxaba, 127
Nxasane, 143
Nxuba (Great Fish River), 155
Nyahokwe, 33, 46, 49
Nyaka, 178
Nyakyusa, 71, 73, 75, 78
Nyambose, 136
Nyamsunga, Uvinza, 46
Nyamwezi, 75
Nzimela clan, 127

officials (white), 3, 20, 90, 93, 306, 321. *See also* High Commissioner
Olifants, R., 166, 194
Omer-Cooper, J., 13, 14, 16, 17, 98, 207–29, 230, 231
oral traditions, 3, 5, 9, 10, 12, 13, 23, 60, 73, 81, 87, 90, 91, 98, 153–9
Orange Free State, 11, 19, 22, 23, 50, 59, 61, 100, 102, 106, 282 *passim*
Orange River, 12, 145, 191, 194, 202, 204, 283
Orpen, C. S., 293
Orpen, J. M., 241, 283, 284
Owen, Capt. W., 186, 187

Pai, 118
Palabora, 7, 36, 49, 54, 66, 118
Palo, Chief, 158, 159, 169
pastoralists, 131–2, 145, 147, 166, 191, 228
patrilineal descent, 75, 76, 78, 79
patron-client relationship, 152, 169
patrons, 71, 76
Patterson, Capt., R. R., 279–80
Pebla, 139
Pedi, 11, 19, 60, 61, 104 *passim*, 117, 122, 192 *passim*; chiefdom, 15, 103; pottery, 68
Penja, 80
Perestrello, 64
Pettman, C., 150–1
Phetla chiefdom, 192
Philippolis, 202, 204
Phillipson, D. W., 6, 8, 9, 24–49, 57
Phiring, 115
Phuthing, 103, 192, 193; chiefdoms, 192
Phutiatsana, R., 284
physical types, 3, 6, 7, 9, 10, 33, 43, 53, 65, 69, 70
Pietermaritzburg, 4, 105
Pietersburg district, 118
Pilansberg district, 103, 104, 108
'Place of Offerings', 33
Platberg, 201
Po chiefdom, 105
Polane, 139, 192
Polena, 139
Political structure: *see under* Khoikhoi, Mpondomise, Ndebele, Ngoni, southern Sotho, Swazi, Xhosa, Zulu
polygyny, 9, 77, 78, 79, 90, 120, 158
Pondoland, 78; coast, 63
Pongola, R., 141, 185, 186
population pressure, 106, 109, 171, 213
Poqo movement, 231
Port Durnford, 315; Natal, 14, 187, 188; St. John, 64, 68
Portuguese documents, 15, 144, 176; frontier, 304; garrison, 177; language, 3; people, 6, 110, 173, 174, 175, 179 *passim*; settlements, 122; shipwreck material, 133, 172; soldiers, 188; trade system, 14, 70
Poshudi, 291
Posnansky, M., 42–3
Potgieter, A. H., 267
Potgietersrus area, Transvaal, 65, 105
pottery, 7, 8, 24 *passim*, 53–60, 63–8, 73, 74, 80, 86, 114, 133, 135
Pretoria, 4, 56, 69, 103, 280
Pretorius, A., 267
Proto-Bantu, 150
Proto-Nguni, 150, 151, 153
Pulana, 118; Kutswe dialect, 118
Pwaga, Uvinza, 46
pygmies, 41, 43

Qulusi clan, 308
Qumbu district, 237
Quobosheane, 194, 197, 205
Qwabe, 127, 130, 142, 143, 184, 217, 218

Radcliffe-Brown, A. R., 89
Radicals, 309
radiocarbon dating, 6, 25 *passim*, 52, 54, 55, 57, 59, 65, 67
rain, 72, 153
Ramaneella: *see* Lesawana
Ramokhele community, 195; Chief, 201, 204
Ranuga, 244
Rarbe, 159
Rathateng, 100, 121
refugees, 164, 201, 203, 204, 257
religion and ritual, 12, 17, 18, 147, 268, 307
Rhodes, C., 281
Rhodesia, 2 *passim*, 24, 29 *passim*, 54, 57 *passim*, 66, 92, 119, 120, 131, 208, 219 *passim*
Ricocco, 38, 47
Riebeeck, J. van, 52, 160, 162
Roan Antelope, 27
Robinson, K. R., 28 *passim*, 73
rock paintings, 24, 41, 50
Rolong, 89, 92, 112 *passim*, 122, 194, 198, 200, 201, 205, 283
Ronga, 135
Rooiberg, 56, 61, 68
Rozwi, 110; state systems, 259
Rustenburg, 102, 103, 104, 113
Ruwenzori, 75
Rwanda, 38, 80, 84

Sabi, R., 269, 273
Safwa, 75
St. Lucia Bay, 80, 135, 178, 319
Salisbury, 4, 30; Lord, 320
Same, 244
San (Bushmen), 8, 9, 13, 16, 41, 43, 69, 107, 132, 133, 140, 145, 146, 150, 151, 155, 166, 167, 211, 258; rock paintings, 133
San Alberto, 64, 65
Sand River, 192, 283
Sandaweland, pottery 39, 49
Sanders, P., 197 fn., 203 fn.
Sanga, 38; pottery, 39, 46, 49
Santos, Jnr., J. R. dos, 37
Sarwa, 81
Schapera, I., 11, 94, 204, 259
Schilpadfontein (Pretoria district), 103
Schofield, J. F., 34, 50, 51, 53, 55, 58 *passim*, 135
Schwellnus, C. M., 54
Scott's Cave, Gamtoos valley, 42, 47, 49
Sebetiele chiefdom, 105
Sebetwane, Chief, 193, 194
Sechele, 277
Seddon, J. D., 42
Sehunelo, Chief, 194, 200, 201
Sekalagadi (lang.), 117
Sekhonyana, 22, 291, 292
Sekonyela, King, 15, 195 *passim*
Sekuata, 108
Sekwati, Chief, 193, 194, 196
Seleka chiefdom, 105, 201, 205
Seleka-Rolong, 194, 199, 200
Senyotong, 196
Senzengakona, 140
Serenje, 26
Shaka, Zulu King, 6, 13 *passim*, 122, 131, 137 *passim*, 177, 186, 187, 188, 208, 214 *passim*, 226 *passim*, 247, 260, 261 302, 306, 308
Shangana-Thonga people, 86
Shangane people, 186–7
Shaw, W., 235, 239
sheep, 3, 12, 32
Shepstone, Theophilus, Secretary for Native Affairs, Natal, 22, 275, 278, 279, 288, 289, 293 *passim*, 306
Shibambo clans, 135
Shippard, Sir Sydney, 270
Shona, 5, 8, 17, 19, 20, 56, 61, 62, 75, 84, 119, 220, 222, 270, 272
Shoshong, 277, 278; Hills, 194
Sia communities, 196; chiefdoms, 192
siachelaba's kraal, 30
Sibiya: *see* Gumede
Sinoia Cave, 30, 46, 49
Situmpa assemblage, 28, 49
slave trade, 176–7, 186–8
Smith, Alan, 14, 171–89
Smith, Dr. Andrew, 195, 202, 204, 263
Smith, M. G., 236, 237
Sneeuwberg, 162
Sobhuza, 17, 213
Soga, J. H., 4, 5, 65, 127, 129, 134, 233
Somerset region, 156
Songea, 81
Songhe, 82
Soper, R. C., 39
Soshangane, 13
Sotho: the term Sotho, 94–7; historical evidence, 87–94, 191 *passim*, 282 *passim*; Pedi, 103–4, 108; -Tswana, 86–125; Southern, 19, 22, 81 *passim*, 101 *passim*, 191 *passim*
Sousoa, 162
South Africa, 2, 3, 4, 9, 13, 35–7, 56, 59, 61, 66, 68, 69, 76, 92–3, 111, 122, 139, 101, 211, 212, 260, 272, 282, 286, 287, 300, 303, 304, 319, 322
South African Museum, Cape Town, 4, 15, 54, 66, 88, 90, 96
South African Public Library, 4
South African Republic, 3, 145
Southall, A., 73
Southern Province plateau, 25
Southey, Sir Richard, Secretary to Cape Govt., 285
Soutpansberg, 7, 36, 51, 57, 66, 193, 196
Standerton, 105
Stanford, W., 235
Stanhope, E., 321
Stanley, F. A., 320, 321
state-making, 14, 16, 97, 104, 105, 111, 141, 180, 208, 260
Stavenisse, 163
Steelpoort, R., 192, 194, 196; Mountains, 212
Stoffberg, 100
stone-walling, 32, 50, 58 *passim*
Stow, G. W., 4, 11, 87, 91, 111, 129, 139

stratification, 54–5
Stuart, J., 144
Sudan, 83
Summers, R., 30, 33, 35
Surat, 173
Sutton, J. E. S., 38
Swazi, 19, 105, 117, 118, 196, 213, 227; Kingdom, 14, 16, 141, 207, 226 *passim*
Swaziland, 7, 35–6, 66, 78, 87, 95, 118, 130, 135 *passim*, 208

Taba Zikamambo, 34, 47
Table Bay, 146, 160 *passim*; peninsula, 146
Tanzania, 3, 39, 76, 83
Tati goldfields, 277
Tau, Chief, 115, 198, 200
Taung (people), 60, 111, 115, 193, 194, 195, 293, 297, 298; (place), 193, 200
Tawana, 110, 164, 194
Tembe, 135, 137, 141, 142, 178, 180, 181, 182, 185
Tembu, 184, 185, 242
Thaba Bosiu, 196, 197, 200, 284, 294, 296 *passim*, 300; Treaty, 288
Thaba Kurutlele, 196
Thaba Mosiu, 196
Thaba Nchu, 195, 201, 204, 205
Thamaga, 115
Theal, G. M., 4, 11, 87, 88, 91, 94, 111, 192
Thekiso, 109
Thompson, G., 202, 239
Thompson, L., 1
Threlfall, W., 186
Thysville, Bas-Congo, 39, 49
Tinley Manor, 62, 63, 65
Tlhako chiefdom, 105
Tlhaloga, 115
Tlhaping, 82, 84, 89, 91, 115, 192–3, 199, 200, 204; /Rolong (lang.), 117
Tlharo, 192, 198, 200
Tlokwa, 193, 199, 201, 202, 205, 238, 283; chiefdoms, 104, 104 fn., 192, 196
Tobias, P. V., 43, 54
Togu, 154–7, 168
Tolo chiefdoms, 238; locations, 247
Tonga, 65, 130 *passim*, 142, 143, 177, 179, 182, 183, 225, 265
Toro, 75
trade and traders, 11, 12, 14, 15, 21, 67, 69, 72, 73, 82, 107–9, 110, 117, 122, 171, 189, 212, 260, 262, 273, 274, 277
Transkei, 51, 146, 151, 152, 153, 231, 233, 234–5, 237
Transvaal, 7 *passim*, 24, 35–7, 50 *passim*, 64 *passim*, 79 *passim*, 101 *passim*, 129, 205, 208, 218, 262, 264, 278, 280, 283, 304, 305, 306, 311, 317, 318
Trevor, T. G., 68
Tsekelo, 22, 288, 291, 293, 294, 295, 298
Tshane, Chief, 193
Tshangula, 41, 47, 49
Tshawe chiefdom, 158, 168
Tshezi, R.: *see* Bushman River
Tshikapa, 39, 49
Tshikapa, Kasai, 39
Tshiwo, 155, 156, 157, 159
Tsoelike, R., 133
Tsolo district, 237, 245; chiefdom, 247
Tsonga, 71
Tswamathe, 287
Tswana, 11, 12, 19, 74, 81 *passim*, 94, 95, 97, 117, 126, 129, 134, 162, 192 *passim*, 245, 262, 272, 292; chiefdoms, 15, 192, 197, 204
Tswapong hills, 104
Tugela river and valley, 65, 136, 143, 184
Tuli, 132 *passim*
Tumbuka, 75, 81, 225
Tunnel site, Gokomere, 32
Turnbull, C., 71
Twa (pygmy), 80
Twickenham Road, Lusaka, 27, 30, 46, 49

Ubiqua (Khoi-San), 146
Uganda, 78, 83
Uitkomst site, 36, 53, 57 *passim*
uKrurmana, 279
Ulundi (1879), 218, 280, 305
Umgazana Cave, 63
Umgeni, R., 143
Umgongo, 218
Umhloti Road midden, 63
Umvoti, R., 136
Umzimkulu, R., 136, 143
Umzimvubu, R., 178
universities, 1 fn., 2, 4, 6, 23, 144
Ur-Bantu, 151
Usutu, 315, 316
Usutu, R., 95
Uvinza, 39, 49

va Mbo, 181
Va Ngoni: *see* Bakoni
Vaal, J. B. de, 36, 37
Vaal, R., 40, 67, 100 *passim*, 121, 191 *passim*
Vambe, 137, 138, 181
Vansina, J., 45, 235, 237
Vatwahs, 186
Venda, 19, 61, 68, 86; -Karanga, 130
Vet rivers, 192
Victoria East, 252
'Victoria incident', 266
Vinnicombe, P., 42
Vipya plateau, 225
Volksrust district, 106
Vrede, 59, 100
Vryheid, 138

Wagner, H., 68
Wakkerstroom, 105
Walton, J., 60 *passim*, 114
Warmbaths, 57
Warmelo, N. J. van, 4, 92, 94, 126, 139
wars: Orange Free State v. southern Sotho, 282 *passim*
Waschbank, 138
Waterboer, A., 200
Webb, C., 22–3, 302–23
Weber, M., 248
Westphal, E., 83
white people in African kingdoms, 1, 3, 15 *passim*, 113, 146, 260 *passim*, 278, 282–3, 289, 299, 300, 322
white commandos, 283 *passim*
white expansion, 17–19
Wilson, Monica, 9, 51, 65, 71–85, 120, 121, 230–1
Winburg, 58
Windhoek, 35
Witwatersrand, 36, 51, 57, 59
Wodehouse, Sir Philip, 22, 282 *passim*
Wolseley, Sir Garnet, 305 *passim*, 312–13, 322
Wood, Sir Evelyn, 308–9, 312

Woodbush Mountains, 193, 196
Wookey, A. J., 89, 91
Wushe, 143

Xhosa, 12 *passim*, 73 *passim*, 127, 130, 132, 145–69, 230 *passim*; chiefdoms, 179, 234, 239, 242; relations with Khoi, 145–69; social organization, 147 *passim*; -Khoi trade network, 160–7

Zaka, Chief, 159
Zambezi basin, 84; river, 2, 29, 35, 119, 129, 135, 193, 205, 222, 265, 266, 269, 272; valley, 3, 25, 29, 37
Zambia, 7, 24, 25–30, 34, 37 *passim*, 84, 133; Early Iron Age, 24, 25–30, 40, 42
Zeerust area, 60
Zelemu, 143
Zezuru, 86
Zhiso Hill, 34, 47, 49
Zibhebhu, 308, 314 *passim*
Zihlando, 215 fn.
Ziko: *see* Gande
Zimbabwe, 5, 32, 46, 49, 55
Zingcuka location, Tsolo, 245
Zinyati River: *see* Buffalo river, 138
Ziwa, 28, 30 *passim*, 47
Ziwedu, 308
Zizi, Basutoland, 139, 140, -Bhele group, 137, 138, 139
Zulu, 23, 73, 78, 126, 130, 132, 142, 172, 185 *passim*, 196, 208, 216, 218, 219, 222, 245, 262 *passim*, 279, 280; Kingdoms, 13, 14, 19, 23, 207, 208, 216 *passim*, 261; -land, 187 *passim*, 207, 208, 213, 214, 226, 261, 278, 302 *passim*
Zungu, 142
Zwangendaba, 17, 127, 221, 222, 224, 266, 267, 275
Zwide, 141, 185, 186, 213, 214, 222